1991

John Dewey

The Later Works, 1925–1953

Volume 14: 1939–1941

EDITED BY JO ANN BOYDSTON

TEXTUAL EDITOR, ANNE SHARPE

With an Introduction by R. W. Sleeper

Southern Illinois University Press

Carbondale and Edwardsville

The text of this reprinting is a photo-offset reproduction of the original cloth
edition that contains the full apparatus for the volume awarded the seal of the
Committee on Scholarly Editions of the Modern Language Association.
Editorial expenses were met in part by a grant from the Editions Program of the
National Endowment for the Humanities, an independent Federal agency.

The paperbound edition has been made possible by a special subvention from
the John Dewey Foundation.

The Library of Congress catalogued the first printing of this work (in cloth) as
follows:

Dewey, John, 1859–1952.
  The later works, 1925–1953.

  Vol. 14 has introd. by R. W. Sleeper.
  Continues The middle works, 1899–1924.
  Includes bibliographies and indexes.

  CONTENTS: v. 1. 1925—[etc.]—v. 14. 1939–1941.
    1. Philosophy—Collected works.   I. Boydston, Jo Ann, 1924–.   II. Title.
B945.D41   1981   191   80-27285
ISBN 0-8093-0986-6 (V. 1) 1426-6 (V. 14)

ISBN 0-8093-1680-3 (paperback)

Contents

Introduction
By R. W. Sleeper

The contents of the present volume are vintage Dewey. Ranging widely over problems of theory and practice, they reveal him commencing his ninth decade at the peak of his intellectual powers. With the full canon of his major works in place, Dewey might have been expected to relax the vigilance with which he had confronted the crises of his culture since before the turn of the century. That he did not is strictly in character. We find him facing new challenges with the same creative energy and compassion, the same integral vision, that had so long distinguished his thought and practice from the work of his contemporaries.

William James taught us something about the importance of such traits in a thinker. "Let me repeat once more," he said, "that a man's vision is the great fact about him." The integrity of vision which binds together the forty-odd essays, reviews, and rejoinders gathered here confirms the fact. Whether John Dewey is dealing with the great issues of war and peace, or with the sometimes petty complaints of his critics, it is with a single purpose and from a singular perspective. While others persist in picking over the bones of old philosophical controversies, Dewey is tackling new problems and proposing fresh solutions. The dust of old disagreements is behind him; his vision remains unclouded. It is stunning evidence of the meliorism that is central to his conception of philosophy from the beginning.

The most impressive feature of the bits and pieces of Dewey's work between 1939 and 1941 collected here is the way that they disclose the coherence of his project. They force us to recognize how thoroughly Dewey had worked it all out. They compel us to see how his treatment of "various problems and various hypotheses" constitutes a coherent "system" (p. 141). It is a system that hangs together, Dewey tells us, because it all comes from a "perspective determined from a definite point of view." It is this perspective that brings coherence to the whole, an *elenchus* that distinguishes it most sharply from the systems of his predecessors from Plato to Peirce. For it is not a Weltanschauung of the architecture and furniture of the universe, nor a *first philosophy* that lays down the foundations of the world order. We can see at once how little interest Dewey has in the categories of thought—or of being—that make up the essential ingredients of other systems, and so how radically different his system is. It finds no use for either the "Scotistic" *reals* that Charles Sanders Peirce made central to his doctrine of Synechism, or the *necessary truths* that William James clings to in the final chapter of his *Principles of Psychology.* Dewey's system is wholly original. It is a system that is wholly in process, movement, and change—as nature itself is—and that grows, emerges, and evolves.

It is a system that develops like the "live creature" that he tells us about in *Art as Experience,* and that involves continuous reconstruction in the ways that he outlines in *Reconstruction in Philosophy.* In *Experience and Nature* Dewey reminded us how things emerge into existence, change, and pass away. They are events, he said, that we transform into objects, fixing them momentarily in shared discourse. In *The Quest for Certainty* he reminded us again how precarious existences are. We deal with them in the risky business of our *knowings,* he said, only in order to reduce the perils of our own existence. And in *Logic: The Theory of Inquiry* he showed us how we might best do it. He concentrated there on the *generic traits* of things that give us a handle on events, and that help us to control them once we find a way.

This is the subject that is central to the essay on "Nature in Experience" that is included here, and that he goes on to develop throughout. In "Time and Individuality" he returns to the theme of qualitative individuality that was central to *Experience and Nature.* It was a theme that was most thoroughly developed in his philosophical logic from the 1903 *Studies in Logical Theory* to the 1938 *Logic,* as well as in his more "practical" treatises on *Human Nature and Conduct* and *Individualism, Old and New.* In the essay on "Propositions, Warranted Assertibility, and Truth," in the course of his trenchant reply to some of Bertrand Russell's more egregious misreadings of his logic, Dewey puts these themes together in terms of his logical semantics. The three essays mentioned are a remarkable display of the scope of the system and its coherence. They remind us how important it is in understanding Dewey to get a sense of the whole. Without it we risk missing, as so many of his critics did, the whole point.

It is unfortunate in this regard that the least successful entry in the present volume is the most familiar, and that so many of Dewey's critics have taken their cues from its content. It is Dewey's "Rejoinder" to his critics that first appeared in the initial volume of Paul Arthur Schilpp's Library of Living Philosophers series. Harried by Schilpp to complete the assigned task under a deadline designed to coincide with Dewey's eightieth birthday, Dewey rushed its completion in a state of exhaustion. Anticipating this condition, Dewey had already decided not to attend the New York City celebration and went off to his daughter's ranch instead, leaving an address entitled "Creative Democracy—The Task Before Us" to be read in his absence (pp. 224–30). Although the "Rejoinder" reflects the patience with which Dewey contended with the urgency of Schilpp's deadline and with the complaints of his critics, it shows little of the freshness of thought and acuteness of perception that mark the birthday address. Nor does it even begin to show the character and originality of the system as a whole. Choosing to limit his attention almost exclusively to the negative criticism contained in the volume, Dewey deals in piecemeal fashion only with the most egregious of the misreadings of his work, sacrificing thereby the opportunity to display the central themes of that work in their unity. Even though Russell, for example, had touched upon the "holistic" character of Dewey's approach to the "problematic situation," the matter is quickly dismissed. It is almost as if Dewey were reluctant to discuss such a subtle and elusive feature of his project in the existing context. Or is it just that Dewey failed to recognize in Russell's unfamiliar vocabulary what had been a central theme of his own project almost from the beginning?

In his earliest essays on logical theory Dewey had repeatedly denounced what he called "apart thought" in the empiricist logics of Mill and his followers as well as in the logics of Kantian transcendentalists. Hegel's refusal to draw a hard and fast line between "theory" and "fact" was the one feature of Hegelian logic that Dewey wanted to save. "Apart thought," for Dewey, had meant the bifurcation of reason from nature and the distinction of the "analytic" from the "synthetic" in logical discourse. It meant, for him, the dualism of the mind and body that he tried to overcome in his 1896 landmark essay on "The Reflex Arc Concept in Psychology," in which he first introduced his concept of the reflex "circuit" involved in inquiry. This "holistic" theme was then developed further in Dewey's contributions to the Chicago Decennial volume of *Studies in Logical Theory* in 1903, reiterated in the *Essays in Experimental Logic* in 1916, and received its most thorough elaboration in the 1938 *Logic*. It is there that it was detected by Russell as a feature of Dewey's conception of scientific method.

It is indeed fortunate, then, that the present volume contains an essay by Dewey that sets the whole matter of his "holistic" approach in perspective. In contrast with the disjointed character of both the criticisms and Dewey's responses to them in the Schilpp volume, the essay on "Nature in Experience" is a model of clarity and responsiveness. Patiently put together in reply to Morris Raphael Cohen and William Ernest Hocking, whose criticisms appear here in the Appendixes, Dewey lays bare in simple terms what counts as his "first philosophy" and explains what his "holism" amounts to. It is perhaps his clearest statement of why it is that metaphysics does not play the foundational role for him that it had regularly played for his predecessors. Because we encounter nature only *in* experience, he points out, it is futile to seek out the foundations of our philosophy in what is antecedent to experience, or in what transcends it. We must look to the logic of experience itself, its character structure and traits, and to the traits of existences that it discloses. He wants us to see how clearly experience manifests all the features of precariousness, stability, and qualitative individuality that he had ascribed to "existences of all kinds" in the context of *Experience and Nature*. He wants us to see just how much of our experience is constituted by our history as "a set of changes marked by development or growth," for once we accept that continuity of experience *is* change we can rid our conceptions of dogma and cant. He wants us to see a way of clearing our creative intelligence from the stifling constraints of tradition by an appreciation of just how deeply change cuts at the same time that we come to grasp the real continuity of the process.

"We are told very little about the nature of things before they are inquired into," Russell complains, but that is what Dewey's "holism" is all about.[1] It is, indeed, why so much of Dewey's "first philosophy" is taken from natural science. Not that Dewey wants to reduce *everything* to science, as some of his critics seemed to think—and some *still* think. It is just that we have so much to learn from it. We must recognize, Dewey says, that "the change from ancient to modern science compels us to interpret ends relatively and pluralistically, because as limits of specifiable histories" (p. 146). Dewey's system is, in a sense, as "historicist," as "relativist," and as "pluralist," as this text implies. But Dewey's project moves in the opposite direction from the "reductionism" that characterizes most other systems to which such labels apply. Dewey is not a "reductionist" at all in the sense that we associate with philosophies that embrace "scientism" and argue that scientific method provides us with an algorithm for solving *all* our problems. But he does insist that we ought to look at the way of going at things that accounts for success in science, *and* what accounts for failure. Dewey is not just thinking of the methods of the sciences either, but what the sciences can tell us about ourselves and about the environments in which we have to live out our lives. We must try to find ways of applying these lessons to our conduct of culture, he tells us, and to the ways in which we live our moral lives as individuals. "I have even gone so far," Dewey says, "as to ascribe the backwardness of the human, the practical, sciences in part to the long period of backwardness of the physical sciences themselves and in part to the refusal of moralists and social scientists to utilize the physical, especially the biological, material that is at their disposal" (p. 148).

Dewey argues here against the sophisticated realism that Cohen's criticism presupposes, just as he had argued all along against the highly attenuated "Scholastic" realism promulgated by Charles Sanders Peirce. But he also argues for the application of Peirce's "fallibilism" across the board. He applies it to the metaphysical background of existence, as well as to the foreground of experience and inquiry. And so he alludes to the "circularity" of the system *tout court*. We take our principles from our practices,

1. Russell, "Dewey's New Logic," *The Philosophy of John Dewey*, Library of Living Philosophers, ed. Paul Arthur Schilpp (Evanston and Chicago: Northwestern University, 1939), 1:139.

Dewey tells us, but our practices comprise the only check that we have on our principles. "That this circle exists is not so much admitted as claimed. It is also claimed that the circle is not vicious; for instead of being logical it is existential and historic" (p. 143). The realism that is implicit here is not that of a philosopher who thinks of an antecedently real world existing independently of our experience and knowledge, but it is a realism of emergent objects and kinds. It is a realism that is put together in piecemeal fashion; a "retail" realism that is in sharp contrast with the "wholesale" realisms of the past. It is realism that is existential and historical. It does not move in the direction that Hocking—and Peirce—called "objective idealism," or to what Hegel called the "Absolute."

Both traditional realism and idealism go wrong because they get their ontology from their logic. It is a consequence of beginning with what Dewey called "apart thought" and that he repeatedly condemned as "*the* philosophic fallacy." It is a fallacy that lies at the root of Russell's philosophy, Dewey claimed, and that vitiates the program of logical empiricism and positivism. Frege had thought that "the laws of logic are the laws of the laws of nature," and his successors had implied as much; most spectacularly, perhaps, in such constructions as Rudolf Carnap's *Der Logische Aufbau der Welt* and the modal logics of "possible worlds." Dewey, by contrast, gets his logic from his ontology of the *actual* world. The great lesson that we have to learn from science, he argued, is that the rules of induction are not extrapolated from the principles of strict implication. We do not get our forms of valid empirical inference from deductive logic at all. Rather, we get our deductive principles by abstractive inference from actual practice. As he often put it, you can get out of your logic only what you have first put into it.

In this reversal Dewey was opposing the whole drift of mainstream philosophical logic from Frege to Carnap that he had long since identified and criticized in Russell's "problem" of the external world and approach to "definite descriptions." And yet it is often assumed that because *Logic: The Theory of Inquiry* makes no use of the system of symbolization made popular by *Principia Mathematica,* Dewey had lost track of what was going on at the leading edge of philosophical logic and mathematical theory. It is a groundless assumption. With remarkable prescience, Dewey had recognized that the direction of the main-stream—that had already led to logical positivism—would fail to find a viable philosophy of science, that the "epistemological industry" would go bankrupt. Its failure was inevitable, according to Dewey, for it lacked an adequate theory of language and of the conceptions and relations that are symbolically rendered.

In his own criticism of logical positivism Willard Quine points out that Dewey was raising this critical objection even as the Vienna Circle was beginning to assemble. Under Gottlob Frege's influence, Russell had promulgated the belief that the meaning of a proposition determines its reference, and that truth is a matter of the correspondence between the formal structure of a proposition and that to which it refers. It was this belief that created for Russell the "problem" of the external world so avidly pursued by both G. E. Moore and himself, and that started Ludwig Wittgenstein on the track to the *Tractatus Logico-Philosophicus*. In slightly altered form it was this belief—that failure of reference is failure of meaning—that led to the "verification principle of meaning" made famous by A. J. Ayer's *Language, Truth and Logic* in 1936. Dewey had been arguing against this belief all along. It was an example of "apart thought" all dressed up in the new clothing designed for *Principia Mathematica*.

Dewey had contended, in his contributions to the 1903 *Studies in Logical Theory*, that meaning is a function of reference and is determined by use. He reiterated this claim in his criticism of Russell's view in the 1916 *Essays in Experimental Logic*. By 1922 it was one central point of his Carus Lectures. In them, Dewey argues against the view—which he ascribes to Russell—that meanings have a kind of "psychic existence." (He had earlier called Russell's "logical objects" the "lost souls" of logical theory.) Meanings emerge from shared discourse, he tells us, and are "primarily a property of behavior." Quine reminds us of the chronological context: "When Dewey was writing in this naturalistic vein, Wittgenstein still held his copy theory of language."[2]

In his discussion of Russell's version of the "correspondence" theory of knowledge in the essay on "Propositions, Warranted

2. W. V. Quine, "Ontological Relativity," in his *Ontological Relativity and Other Essays* (New York: Columbia University Press, 1969), p. 27.

Assertibility, and Truth" that is included here, Dewey raises his objection to "apart thought" once again. Language is not *externally* related to the world, as Russell imagines, but is processively *involved* with it. The language-world relation is *internal* to nature in experience. It is not that words attach themselves to things, but that *we* do in our transactions with them. "Wondering at how something in experience could be asserted to correspond to something by definition outside experience, which it is, upon the basis of epistemological doctrine, the sole means of 'knowing,' is what originally made me suspicious of the whole epistemological industry" (p. 179). In an "operational and behavioral" sense, the only one that is "entitled to be called a correspondence theory of truth," Dewey is quite ready to accept that propositions have meaning as *means*. They are the means of conducting our transactions with things. It is this kind of transactional "correspondence" that he had called a "conjugate" relation in *Logic: The Theory of Inquiry.*

Interpretation of Dewey's doctrine of propositions has oscillated between "instrumentalism" and "operationalism," but as this same essay shows it is neither—or both. Dewey offers a solution to the problem that Nelson Goodman identified as "The Problem of Counterfactual Conditionals" in a famous paper in 1946. What Dewey's doctrine does with what he prefers to call "if-then" propositions is construe them as plans that we accept or reject depending upon how they work out in practice. These plans, no more than those that Goodman calls the *Ways of Worldmaking,* are ways of arriving at certitude. Like the process that Goodman calls "entrenchment," Dewey's process of inquiry provides warrants for actions and choices that turn out to be more right than wrong. In his 1916 *Essays in Experimental Logic* Dewey had put it this way: "Inference is the advance into the unknown, the use of the established to win new worlds from the void."[3]

In the preface to *Logic: The Theory of Inquiry* Dewey refers to

3. "Some Stages of Logical Thought," *Essays in Experimental Logic* (Chicago: University of Chicago Press, 1916), p. 215 [*The Middle Works of John Dewey, 1899–1924,* ed. Jo Ann Boydston (Carbondale and Edwardsville: Southern Illinois University Press, 1976), 1:171]. See Hilary Putnam's comparison of Wittgenstein, Dewey, and Goodman in his foreword to Goodman's *Fact, Fiction, and Forecast,* 4th ed. (Cambridge: Harvard University Press, 1983), pp. viii–ix.

"the need for development of a general theory of language in which form and matter are not separated; and . . . to the fact that an adequate set of symbols depends upon prior institution of valid ideas of the conceptions and relations that are symbolized." He goes on to deliver this decisive comment on the danger of excessive formalism: "Without fulfilment of this condition, formal symbolization will (as so often happens at present) merely perpetuate existing mistakes while strengthening them by seeming to give them scientific standing." It is an irony of history that this powerful critique of the dominant philosophical logic of the period should have been so readily dismissed as not belonging to logic at all. Russell thought that it belonged to psychology, and C. I. Lewis wished that Dewey would not call logic "what is a much wider thing." It was, of course, both a part of psychology *and* a much wider thing. For in *Logic* Dewey had produced the very theory that he called for in the preface. He had developed a general theory of language in which "form" and "matter" are not separated, and he had instituted an analysis of the conceptions and relations that comprise the subject matter of logical theory.

Richard Rorty points out that Dewey was "waiting at the end of the dialectical road which analytic philosophy traveled."[4] And what the essays and rejoinders in the present volume disclose is that he was ready to block that road from the beginning. The operational and behavioral conception of meaning which analytical philosophy arrives at, through the work of such different philosophers as Wittgenstein, Goodman, and Quine, had been part of Dewey's project all along. It is not that Dewey wanted to deny the great value of formal analysis any more than they did. But, like them, he wanted us to see how mistaken it is to superimpose our formal analysis upon our natural language. Dewey was not trying to deprive the sciences of access to the norms and criteria of formal logic. He was not an *antiformalist* in that sense at all. It is just that he wanted us to realize how much the norms and criteria of formal analysis owe to the biological and cultural matrix from which they arise. He wanted us to see how little they owe to "apart thought."

It is futile, Dewey argued, to begin with "self-evident" prin-

4. Rorty, *Consequences of Pragmatism* (Minneapolis: University of Minnesota Press, 1982), p. xviii.

ciples and axioms, with rules of strict implication, and then expect that we can somehow get our rules of inductive inference
from them. That puts the cart before the horse. The way to begin is
the other way around. Dewey wanted us to see how much our
natural discourse owes to our own creative intelligence and how
much it reflects the logical structure of our experience. He viewed
our language and the logic which it embodies as a man-made
structure, one that is no less wondrous for being so. In a popular
essay on "Events and Meanings" written for the *New Republic* in
1922 he put it this way: "By sufficient preliminary conversation
you can avert a catastrophe. . . . Apart from conversation, from
discourse and communication, there is no thought and no meaning, only just events, dumb, preposterous, destructive" (*Middle
Works* 13:279, 280). And in the more measured phrases of *Experience and Nature:*

> Of all affairs, communication is the most wonderful. That
> things should be able to pass from the plane of external push-
> ing and pulling to that of revealing themselves to man, and
> thereby to themselves; and that the fruit of communication
> should be participation, sharing, is a wonder by the side of
> which transubstantiation pales. (*Later Works* 1:132)

John Dewey laid no claim to have originated what is today called
the social theory of language, but he did see in that theory "The
Basis for Hope" (pp. 249–51).

In his superb introduction to *The Quest for Certainty* in the
Later Works, Stephen Toulmin shows how different Dewey's philosophy looks when compared with the methods, arguments,
and purposes of Peirce and James. He points out how "misleading it can be to lump them all together, as the single school of
'pragmatists,'" and he stresses the extraordinary "farsightedness,
perception and originality" of Dewey's work, features that are of
a kind that could scarcely have been recognized in his own time,
and that have barely been acknowledged in our own. Toulmin
goes on to suggest that we gain in understanding Dewey from
a comparison of his achievements with those of his "younger
contemporaries, Ludwig Wittgenstein and Martin Heidegger"
(*Later Works* 4:ix). He wants us to see how the cutting edge of
Dewey's critical thought in the Gifford Lectures anticipates so

many of the concerns of Wittgenstein and Heidegger in under-mining the epistemological foundations of the Cartesian and Lockean traditions, and how clearly the constructive side of Dewey's work relates to the creative use of "language games" by Wittgenstein and to Heidegger's insights as to how we "consti-tute" the objects of our understanding.

While these comparisons accurately reflect some of the ways in which Dewey departed from his pragmatic predecessors, there are other ways that are no less important. They are ways in which his conception of philosophy contrasts both with that of his predecessors and of his "younger contemporaries" as well. For Dewey's conception of philosophy seems always to have in-volved him in the reconstruction of the culture that he criticized in ways that their conceptions did not. It is not that they failed to offer therapeutic suggestions and remedies for the diseases that they diagnosed, it is just that they left the applications of these suggestions and remedies to others. They did not *engage them-selves* in the process as Dewey always did.

Dewey's conception of philosophy includes not just a *critical* component but a *transformational* thrust as well. Philosophy must not merely reflect and respond to its cultural context, to the processes of change taking place all around it; it must engage in those processes and act upon them. It does so by participating in the conversation, in the shared discourse that determines the course to be taken. It is a conception of philosophy that we rec-ognize in such different thinkers as St. Augustine and Karl Marx, in Jean-Paul Sartre and Paul Tillich, a conception that we some-times think of as the lasting contribution of Socrates to philoso-phy. That it was integral to Dewey's conception is amply evident in the contents of the collection in hand that range from a state-ment on "Art as Our Heritage," published in the *Congressional Record,* to a "Statement on Academic Freedom" made in criti-cism of President Nicholas Murray Butler of Columbia University and printed in the *New York Times.* One thinks of Dewey's life-long battle against the stagnation of educational institutions, and his efforts to transform them as part of his strategy for social change that form the background of the essays on "Education: 1800–1939" and "For a New Education." They are all of a piece with his leadership of a parade of "Suffragettes" down Fifth Ave-nue in the 1920s, and his chairmanship of the Commission of Inquiry in 1937 that had been set up to hear Leon Trotsky's defense against the charges that had been brought against him in the Moscow "purge" trials under Stalin. It is not easy to imagine Dewey's "younger contemporaries" in any of these roles, unless we should happen to think of Russell.

The bond between Dewey and Russell is a curious one. Devoid of any trace of sentiment or mutual affection, and marked by the most serious philosophical differences, they found themselves on the same side of a moral issue on more than one occasion. Although they were divided on the question of pacifism in 1914, Russell wrote to Lady Ottoline of his first meeting with Dewey at that time: "To my surprise I liked him very much. He has a large slow-moving mind, very empirical and candid, with something of the impassivity and impartiality of a natural force."[5] This appreciation of Dewey's mind was extended to include Mrs. Dewey as well, in 1920, when they met in China. The Deweys had gone to China at the invitation of Hu Shih and other former Columbia students, who were trying to reform Chinese educational practices, and they remained there for the better part of two years. Dewey lectured for the most part at the National Peking University, but was traveling in Hunan Province when Russell arrived with his secretary, Miss Dora Black. Russell tells of their meeting in China this way: "The first time I met Professor and Mrs. Dewey was at a banquet in Chang-sha, given by the *tuchun*. When the time came for after-dinner speeches, Mrs. Dewey told the *tuchun* that his province must adopt co-education. He made a statesmanlike reply, saying that the matter should receive his best consideration, but he feared the time was not ripe in Hunan."[6]

The fact that Russell was traveling with a woman to whom he was not yet married caused consternation in the British and American settlements in Peking. George Dykhuizen tells us that "This struck Mrs. Dewey as very unfair, her argument being that if Russell was socially acceptable, Dora Black should be also. Consequently, her invitations to the Dewey home included both Miss Black and Russell despite the disapproval of many of her friends." When Russell fell ill with pneumonia and was not ex-

---

5. Ottoline Morrell Papers, #1008, 22.3.14, Humanities Research Center, University of Texas at Austin. Quoted from *Middle Works* 7:496.

6. Quoted by George Dykhuizen, *The Life and Mind of John Dewey* (Carbondale and Edwardsville: Southern Illinois University Press, 1973), p. 198.

pected to survive, it was reported in Peking that Dewey was at his bedside and had taken down his last will and testament. The London papers carried a report that death had come on March 28, 1921, and the *Manchester Guardian* published a fulsome obituary that no doubt contributed immensely to Russell's speedy recovery.[7]

The events described in the present volume in the essay on "Social Realities *versus* Police Court Fictions," and Dewey's reaction to them, were not unprecedented, then. But something should be said about Dewey's response beyond what is here recorded. For, after the "Russell Case" was concluded, and an appeal had failed, Russell found himself in a position of financial embarrassment. Coming to his rescue, Dewey secured for him an appointment at the Barnes Foundation in Merion, Pennsylvania. Although that position was not an entirely suitable one from either the foundation's standpoint or from Russell's, and was soon to be terminated (with ensuing litigation), Dewey's personal generosity in the instance remained unimpeached. It, like the defense of Russell's appointment to City College, and of the college's right to offer it in the first place, was but another in a long series of tests of principle that Dewey put into practice—and of practice that informed his conception of principle. Years earlier, when Maxim Gorki had visited New York City in an effort to rally support for the revolution then taking place in Russia and had been refused even hotel accommodation in the city, Dewey offered his home to Gorki and his mistress. In the public outcry that followed in which even Mark Twain complained that Dewey had gone too far, for "laws can be evaded and punishment escaped, but an openly transgressed custom brings sure punishment," Dewey remained firm.[8] As John McDermott has observed of the incident: "The publicity in this instance was unusual but the hospitality was not, for the Deweys often housed on a temporary basis people fleeing or making one revolution or another, be they Irish or Chinese."

The relationship between law and custom had indeed been a central concern of Dewey's since 1893, when he had reviewed

7. Dykhuizen, pp. 198–99.
8. John McDermott, ed., *The Philosophy of John Dewey* (New York: G. P. Putnam's Sons, 1973), p. xxi.

Oliver Wendell Holmes's treatment of the problem in his treatise on *The Common Law*. Under the title "Anthropology and Law" (*Early Works* 4:37–41) Dewey had early adopted the central theme that he reiterates here in the essay on "My Philosophy of Law." It is that the relationship between law and custom is the same in pattern as that between theory and fact; he thought that we should treat law in the same "experimental" way that we treat theory. We opt out of that circular pattern for the same reason that we opt for "apart thought" in our logic of inquiry. We want a standard or criterion which is not subject to the variance of actual experience, not vitiated by the evanescence of actual conditions. And so we postulate a "source" of law that lies outside of actual experience, and an "end" of law that transcends the actual conditions of life. The history of the theory of "natural law" confirms the practice, Dewey says, with the result that its content remains largely irrelevant to changing needs and actual practices. By contrast the "common law" arises from custom, and is "preserved and modified through the agency of natural selection" (*Early Works* 4:40).

Just as he had rejected "natural law" theory early on, Dewey had also rejected its most popular rival. The "positive law" theory, advocated by Jeremy Bentham and his colleague John Austin, errs in the opposite direction from that followed by the advocates of "natural law." By reducing law to whatever the "sovereign commands," legal positivism had hoped to counter the arguments of all those who found that the source of the law is in the "Divine Will" or in the fixed order of Nature (writ large). This appeal to a transcendent source of authority for legal rights, Bentham argued, blocked the program of legal reform in which he was engaged and which would have vested rights in the "sovereignty" of the individual. The doctrine of "natural rights," Bentham wrote, "is simple nonsense: natural and imprescriptible rights, rhetorical nonsense,—nonsense upon stilts."[9] Dewey rejected the extreme individualism implicit in this conception of sovereignty on the grounds that it failed to acknowledge the social reality that Rousseau had tried to recognize in his notion of the "General Will." As for "sovereignty," Dewey wrote in his 1894 essay on "Austin's Theory of Sovereignty," it must find resi-

---

9. *The Works of Jeremy Bentham,* ed. John Bowring (New York: Russell and Russell, 1962), p. 501.

dence "in the whole complex of social activities . . . the social whole, or true sovereign" (*Early Works* 4:90).

Having carved out a path between "natural law" and "legal positivism" in these early essays, Dewey never wavered from it in his subsequent and not infrequent work on legal problems, both jurisprudential and legislative. Repeatedly, Dewey put to legal philosophy the three questions that he had formulated in his early essays: What is the source of law? What is the end or purpose of law? By what means is the law to be applied? They are the three questions that form the conceptual core of the essay on "My Philosophy of Law" in which "The standpoint taken is that law is through and through a social phenomenon; social in origin, in purpose or end, and in application" (p. 117).

Dewey argued these questions, and the social answers to them, in an essay on legal reasoning in 1914 called "Nature and Reason in Law" (*Middle Works* 7:56−63), and again in 1926 in an essay on "The Historic Background of Corporate Legal Personality" (*Later Works* 2:22−43). But perhaps the clearest example of how closely Dewey's legal philosophy follows his philosophy of logic is his 1924 essay on "Logical Method and Law" (*Middle Works* 15:65−77), which was first published in the *Philosophical Review* and appeared shortly after in the *Cornell Law Quarterly*. By that time Dewey had been widely recognized as a proponent of a "school" of jurisprudential thought known as "legal realism" that had its headquarters at the Columbia Law School. The essay was an attempt to show the consequences for legal reasoning of the criticism that Dewey had been making of traditional logical theory since before the turn of the century. He wanted his readers to understand that logic must be thoroughly reconceptualized as an *empirical* undertaking. It must examine ways of solving problems, not in order to discover some single method or set of formal rules or some all-encompassing algorithm such as the syllogism was once thought to be. We start with a confused situation, not with a set of neatly ordered premises. "Thinking," he said, "may be defined either as a development of premises or development of a conclusion; as far as it is one operation it is the other" (*Middle Works* 15:72). He was reaffirming the "circularity" of the process, and showing how it applies both to the lawyer as advocate and to the judge who "finds" the law by making it.

In "My Philosophy of Law" Dewey is still arguing the middle path of "legal realism" that had so influenced American jurisprudence from Justice Holmes to Justice Douglas, that brought the social sciences to bear upon the law in the Warren Court—most notoriously, perhaps, in *Brown v. Board of Education* and the school desegregation cases. "On the view here presented," Dewey says, "the standard is found in consequences, in the *function* of what goes on socially. If this view were generally held, there would be assurance of introduction on a large scale of the rational factor into concrete evaluations of legal arrangements" (p. 122). It is the view adopted by such legal scholars as Jerome Frank and Karl Llewellyn not long since, and upon which the disparate views of Ronald Dworkin and H. L. A. Hart seem convergent in our own time—the convergence of the "right based" theory of justice on the one hand with the "goal based" theory on the other. Abraham Edel has described it this way: "In general, the ultimate matrix of legal theory is the totality of social experience and reflection upon it. The life of the law is not logic, nor an abstract way of looking at the law. But it is not experience either. It is the reflection on experience in the effort to guide further experience. No model should become so entrenched as to hamper this process." [10]

It is just this holistic reflection on experience designed to guide further experience that is at the core of Dewey's conception of philosophy across the board. It links his treatment of the Constitution with his introduction of Thomas Jefferson, his defense of Bertrand Russell against the Police Court "Fictions" with his treatment of Cowdry's *Problems of Ageing,* his conception of reconstruction in philosophy with Karl Mannheim's conception of social reconstruction. It shows how the "problems and hypotheses" that Dewey had been tackling all along "hang together" and contribute to the task of "creation of a freer and more humane experience in which all share and to which all contribute" (p. 230). It is this vision which is the great fact about John Dewey, and about the "definite point of view" which informs his philosophy and the originality of his perspective. [11]

10. Edel, *Archiv für Rechts- und Sozialphilosophie, Supplementa,* Vol. 1, Part 1, Contemporary Conception of Law, 9th World Congress, Basel, Switzerland, 27 August–1 September 1979, p. 96.
11. Three themes that are central to the essays collected in this volume—metaphysics, language, and logic—are dealt with more extensively in R. W. Sleeper, *The Necessity of Pragmatism: John Dewey's Conception of Philosophy* (New Haven: Yale University Press, 1986).

Essays

Experience, Knowledge and Value: A Rejoinder

To combine acknowledgment of indebtedness to the writers who have taken so much pains in expounding and criticizing my views with reply to adverse criticisms is not an easy task. I am confident I can count on their and the readers' appreciation of this difficulty. I do not share, I confess, the optimism expressed in the Announcement of the Series of which this is one volume, regarding the possibility of terminating controversy. As the history of philosophical discussion shows, it is quite possible that what is said in answering one objection and clearing away one misconception will give rise to others. Yet, as the same Announcement also says, an undertaking of this kind, providing as it does for interpretation on the part of both friendly and adverse critics, should facilitate a "meeting of minds" so that whatever happens to the views and doctrines of a given writer on philosophy (in this case, mine), the larger continuing cause of philosophic inquiry should be forwarded.

It may assist understanding of the comments and replies found in the following pages if I say something about the method adopted in arranging my remarks. The first idea that occurred to me was to take up each contribution separately, and reply *seriatim* to the several points made in each. But it soon appeared that such a course would demand many quotations from both my own writings and those of my critics, with the necessity for more or less extensive exegesis of passages cited:—proverbially the source rather than close of controversy. As Mr. Piatt says in his article, too frequently "clarifications of meanings fail to clarify and merely repeat the initial difficulty." It is not easy at the best to move from a system of ideas having one centre and order

[First published in *The Philosophy of John Dewey,* Library of Living Philosophers, ed. Paul Arthur Schilpp (Evanston and Chicago: Northwestern University, 1939), 1:517–608.]

into a system having a different focus and arrangement. Neither a critic nor myself is responsible for the fact that every philosophical word employed is charged, in the degree of its importance, with ambiguities resulting from centuries of controversial discussions. In addition, adoption of the kind of procedure just mentioned may easily obscure the matters at issue by covering them up with a multiplicity of details so that the forest is not seen because of the trees. For a time, then, I entertained the contrary hope that I might be able to discuss a number of general issues, which the various papers show are in need of clarification, with only incidental reference to special criticisms. My experience in trying this method proved however that there was danger that my reply would be so very general as not to come to grips with specific criticisms. Moreover, the variety of points touched upon and the diversity of the philosophical perspectives in which they are presented formed a serious practical obstacle. I have adopted accordingly a sort of compromise procedure—in the not too confident hope that it may not turn out in the end to combine the worst features of the other two methods. I have selected some main heads under which to restate my views in reference to criticisms passed upon fundamental principles in my philosophy, and then under each head have attempted to meet with specific comments a variety of special criticisms.[1]

In the hope that it may be of help in following what is said and also in understanding the distribution of space given to different contributors, I attempt a rough classification of the papers which precede. Drs. Ratner, Geiger, Childs and Kilpatrick have at various times been members of classes taught by me at Columbia University. Some of them have been colleagues as is the case with Dr. Randall. It would be a serious reproach to me if my associates had not attained a juster understanding of what I had said in my written work than is likely to exist in the case of those who have only the latter to consult. Dr. Piatt was a student at the University of Chicago after I left there and had the great advantage of the teachings of Professors Tufts, Mead and Moore. Just because my obligations to these contributors are great I have said much less about their articles than about those in the third group

---

1. In my rejoinders to some of the specific criticisms, I shall presuppose familiarity with the text of the contributors' articles since space forbids reproduction of the details of their argument.

mentioned below. In many respects a careful reading of their articles will serve as more effectual replies to some of the adverse criticisms than anything I can say. After all allowance is made for the loyalty of students to old teachers—a loyalty often carried to excess—I have to express my appreciation of the way in which these contributors have seen and reported the direction in which my thoughts have moved, of their sense of what it is I was doing and what it is I was after. In lieu of extended comments, I must ask them to accept my thanks, and with mine that of all readers who are concerned to know what my views actually are.

In the second group are a number of writers whose expositions of the topics with which they deal are essentially correct in some or many points, even though accompanied with disagreement with the conclusions I have reached. To these persons, comparative strangers, are due my thanks for the pains they have taken to become acquainted with my writings and to report faithfully their general tenor. Dr. Allport, an expert psychologist, has performed this service for one who long ago ceased to profess expertness in a highly specialized technical field. Dr. Parodi in his careful account of the relations of knowledge and action in my theory has lightened my task of reply by correcting in advance some misconceptions put forward by other contributors who touch upon the subject. Dr. Savery has provided a valuable supplement to the other contributions by placing my views in historic perspective in their relation to Peirce and James, while also correcting in advance, by his brief but pertinent remarks upon pluralism, continuity and contingency, some common misapprehensions. Professor Whitehead has written with his characteristic generosity of spirit.

In the third group fall the articles of a more definitely adverse kind—those of Drs. Reichenbach and Pepper in part, and of Russell, Murphy, Santayana, Stuart and Schaub in almost their entirety. It will readily be understood, then, why much more space is given to them than to the writers who are more sympathetic or more correct in their expositions of my views. My indebtedness to this third group is of a different kind. I am obliged to them for the stimulus of their challenges and for the opportunity to try and set myself right on some points where in the past I have obviously failed not only to carry conviction, but (a more important matter) to make clear my actual position.

A. Introductory

As an introduction to the leading issues (Experience, Knowledge in its relation to experience, and Ethics) which constitute the main heads of my reply, I shall say something about the problems which have directed the course of my philosophical thinking—a procedure almost obligatory upon one who has emphasized the role of problems to the extent I have done. And in this particular connection I am especially grateful for the contributions of Drs. Ratner and Randall. I have been engaged by means of published writings in developing the essentials of my present philosophical views for at least thirty-five years, beginning with my essays in the *Studies in Logical Theory* in 1903. Inconsistencies and shifts have taken place; the most I can claim is that I have moved fairly steadily in one direction. Dr. Ratner has put his finger upon the main "shift" in my writings. It affects not only the special topic of philosophy but the more general one of knowledge. At various places in my writings I have said that, from the standpoint of empirical naturalism, the denotative reference of "mind" and "intelligence" is to funding of meanings and significances, a funding which is both a product of past inquiries or knowings and the means of enriching and controlling the subject-matters of subsequent experiences. The function of enrichment and control is exercised by incorporation of what was gained in past experience in attitudes and habits which, in their interaction with the environment, create the clearer, better ordered, "fuller" or richer materials of later experiences—a process capable of indefinite continuance. Dr. Ratner is quite right in indicating that the word "intelligence" represents what is essential in my view much better than does the word *knowledge,* while it avoids that confusion of knowing—inquiry—and attained knowledge which has led some of my critics astray in their accounts of my position. At present, after reading criticisms of the kind of *instrumentalism* that is attributed to me, it is clear that I should, from the start, have systematically distinguished between knowledge as the outcome of special inquiries (undertaken because of the presence of problems) and *intelligence* as the product and expression of cumulative funding of the meanings reached in these special cases. Nevertheless, there are in my earlier writings many indications of the distinction and of the role it plays, as well as references to the principle of organic habit as the physical agency by which the transition from one to the other is effected. I cite two passages: "The function of knowledge is to make one experience freely available in other experiences. The word 'freely' marks the difference between the function of knowledge and of habit," while sentences which follow show that the difference is not ultimately one between habit and intelligence but between routine habits and intelligent ones.[2] From a later, though not latest, writing I cite the following representative passage:

> The history of human progress is the story of the transformation of acts which, like the interactions of inanimate things, take place unknowingly to actions qualified by understanding of what they are about; from actions controlled by external conditions to actions having guidance through their intent:— their insight into their own consequences. Instruction, information, knowledge, is the only way in which this property of intelligence comes to qualify acts originally blind.[3]

I did not hit upon my position as a ready made and finished doctrine. It developed in and through a series of reactions to a number of philosophic problems and doctrines. During the early nineties, practically all important philosophizing in the English language was influenced by Neo-Kantian and Hegelian idealism. Pragmatism and all versions of realism are of later growth. In my own case change of residence from Chicago to New York in 1905 brought me in direct contact with the Aristotelian realism of Woodbridge and the monistic realism of Montague. There was a new challenge and a new stimulus. It is perhaps natural that I should not agree with the judgment expressed by Dr. Murphy that my discussion of certain important issues "is not intelligible until we refer it back to the idealistic and realistic philosophies in relation to which it was developed." But I gladly admit that my philosophic views did not develop in a vacuum and that I took seriously philosophic doctrines that were current. Undoubtedly, study of the problems they presented played a part in the devel-

2. *Democracy and Education* (1916), 395 [*Middle Works* 9:349]. The whole discussion of the topics of Method, Subject-matter and Theories of Knowing is relevant.
3. *Quest for Certainty* (1929), 245 [*Later Works* 4:196].

opment of my own philosophic method and doctrines. For I felt myself under an obligation to develop my personal intellectual predilections in a way that took cognizance of strong points in other teachings while trying to avoid what appeared to me to be their weak points.

As, however, will be made evident later, it was not the issue of idealism *versus* realism that constituted my problem, but the bearing of these theories (as well as that of the older classic tradition) upon two issues which chiefly preoccupied me. Personally, I do not feel that a defence of the habit of taking seriously important historic systems is necessary. But it is important, even necessary, to appreciate what phases of historical thought—past and present—enter deeply into determination of the thinking of any philosopher. Consequently, I am deeply grateful for two things that stand out in Dr. Randall's account. One of them is the general and basic consideration that I regard the philosophy of any period as a reflex of larger and more far-reaching cultural achievements, needs, conflicts and problems. The other as stated in his own words is the fact that there is "one central conflict as the focus for understanding all Western philosophies. It is the ever repeated struggle between the active force of scientific knowledge and technical power and the deflecting force of the lag and inertia of institutionalized habits and beliefs." Because of the centrality of this struggle and the problem of readjustment set by it, I have approached (as Randall says) our cultural "heritage as a critic and reconstructor of tradition" so that "he is forever bringing men's past experience with ideas to the test of present experience." Whether I am right or wrong in this attitude and whether or not I have exaggerated the extent to which vital cultural problems—which ultimately decide important philosophical problems—now centre about the reworking of traditions (institutions, customs, beliefs of all sorts), to bring them into harmony with the potentialities of present science and technology,—here is the setting in which my chief problems have arisen.

The form taken in my philosophical system by this underlying socio-cultural problem is seen in what I have said about the two issues which to my mind have controlled the main course of modern thought: [4] "The problem of restoring integration and co-

4. There are also, it goes without saying, in the course of modern thought, a large number of questions of a more definitely technical sort, some of which are more closely connected with the main issue I state below and some more remotely. My

operation between man's beliefs about the world in which he lives and his beliefs about values and purposes that should direct his conduct is the deepest problem of any philosophy that is not isolated from that life."[5] What is here designated by the phrase "beliefs about the world" is made explicit in a sentence of the next page: "Its [philosophy's] central problem is the relation that exists between the beliefs about the nature of things *due to natural science* and beliefs about *values*—using that word to designate whatever is taken to have rightful authority in the direction of conduct."[6] The other main problem has in verbal statement a more technical sound. It is "the problem of the relation of physical science to the things of ordinary experience."[7]

This latter problem is closely connected with the first in as far as things desired and enjoyed—and disenjoyed—are among the things of ordinary experience and also provide the material of valuation-judgments. It involves, however, a somewhat distinctive set of problems, connected with the pre-experimental and pre-technological leisure class tradition, according to which the characteristic object of knowledge has a privileged position of correspondence with what is ultimately "real," in contrast to things of non-cognitive experiences, which form the great bulk of "ordinary experiences." Most of the dualisms forming the stock problems of modern epistemological theory have originated, as I have tried to show, out of the assumptions which generate these two problems. If, however, the philosophical theory of experience is brought up to date by acknowledgement of the standpoint and conclusions of scientific biology and cultural anthropology and of the import of the experimental method in knowing, these problems, I have argued, are "solved" by recognition that they depend upon premises inherited from traditions now shown to be false. Some of the gratuitous dualisms done away with, I have argued, are those of the objective and subjective, the real and apparent, the mental and physical, scientific physical objects and

technique has grown directly out of the problems and methods of historic philosophies. I hardly know any other way in which a competent technique can be formed; although it is possible that at times I have overdone the importance of obtaining technical skill. At least, were I to criticize my own writings, I should bring that charge rather than that of complete looseness which some critics find in what I have written.

5. *Quest for Certainty,* 255 [*Later Works* 4:204].
6. *Ibid.,* 256 [*Later Works* 4:204].
7. *Ibid.,* 252 [*Later Works* 4:201].

objects of perception, things of experience and things-in-themselves concealed behind experience, the latter being an impenetrable veil which prevents cognitive access to the things of nature.[8]

The source of these dualisms, I have contended, is isolation of cognitive experience and its subject-matter from other modes of experience and *their* subject-matters, this isolation leading inevitably to disparagement of the things of ordinary qualitative experiences, those which are esthetic, moral, practical; to "derogation of the things we experience by way of love, desire, hope, fear, purpose and the traits characterizing human individuality"[9]— or else in an effort to justify the latter by assertion of a super-scientific, supra-empirical transcendent *a priori* realm. Now I did not invent these problems; I found them controlling, often covertly rather than openly, the course of philosophic reflection and thereby determining conclusions reached. If the urgency of these problems is ignored or slighted (urgent in philosophy because urgent in actual cultural life when the latter is submitted to analysis), the context of the larger part of what I have written will be so missed that what I have said will seem to be a strange, a gratuitously strange, intellectual adventure, redeemed—if at all— only by the presence of a certain technical skill. For what has governed my discussion of historical systems—at first idealistic and realistic theories of knowledge and later the classic tradition as it has come down to us from Greece—is the belief that the cultural causes, scientific, political and economic, which led to the doctrine of the supremacy of the cognitive experience and the consequent supposed necessity for relegating the things of all non-cognitive experiences to an inferior status, no longer apply. On the contrary, I believe that the factors of the existing cultural situation, scientific, technological, and "social," are such that philosophic theories which in effect, even if not in intent, are products of pre-scientific and pre-technological, dominantly leisure class conditions, are now as obstructive as they are unnecessary.

I do not find that my critics have much to say about my criticism of the virtual irresponsibility of theories produced by isola-

8. Cf. the standpoint from which Santayana criticizes my view, a standpoint viti-ated by its own uncritical assumption that the splits involved are matters of ordinary common sense acknowledged as such by every "candid" thinker.
9. *Ibid.*, 219 [*Later Works* 4:175].

tion of cognitive experience, and by assertion of the exclusively "real" character of its subject-matter in contrast with that of the things of ordinary, chiefly non-cognitive, experience. But these ideas when they govern philosophy (as a distinctive mode of knowledge) are the source of the notion that its business is to tell something about "ultimate reality" not told about in the natural sciences, so that in the end philosophy is separated from the sciences as well as set over against the things of ordinary experiences. I do not wish to intimate that no correct statements and valid criticisms of special points in my philosophic positions can be made unless their general setting is noted. But some of the accounts given of my ideas, together with the criticisms based on them, seem to me to have their source in the failure to take into consideration the contextual problems by which my statements have their import determined—a failure especially marked, as is shown later, in the case of Dr. Murphy, in spite of his professed respect for the principle of Contextualism.

Among the contemporary factors which enable us to get away from issues that lack present support and relevance is the influence of biology and cultural anthropology in transforming traditional psychological views. The point to be borne in mind in this connection is the respective bearings of the old "subjectivistic" psychology and the new behavioral one upon the philosophical conception of experience. It is to me a very curious fact that some of my critics take for granted a mentalistic view of experience; so that they cannot help attributing to me that view when I speak of experience. In addition they so largely ignore the difficulties inherent in their own subjectivism:—difficulties that are recognized by Santayana, and that drive him into complete scepticism, tempered by a sudden and unmediated practical jump of pure faith into the things of nature—a kind of arbitrary pragmatism from which I shrink. For it seems to me identical with the pragmatism sometimes attributed to Kant, although with the substitution of animal for moral faith on one side, and of a natural for the noumenal world on the other. The biological-anthropological method of approach to experience provides the way out of mentalistic into behavioral interpretation of experiencing, both in general and in its detailed manifestations. With equal necessity and pertinency, it points the way out of the belief that experience as such is inherently cognitional and that cognition is the sole path that leads into the natural world. Anybody who accepts the socio-biological point of view is bound, I think, to raise sooner or later the questions I put forward in *Studies in Logical Theory* about the relations between dominantly esthetic, moral and affectional modes and subject-matters of experience and the cognitional mode and its subject-matter. I can see how this issue can be considered without arriving at the idea of "Instrumentalism." But I believe the conclusion of any serious analysis will make the cognitional mode intermediate between an earlier, less organized, more confused and fragmentary sort of experienced subject-matter and one more ordered, clearer, freer, richer, and under better control as to its occurrence.

The other fundamental consideration is drawn from a study of modern scientific method in its contrast with Greek and medieval theory and practice of knowing. It is, of course, the importance of experimental method. If in this connection I have emphasized physical knowledge, it is not (as I have said many times) because the latter is the only kind of knowledge, but because its comparative maturity as a form of knowledge exemplifies so conspicuously the necessary place and function of experimentation; whereas, in contrast, beliefs in moral and social subjects are still reached and framed with minimum regard for experimental method.

I am aware that it is now not unusual to say that the value of experimental method is such a familiar commonplace that it is not necessary to dwell upon its implications; that putting it in antithesis to the theory of immediate knowing is but a case of slaying the dead. I wish this were so. If it were, I should feel that I had accomplished a large part of the purpose I set out to accomplish, and that philosophy would henceforth be free from this phase of epistemological doctrine. But I find the belief in immediate knowledge still flourishing, and I also find that a writer like Mr. Bertrand Russell can link my theory of knowledge and the place of experimentation (doing and making) in knowledge primarily with an age of industrialism and collective enterprise, so especially marked in this country as to make my philosophy peculiarly American. This view is a repetition of a position he took long ago. When, in 1922, he said that he found the "love of truth obscured in America by commercialism of which pragmatism is the philosophical expression," I remarked that the statement seemed to me to be "of that order of interpretation which would say that English neo-realism is a reflection of the snobbish aristocracy of the English and the tendency of French thought to dualism an expression of an alleged Gallic disposition to keep a mistress in addition to a wife." [10] And I still believe that Mr. Russell's confirmed habit of connecting the pragmatic theory of knowing with obnoxious aspects of American industrialism, instead of with the experimental method of attaining knowledge, is much as if I were to link his philosophy to the interests of English landed aristocracy instead of with dominant interest in mathematics.

Similarly, when I read that I eschew discussion of a certain problem because "my *purpose* is practical," I am quite sure that all I have said—amounting first and last to a good deal—to the effect that my pragmatism affirms that action is involved in *knowledge,* not that knowledge is subordinated to action or "practice," has gone for naught—as it could hardly do if the emphasis upon experimental method were taken seriously. And I should not be obliged to devote to the topic of *truth* the space later given to it, if what I have said about *consequences* were put in the context of experiment. The outcome of the operations that are guided by a hypothesis is the only context in which consequences in my theory have anything to do with truth. Nor, were the point recognized, should I be compelled to repeat once more that, instead of holding that knowledge is instrumental to action and truth to personal satisfaction, what I have uniformly insisted upon is that knowledge when attained is the only medium to controlled enrichment and control of subsequent experiences of a qualitative non-cognitive type. As it is, however, I seem obliged to cite a passage like the following:

> Many critics take an "instrumental" theory of knowledge to signify that the value of knowing is instrumental to the knower. This is a matter which is as it may be in particular cases; but certainly in many cases the pursuit of science is carried on, like other sports, for its own satisfaction. "Instrumentalism" is a theory not about personal disposition and satisfaction in knowing but about the proper objects of science, "proper" being defined in terms of physics. [11]

10. Reprinted in *Characters and Events,* Vol. II, 543 [*Middle Works* 13:307].
11. *Experience and Nature,* 151 [*Later Works* 1:121].

And again,

> To say that knowledge as the fruit of intellectual discourse
> is an end in itself is to say what is esthetically and morally
> true for some persons, but it conveys nothing about the
> *structure* of knowledge; it does not even hint that its *objects*
> are not instrumental. These are questions that can be decided
> only by an examination of the things in question.

Earlier in the same paragraph, it is said to be "a priceless gain
when it (gaining of knowledge) becomes an intrinsic delight,"
while it is also pointed out that the more this possibility is emphasized, the more imperative becomes the social problem of discovering why it is that such a relatively small number of persons
enjoy the privilege.[12] In short, I think I have lived up, with reasonable faithfulness, to the principle stated in the ensuing passage: "Genuine intellectual integrity is found in experimental
knowing. Until this lesson is fully learned, it is not safe to dis-
sociate knowledge from experiment nor experiment from experience."[13] I shall indeed be most happy when the day comes when
all I have said on this topic becomes superfluous.

B. Experience and Empirical Method in Philosophy

After this introduction, intended to place some of my
leading ideas in their proper context, I come to the first of the
three chief subjects to be taken up in my reply. Dr. Piatt remarks
in his paper that understanding my position would be facilitated
if more attention were paid to my naturalism and less to my empiricism. I fully agree, with the proviso that my idea of experience and hence of empirical method is naturalistic. I have already
mentioned the potential effect of biological and anthropological
knowledge in transforming the older psychological and philo-

12. *Ibid.*, 203 [*Later Works* 1 : 158]. The belief that a theory of knowing which in
its origin was inherently a leisure class theory has influence in justifying the
state of society in which only a few are thus privileged, hence in perpetuating
the latter condition, *is* a part of my complete theory. If that be commercialism,
I do not know what humanism would be.
13. *Essays in Experimental Logic*, 74 [*Middle Works* 10 : 365].

sophical idea of experience. The modification thus effected is directly relevant to Mr. Russell's notions that my philosophy is holistic and that my empiricism leads to subjectivism; to the interpretation placed by Mr. Pepper upon my use of such words as coherence, integration, wholes, etc.; to Mr. Santayana's charge that my theory of experience commits me to a view that everything is "immediate foreground" so that there is no room left for nature as background; and, in a less direct way, to some of Mr. Reichenbach's criticisms. I shall accordingly discuss the criticisms which bear upon this point, concluding this section of my reply with a few remarks suggested by Mr. Allport's careful study of my psychological views.

I. For many years I have consistently—and rather persistently—maintained that the key to a philosophic theory of experience must proceed from initially linking it with the processes and functions of life as the latter are disclosed in biological science. So viewed, I have held that experience is a matter or an "affair" (*pace* Mr. Santayana) of interaction of living creatures with their environments; *human* experience being what it is because human beings are subject to the influences of culture, including use of definite means of intercommunication, and are what in anthropological jargon are called *acculturated* organisms. I am naturally somewhat surprised, accordingly, when I find that Mr. Santayana sets forth as something he takes to be in complete opposition to my position, the idea expressed in the following sentence: "Every naturalist knows that this waking dream [immediate experience of things] is dependent for its existence, quality, intensity and duration on obscure processes in the living body, in its interplay with the environment; processes which go back, through seeds, to the first beginnings of life on earth." For in some fundamental respects this view of experience seems to be just that which I have consistently taken, his word *interplay* being synonymous with my word *interaction*. However, the phrase "waking dream" gives pause to complete identification of our two views, where the advantage, from the standpoint of common sense, seems to be on the side of my view.

However, there is a certain ambiguity in the sentence quoted from Mr. Santayana, which possibly throws light upon why he takes experience to be but a waking and specious dream. The ambiguity is found in the phrase "obscure processes in the living body"; for, if these obscure processes are isolated from connection with organic activities which, in their interaction with environment, constitute *life,* dependence of experience upon obscure occurrences in the *inside* of the organism certainly does cut experience off from intrinsic connection with environing conditions and render it a mere parasitic attachment to a private body. However, this interpretation of the phrase as an explanation of why Santayana regards experience as a dream, as specious, as a veil drawn between us and nature, is speculative. It is safer to suppose that he starts from the traditional "mentalistic" view of British psychology; and yet he takes sufficient cognizance of biological facts to connect *it* with the body in its interplay with environment. For the product of this combination—of Lockeian psychology with a reference to the organism—is a view in which an experience is a dream, while the dream is a product of interplay of a body with environing conditions.

Since, on the contrary, I begin with experience as the manifestation of interactions of organism and environment, it follows that the distinction between the things of a dream and of waking life is one to be itself stated in terms of different modes of interaction, so that it is pointless to call them both "dreams." At all events, it is only because he attributes to me the idea of experience which he himself holds—a view that seems to me to involve a complete abandonment of the professed naturalistic standpoint—that he draws the conclusions he sets forth from what he takes to be my view.[14]

Because of Mr. Santayana's own view of experience and his notion that no intelligent person can have any idea of "experience" save that put forth in orthodox British "mentalism," he attributes to me the monstrous position that "only the immediate is real"; a view that is obviously contradicted by the idea of experience as an interaction of organism and environment. Then when he finds that the implications of the latter view are in fact carried out in my writings, he decides that in addition to pure

14. Mr. Santayana's paper is an almost literal reprint of an article published by him in 1925 in the *Journal of Philosophy.* As he makes no reference in reprinting it to my reply in the same *Journal* in February 1927, I am obliged to refer the reader to that article of mine for detailed discussion of many points in his contribution to this volume not here dealt with ["Half-Hearted Naturalism," *Journal of Philosophy* 22 (3 February 1927): 57–64 (*Later Works* 3 : 73–81)].

subjectivism I hold to an external behaviorism in which there is nothing immediate or consummatory and to identification of experience with conventions. Such a combination of contradictions, did it represent my philosophy, would confer a certain preeminence, although not an enviable one, upon my ideas. It is, however, Mr. Santayana's premises, not mine, which make experience merely immediate, specious and illusory, with Nature so completely screened by it that the only possible Naturalism is a gesture of genuflection aimed blindly in the direction of an object of pure faith.

However, lest my reply here merely take the form of an *ad hominem* comparison of the respective merits of our two views, let me say a few words of a more general character. If the things of experience are produced, as they are according to my theory, by interaction of organism and environing conditions, then as Nature's own foreground they are not a barrier mysteriously set up between us and nature. Moreover the organism—the self, the "subject" of action,—is a factor *within* experience and not something outside of it to which experiences are attached as the self's private property. According to my view a characterization of any aspect, phase, or element of experience as *mine* is not a description of its direct existence but a description of experience with respect to some special problem for some special purpose, one which needs to be specified.[15] So much for alleged subjectivism, though I cannot refrain from once more asking how those who hold a purely "subjectivistic" idea of experience provide means for ever getting outside of its charmed circle. Mr. Santayana, at least, sees the need of some device and hence provides "animal faith" as the recourse of otherwise helpless "experience."

The account does not close here. I have repeatedly stated that an indispensable part of my theory is the fact that experience as an interaction consists of connections between doing-undergoing-doing . . . , and that the connections between the two, when they are noted and formulated, give rise to the distinctively cognitive experience; namely, a perception of relations which are me-

15. Although the required specification is not particularly an issue here, I point out that I have several times suggested that reference of a specified experience to "me," like a reference to "you," arises in those social interactions in which there is need for assuming *responsibility*.

diated and mediating. I have pointed out the fallacy of supposing that because an experience is immediate in its existence—or is directly just what it is and nothing else—its *subject-matter* must be immediate. My theory of the relation of cognitive experiences to other modes of experience is based upon the fact that *connections* exist in the most immediate non-cognitive experience, and when the experienced situation becomes problematic, the connections are developed into distinctive objects of knowledge, whether of common sense or of science.[16] The significance of experience as foreground is that the foreground is of such a nature as to contain material which, when operationally dealt with, provides the clews that guide us straight into Nature's background and into Nature *as* background. If philosophical writers would and could only forget their own dominating foreground of mentalistic psychological interpretation of experience, the historic course of the experiential development of the sciences out of experiences of the sort found among savage peoples would suffice to prove that experience is in fact of this sort. The proof would be reinforced by noting what happens whenever out of experiences previously had there develops a new experience based upon and containing juster and deeper cognitive insight into the world in which we live.

Some of my critics say that my philosophy does not tell much about the environing world which is discovered when experience takes on the cognitive phase. I hope this statement, though offered as an indictment, is correct. For, according to my view, the actual inquiries constituting the sciences of astronomy, archaeology, botany, down through the alphabet to the *zed* of zoology, are the procedures which tell us about the environing world; they tell because they follow out clews present in actually had experiences. The business of philosophy, in logic or the theory of knowledge, is not to provide a rival account of the natural environment, but to analyze and report how and to what effect inquiries actually proceed, genetically and functionally, in their experiential context. In this connection, I quote the following extraordinary passage from Santayana's essay: "Suppose I say

16. Long ago I learned from William James that there are immediate experiences of the connections linguistically expressed by conjunctions and prepositions. My doctrinal position is but a generalization of what is involved in this fact.

that 'everything ideal emanates from something natural.' Dewey agrees, *understanding that everything remote emanates from something immediate.* But what I meant was that everything immediate emanates from something biological." Eliminating the effect of an *aura* that clings to the word "emanates," the view stated in the last sentence is also mine. But I recognize frankly the circular movement involved, and that the experience which results from interaction with environing conditions contains within itself relations which when followed out tell us about the biological and about the further background—astronomical and geological. In other words, the proof of the fact that *knowledge* of nature, but not nature itself, "emanates" from immediate experience is simply that this is what has actually happened in the history or development of experience, animal or human on this earth—the only alternative to this conclusion being that in addition to experience as a source and test of beliefs, we possess some miraculous power of intuitive insight into remote stellar galaxies and remote geological eons. In the latter case, it is strange that astronomers and geologists have to work so hard to get first certain direct observational experiences and then to get those other experiences by whose aid they interpret and test the evidential value of what is observed. I am compelled to decide that the chief difference between myself and some of my critics is that I succeeded finally in freeing myself from observation of certain facts only through the medium of the traditional "subjective" view of experience, while these facts are still seen by my critics through the refracting medium of an uncriticized psychological doctrine.

II. When I turn to Mr. Reichenbach's paper, discussion finds itself in a context where there is agreement upon certain basic points. We have empiricism in common, and he also agrees with me—as against early logical positivists and Mr. Russell, at least in one of his periods—that experience as such cannot be reduced to sense data, since immediate reality in experience consists "of things, not of qualities." To a certain extent, I think, the further difference between us is lexicographical, due to different habitual associations with certain words, illustrated by the fact that he interprets "subjective" to mean—if I understand him aright—that which is influenced or affected by the action of the organism in that particular respect or capacity; whereas I give the word an objectionable metaphysical or epistemological meaning. However, since Mr. Reichenbach also makes the word synonymous with *apparent* and places what is designated by it in antithesis to the *objective* and *real,* the difference between us is not wholly linguistic, even though Mr. Reichenbach expressly repudiates the traditional metaphysical meaning of the words. In any case, since Mr. Reichenbach bases his justification for use of the words upon my idea about the relation of the distinctive object of science to the subject-matter of perceptual experience, the need for special discussion of the latter point is clearly indicated.

The foundation of his criticism is the belief that my identification of the scientific object with *relations,* instead of with some kind of existing non-relational things, commits me to the doctrine of the *"non-reality"* of scientific objects. This point is so fundamental that I am grateful to Dr. Reichenbach for the opportunity to discuss the matter. For I certainly have never intended to say anything which could lead directly or indirectly to a belief that I hold a "non realistic interpretation of scientific concepts." On the contrary—as is indicated in what I have said in immediately preceding pages—the actual operative presence of *connections* (which when formulated are *relational*) in the subject-matter of direct experience is an intrinsic part of my idea of experience. I am obliged, then, to conclude that Dr. Reichenbach holds to that traditional particularistic empiricism according to which "relations" have not the empirical reality possessed by things and qualities, so that attribution of the same view to me logically makes relational objects unreal. This interpretation is borne out by Mr. Reichenbach's reference to the "nominalistic reduction" of "abstracta to concreta," which he assumes to be involved in the empiricism common to both of us. But just here is where the view of experience as the manifestation of interactions of an acculturated organism—in the case of human experience—with environment differs from traditional empiricism. Mr. Reichenbach, as I see his position, has advanced beyond traditional psychological empiricism to the point of admitting *things* as material of direct experience instead of just separate qualities. But he has not gone on to the point of admitting that *actions* and modes of actions, ways of operating, are also contained in what is directly experienced. Yet if one starts with the biological-cultural approach to the theory of experiencing, the presence of native and acquired (like habits) *general* ways of behavior is an unescapable datum.[17]

Mr. Reichenbach, however, quotes from my writings a passage whose interpretation may seem to justify attribution to me of denial of the reality of scientific objects. The passage reads: "The physical object, as scientifically defined, is not a duplicated real object, but is a statement . . . of the relations between sets of changes the qualitative object sustains with changes in other things." Now the treachery of words is such that this sentence taken by itself may seem to read like an assertion that the scientific object is not "real," in spite of what is suggested by the word "duplicated." The context in which the passage is located has to do with one of the two problems mentioned in my Introduction as central in modern philosophy; namely, the relation of the "conceptual" objects of physical science to things of ordinary perception. I cannot be accused of inventing this problem. Moreover, one solution for it has been a doctrine which makes perceived and "conceived," or scientific, objects rival claimants for the position of being the "realities" knowledge is about. The sentence quoted is a denial of the validity of that view. What lies back of it is the belief that the qualitative traits of the things of ordinary common sense knowledge are not only legitimate but necessary in connection with one kind of problems,—those of use and enjoyment—, while the so-called "conceptual" objects of science are legitimate and necessary for the kind of problems with which scientific inquiry is concerned. Hence they are not rival claimants for occupancy of the seat of "real" knowing; and one does not duplicate in "true" or objective fashion what the other presents in a merely apparent and subjective fashion.[18] Or, as I have put the matter elsewhere, "The procedure of physics itself, not any metaphysical or epistemological theory, discloses

17. Peirce's pragmatic empiricism is of course explicit on this point. James sometimes wavers, but his emphasis upon continuity and upon the motor factor are such as to take his theory definitely out of particularistic or nominalistic empiricism.

18. That there is nothing peculiar to my form of pragmatism in the position taken about the scientific physical object may be seen in the fact that a writer like Broad can say "What really matters to science is not the inner nature of objects but their mutual relations." *Scientific Thought*, 39.

that physical objects cannot be *individual* existential objects." [19]
The phrase the "procedure of physics" is intended to point to the
fact that the Newtonian-Lockeian supposed primary *qualities* of
mass, solidity, extension, etc., are now treated in physical science
not as qualities but as strictly relational.

What is meant by my statement that a scientific physical object
is not a rival or duplicate of an object in the perceptual field may
perhaps be made clearer if I mention a passage of mine which
Mr. Reichenbach does not quote but which, I find, has been a
stumbling-block to some readers in the past. The passage is the
following: "The perceived and used table is the only table." [20]
Now this passage, because of the use of the word *only,* might be
taken to deny that a scientific physical object exists. If the passage had read: "The perceived and used table is the only *table,*"
the italics might have warded off misinterpretation. For it would
have indicated that it was not the existence of a swarm of atoms
(electrons, etc.) in rapid movement which was denied, but the
notion that this swarm somehow constitutes a ghostly kind of
table, instead of being just what it is in terms of electrons, deu-
terons, etc. One would hardly put books or dishes on the latter or
sit down before it to eat. That the table *as* a perceived table is
an object of knowledge in one context as truly as the physical
atoms, molecules, etc., are in another situational context and
with reference to another *problem* is a position I have given considerable space to developing. [21]

Pragmatic philosophers did not invent the idea of the nature of
the scientific object here put forth. Long ago attention was called
to the fact that English physicists tend to seek for literal models,
while as a rule French physicists are content with interpreting
physical objects symbolically rather than literally. Duhem, for example, many years ago presented a view which amounted in
effect to saying that scientific objects are symbolic devices for
connecting together the things of ordinary experience. Others
have held that they were devices for facilitating and directing

19. *Quest for Certainty,* 241 [*Later Works* 4 : 192]; a passage in which, I hope, the
word "individual" protects the sentence from the misunderstanding the other
sentence may give ground for—for *individual* is here contrasted with *relational* as general.
20. *Quest for Certainty,* 240 [*Later Works* 4 : 191].
21. The position that perceived objects are not as such cognitional is consistent
with the position that *what* is perceived may be involved in inquiry.

predictions. Now my view does not go as far as these. Its import may be gathered from the following illustration. Suppose one of those persons of extraordinarily keen vision who abound in the Grimm fairy tales were in fact to *see*, sensibly to perceive, an object which had all the qualities a physicist attributes to the atom. He would surely see something. But would he see an atom in the definite sense of seeing that which is *an object of physical science?* I can find but one possible answer, namely: "It depends. If he himself has had a scientific training and if in sensibly perceiving this particular thing he explicitly *identifies* it as having all the *relational* properties required by the scientific theory of atomic structure and with no properties incompatible with the latter, the answer is Yes. But if he sees it merely as another man of lesser power of vision sees a rock, the answer is No." In other words, it is not just the thing as perceived, but the thing as and when it is placed in an extensive ideational or theoretical context *within which it exercises a special office* that constitutes a distinctively physical scientific object.

The exigencies of discussion have taken me beyond the topic of experience over into the topic of knowledge, discussed at greater length later in my reply. I return now to the connection that exists in my theory between the scientific physical object and the qualitative experienced situation. For, according to my view of the latter, the definitely relational objects of science are produced when *connections* existing in the immediate situation are noted and formulated, the latter process involving elaboration in discourse. If, however, the operational presence of *general* modes of activity (constituting *connections*) in the material of ordinary experience is ignored (if, in the sense in which "thing" is an equivalent of the Latin *res*, it is not noted that a *way* of behaving is a "thing"), then the general and relational character of scientific objects must be denied by a professed empiricist. Such a denial has been and will continue to be the occasion for the promulgation of transcendent aprioristic rationalism.[22]

I am sorry that I cannot give to the illustrations presented by

22. This is perhaps as good a place as any to say that in the sense in which Piatt uses the word *rationalism* my theory is rationalistic, though I much prefer the word *intelligence* to *reason* because of the long anti-empirical history back of the latter word. The kind of "*a priori*" which Mr. Piatt mentions (and which *is* involved in my theory) is so radically different from the fixed *a priori* located in

Mr. Reichenbach the attention they deserve. About the alleged perceptual bent stick in water, let me say that the *ray of light is* bent—there is no illusion or "appearance" about *that*. It is not *scientific* knowledge which substitutes bending of light, as it passes from one medium to another, for bending of the stick. For "bent" and "crooked" in objects of perception are matters of *motor* adaptive responses. I doubt if any oarsman ever failed to make the correct response, the response being "correct" because it produces the consequences intended in the act of using the oar. The boatman, then, never supposed the *oar* was bent. A fisherman who catches fish by spearing them requires but a few trials, with no help from "science," to form a habit that is expressed in effective motor adjustments.[23] What science does is not to correct the thing of ordinary experience by substituting another thing but to *explain* the former. Moreover, the object as perceived can be explained only by giving the "appearance" full standing as it occurs; and explanation takes the form of a correlation, general in nature, between changes in the density of media and changes in the refractive index of light; the correlation being the scientific "physical object" in this case, so that the illustration would seem to prove my definition.[24]

Another instance cited by Mr. Reichenbach seems to me most naturally interpreted in my sense rather than in his—the instance namely of a needle on a dial, the motion of which is most regularly employed as a register of velocity or to serve as a speed-

---

and furnished by the inherent nature of Mind, *Intellectus, Purus,* Reason as *Nous,* figuring in the history of thought, that it seems to me the words rationalism and *a priori* should be either avoided, or else used only with explanatory qualification.

23. It seems to me that the problem with which Mr. Reichenbach is concerned is of the same order as one that used to be discussed in psychological texts: How does it happen we see things upright when "images" on the retina are inverted? The problem arose only because the phenomena were placed in a cognitive context instead of in a stimulus-response context. We don't first see and "know" that the images are inverted, and then correct by appealing to scientific knowledge. We *learn* to make effective motor responses, and if and when *they* are acquired the nature of the stimulus is for perceptual experience a matter of no bearing or relevancy.

24. The meaning of *explanation* as here used is functional—that of bringing a given set of cases into relation with sets that are of a different kind with respect to qualitative considerations so that free and systematic inference is possible.

ometer. The index may, however, be moved by changes induced by a magnet without the occurrence of locomotion in space. I am unable to see the relevancy of distinctions of the *real* and apparent, the *objective* and *subjective* in cases like this. If a person who has formed the habit of making a motor response to the movement of an index hand as a sign of a rate of speed should apply that habit when the change of position of the index hand is a sign of something quite different, there is certainly a maladjustment in a stimulus-response situation. A habit formed under a given set of conditions, which have been constant in the past, does not work when the conditions in which that habit is effective are suddenly changed—and yet *as* a habit it will tend to operate. This is a very common source of mistakes—that is, of taking things amiss in action. Why it should be necessary to have recourse to the categories of "subjective" and "objective," "real" and "apparent," in connection with such cases I do not see;— save that the systematic neglect by traditional psychology of motor and active elements in the make-up of experiences has deprived those who accept such a psychology of the natural—and naturalistic—means of describing what happens.

III. There is some ground for thinking that my emphatic affirmation of the "reality" of the *qualities* of directly experienced things has had some effect in leading Reichenbach to suppose that I deny or am doubtful about the "reality" of scientific objects. In this respect, I agree with him that it would have been better to employ a more neutral word than "real," namely *existential*. But I fear that this linguistic change does not remove the actual difference between us. When I used the word *real* in the following passage (which he quotes from me), I used a word that is unfortunately highly ambiguous, so that I must accept partial responsibility for any misunderstanding occasioned: "Dreams, insanity, and fantasy are natural products, as 'real' as anything in the world." I now see that I should not have depended upon the use of quotation marks about *real* to protect the sentence from misconception, even in connection with the phrase "natural products." The meaning of the passage is less ambiguously conveyed in a sentence on the page previous to the one from which it is quoted, where all qualities, the tertiary and those usually called "subjective," are said to be "as much products of the *doings of nature* as are color, sound, pressure, perceived size and distance."[25] It means that as manifestations of interactions of a naturally existent organism and existent environing conditions all experienced materials stand on exactly the same level. But it does *not* mean that with respect to their *evidential* value, their function as dependable signs, they stand on the same level. On the contrary, I have repeatedly insisted that experiential control of what is directly given, a control which analyzes that material into simpler, more "elementary" data, is necessary for valid inference and hence whenever cognition comes into the picture. Hence I have held that any signification justifiably assignable to the words "real" and "apparent," "subjective" and "objective," has to do with experienced materials in their evidential, signifying function, and does *not* belong to them in their original and innocent occurrence. For this reason I do not see that my acceptance of the word *"existential"* in place of the ambiguous and hence objectionable word *"real"* would, in spite of its being an improvement in expression, remove the basic difference between us. For what to me is a difference arising *within* the reflective or cognitive use of primary experiential material, is to Mr. Reichenbach a difference between that primary material itself, which is inherently only "apparent," and the material of cognition as "real."[26]

Hence I agree fully with the statement that "the distinction between 'appearance' and 'reality' is a basic need for constructing a consistent picture of the everyday world, in particular the world of action." But (aside from wishing that less ambiguous words be found) I point out that the problem of forming a *consistent picture of the world* obviously falls within a definitely cognitive con-

25. *Quest for Certainty*, 239 [*Later Works* 4:191].
26. As a verbal matter, the words *apparent, real, subjective, objective* are so loaded with metaphysical and epistemological debris, that the force of the distinction would, it seems to me, be much better indicated by words like *dependable* and *unreliable qua* evidential; *relevant* and *irrelevant; effective* and *futile; directive* and *misleading*—all being used in a specified *functional* sense. That sometimes material is undependable in its evidential function because it is overloaded with qualities that are due to the organism's share in the organic-environment interaction is certainly true—as in the tendency to clothe natural occurrences with animistic properties. But elimination of this source of error does not involve, as far as I can see, any other principle than that involved in every experimental determination of data as appropriate and effective.

text, and is thus secondary and derived as compared with the materials of primary non-cognitive experiences. In leaving this phase of the matter, I may say that, so far as I am aware, there is nothing peculiarly pragmatic in this special phase of my general doctrine, but that the position I have taken follows directly from a thoroughly naturalistic treatment of experience in general, and of experiences in their plural occurrence. I am, however, more concerned here to make my own position clear, leaving its correctness or incorrectness to be judged after it has been made clear, than to engage in controversy with Mr. Reichenbach on this particular point.[27] So I conclude with saying that the plausibility of the contention that the qualitative objects of direct experience are "*replaced*" by other objects through the intervention of inferential processes, of the same type that lead to scientific objects, depends upon a confusion of the function performed by *adaptive motor responses* in things of ordinary experience with the function performed by controlled and systematic *inference* in cognitive experience of the scientific type.

By way of further clearing up my own position I would point out that I hold that the word "subject," if it is to be used at all, has the organism for its proper *designatum*. Hence it refers to an *agency of doing,* not to a knower, mind, consciousness or whatever. If the words "subject" and "object" are to be set over against each other, it should be in those situations in which a person, self, or organism as a *doer* sets up purposes, plans, to realize the execution of which is resisted by environing conditions as they exist. An *object,* as Professor Gildersleeve wittily suggested a good many years ago, is that which *objects:* that which gets in the way of the carrying out of some plan entertained by a person—where the word *person* has the denotative force of John Smith and Mary Jones. A *person* on this view is one existing thing in the world—one "object" among other objects whose distinguishing traits are to be learned by inquiry, just as the difference between cats and dogs as things in the actual world

27. Yet I cannot refrain from saying that (as Reichenbach's *Experience and Prediction* clearly shows) upon his view the existence of an "external world" is a *problem* for philosophy, whereas according to my view the problem is artificially generated by the kind of premises I call epistemological. When we *act* and find environing things in stubborn opposition to our desires and efforts, the externality of the environment to the *self* is a direct constituent of direct experience.

is learned. I submit that if the words *personal* and *impersonal* were uniformly prefixed to things ("objects" in the sense in which they are linguistically identified with things) instead of the words "subjective" and "objective," an artificial, because gratuitously instituted, problem would be eliminated.

There remains in connection with this part of Mr. Reichenbach's paper, the matter of "tertiary qualities" in relation to valuation. It is of course an inherent part of the naturalistic view of experience that affective qualities are products of the doings of nature—of the interaction of an organism and environmental conditions. It also follows that as direct qualities their reference is primarily to the carrying on of life processes—I hardly need do more than allude to the qualities of things as loved and feared. *If* the object of science is something which is related as a real thing to a thing of direct experience as merely apparent, and if it has to be made, by means of inferential processes, to replace the latter, it is clear that no such scientific replacing object exists in the case of things of desire, affection and direct enjoyment. From this point of view the possibility of scientifically valid objects of valuation as a form of knowledge is ruled out from the start. But if the scientific object is a generalized constant correlation of sets of changes, there is no insuperable object set up by premises laid down in advance. Correlations between changes that form *conditions* of desires, etc., and changes that form their *consequences* when acted upon, have the same standing and function in this field that physical objects have in their field.

There are many *practical* difficulties to be overcome in developing the methods of inquiry that will enable conclusions regarding such correlations to be reached. But as distinct from the position taken by Mr. Reichenbach there is no inherent theoretical bar on my view to some day succeeding.[28]

IV. Other criticisms of my theory of experience are connected with the fact that I have called experiences *situations,* my use of the word antedating, I suppose, the introduction of the *field* idea in physical theory, but nevertheless employed, as far as I can see, to meet pretty much the same need—a need imposed by subject-

---

28. I deal with this matter very briefly because a monograph on this topic, stating my views in detail, has recently been published: *Theory of Valuation,* in the *International Encyclopedia of Unified Science,* Vol. II, No. 4 (Chicago, 1939) [*Later Works* 13 : 189–251].

matter not by theory. The need in both cases—though with different subject-matters—is to find a viable alternative to an atomism which logically involves a denial of connections and to an absolutistic block monism which, in behalf of the reality of relations, leaves no place for the discrete, for plurality, and for individuals. In philosophy there is also the need to find an alternative for that combination of atomistic particularism with respect to empirical material and Platonic *a priori* realism with respect to universals which is professed, for example, in the philosophy of Mr. Russell. According to the naturalistic view, every experience in its direct occurrence is an interaction of environing conditions and an organism. As such it contains in a fused union some*what* experienc*ed* and some processes of experienc*ing*. In its identity with a life-function, it is temporally and spatially more extensive and more internally complex than is a single thing like a stone, or a single quality like red. For no living creature could survive, save by sheer accident, if its experiences had no more reach, scope or content, than traditional particularistic empiricism provides for. On the other hand, it is impossible to imagine a living creature coping with the entire universe all at once. In other words, the theory of experiential situations which follows directly from the biological-anthropological approach is by its very nature a *via media* between extreme atomistic pluralism and block universe monisms. Which is but to say that it is genuinely empirical in a naturalistic sense.

Mr. Russell, however, finds that what I write about situations as the units of experience springs from and leads directly to the Hegelian variety of absolutism. One indirect reason he presents for this belief, when it is put in the form of an argument, runs somewhat as follows: Mr. Dewey admits not only that he was once an Hegelian but that Hegel left a permanent deposit in his thought; Hegel was a thoroughgoing holist; therefore, Dewey uses "situation" in a holistic sense. I leave it to Mr. Russell as a formal logician to decide what he would say to anyone who presented this argument in any other context. The following argument answers perhaps more to Mr. Russell's idea of inductive reasoning. British philosophy is analytic; Dewey not only leans to the Continental synthetic tendency but has vigorously criticized British analytic thought; therefore, his identification of an experience with a situation commits him to "holism."

Coming to a more relevant matter, the interpretation put by Mr. Russell upon quotations of passages in which I have used the word *situation* contradicts what, according to my basic leading principle, is designated by it.[29] This position, however, is not just a necessary implication of that principle. The pluralistic and individualized character of situations is stated over and over again, and is stated moreover in direct connection with the principle of the experiential continuum. Take for instance the following passage:

> Situations are precarious and perilous because the persistence of life-activity depends upon the influence which present acts have upon future acts. The *continuity* of a life-process is secured only as acts performed render the environment favorable to subsequent organic acts. . . . All perceived objects are individualized. They are, as such, wholes complete in themselves. Everything directly experienced is qualitatively unique.[30]

I lay no claim to inventing an environment that is marked by both discreteness and continuity. Nor can I even make the more modest claim that I discovered it. What I have done is to interpret this duality of traits in terms of the identity of experience with life-functions. For in the process of living both absorption in a present situation and a response that takes account of its effect upon the conditions of later experiences are equally necessary for maintenance of life. From one angle, almost everything I have written is a commentary on the fact that situations are *immediate* in their direct occurrence, and mediating and mediated in the temporal continuum constituting life-experience.

I have pointed out that one person cannot communicate an experience as immediate to another person. He can only invite that other person to institute the conditions by which the person himself will *have* that kind of situation the *conditions* for which

29. Mr. Savery has not had Mr. Russell's difficulty in understanding my point of view. Cf. his remark "Concatenism is, then, a *via media* between monism and monadism. It is the only form of pluralism that is intellectually tenable." There can be no genuine continuity unless an experience, no matter how unique or individualized in its own pervasive quality, contains within itself something that points to other experiences—or, in Mr. Savery's phrase, unless experiences "*overlap*" with respect to their subject-matters.
30. *Quest for Certainty*, 234 [*Later Works* 4:187].

are stated in discourse. Even if this difficult condition is fulfilled, there is no assurance that any one will so act as to have the experience. The horse led to water is not forced to drink. This predicament has to be faced by the experimentalist in physical inquiry. He, however, can describe the experimental set-up, the material involved, the apparatus employed, the series of acts performed, the observations which result and state the conclusions reached. But even so it is up to other inquirers to take this report as an invitation to *have* a certain experienced situation and as a direction as to how to obtain it. *This predicament is inherent, according to genuine empiricism, in the derived relationship of discourse to primary experience.* Any one who refuses to go outside the universe of discourse—as Mr. Russell apparently does—has of course shut himself off from understanding what a "situation," as directly experienced subject-matter, is.

An almost humorous instance of such refusal and its consequences is found when Mr. Russell writes: "We are told very little about the nature of things before they are inquired into." If I have said or tried to say the tiniest bit about the "nature of things" prior to inquiry into them, I have not only done something completely contradictory to my own position but something that seems to me inherently absurd. Or if, as is possible, what the passage means is that, even after inquiry has been carried on, I still do not tell what things were like *before the time in which the inquiry* was undertaken, I can only say that I have always supposed that this sort of telling is the specific business of the inquiries themselves. I plead guilty to not having written into my philosophical writings an encyclopedia of the conclusions of all the sciences. Whatever Mr. Russell may have meant by the sentence quoted, my position is that *telling* is (i) a matter of discourse, and that (ii) all discourse is derived from and inherently referable to experiences of things in non-discursive experiential having;—so that, for example, although it is possible to tell a man blind from birth *about* color, we cannot by discourse confer upon him that which is had in the direct experience of color— my whole position on this matter being a generalization of this commonplace fact.

When Mr. Russell adds to the sentence just quoted from him, the phrase "we know, however, that, like dishonest politicians, things behave differently when observed from the way they behave when no one is paying attention to them," I do not suppose he is intending to say that, according to the Heisenberg principle, minute particles moving at high velocities behave like dishonest politicians. I take it he is referring to something he regards as a legitimate inference from my position. In the latter case, it is probably well for me to state once more what my view is. It is that scientific knowledge has an effect upon things *previously directly-experienced-but-not-known*. Now this I should have supposed to be a commonplace, although a commonplace which philosophers have mostly not deigned to notice. It is commonly believed, for example, that persons behave somewhat differently when they know they are mad than when they are mad without knowing it, and that a man who knows he is hungry will not behave in the identical way he behaves when he is hungry without being aware of it. Likewise with the knowledge of illness; the different kind of response engaged in is, *ipso facto,* a modification of the subject-matter of a previous non-cognitive experience. And, although the point involves trenching upon the topic of the second section of my reply, namely knowledge, I add here that I have not been guilty of the Irish bull with which I am occasionally charged. I have not held, as is intimated in Mr. Russell's allusion to knowledge of sun and planets, that knowing modifies the *object of knowledge*. That a planet *as known* is a very different thing from the speck of light that is found in direct experience, I should suppose to be obvious;—although, once more, one of those commonplaces of which philosophers engaged in pursuit of an artificial problem have failed to take proper note. The fact that critics so readily forget that the planet, rock (or whatever it is that is used, and which they imagine I hold to be modified by knowing), is *already* an object of knowledge indicates that they hold that the entire subject-matter of philosophical theory is exhaustively contained within the field of discourse. An empiricist will hold that subject-matter to be *philosophically* understood has to be placed in its reference to subject-matter of directly experienced situations.[31]

In this connection Mr. Russell's belief that I hold that the "raw

31. Stated in another way, the material of sensations, impressions, ideas as copies, etc., with which traditional empiricism has operated is material already taken out of the context of direct experience and placed in the context of material within discourse for the purpose of meeting the requirements of discourse.

material remains *unknowable*" is peculiarly indicative. For it affords final proof that Mr. Russell has not been able to follow the distinction I make between the immediately had material of non-cognitively experienced situations and the material of cognition—a distinction without which my view cannot be understood. A typical illustration of what I mean by such non-cognitive experiences is found in my not infrequent statements to the effect that the assumption of the ubiquity of cognitive experience inevitably results in disparagement of things experienced by way of love, desire, hope, fear and other traits characteristic of human individuality. Instead, however, of holding that this material is *unknowable,* my view is that when the situations in which such material exists become *problematic,* it provides precisely that which is *to be* known by being inquired into. But apparently Mr. Russell is so wedded to the idea that there is no experienced material outside the field of discourse that any intimation that there is such material relegates it, *ipso facto,* to the status of the "*unknowable.*"

Although the point now to be explicitly mentioned concerns my theory of knowledge rather than my theory of experience, it is so directly connected with the "holistic" meaning Mr. Russell reads into the word "situation" as used by me, that it is taken up here. Mr. Russell asserts that my use of the word "situation" commits me to the view that the entire universe is the only "real" object of knowledge, so that logically I am committed to the view expressed by Bradley. It so happens that I have explicitly stated the fundamental difference between my view and that of the Bradleyan type. I quote the passage because it shows, unless I am mistaken, that the source of Russell's misconception of my view is his imperviousness to what I have said about the *problematic* quality of situations as giving both the occasion for and the control of inquiry.

The theory [that is, of the type just mentioned] thus radically misconstrues the unification towards which inquiry in its reflective mediate stage actually moves. In actual inquiry, movement toward a unified ordered situation exists. But it is always a unification of the subject-matter which constitutes an *individual problematic situation.* It is not unification at large.

If, however, "the feature of unification is generalized beyond the limits in which it takes place, namely *resolution of specific problematic situations,* knowledge is then supposed to consist of attainment of a final all-comprehensive Unity, equivalent to the Universe as an unconditioned whole." [32]

V. Mr. Pepper in his comments on my esthetic theory makes words like *coherence, whole, integration,* etc., the ground of his criticism, rather than *situation.* But since his charge of an "organicism" has something in common with Russell's charge of "holism," I shall deal with his criticism at this point. I have, however, to introduce my remarks by saying something about the topic of method in connection with esthetic theory. Mr. Pepper refers to an attempt on his part at one time to derive a theory of esthetics, at least in outline, from the "implications of the general pragmatic attitude in the face of relevant facts," and being led thereby to predict what a good pragmatist would say upon this subject. I cannot charge Mr. Pepper with trying to *deduce,* in a way opposed to pragmatic empiricism, esthetic theory from general premises in isolation from experienced subject-matter. His phrase "in the face of relevant facts" protects him from this charge. Nevertheless I think his adoption of that method is the source of the criticisms he brings against me. For when he finds in my *Art as Experience* ideas put forward and words used that were not predicted in his scheme, he assumes that I have combined an anti-pragmatic position with a genuinely pragmatic one, oscillating between the two. Now in my chapter in *Art as Experience,* I expressly objected to typical and to current philosophies of esthetics on the ground that they were not formed by examination of the subject-matter of esthetic and artistic experience but by deducing what the latter *must be* from antecedent preconceptions. The idea did not occur to me to employ myself the procedure I criticized when it was adopted by others.

These remarks, I hope, serve to clarify the issue, which is whether *words* I have used in describing and analyzing esthetic subject-matter apply to genuine traits of the subject-matter; so that, whether or not some of them have also been used by idealist (organicist) writers on esthetics, they have a meaning consistent

32. *Logic,* 531 [*Later Works* 12:523] (italics not in original text). The passage, however, is almost at the close of the book so that it may have escaped Mr. Russell's attention.

with naturalistic and pragmatic empiricism.[33] With respect to these issues, I call attention to the fact that in earlier writings I pointed out that the very type of philosophy Mr. Pepper attributes to me arose historically precisely from the fact that Greek thinkers took categories which *are* applicable to works of art and to their enjoyed perception and then extended them to the whole universe where they are not applicable.[34] In other words, it *is* an integral part of my analysis of the material of esthetic experience that *it,* in distinction from the material of scientific and moral experience *as such,* has traits of qualitative wholeness, integration, etc., as genuinely characteristic of it. This point is the one to be critically appraised and objected to if my esthetic theory is erroneous. However, it is a point Mr. Pepper nowhere discusses. Apparently, my use of certain *words* suffices to render unnecessary discussion of the subject-matter which is the only criterion for judging the applicability of theories.

In my *Quest for Certainty* I wrote as follows:

> There are situations in which self-enclosed, discrete, individualized characters dominate. They constitute the subject-matter of esthetic experience; and every experience is esthetic in so far as it is final, or arouses no search for some other experience. When this complete quality is conspicuous the experience is denominated esthetic.[35]

Were one to try to guess in advance what I would be likely to say in a more extended discussion of art and esthetics, this passage might form a point of departure. The question it raises is one of fact. Are there experiences of this kind? In the third chapter of my *Art as Experience,* this latter question is discussed at consid-

---

33. It may be pointed out that a large group of biologists have reached, on what they take to be experimental scientific grounds, conclusions they call *organismic,* as over against previous "cellular" conceptions comparable in biology to old views of atomism in physics. I do not know whether Mr. Pepper would bring against them the kind of charge he brings against me, since they also use with great freedom words like *whole, integration,* etc. There is, it seems to me, as much warrant in the one case as in the other.

34. Cf., for example, in Chapter III of my *Experience and Nature* (and, quite explicitly, the last chapter of my recent *Logic*), the following sentence. "Their thinkers [those of Greece] were as much dominated by the esthetic characters of experienced objects as modern thinkers are by their scientific and economic (or relational) traits."

35. P. 235 [*Later Works* 4:188].

erable length. The answer given is that every experience to which the name *an* experience emphatically applies is of this nature. Such experiences, of course, can only be *had* and be pointed towards by discourse. But several pages are spent in indicating the traits to be looked for in them, as against experiences that are tight and constricted on one side, and loose, slack, sprawling on the other side. Throughout all subsequent chapters the words *whole, complete, coherence,* refer exactly and exclusively to the materials of these experiences which are individualized and entire in the sense pointed out.[36]

The sole question at issue is then one of fact: Do or do not the objects of distinctively esthetic experiences have characteristics to which the words *whole, integration, complete* apply in that *special sense* which has been indicated?—a sense which is *special* just because it belongs to experiences as esthetic and *not* to experiences of other kinds, and certainly not to the world at large as objects of distinctively *cognitive* experience.

What I have just said exempts me, I believe, from responsibility of taking up one by one all the points made by Mr. Pepper, since in each case I could only point to the special signification given the words used in the context of having an esthetic experience, and raise the question of whether this subject-matter justifies use of the words in the sense given them. I shall deal briefly, however, with three of his points. (i) Instead of denying the importance of *conflict* in esthetic experience, I have emphasized its indispensable function—see for example the references under *Resistance* in the Index. What I have done is to distinguish between the cases of conflict that lead to dispersion and disruption (of which for example modern psychiatry gives so many examples), and those cases in which conflict and tension are converted into means of intensifying a consummatory appreciation of material of an individual qualitative experience. The distance which separates such a view from a "theory of harmony culminating in the great cosmic harmony of the absolute" is so vast as to confirm the impression that Mr. Pepper was led astray by ig-

---

36. For example it is pointed out that the subject-matter of an experience of knowing, while the knowing is in progress, is such as to arouse search for some other experience, but that every conclusion reached after active search is experienced as a finding of what has been searched for and in so far has esthetic quality.

noring what I said about the uniquely qualitative individualized and discrete aspect of the situations which have esthetic traits.

Then (ii) there is my distinction between the raw material of a work of art which is said to belong to a "common world," and not to be *private*—since it *is* common—, and the individual response of the personal and individualized vision and shaping activity of the artist by which otherwise common material is transformed into a work of art. Because I say—at least this is the only reason I have discovered—that treating the antecedent *raw material* as private, belonging merely to the artist's own consciousness, takes us to "the state of the mad-house," Mr. Pepper finds something peculiarly organistic in this passage. The context shows clearly that I am distinguishing between *pre*-artistic material—which is common to the experience of many human beings—and the material of the work of art *as such* in which common material has been transformed into something individual, unique, through the vision and creative procedures of an artist.[37] The discussion in my text has for its context the old problem of the "representative" character of a work of art; my conclusion being that the material of the work of art as such is *not* representative of what existed before in experience since it represents a transformation of the material had in ordinary (common) experiences by transfusion through a *new* and individual mode of experience. If this view is wrong, *it* is the view to be criticized.[38]

Mr. Pepper is troubled (iii) by the fact that coherence of relations, even of inner relations, figures in my account of artistic form—for is not coherence a mark of the idealistic theory of knowledge, and "inner relations" the sign of its metaphysics? Let us, however, "look at the record"—in this case, my text. After defining form in terms of relations and esthetic form in terms of

37. I used, in single quotes, the word 'universal' as a synonym of "*common*." It may be that Mr. Pepper was unable to distinguish the word thus used from the "concrete universal" of idealistic philosophy.

38. There is a touch of the humorous in the fact that Mr. Pepper reverses in this connection his previous dictum that for "organicism the coherence of feelings is central, while for pragmatism it is secondary and instrumental. And for pragmatism quality is central and for organicism only a sort of corollary." It is a reversal because when I say that the private, the feelings, is not the subject-matter of a work of art, but things which, like qualities of color, sound, etc., are *common*, Mr. Pepper accuses me of deserting pragmatism for organicism.

"completeness of relations in a given medium," I go on directly to say:

> But "relation" is an ambiguous word. In philosophical discourse it is used to designate a connection instituted in thought. It then signifies something indirect, something purely intellectual, even logical. But "relation" in its idiomatic usage denotes something direct and active, something dynamic and energetic. It fixes attention upon the way things bear upon one another, their clashes and unitings, the way they fulfill and frustrate, promote and retard, excite and inhibit one another.[39]

It hardly seems necessary to say any more about coherence and inner relations as they actually enter into my theory. I close by saying that I do not believe that any school of philosophy has a monopolistic hold upon the interpretation of such words as "whole, complete, coherence, integration," etc. I am also convinced that the school of objective idealism has borrowed these traits from esthetic experiences, where they do have application, and has then illegitimately extended them till they became categories of the universe at large, endowed with cosmic import. I am not prepared to deny to writers of this school genuine esthetic insights; and in so far as these insights are genuine, it is the task of an empirical pragmatic esthetics to do justice to them without taking over the metaphysical accretions.

VI. What I have to say in connection with Dr. Allport's paper about my psychological view fits in here perhaps as well as anywhere else. First I want to say that I am gratefully appreciative of the painstaking study and faithful exposition an expert in this field has made of my scattered and, of late years, unprofessional writings. His criticisms are also just. Especially do I admit the truth of his remark that, although I have said that I regard psychology as indispensable for sound philosophizing at the present juncture, I have failed to develop in a systematic way my underlying psychological principles. Some at least of the criticisms of my theory of experience might have been averted if I had set forth my socio-biological psychology so as to show how and why, upon the negative side, many philosophical ideas still put

39. *Art as Experience*, 134 [*Later Works* 10:139].

forth as fundamental and as all but axiomatic represent uncritical acceptance of psychological theories formed two centuries ago; and, upon the positive side, so as to show how and
why I believe a sound psychology provides the basis for a theory
of the nature of experiencing, and of its different modes and their
connections with one another. I have made the mistake of treating as incidental certain psychological matters which are central
in the present state of philosophy. I had no right to assume that
philosophical readers were sufficiently in touch with newer developments in psychology so that my references to the latter could
be left with little elaboration. I now see how far contemporary
philosophy as a whole is from having appropriated and digested
the main principles set forth even in the psychology of William
James.

The need for explicit statement is the greater because writers
who proclaim the complete independence of philosophy from
psychology are often the very ones who can be most seriously
charged with uncritical use of outmoded psychological ideas, as
if they were matters of course too assured to need examination.
This statement is particularly applicable wherever the ideas of
subjective-objective, mental-physical come into play, and wherever such a term as "sense-data" is employed as an objective or
natural substitute for the older mentalistic word *sensations*. The
influence of pre-biological psychology affects also the meanings
attached to *ideas* and *conceptions*. As I remark from time to
time in the course of my present reply, from the standpoint of a
biological-cultural psychology the term "subject" (and related
adjectival forms) has only the signification of a certain kind of
actual existence; namely, a living creature which under the influence of language and other cultural agencies has become a person interacting with other persons (concrete human beings).

In my theory of experience and of the experiential continuum,
this way of regarding the subject (or self, or personal being, or
whatever name is employed) is fundamental. For, although the
psychological theory involved is a form of Behaviorism, it differs
basically from some theories bearing the same name. In the first
place, behavior is not viewed as something taking place in the
nervous system or under the skin of an organism but always, directly or indirectly, in obvious overtness or at a distance through
a number of intervening links, an interaction with environing

conditions. In the second place, other human beings who are also acculturated are involved in the interaction, including even persons at a great distance in space and time, because of what they have done in making the direct environment what it is. Were the presence of remote environmental influences, impersonal and personal, within direct experience recognized by my critics some of the objections brought would collapse, especially those which rest upon dialectical manipulation of the idea of "immediacy." For although distant conditions are not present *in propria persona,* they are present through their effects so that the latter provides matter usable as clews and evidential indications that conduct inquiry to knowledge of the indefinitely remote.

Returning now to specific criticisms of Dr. Allport, I am obliged to admit what he says about the absence of an adequate theory of personality. In a desire to cut loose from the influence of older "spiritualistic" theories about the nature of the unity and stability of the personal self (regarded as a peculiar kind of substantial-stuff), I failed to show how natural conditions provide support for integrated and potentially equilibrated personality-patterns. That this potentiality often fails of realization is sufficiently proved by psychiatric evidence. But the same evidence shows that conditions which produce integrated personality-patterns are as natural as are those which produce pathological human beings, the differences being due to different kinds of *interactions.* The same evidence is equally convincing as to the role of interactions with other persons in determining unified or divided personality patterns. Dr. Allport criticizes my writings in the field where the psychology of persons in their social (inter-personal) relations is peculiarly weighty, on the ground that I have failed to show the compatibility of a community of integrated persons with the variety of segmental types of publics which are due to specialization of interests and divisions of labor. I certainly admit that at the present time the problem is unsolved, and would go so far as to say that as a practical problem it is *the* problem of our day and generation. Need for a theory that would point the way in which efforts at practical solution should be directed is manifested in the present widespread reaction from atomistic "liberal" theories to totalitarianism. But I cannot admit that the incompatibility between individual human beings integrated in themselves and a community life marked by diversity of voluntary groups representing different interests is *inherent.* It is an incompatibility which is historic and which is always changing its constituents so that the problems it sets have forever to be solved anew in construction of new forms of social relationships.

C. The Theory of Knowledge

I. In taking up the second of the main heads under which I am arranging my comments, I begin with Dr. Murphy's criticisms as they bear directly upon my theory of knowledge. In the case of his paper in particular, I have to remind readers of a caution, already given, about the need of keeping in close touch with the text of the original contributions. For although he quotes, in connection with his discussion of special topics, a number of passages from my writings, in his statement of my basic theory of knowledge he neither quotes passages nor gives references in support of his interpretation. Accordingly, although I quote his report of my supposed theory at some length, I must also ask readers to go directly to his paper. His general charge is that "the non-philosophical reader who studies the theory of 'inquiry' in his [my] *Logic,* or the theory of Nature in *Experience and Nature* will not find what on the basis of the prospectus offered he had a right to expect." Now I do not know what criterion is implicit in the reference to a non-philosophical reader nor in the not infrequent references made to an "ordinary theory" of knowing. However, save perhaps as an indication of a certain undefined predilection on Mr. Murphy's part, these allusions are not important. For the sequel makes it clear that Mr. Murphy believes that a philosophical reader will be similarly frustrated. He restates as the ground of his criticisms the alleged fact that, in spite of my nominal opposition to what I call epistemology, my theory of inquiry-knowing is so entangled in the latter that I have come far short of presenting an intelligible theory of knowing.

What, then, according to Mr. Murphy *is* my theory of inquiry? Instead of taking us, he says, "as it should to such specific sorts of inquiry as serve in practice as our means of finding out about the environment or the consequences of human behavior in it," my procedure, he claims, is as follows:

It [my theory of inquiry] refers us instead to a theory about the rôle of ideas as instruments to be used in so altering a present indeterminate situation that an enjoyed future experience, itself non-cognitive but worth while on its own account, will reliably ensue, through the use of procedures which have proved their instrumental value in this capacity.

At this point I regret all the more the complete absence of substantiating or verifying references because I have tried in my *Logic* to do exactly the thing Mr. Murphy says I have not done:— namely, that according to it "'I am about to have known' is the pragmatic equivalent for 'I know.'" It is certainly true that with Furthermore, I am so far from recognizing my theory of inquiry in the report Dr. Murphy makes of it, that, as presented, it seems to me quite as unintelligible as it does to Mr. Murphy, and, I presume, as it does to the reader. In lieu of verifying references, Murphy repeats twice his interpretation of my view on the nature of inquiry, saying that the "'ordinary' theory of knowing" (whatever that may be) is "replaced by a reference of ideas to future experience and to the means of so altering a present situation that a desired and anticipated future will reliably ensue"; and,

> we have already seen [presumably in the passages just quoted] he regards it [knowing] as a use of ideas as signs of possible future experiences and means for effecting the transition to such experiences in a satisfactory manner. These future experiences, in so far as they terminate inquiry will not be cases of "knowing," that is of the use of given experiences as signs of something else.

I regret my inability to identify any part of my theory of knowing in the above passages. In fact I cannot identify any consistent and intelligible theory whatever by means of the sentences just quoted. If I found them advanced by any writer, my criticism would have to take the form of asking what in the world they are supposed to mean. However, since I cannot rewrite here my whole *Logic*, I shall point out in summary fashion a number of specific points in which the view attributed to me, so far as I can understand it, differs radically from that which I have placed on record in my writings. (1) Instead of saying that "*ideas* are signs of future experiences," I have denied their capacity to act as signs or evidence, pointing out that signifying capacity belongs *only* to observed facts or data. (2) Since Mr. Murphy makes no allusion to the latter in what purports to be an account of my theory of inquiry, I call attention to the fact that instead of saying that "given experiences are signs of something else," I have insisted that "given experiences" have to be experimentally analyzed in order to yield evidential signs. (3) Just what is meant by the statement that upon my view ideas ultimately refer to future experiences, I do not know. What I have said is that ideas are correlated, in strictly conjugate fashion, with discriminated material of observation, the former serving to indicate a possible mode of operative solution and the latter serving to locate and delimit a problem, so that a resolved situation is attained (if it *is* attained) by the operational interaction with each other of observed and ideational contents. If "ultimate reference" means that ideas *alone* do not determine an existential proposition, the statement is in accord with my view—just as I have also held that data alone do not constitute the object of a final and complete judgment. (4) The references in Mr. Murphy's account to future experiences as anticipated, desired and enjoyed are apparently intended to state the heart of my doctrine. But the references are so loose that I do not know what they mean sufficiently to be able to correct them. I shall, therefore, simply restate briefly the view that is repeated any number of times in my *Logic*.

The only kind of experience that is *anticipated or desired* is the operational production of that situation in which the specific problem under inquiry is solved, so that warranted assertion takes place. The only *enjoyment* that has any relevancy is that which a person may happen to obtain in appreciation of a resolved situation as consummatory of the inquiries that led up to it. This personal enjoyment has nothing to do with the logical or cognitive function of the attained resolved situation; yet the fact that solution of problems is capable of yielding keen enjoyment is a highly fortunate circumstance in promoting the disposition to inquire. (5) The statement that, according to my theory of inquiry-knowing, "future experiences as far as they terminate inquiry are not cases of 'knowing'" is either the tautology that knowing-inquiry terminates when it does terminate, or, if it is taken to refer to *knowledge as attained* in distinction from knowing in process, is a flat contradiction of my actual position, according to which *only* the subject-matter in which inquiry terminates (in fulfilment of its own conditions) is knowledge. Nowhere in any of Murphy's statements about my theory of inquiry as knowing is there any reference, even an incidental one, to that which is the controlling factor in my entire view, namely the function of a *problematic* situation in regulating as well as evoking inquiry. Although the disastrous effect of this omission is most clearly in evidence in the cases of the third and fourth of the above mentioned points, leaving it out of account makes nonsense of my theory of ideas in themselves and in their reference to a terminal conclusion. If it were not that the same omission of this controlling factor of my whole logical doctrine is found in Mr. Russell's comments, I should have supposed that I had repeated so often the statement about its importance in determination of inquiry and of the adequacy of any conclusion reached that its regulative function could not be missed.

The failure on Mr. Murphy's part to refer to it is the more striking in his case because of his nominal acceptance of the principle of Contextualism. For the problematic situation is *the* context in which everything I say about knowing is placed and by reference to which it is to be understood. It controls the meaning of "ideas," the factor to which Mr. Murphy practically confines his account of my view. It controls my theory of the place and function of facts or data, about which he says nothing, although according to my view ideas are so related to observed facts that they can be understood only in this reference. It controls the nature and function of those "future experiences" which appear so mysteriously out of nowhere in Murphy's account of my position. Finally, it controls the meaning to be put upon the *operations* by means of which the terminal conclusion "reliably ensues." Since I have held that the relative defects of both the idealistic and realistic epistemologies is the result of their failure to set knowing in this context of problematic situations, it is quite possible that Murphy's notion that my theory of knowing is a product of preoccupation with these epistemologies springs from his failure to note the context which actually controls my theory, both in general and in all its constituent details.

This failure is responsible for Mr. Murphy's repeated statement that my theory neglects the fact that "the ideas used and analyses performed in the course of inquiry are instrumental to finding out whatever the particular inquiry was investigating." This truism is the starting point of my whole theory. More chapters of my *Logic* are devoted to stating what happens when one investigates, say, "some (hitherto) unperceived antecedent existence," or "the structure of some purely hypothetic logical system," or some past event like the "batting averages of all members of the New York Yankees in 1921," or "the cause of infantile paralysis"—(my own example being the cause of malaria)—than to all other topics put together. Consequently, I am at a loss to understand the point of view from which Mr. Murphy's criticisms are made. Does he hold that there is no such thing as a theory of knowing beyond pointing to the *fact*[40] that when persons inquire, what they do is instrumental to finding out about whatever it is they are investigating? Does he hold that there exists only a multiplicity of special inquiries and that it is futile to search for any common logical pattern? Does he mean that there is some "ordinary theory of knowing" which is so satisfactory and so generally accepted that it serves as a criterion for judging every theory which is put forth? I do not know the correct answer to these questions. I had supposed that there are in existence a vast multitude of inquiries, investigations of quantities and qualities, of past events, of things that coexist, of mathematical topics, of social events, etc., which constitute the material of all the sciences; and that the business of logic is to investigate these different inquiries, in connection with the conclusions they arrive at, so as to frame a general theory of inquiry based upon and justified by what happens in these particular cases. If Mr. Murphy holds that no such generalized inquiry into inquiry is necessary or possible, I can see that he would regard my theory as superfluous. But I have difficulty in believing that he holds that a generalized logical theory is rendered unnecessary by the fact that one can point to a great number of cases of actual knowing. Moreover, there are in existence not only a large number of cases of inquiry or knowing, but also a considerable number of different *theories* about knowing and I supposed it was the business of one presenting another theory to take some notice of these. For, instead of holding, as Mr. Murphy intimates, that all of them, from Plato through Locke to the present, are of no value, I have held that *all* of them have laid hold of *some* actual

---

40. What Mr. Murphy regards as the "ordinary theory of knowing" does not seem to me to be a theory at all but one of the most obvious of the facts which the theory of knowledge is about.

constituent of knowing, but have failed to place it in the context in which it actually functions—a matter discussed at some length in the final chapter of my *Logic*.

There is some evidence that Mr. Murphy's failure to state my theory of knowing in its connection with the context which determines its meaning—both in general and in all its constituent parts—is due to his carrying over into his report of my view about knowing-as-inquiry-in-process what I say about the function of knowledge as a mode of experiencing in its relation to other non-cognitive modes of experience. For example, he endorses what he finds Lovejoy to have said about my theory, namely, that according to it "'I am about to have known' is the pragmatic equivalent for 'I know.'" It is certainly true that with reference to know*ing*, as inquiry *in process*, I have held that its reference is to an object not as yet reached and hence future. To transfer to my view of knowledge when *attained* the reference to a future object involved in inquiry still *in process*, is much as if I were to say that, according to Mr. Murphy's view, "I am engaged in the process of trying to discover is an equivalent for: I already know what it is I am trying to discover." It is a truism that, while one is engaged in knowing, the things to be known are still future. This belief is not then a peculiarity of my view over against any other view. What *is* characteristic of my view is that it defines the conclusion for which inquiry is a search as that which resolves the problematic situation in which search occurs.

The transfer of what is said by me about the function of attained knowledge to an alleged account of knowing-inquiry-in-process may account for other errors in Mr. Murphy's statement. For example, right after the passage in which he speaks of the process of inquiry as instrumental to finding out about whatever a particular inquirer is investigating, he goes on to say something about "the worth of knowledge for improving man's estate being different from its worth as a conclusion based on evidence and proper method." Of course there is a difference, a difference in context and hence in kind. The first matter is a matter of know*ing*-inquiry in process. The distinctive thing in my theory of knowing, as set forth in the *Logic*, is its exposition of the *particular ways* in which various kinds of factual and ideational propositions function as instruments to attainment of conclusions resting on evidence and/or the use of a proper method. The instrumental worth claimed by me to exist in the functional relation of attained knowledge to non-cognitive forms of experience is another matter, having to do with another philosophical problem. I did not invent the problem of the possibility of controlling the occurrence or existence of consummatory experiences, of experiences that are marked by intrinsic values. I did not invent the problem of how such experiences can be enriched by clarifying and deepening their contained meanings, nor that of extending the range of persons and groups who enjoy such values.[41] For these are problems of every *moral* theory in its social aspects, of every social theory in its moral aspects. What is characteristic of my theory is simply the emphasis placed upon the knowledge mode of experience, defined in terms of the outcome of competent inquiry, as that which accomplishes these functions; an emphasis which goes so far as to say that intelligence, as the fruit of such knowledge, is the *only* available instrumentality for accomplishing them. The contrast is with those theories which hold that transcendent *a priori* principles, rational intuitions, revelations from on high, adherence to established authorities in state and church, inevitable social revolutions, etc., are the agencies by which experienced values are to be made more secure and more extensively enjoyed.

I had supposed that the contexts within which reference is made, on the one hand, to the instrumentality of propositions in the *process* of inquiry, to knowledge as warranted solution of a problem, and, on the other, to the instrumentality of *attained* knowledge, through development of intelligence, to enrichment of subsequent experiences, were such as to prevent transferring what is said about one kind of instrumentality to the other. It may be that I have not taken sufficient pains to make clear the transition from the discussion of one point to that of the other. There are, moreover, certain factors common to both kinds of instrumentality which may have induced confusion in the minds of some readers. Within the progress of inquiry, for example, intelligent action as the product of previously attained knowledge is constantly taking effect. The termination of inquiry, with respect to the procedures of inquiry that have led up to it, is a re-

41. "Improving man's estate" is but a vague name for the three specified things just mentioned: Extension of range of persons enjoying consummatory experience, enrichment of their contents, and increased control of their occurrence.

solved situation whose *primary* status and value is cognitional. But the terminal material is also a directly had situation, and hence is capable of treatment on its own account as an enriched experience. It is quite possible that I have not always made the particular universe of discourse which is the context of a given discussion as distinct as these overlappings demand it should be made. There is also the point made in Dr. Ratner's contribution about a shift from the use of the word "knowledge" in my earlier writings to the word "intelligence" in my later. If I had uniformly made it clear that attained knowledge produces *meanings* and that these meanings are capable of being separated from the special cases of knowledge in which they originally appear and of being incorporated and funded cumulatively in habits so as to constitute *mind,* and to constitute *intelligence* when actually applied in new experiences, it is quite likely my view would have been less exposed to misunderstanding. The function of knowledge-experience as the mode of experience which, through formation of intelligence in action, is the sole instrumentality for regulating the occurrence and distribution of consummatory experiences and for giving them increased depth of meaning, might then have stood out in a way which would not permit of misunderstanding.

I do not mean that this distinction of functions is not frequently clearly stated, but that it is possible that my mode of statement at times has put an undue tax upon the attention of readers in keeping track of transitions. Of my explicit statements the following passage is representative:

> Experienced situations come about in two ways and are of two distinct types. Some take place with only a minimum of regulation, with little foresight, preparation and intent. Others occur, because, in part, of the prior occurrence of intelligent action. Both kinds are had. . . . The first are not known; they are not understood. . . . The second have, as they are experienced, meanings that present the funded outcome of operations that substitute definite continuity for experienced discontinuity and for the fragmentary quality due to isolation.[42]

42. *Quest for Certainty,* 243 [*Later Works* 4:194]; *cf.* 250, 259, 245 and 218–222 [*LW* 4:199–200, 206–7, 195–96, 174–77]. I quote a passage from p. 218 [*LW* 4:174], and another from the conclusion of the discussion [*LW* 4:175]: "Apart from knowledge the things of our ordinary experience are fragmentary, casual, unregulated by purpose, full of frustrations and bar-

I obtain a certain humorous enjoyment from reading criticisms which combine condemnation of my "pragmatism" for its alleged sacrifice of knowledge to practice with condemnation of my "instrumentalism" for greatly exaggerating the potential function of knowledge and of intelligence in direction and enrichment of everyday experiences. My position may be badly taken, but it is not so loose in its joints that the bones of the argument stick out at right angles to one another.

Mr. Murphy is not alone in being troubled by my denial that antecedent conditions constitute the object of knowledge. *If* I have written anything affirming that antecedent objects are not capable of being known and are not as matter of fact known, *if*, in Mr. Murphy's language, I have asserted their "inaccessibility," any one, myself included, ought to be troubled. But the trouble arises from confusion of the contexts in which certain statements are made. There is in a given practical and scientific inquiry the question as to what the objective of knowing is for that particular inquiry. There is the question in the form of inquiry constituting logical theory as to what the object of knowledge is and means—a problem I did not invent. Instead of denying that unperceived antecedent conditions are objectives of knowledge in the first context, I have very explicitly stated that no problem as to existential matters can be resolved except by inquiries which *ascertain antecedent conditions not previously observed.* I have also then pointed out that such objects do not fulfill the conditions which must be satisfied in a philosophical logical theory as to the *generalized* meaning of the category "object of knowledge." That is, as in a sentence quoted in Mr. Murphy's account but not discussed by him, I have said that such objects are not *final and complete* with respect to satisfying the conditions that must be satisfied, in philosophical inquiry, by a candidate for the position of object-of-knowledge in this latter context.

---

riers. . . . But we return from abstractive thought to experience of them with added meaning and with increased power to regulate our relations to them. Reflective knowledge is the *only* means of regulation. Its value as instrumental is unique." And, from the conclusion [*LW* 4 : 177]: "It is congenial to our idiom to call the reflective conclusions of competent methods by the name of science. But science thus conceived is not a final thing. The final thing is appreciation and use of things of direct experience. These are *known* in as far as their constituents and their form are the result of science. But they are also more than science. They are natural objects experienced in relations and continuities that are summed up in rich and definite individual forms."

From the time of my earlier essays, first printed in the *Studies in Logical Theory*, I have pointed out that material dealt with in inquiry passes through a series of temporal phases and that what is said of the material in one phase cannot be applied to material in another phase without production of confusion. There is the initial phase of a non-cognitive situation out of which knowing develops; there is the terminal stage of the attained knowledge; and there is the intermediate phase in which subject-matter is what it is *as* conditioned by inquiry (and hence is tentative, provisional, conditional, pending completion of inquiry). In my recent *Logic*, the words *subject-matter, object, and contents* are used technically to designate these different statuses of experienced material. Obviously such distinctions appertain to the logical-philosophical analysis of knowing; an investigation of a particular problem does not need to make them explicit because, as I pointed out in my early essays, the immediate exigencies of the conduct of his inquiry prevent an inquirer giving to the material of one phase the properties belonging to that of another phase. *Epistemological discussion, however, as I pointed out, is definitely marked by confusions arising from this source.* Hence the necessity for making clear what is the object-of-knowledge in its definitive sense. If the distinction between the particular object of a particular inquiry as such and the object of knowledge in its philosophical-logical sense is denied, then, as already indicated, there is *no* philosophical problem or theory of knowledge. It suffices to enumerate, without analysis, all the special cases of knowing for which one has time. As for myself, throwing out epistemological bathwater I had no intention of also throwing out the baby.

There are a few cases in which, in speaking of the object of knowledge in the sense it bears in philosophical discussion, I have prefixed the word "true." Two of these cases are quoted by Mr. Murphy and are interpreted by him as if "true" here refers to what is ascertained to be true in a particular inquiry. In speaking of certain controversies, I said: "They spring from the assumption that 'the true and valid object of knowledge is that which has being prior to and independent of the operations of knowing.'" This sentence, when isolated from its context, might be understood to refer to the object of a specific inquiry, instead of, as is intended, to the characteristic object of the *knowledge-*

function as determined in philosophical theory.⁴³ Reference to its context shows that the expression "true object" is relevant to a philosophical issue—though not to that of idealism-realism. The issue to which the passage is relevant is stated as follows in a nearby paragraph:

> The claim of physical objects, the objects in which the physical sciences terminate, to constitute the real nature of the world, places the objects of value with which our affections and choices are concerned at an invidious disadvantage. . . . The net practical effect is the creation of the belief that science exists only in the things which are most remote from any significant human concern, so that as we approach social and moral questions and interests we must either surrender hope of the guidance of genuine knowledge or else purchase scientific title and authority at the expense of all that is distinctly human. (*Quest for Certainty*, 195–196 [*Later Works* 4:156–57].)

There are contributors to this very volume who deny in a thoroughgoing way the possibility of any valid cognitive determination whatever of valuations, and who in consequence relegate all moral affairs, personal and social, to the status of private desires or else to the use of coercive force. It is a well known fact that others, perhaps not represented in this volume, deny the competency in moral inquiry of the methods used in practical and scientific knowing and in consequence insist upon the necessity of non-empirical validation for moral judgments. The existence of such theories gives pertinency to a theory which holds that the same methods of inquiry that yield ordinary practical and scientific conclusions are capable of application in reaching moral judgments, so validated as to fall within the scope of verifiability.

---

43. That I hold that a logical theory of knowledge can be formed only in terms of the *object* of knowledge as that is ascertained in critical analysis of actual cases of knowledge is not a matter for which I have any apologies to offer. To my mind, the framing of a theory of knowledge in terms of properties of its characteristic *object* is the only alternative to epistemological theories of knowledge that claim to decide its nature by analysis of "mind," "consciousness," mental states like "sensations and ideas," etc. To start from the fact that there are in fact objects of knowledge as distinct from objects of mere opinion or of fear and hope is the only way of avoiding the futile question as to how knowledge is possible.

When it is said, therefore, that "the true object of knowledge lies in the consequences of directed action," the context is a philosophical logic of inquiry, *based upon what is found out in specific inquiries* as to the necessity for experimentation (directed action) if a valid conclusion is to be reached. If the context in which the passage occurs fails to make this point clear, I am glad of the opportunity to say (i) that I hold a philosophic logical theory of knowledge can be framed only in terms of properties that analysis finds to belong to attained objects of knowledge; and (ii) that physical scientific objects, when taken as models for framing such a theory, prove, through their dependence upon experiment (which is *ipso facto* a transformation of antecedently experienced materials), that existential consequences must be taken into account in forming the theory; (iii) that instead of denying that antecedent conditions are accessible to inquiry or knowing, I hold that all physical scientific objects are precisely generalizations, on a statistical basis, of such antecedent conditions, but (iv) that they nevertheless do not stand alone, or as "final and complete" fulfilments of the conditions involved in inquiry. To conclude this phase of my reply I quote, then, the following passage:

> We know whenever we do know; that is, whenever our inquiry leads to conclusions which settle the problem out of which it grew. This truth is the end of the whole matter— *upon the condition that we frame our theory of knowledge in accord with the pattern set by experimental inquiry.*[44]

II. A close counterpart of Mr. Murphy's method of dealing with what I say about "ideas" is found in Mr. Russell's treatment of what I say about "apprehension." In both cases, there is neglect of the reference of "ideas" and "apprehensions" to a problematic situation and to their function in resolution of such a situation. If the reader will refer to Mr. Russell's paper he will find quotations from me in which I expressly recognize the existence of direct perception of objects and of direct apprehensions

---

44. *Quest for Certainty*, 198 [*Later Works* 4:158]; italics not in original text. In view of the fact that nothing is said in what purports to be an account of my view about problematic situations and problems, it is perhaps not surprising that almost nothing is said about the role that *experimental* science plays in my theory.

of meanings and of things. Mr. Russell also quotes in this connection what I said about the dependence of such cases upon causal conditions, *i.e.,* organic mechanisms formed by previous cases of mediated knowledge of the same objects. The point here is that we now *directly* grasp a book as a book and a typewriter as a typewriter, because of operation of organic mechanisms which were produced by a series of mediated inquiries by which at an earlier time we came to identify and discriminate these things as of the kinds in question. But Mr. Russell's remarks say nothing at all about the point made by me in the next sentences after the ones he quotes:

> But the important point for the purpose of the present topic is that either an immediate overt response occurs, like using the typewriter or picking up the book, or that the object directly noted is *part of an act of inquiry* directed toward knowledge as warranted assertion. In the latter case [the only cognitional one], the fact of immediate apprehension is no logical guarantee that the object or event directly apprehended is that part of the "facts of the case" it is *prima facie* taken to be. . . . It may be irrelevant in whole or part. . . . In other words, immediate *ap*prehension of an object or event is no more identical with knowledge in the logical sense required than is immediate understanding or *com*prehension of a meaning. (*Logic,* 143–144 [*Later Works* 12:146–47].)

It is possible that without taking still more of the context into account the force of the sentences just quoted will not be evident. So I add some further explanatory remarks, at the same time asking any interested reader to go to the complete original text. "But" in the passage just cited places the *important* point in opposition to one not important "for the purpose of the present topic," which purpose is the proper logical interpretation of direct apprehension. That which by contrast is said to be not important with respect to that problem is precisely the nature and action of the organic mechanisms to which Mr. Russell devotes his attention. That which is said to be important is the fact that if there is *knowing* involved—instead of direct motor response to a given stimulus—the thing apprehended is a means of knowing something else—in other words, is a mediating factor in arriving at knowledge of something else. The question involved is one of fact. Is there any case in which the occurrence of a directly apprehended object constitutes a *final* object terminating knowing? If not, to be a directly apprehended thing and to be *that* thing which provides the evidential data in a given case are not equivalents. The reference to the logical similarity between *app*rehension of a thing and *com*prehension of a meaning carries out the point. One may have, say, the direct comprehension of the meaning "sea serpent," but it does not warrant a proposition that sea serpents exist. Similarly one may directly apprehend a long thing gliding over the water, but its apprehension will not prove the object apprehended to be evidence warranting an existential proposition that a sea serpent exists. It is, I suppose, a familiar fact that more mistakes arise in scientific investigation from taking actually perceived things to be good evidential data in the inquiry at hand than from hallucinatory perceptions. One may see a lot of things and still be in doubt *what* seen things, if any of them, are relevant to reaching a sound conclusion.

Instead of discussing this point, which is said to be the *important* one with respect to the problem of immediate knowledge or of beliefs not mediated by inquiry, Mr. Russell discusses the point of causal production which is just the point which in contrast I take *not* to be important for the issue in question. Unless I am mistaken, Mr. Russell has himself upon occasion pointed out that causal issues should not be substituted for logical ones. As far as causal conditions are concerned, it makes no difference to my argument what they may be, as long as it is granted that habits are formed that enable us to spot familiar objects on sight. I have, therefore, no ground for quarreling with Mr. Russell's particular view on this point. *If* I held a holistic view, his reference to independent causal chains would be highly pertinent. But since I do not hold that position, and since in my own treatment, when I deal with the topic of causation, I expressly insist upon a plurality of sequences, I need only remark that Mr. Russell's considerations reinforce the point I have made about the logical aspect of the matter. For a given set of causal conditions, or the organic mechanism operating in a given case, may (as is obvious in the case of a hallucination) produce an object which is directly apprehended but which is just *not* the datum needed as evidence in the problem at hand, thereby proving it is not the "complete and final object of knowledge."

If I now cut somewhat short my discussion of the criticisms passed by Russell upon my theory of truth, it is partly because my discussion up to this point indicates the particular context— that of problematic situations—in which my view is set and which must be taken into account in discussing my view; and partly because former, rather extended, corrections of misconceptions on this point have indicated that nothing I can say will eliminate them from the minds of some of my critics. The rather elaborate exegesis of Mr. Russell of my presumed view as to truth would have been rendered unnecessary if Mr. Russell had only taken seriously the passage he, curiously enough, quotes from the Preface of my *Logic*—I say "curiously" because apparently he uses the passage only as a means of identifying me as a pragmatist, but not as a means of understanding what I mean by any pragmatic theory of "consequences" which I accept. The passage reads as follows:

> The word "Pragmatism" does not, I think, occur in the text. Perhaps the word lends itself to misconception. At all events, so much misunderstanding and relatively futile controversy have gathered about the word that it seemed advisable to avoid its use. But in the proper interpretation of "pragmatic," namely, the function of consequences as necessary tests of the validity of propositions *provided* these consequences are operationally instituted and are such as to resolve the specific problem evoking the operations, the text is thoroughly pragmatic.

If I mention that the word *provided* is italicized in the original text it is because Mr. Russell, in spite of the reference in this very passage to "misunderstanding and relatively futile controversy" has paid no attention to what is stated in the proviso, and so repeats notions about pragmatism which he formed long ago and has frequently stated, despite my express repudiation of them at least as many as thirty years ago.

The proviso about the kind of consequences that operate as tests of validity was inserted as a caution against just the kind of interpretation which Mr. Russell gives to my use of consequences. For it explicitly states that it is necessary that they be *such as to resolve the specific problem* undergoing investigation. The interpretation Mr. Russell gives to consequences relates them to personal desire. The net outcome is attribution to me of generalized wishful thinking as a definition of truth.[45] Mr. Russell proceeds first by converting a doubtful *situation* into a personal doubt, although the difference between the two things is repeatedly pointed out by me. I have even explicitly stated that a personal doubt is pathological unless it is a reflection of a *situation* which is problematic. Then by changing doubt into private discomfort, truth is identified with removal of this discomfort. The only desire that enters, according to my view, is desire to resolve as honestly and impartially as possible the problem involved in the situation. "Satisfaction" is satisfaction of the conditions prescribed by the problem. Personal satisfaction may enter in as it arises when any job is well done according to the requirements of the job itself; but it does not enter in any way into the determination of validity, because, on the contrary, it is conditioned by that determination.

There is a distinction made in my theory between validity and truth. The latter is defined, following Peirce, as the ideal limit of indefinitely continued inquiry. This definition is, of course, a definition of truth *as an abstract idea*. This definition gives Mr. Russell a surprising amount of trouble, due I think to the fact that he omits all reference to the part played in the theory of Peirce— which I follow—by the principle of the continuity of inquiry. Apparently Mr. Russell takes the statement to apply *here and now* to determination of the truth or falsity of a given proposition—a matter which, in the sense of validity as just stated, is determined, on my theory, by a resolved situation as the consequence of distinctive operations of inquiry. For Mr. Russell says: "I do not see how we can guess either what will be believed, or what would be believed by men much cleverer than we are," as if something of the nature of that kind of guess at a future belief is so implied in the definition that the impossibility of making the guess is a refutation of the definition. The contrary is the case. The "truth" of any present proposition is, by the definition, subject to the out-

45. The following lines from Parodi's contribution show that long before the *Logic* was written some readers were able to derive from what I wrote a correct idea: "Truth is not verified just by any kind of satisfaction, but only by that satisfaction which is born of the fact that a working hypothesis or experimental method applies to the facts which it concerns and effects a better ordering. No misconception concerning the instrumental logic of pragmatism has been more persistent than that one which would make of it merely a means for a practical end."

come of continued inquiries; *its* "truth," if the word must be used, is provisional; as *near* the truth as inquiry has *as yet* come, a matter determined *not* by a guess at some future belief but by the care and pains with which inquiry has been conducted up to the present time.[46] Admission of the necessary subjection of every present proposition to the results to be obtained in future inquiry is the meaning of Peirce's reference to "confession of inaccuracy and one-sidedness" as an ingredient of the truth of a present proposition. In other words, a person who makes this admission is nearer the truth than any person is who dogmatically claims infallibility for the conclusion he entertains here and now.

Mr. Russell's inversion of what Peirce actually says upon occasion takes an amusing form. Peirce having, for example, defined truth in terms of the ideal limit *of inquiry*—ideal since not now actually attained—Mr. Russell says: "If the definition is interpreted strictly, every proposition investigated by no one is 'true'"; from which it would appear that a *strict* interpretation consists in stating the contrary of a given proposition. The exclusive devotion of Mr. Russell to discourse is manifested in his assumption that *propositions* are the subject-matter of inquiry, a view assumed so unconsciously that it is taken for granted that Peirce and I likewise assume it. But according to our view—and according to that of any thoroughgoing empiricist—*things and events* are the material and objects of inquiry, and propositions are *means* in inquiry, so that as conclusions of a given inquiry they become means of carrying on further inquiries. Like other means they are modified and improved in the course of use. Given the beliefs (i) that propositions are from the start the objects of inquiry and (ii) that all propositions have either truth or falsity as their inherent property, and (iii) then read these two assumptions into theories—like Peirce's and mine—which deny both of them, and the product is just the doctrinal confusion that Russell finds in what we have said.

It does not follow of course that our views are the correct ones. But since they are after all the views which we hold, it is they, if anything, which should be criticized. It is hardly necessary to carry comment further. But Mr. Russell's allusion to the opinions

---

46. The definition is directly connected of course with Peirce's principles of "fallibilism," and his emphasis upon the probability coefficient of all propositions.

of "the last man left alive," as if the reference had some relevance to Peirce's definition of truth *in terms of continued inquiry*, repeats his misunderstanding. His view that, according to our definition, the truth of the theory of relativity will be determined by Hitler's victory or defeat—the latter cutting inquiry off short—shows what can happen in the way of inversion of meaning when a critic declines to treat a view in its own terms, even as independent hypothesis, but insists upon translating it into terms of his own theory before considering it. For the technical purposes of strictly formal logic an assumption that every proposition is of itself, or intrinsically, either true or false may not do harm. But it is the last view an empiricist can possibly take who is concerned with truth and falsity as having *existential* application, and as something determined by means of inquiry into material existence. For in the latter case the question of truth or falsity is the very thing to be determined.

III. I regret that it is not possible within the limits of my reply to deal adequately with Mr. Reichenbach's comments on my theory of induction in connection with his presentation of his own view. I am, however, inclined to think that the difference between us is far from insuperable. When I criticized the theory of induction by simple enumeration I was criticizing that theory in its traditional formulation. The statement of that theory given by Reichenbach involves quite fundamental revision of it in its traditional form. If those who held it meant by it what Mr. Reichenbach finds in it, they failed to make their point clear. Now, my emphasis that the heart of the inductive process is the experimentally controlled analysis by means of which a given case is constituted to be a representative or exemplary instance (a sample or a specimen) admits the importance of *other* observed cases as means of the analysis which finally yields the representative instance. If I had treated the topic of probability in that immediate context, I should have been forced to recognize that an *indefinite number* of such other cases are, in theory, involved in determination of the representative case. If the theory of induction by simple enumeration *is understood in this particular sense*, I do not see that there are fundamental differences between Mr. Reichenbach's view and mine, though there are doubtless differences in detail. If there is such agreement, I should not allow what seems to me the inadequacy of the word "enumeration" for conveying the analytic function of enumerated cases to stand between us.

IV. I am so much indebted to Dr. Savery for his exposition of my main ideas in their historical perspective, together with his generous appreciation of the source of such inconsistencies as appear in successive writings, that I should gladly forego reply to his criticisms were it not that abstinence might seem to indicate lack of regard for them. I begin with the matter of verification. When a proposition about a thing in some specified respect is definitely in question, "confrontation" seems to me to be a good term by which to describe the nature of verification. If I doubt, for example, whether the outside walls of a certain house are colored white or brown, confrontation with the actual house settles the matter. It seems to me, however, that in the case of an *hypothesis* verification is of a more complex character than this; it *involves* confrontation, but only as one constituent. The point of this remark comes out most clearly when the hypothesis is a theory of considerable scope. A certain phase of Einstein's special theory of relativity was confirmed by observation of something that happened in the eclipse of Mercury. I doubt if any one could say more than that the confrontation which occurred tended toward confirmation. A negative result would have been a disproof of the theory *as previously stated,* but it would not have precluded a modification of it. I do not see how a theory can be said to be verified unless *a set of instances, positive and negative, inclusive and exclusive,* has been instituted. If this view is correct, it is the *function* of confrontations as experimentally determined consequences that confers upon them verifying power. In my *Logic* this function is said to be the "capacity of an idea or theory to order and organize particulars into a coherent whole"—it being understood, of course, that this organization is not "mental" but is existentially effected by suitable experimental operations. In the context in which the sentence just quoted occurs, it is put in opposition to the idea that hypotheses are capable of being "verified by particular objects in their particularity" (157 [*Later Works* 12 : 159–60]). That is to say, I hold that confrontation is a necessary but not a sufficient condition for verification of an hypothesis. The remarks I make about ultra-positivistic views, while not identical in import with the point just made, have a similar bearing. For they indicate that the primary value of

hypotheses and theories is found in their power to direct observation to discovery of newly observed facts and in their power to
organize facts in such a way as to forward the solution of a problem. If I were to say that logical theory has exaggerated the importance of verification of ideas at the expense of some other uses
of the latter, I should probably be understood by some persons to
confirm their notion that I think rather lightly of truth. But as far
as *scientific* hypotheses and theories are concerned, it is clear to
me that the indubitable and supreme value of truth in its *moral*
sense has often been uncritically carried over into the context of
scientific inquiry and into the logical values of ideas and theories.
What a scientist asks of his hypotheses is that they be fruitful in
giving direction to his observations and reasonings. Confrontation with an observed fact which does not square with an hypothesis is consequently just as welcome as one which does—
since it enables him to introduce modifications into his idea that
renders the latter more efficient in future conduct of inquiry.
Whereas if a liar is confronted with something which contradicts
what he says, there is one hundred per cent nullification of what
he has said, with no opportunity allowed for additional development because of the negative confrontation that has occurred. In
science, discovery of an exception, of a fact that contradicts a
theory in the form in which it has been previously held, is a positive means of advance. It is not only welcome when hit upon but
is actively searched for.

This matter of verification is intimately connected, as Savery
points out, with the more inclusive matter of the theory of knowledge. Accordingly I refer the reader to what he says on that point,
especially about the matter of futurity in relation to knowledge.
The point involved here as to futurity is not identical with that
previously discussed. For example, in connection with the otherwise ambiguous phrase that "all knowledge is of the future," he
cites my statement that the proposition "This is red" has for its
logical equivalent "This has changed color from the quality it
previously had." Obviously in this case what is known is something which *has* occurred. It may, then, help to clear up my theory if I point out three distinct contexts in which futurity appears in theoretical analysis of knowledge. One of them is the
obvious case mentioned earlier. While inquiry is still in progress,
its object, as the conclusion of inquiry, is, truistically, in the fu-

ture. The second case is far from being truistic. It is exemplified in the case just cited regarding the color quality of a thing. Here the point is that the *material* subject-matter of an existential proposition is found to be *temporal* when the proposition is analyzed. As temporal it involves a change from what a thing was to something temporally future (but not to our knowing), *i.e.*, temporally future to what *it* was. In other words, any existential change is from a *past* into a present, something future to its past, so that "is," in an existential proposition, is just as temporal in its reference as "was" or "will be." Consequently it is dated and has no meaning when taken out of connection with the futurity, or "will be" of what was. The third distinction of futurity in connection with knowledge is that consequences still to be obtained as the outcome of experimental operations in inquiry serve to test ideas, hypotheses, theories, that are entertained. The immediate *reference* of an idea is not to these future consequences, but to facts, data of observation. But the *validity* of its reference to any given set of facts is determined by the consequences that result when the given idea and the given facts operationally interact in institution of a new experienced situation—a view clearly implying that the reference of the idea to facts is already there as a condition. These three kinds of connection with futurity are found in a theory of knowledge reached by analysis of what takes place in inquiry. The potential bearing of attained knowledge through the medium of intelligent action upon subsequent noncognitive value-experiences belongs not in the theory of knowledge as such but in the theory of the relation of the knowledge function of experience to other modes of experience.

A further important question raised by Mr. Savery has to do with the existential character of scientific objects. One phase of this question was dealt with in connection with Reichenbach's criticism. Mr. Savery, however, raises the question in a somewhat different form so that it is possible that the answer already given—to the effect that scientific objects are statistically standardized correlations of existential changes—may not answer the question as he puts it. But that reply suggests that I cannot accept the problem in the form in which Mr. Savery phrases it, namely whether scientific objects are existential *or* operational. For in my view they are existential *because* they formulate operations which actually take place. The particular passage Savery quotes from me in this connection is concerned with "conceptual" subject-matters, and it is to them *as conceptual* that descriptive character is denied. Hence when he says that "such a view yields pure positivism"—in the sense, I take it, of pure phenomenalism—he unwittingly transfers to *knowledge* what is said about *theories*.

D. Ethical and Allied Topics

Critics of my theory of knowledge have found the idea that qualitative transformation of antecedent conditions is required for its attainment to be a stumbling-block. It is accordingly interesting, if not surprising, that Dr. Stuart, a critic of my theory of moral judgment and action, comes close to finding that absence of this category—or something similar to it—is the source of the defects of my moral theory. For, being aware, and properly so, of the difference between operations that manipulate what is given or that merely adapt conditions to old ends and habits and operations that re-adapt habits to new ends, he thinks that my theory has thrown in its lot with the former. Now it is quite true that I hold there is a common logical pattern in scientific and moral knowing. But instead of first accepting the traditional theory of knowing according to which it is an accommodation of the self and its beliefs to conditions already fixed, I have held that scientific knowing involves deliberate modification, through working ideas, of what previously existed—pointing to the necessary role of experiment in natural science as evidence. Since there seemed to be a certain similarity between this conclusion and the idealistic theory that mind constitutes the objective world, the commonest early interpretation of my view was that it consisted of a rather gratuitously devised, verbally novel, version of idealistic epistemology. The actual point of my theory may however be found in a transfer of traits which had been reserved for the function of moral judgment over to the processes of ordinary and scientific knowing. It is, accordingly, my belief that the difference between Dr. Stuart and myself is not where he puts it, but lies in the fact that his view of scientific knowing is such that it compels him to set up a rigid dualism between it and moral knowing, while I find the features which he reserves for the latter to be implicit, or involved, in all inquiry whatever. In any case, many of the criticisms of my theory of knowing have arisen from my insistence on the function of transformation, reconstruction, readjustment, of antecedent material in knowing, while an alleged absence of these categories seems to be the source and ground of Mr. Stuart's criticisms of my ethical views.

Mr. Reichenbach in his article makes a statement which shows an acute appreciation of an important, perhaps fundamental, "directive tendency" in my philosophy. He says: "In restoring the world of every-day life as the basis of knowledge, Dewey does not only want to establish knowledge in a better and more solid form. What he intends, and perhaps to a greater extent, is establishing the sphere of values, of human desires and aims, on the same basis and in an analogous form as the system of knowledge." This passage proves that Reichenbach grasps the direction in which my thoughts have moved. It marks a realization of the role played in development of my ideas by that problem which, in my introductory remarks, I said is the central problem of modern philosophy, because it is the central problem of modern life.

Were I anonymously to turn critic of my own philosophy, this is the place from which I should set out. I should indicate that after insisting upon the genuineness of affectional and other "tertiary" qualities as "doings of nature," Dewey then proceeds to emphasize in his theory of knowing, as that is manifested in both science and common sense, the operations of transformation, reconstruction, control, and union of theory and practice in experimental activity which are analogous to those involved in moral activity. Without continuing this line of criticism and then defending myself against it, I express my indebtedness to Dr. Stuart's paper for the opportunity to remove any doubts that may exist as to the direction in which I read the community of pattern which I find in physical and moral judgment.

Since apparently it is use of the word "Naturalism" to characterize my general position which has led Stuart off the track, I call attention again to the fact that instead of presenting that kind of mechanistic naturalism that is bound to deny the "reality" of the qualities which are the raw material of the values with which morals is concerned, I have repeatedly insisted that our theory of Nature be framed on the basis of giving full credence to these qualities just as they present themselves. No one philosophic theory has a monopoly on the meaning to be given Nature, and it is the meaning given Nature that is decisive as to the kind of Naturalism that is put forward. Naturalism is opposed to idealistic spiritualism, but it is also opposed to super-naturalism and to that mitigated version of the latter that appeals to transcendent *a priori* principles placed in a realm above Nature and beyond experience. That Nature is purely mechanistic is a particular metaphysical doctrine; it is not an idea implied of necessity in the meaning of the word. And in my *Experience and Nature* I tried to make it clear that while I believe Nature *has* a mechanism—for otherwise knowledge could not be an instrument for its control—I do not accept its *reduction* to a mechanism.

There are passages in Mr. Stuart's paper which seem to assume that I *must* give Nature and Naturalism a meaning that reduces it to a mechanism or something close to it. For he speaks as if I admitted a special field of morals only as "a grudgingly tolerated annex to biology," and he devotes considerable attention to a passage in my *Logic* which he takes to reduce all thinking to a merely biological phenomenon—in spite of the fact that the title of the chapter in which the passage quoted occurs is "The Biological Matrix of Inquiry" and that the next chapter on "The Cultural Matrix" deals expressly with the radical change wrought when biological conditions and activities are taken up into the distinctively human context of institutions and communication. Moreover, in close connection with the very passage he quotes, it is stated that, even on the biological plane, there is more than mere restoration of what previously existed, namely, production of *new* conditions in both *organism* and environment.[47] The most surprising venture of Mr. Stuart's in this line of interpretation is found in the view of deliberation he attributes to me. He holds I am capable of regarding it only from "without," thereby reducing it to a purely "muscular" phenomenon. At the outset of his paper, Mr. Stuart quotes a number of passages from me where I expressly differentiate modes of mental behavior from

47. The meaning of my insistence, as against Rignano, that it is the *relation* of organism and environment that is restored seems to have escaped Mr. Stuart. For without restoration of the relation of harmony or equilibration, life cannot continue while specific *conditions* constituting both organism and environment have to be made over in some degree in order that *this* relation may be re-instated. In other words, *trans*formation has a natural biological basis.

other forms on the ground that they are responses to the *doubt-ful* as such. It is surprising that within a few short pages Mr. Stuart completely forgets this differentia, since it is especially conspicuous in marking off deliberative from merely muscular behavior.

At all events, Mr. Stuart finds "implicit in the naturalism which is the dominant theme" of my later writings a conception of the nature of the "supremacy of method" which is as close to the opposite of my actual view (a view which in my inability to foresee all possible interpretations I had supposed to be clear) as is possible. For he believes that what is implicit in my naturalism is that my idea of the supremacy of method is in no way inconsistent with the view that method, considered as a procedure of the actual knower, engaged not in epistemological inquiry, but in the direct solution of a first-hand problem in his experience, is not and cannot be "supreme." The contrary is the case. The whole point of my position is precisely that method *is* supreme in direct solution of every first-hand problem in experience, so that epistemological inquiry—*logical* inquiry in my terminology—has solely the business of pointing out the characteristic features of the method which is supreme in these first-hand investigations. From an inversion of what I intended and supposed I had clearly stated in my chapter upon "The Supremacy of Method" follow the further misconceptions of my ethical views upon which Dr. Stuart bases his criticisms.

The issue is perhaps made clearer by an earlier passage in which he says that methods are justified by their success, and "results derive none of their worth from the method by which they have been brought to pass." This view apparently he takes to be so axiomatic that I must also hold it as a matter of course:— even though I have repeatedly stated (as in the first chapter of my *Logic*) that conclusions owe their scientific worth to the method by which they are reached, while the only result an inquirer intends who observes the conditions which are set by inquiry itself is resolution of the problematic situation in question. How Stuart, or any observer of the procedures of the sciences, can say that for an individual inquirer "no method can be supreme," since "what is legislative is the result which he desires and intends," I cannot imagine. For if it means that attainment of some special result controls scientific inquiry, the remark is as good a description of violation of scientific method as can be found.[48]

In reducing what I say about method to an identification of it with "a formula of skill to be used as needed," the supremacy of method is so denied that I should have supposed Mr. Stuart would have been moved to wonder why I used such a totally inappropriate title. In any case what I hold, to repeat, is that method in knowing of physical objects is not a formula for conducting skilful manipulations, subordinating either the self to pre-existing material or the latter to some pre-existing impetus of the self, but is reconstructive of antecedent situations, a reconstruction in which the self as knower is changed as well as the environing conditions. The function of the chapter on "The Supremacy of Method" is thus quite literally to prepare for the discussions of the next chapter, which is entitled "The Construction of Good." That is to say, precisely because I hold that experimental method as union of theory and practice, of ideas and operations directed by them, has supremacy over an antecedent situation, I also hold that one and the same method is to be used in determination of physical judgment and the value-judgments of morals. In consequence I hold that enjoyments, objects of desires as they arise, are *not* values, but are problematic material for construction—for creation if you will—of values. The dualism between scientific and moral knowing arose, as I point out, before the rise of the experimental method in scientific knowing. The theory of scientific knowing that reflected this condition— pre-scientific in substance—limited knowing to ascertainment of antecedent reality, while a theory of knowing as *experimental* displays and proves the "supremacy of method." Thus once more the very point in my theory of knowing whose presence has called out the criticisms of other contributors is assumed by Mr. Stuart to be so utterly absent in my theory of scientific knowing as to vitiate my theory of morals. My assertion of the supremacy of method is identical with my assertion that "intelligent action is the sole ultimate recourse of mankind in every field whatever." For intelligent action, made manifest as it is in the experimental method of science, while it recognizes the necessity for discover-

48. The inversion of my view is marked in the last section of Stuart's paper, in which he refers to "*predetermined* ends."

ing antecedent conditions, it employs them when discovered as *means* for construction of a new unified and ordered situation. Or as is stated in the very chapter under discussion: "Knowledge of special conditions and relations is instrumental to the action which is in turn an instrument of production of situations having qualities of added significance and order."[49] Almost at the end of the same chapter, there occurs the following passage, serving as a transition to the discussion in the next chapter of "The Construction of Good." "What possibilities of controlled transformation of the content of present belief and practice in human institutions and associations are indicated by the control of natural energies which natural science has effected?"[50] In this passage is indicated a real difference between Mr. Stuart and myself. I hold that a philosophy of knowing based upon experimental method makes it possible to utilize the conclusions of science about natural energies so that the latter may become positive means of constructing values, of controlling (as I have said in previous pages) the occurrence of enriched values. Mr. Stuart seems to recur to the essentially Kantian dualism of scientific and moral knowing, a view which implies the complete indifference of what is found out about natural structures and events to formation and attainment of moral ends. This "splendid isolation" of moral values is bought at too high a price.

As far as I can make out, Mr. Stuart believes that I begin with two separate entities, those commonly called knowing-subject and object-to-be-known, and that I then think of knowing as some kind of transaction carried on between these two end-terms. This appears to be his view, and he further distinguishes knowledge of physical objects as involving subjection of the self, as knower, to conditions set by what is to be known, whereas in moral knowledge the reverse is the case—the self insisting upon subordination of existing material to an end *it,* in its very capacity as Self, sets up. At all events, he states my view as follows:

---

49. *Quest for Certainty,* 250 [*Later Works* 4:200]. The purport of the discussion is shown in a conclusion, drawn from the transformative power of the inferences of scientific method, to involve the elimination of the dualism between the categories of freedom and purpose which, upon the old theory, caused scientific and moral knowing to be thought of as two wholly separate kinds.

50. *Ibid.,* 252 [*Later Works* 4:202].

If conditions when encountered are found not "wholly good," it is because some *present end of the individual* finds itself adversely affected by them. In such a situation we have, according to the scheme of Professor Dewey's naturalism, the drive or inertia of the *"organism's" disturbed or interrupted activity* seeking to push forward. Pushing forward, it spreads out in continuously ramifying trains of attentive and *manipulative* behavior by which the *environment* is explored and reconstructed.[51]

The same point of view is found when he says, speaking of my supposed view, that "a situation presents itself *to the knower* as doubtful" or precarious, as if I held the situation to be *outside* the knower, and again when he says, nominally reporting my view, that "precariousness apprehended" is the "occasion for the *knower's* resort to *method*." He also frequently speaks of some "intrusion" furnishing the occasion for the self's engaging in knowing. It is this background which leads him to suppose that I believe in the *supremacy* of method only in that rather trivial— or at least definitely secondary—sense in which, according to him, it does not apply to inquiry engaged in "direct solution of a first-hand problem in experience"—which is exactly where it does apply. From this attributed interpretation—and from it alone—follows the conclusion that to me knowing, even in the case of moral judgment, consists only in using a method of manipulative skill for getting rid of the external conditions which interfere with, disturb, intrude upon the self and the knower.

I can readily understand that Dr. Stuart may have worked out his own view of moral knowing in contrast to such a view as has just been stated, and I can certainly see how, if he takes such a view to be the correct statement and the "ordinary theory" of what takes place in scientific knowing, he should insist upon a rigid dualism between scientific and moral knowing. I do *not* see how he came to attribute this view to me since it is so nearly the

51. Italics not in original text. They are emphasized to indicate how definitely Stuart reads into my theory an original separation of self and object, organism and environment, and regards that disturbance which initiates knowing to be something produced in the former by some change in the latter; as over against my actual theory in which the disturbance is of a *situation* in which organism and environment are functionally united. (Cf. passage on p. 305 [Schilpp] above.)

opposite of the one I have set forth. Aside from his questionable deduction of what a naturalistic view must be, it is probable, judging from his quotations of passages found in the earlier part of the chapter on "The Supremacy of Method" that he was also misled by taking part of my view for the whole of it. For in the early part of that chapter I give a rather summary account of behavior, emotional, volitional, cognitive, from the *psychological* standpoint—that is from the standpoint of the organic factor in the total life-function. In this account psychological phenomena are interpreted as *behavioral responses to the doubtful as such.* However, this account is so far from being a statement of the *method* of knowing—that which has rightful supremacy—that it deliberately commences with conditions as they exist *after* a total qualitative existential situation has been disrupted from within and in consequence the self—organism—and environing conditions being no longer unified in that situation are set practically at odds. It then proceeds to describe the characteristic phenomena of the former from the standpoint just mentioned— behavioral responses to the doubtful—dealing, accordingly and deliberately so, only with a partial factor of method. So far is the account given in this connection from being the whole story, that this section of my discussion was occasioned by the need of advancing some theory of the phenomena ordinarily called mental or psychological in which the "self," "subject," "mind," "knower" is *not* (as I have held it is not) an original separate entity set over against objects and the world. Even from the standpoint of this intentionally partial account—partial because stated from a special angle—there is no justification for the introduction of the categories of "intrusions" and "manipulations." The doubtful is not an intrusion, and the last thing a behavioral response can do to or with the doubtful is to manipulate it. Only the definitely and mechanically settled can be manipulated by rules of skill. I believe that Francis Bacon did hold that rules of skill could be worked out so that all persons could be put by training on practically the same level, just as persons can learn proficiency in use of tools like a hammer or plane. But when a scientific inquirer is faced with a problematic situation rules of skill are just what are precluded by the very fact that the situation is so pervasively problematic.

In one passage, Mr. Stuart expressly points out that according to me determinations like *mind, body,* and the *outer world* emerge and function *within* "the situation taken as a whole in its problematic character." Taken by itself this passage might lead one to wonder how it was that he did not see that the distinction of *organism* and *environment, knower* and *that-to-be-known,* also arises and functions within the total problematic situation as a means to its resolution—a process by which *both* are in some degree modified or reconstituted. But his previous sentence explains why he did not grasp my actual view. For it reads "The precarious *environment* must accordingly be faced with such detachment and fortitude as the *agent* can muster and then grasped *as a whole* as problematic."[52] Not only does this passage prove that Mr. Stuart attributes to me from the very start a differentiation and opposition of "knower" and "the-to-be-known" but also supposes that it is the *environment* which is grasped as problematic—while according to my view a *situation* is problematic prior to any "grasping" or "apprehension" whatever, the first act of knowing being to locate *a problem* by selective or analytic discrimination of some of the observable constituents of the total situation.

It should then be clear that my view of the nature of knowing goes further than does that of Dr. Stuart in providing the groundwork and groundplan of a theory of moral knowing similar in general features to that he set forth in his article as if in opposition to mine. For his theory sets up an impassable dualism between the two kinds of judging, while mine asserts continuity, which, as I have said, involves difference as well as community. The formation of a self new in some respect or some degree is, then, involved in every genuine act of inquiry. In the cognitive situation as such the overt and explicit emphasis falls upon the resolution of the situation by means of change produced in environing conditions, whereas in the distinctively moral situation it falls upon the reconstruction of the self as the distinctively demanded means. But the difference is in any case one of *emphasis.* There are occasions when for the proper conduct of knowing as the controlling interest, the problem becomes that of reconstruction of the *self* engaged in inquiry. This happens when the pursuit of inquiry, according to conditions set by the need of following

52. See p. 294 [Schilpp] above; italics mine.

subject-matter where it leads, requires willingness to surrender a theory dear to the heart of an inquirer and willingness to forego reaching the conclusion he would have preferred to reach. On the other hand, the problem of reconstructing the self cannot be solved unless inquiry takes into account reconstitution of existing conditions, a matter which poses a problem in which scientific knowledge is indispensable for effecting an outcome satisfying the needs of the situation.

In propounding a theory of knowing I have insisted that inquiry itself involves *in its own nature* conditions to be satisfied. The autonomy of inquiry is equivalent to demand for integrity of inquiry. It is this fact that leads to the definition of truth in its intellectual or cognitive sense in terms of fulfilment of conditions intrinsic to inquiry. But the will, the disposition, to maintain the integrity intrinsic to inquiry is a moral matter. In this regard, the operations of valuation which I have affirmed to be involved in any case in knowing—in choice of data and hypotheses and experimental operations to be performed—pass into definitely moral valuations whenever the existing habits and character of an inquirer set up obstacles to maintenance of integral inquiry. Reconstitution into a self in some respects new is then not incidental but central. I suggested earlier that the current theory of verification and of the cognitive truth of propositions—validity as I call it—suffers from having read into it the moral meaning of truth. But whenever the immediate problem in conduct of inquiry for the sake of obtaining knowledge involves the will to search for evidence, to weigh it fairly, not to load the dice, to control a preference for one theory over another so that it does not affect the conclusion reached, the category of truth in its *moral* sense is supreme. This is a reason why denial of the possibility of validly grounded valuation propositions involves, as its logical consequence, suicide of scientific knowing, a logical destruction which is not averted by insisting that propositions are inherently true or false.

Perhaps I can illustrate my meaning by referring to an incidental remark of mine of which Mr. Stuart makes a great deal, the remark, namely, that "were existing conditions wholly good, the notion of possibilities to be realized would never arise." Now I think that common experience and the evidence of history testify that the occurrence of problematic situations, necessitating the

putting forth of effort in thinking, was usually regarded as *bad,*
as obnoxious, until the pursuit of inquiry was found to be a good
on its own account. When inquiry is found to be a good, then the
occurrence of problematic situations is welcomed as contribu-
tory to enjoyed possession of a good. I cannot find in the sentence quoted the ominous meaning it seems to bear to Mr.
Stuart. "Were conditions *wholly* good" lays down a completely
generalized and comprehensive condition. Its scope is not limited
to conditions as they present themselves at a specified time. It
applies to the total enduring experience of any person. Any one
who has ever experienced conditions that are not wholly good
will, in the degree of his capacity to learn, be aware that conditions may not be wholly good in situations where on the surface
there seems to be nothing the matter. Just as the inquirer as such
will be on the lookout for *problems,* so the conscientious person will be on the lookout for something better instead of being
content with customary goods. There is, in other words, none of
that incompatibility which Mr. Stuart seems to find between
what I have said in my chapter in Dewey and Tufts' *Ethics* about
the conscientious person and what I have said would happen if
conditions "were wholly good." No one lives in a world in which
he has found everything at all times perfect. If he understands
the meaning of this fact he has learned to be alive to possibilities.
The potential *better* will then be regarded as the good—and the
only good—of any situation, a statement as applicable to scientific inquiry as to any moral matter. A disposition framed when
conditions are overtly not wholly good is capable, like the experimental method itself, of exercise when, on the surface, they
seem good.

It will be noted that I have given much more attention to Mr.
Stuart's idea about my theory of knowing than to his special
criticisms of what he takes to be my ethical position. The reason
is that Mr. Stuart's belief that I deny the "incommensurability"
and disparity of ends and values, and hence reduce what seem to
be conflicts to a difference negotiable by "manipulation of intru-
sive" factors is the product of his misconception of my theory of
inquiry. For according to this theory, the conflict which is involved in any problematic situation is such as to be resolvable
only by qualitative transformations. I have indeed emphasized, in
what I have said about morals, especially in their social aspect,

the idea that production of new environing conditions is a prerequisite of the creation of an enduring new self. But that emphasis was not by way of disparaging the importance of a new self but by way of protest against the "subjectivistic" morals which identify "meaning well" with morality, and which thereby deny importance to active effort which always makes some change in previous conditions—exactly as does experiment in scientific inquiry.[53] If there is a difference between us as to the basic problem in the moral situation being the problem of what the self shall become and be (as the *end* at stake), it is in the fact that I treat the difference between this problem and that of adjusting means with reference to an accepted end as *relative*, not absolute. I quote the following passages from Dewey and Tufts' *Ethics:* "The person who completely ignored the connection of the great number of more or less routine acts with the small number in which there is a clear moral issue, would be an utterly independable person"; and again, "Every act has potential moral significance because it is, through its consequences,[54] part of a larger whole of behavior"; and again,

> Every choice sustains a double relation to the self. It reveals the existing self and it forms the future self . . . shapes the self, making it, in some degree, a new self. This fact is especially marked at critical junctures, but it marks every choice to some extent, however slight.[55]

And once more this position follows directly from the reconstructive function of inquiry in obtaining tested knowledge. Now I do not wish to infer that Dr. Stuart does in fact make a sharp separation between "economic" situations, in which the problem refers simply to conflict of *means* with respect to an accepted and unquestioned end, and "moral" situations where conflict of incommensurable ends sets the problem of determining what the self *shall* be. I only say that *if* he holds to such a separation, I go further in the direction he points out as necessary to genuine

---

53. The trouble with the Kantian *Good Will* does not lie in its emphasis upon active disposition and resolute character, but in its separation of will from all empirical conditions of desire and purpose.

54. Consequences, namely, upon formation of habits and hence formation of a self.

55. *Ethics*, 178, 179, 317 [*Later Works* 7:168, 169, 286–87].

moral knowing than he does. For I do not admit anything but a strictly relative distinction between means and ends. Consequently when I have touched upon economic and political problems in writing upon social philosophy I have held that all such problems are problems of valuation in the moral sense. It is in *this* context that I have dwelt upon *intelligent action* as the sole and supreme method of dealing with economic and political issues, and have tried to take that statement out of the region of innocuous truisms by linking up the possibility of intelligence in action with that ascertained knowledge of conditions and consequences which is obtained by the use of the methods which stand out conspicuously in the physical sciences. We are thus brought back to that instrumental view of attained knowledge which has given so much trouble to some of my critics.[56]

II. Dr. Geiger's paper is welcome because of its recognition of the moral context of economic and political issues in my social philosophy, *moral* being here viewed as a matter of choice ensuing upon valuations. The importance of the practical questions he raises at the close of his exposition is not to be denied. To my mind they come to this: Is the disproportion between the application of the scientific experimental method to the physical conditions of human associations and its lack of application in direct social affairs such that, in the present state of the world, it is hopeless to expect a change? I know of no sweeping answer to this question. But the problem is one of degree, not of all or none. It cannot be denied that in our social life a great imbalance has resulted because the method of intelligent action has been used in determining the physical conditions that are causes of social effects, whereas it has hardly been tried in determination of social ends and values. One might point out that the use of other principles, custom, external authority, force, so-called absolute ideals and standards—out of the range of empirical adjudication because absolute—in lieu of intelligent action, has played the

---

56. I have said nothing here about Mr. Stuart's criticism of my view of the role of consequences. In principle, their role in morals is the same as in scientific inquiry. They are important not as such or by themselves but in their function as *tests* of ideas, principles, theories. It is possible that at times, in opposition to *ipse dixit* "intuitions" and dogmatic assertion of absolute standards, I have emphasized the importance of consequences so as to seem to make them supreme in and of themselves. If so, I have departed from my proper view, that of their use as tests of proposed ends and ideals.

chief part in the production of the situation which makes it so extremely difficult to use the method of intelligent action. While this fact does not modify the conditions which create the difficulty, application of the method, like charity, begins at home. The application is to the methods *we* are to apply in *our* economic and political predicaments, not as to what people on the other side of the world are going to do.[57] If, instead of letting our imagination roam abroad to dwell upon the difficulties other nations and persons experience in using the method, we fasten attention upon our own problems, the difficulties in the way of its use are much less. To consider the state of the world at large in this or any similar connection is itself a procedure that violates the supremacy of method. For we are here in a specific social and historic situation which compels a choice based on valuations, and it is we, with respect to our own specific problems, who have to form the valuations and to make a choice.

In any case, the question is not, as critics have sometimes put it, one of intelligence, or knowledge, versus action, but one of *intelligent* action versus some other kind of action—whether it relies on arbitrament by violence, or "dialectical materialistic inevitability," on dogmas of race, blood, nationality, or supernatural guidance. The method of intelligent experimental action is criticized on the ground that class interests are too strong to permit its use, so that the only alternative is the method of class war with victory to the strongest. It is not enough to counter this argument by saying that most of those who hold it are indulging in a dialectical game and have rarely faced what the concrete consequences of this appeal to violence would be. But when some dogma—called a "law"—of inevitable historic evolution is appealed to, it can be replied that the issue is not whether there will be clashes and conflicts of interests but how they are to be met and what *kind of action,* probably involving under certain conditions positive use of force, shall be undertaken. The alternative is not an extreme pacifism which makes a fetish of passivity. The

57. I wish to take this opportunity to express my full agreement with what Dr. Randall says in his paper about the importance of developing the skills that, if they were produced, would constitute political technology. The fact—which he points out—that I have myself done little or nothing in this direction does not detract from my recognition that in the concrete the invention of such a technology is the heart of the problem of intelligent action in political matters.

basic difference is that one theory, that of inevitable class conflict and inevitable victory for one class, takes situations in a mechanical and wholesale manner, whereas the method of intelligent action insists upon analysis *at each step* of the concrete situation then and there existing, basing its hypothesis as to what should be done upon the results of that analysis, and testing moreover the adequacy of the hypothesis at every step by the consequences that result from acting upon it. The question is one of choice—choice between a procedure which is rigid because based on fixed dogma, and one which is flexible because based upon examination of problems actually experienced and because proposing policies as hypotheses to be experimentally tested and modified.

I return to Mr. Geiger's paper with a few words about the issue of the critical versus the gradual. I do not think the antithesis is well taken. There is something critical in every problematic situation; it marks a qualitative turn, a divergence; it is of the nature of a "mutation" rather than of a Darwinian "variation." Crises differ greatly of course, in the depth and range of the conflicting issues involved in them. But the critical quality remains in spite of differences of degree. The *execution* of any policy for directing change to one outcome rather than to another is nevertheless a gradual affair; the more critical the emergency, the more gradual will be the execution of the plans and policies by which it is finally resolved. The idea that the resolution of a crisis is of the same abrupt nature as is the occurrence of the crisis is a Utopian confusion. A revolutionary event is a crisis of high intensity. But the idea that the revolution in its immediate occurrence, as of a given date, 1789 or 1917/18, is anything more than the beginning of a gradual process is a case of Utopian self-delusion. The method of intelligent action has to be applied at every step of that process in which a revolution "runs its course." Its final outcome does not depend upon the original abrupt revolutionary occurrence but upon the way intelligent action intervenes at each step of its course—as all history shows in spite of *ex post facto* "inevitabilities" constructed *after* choice has manifested its effects. Perhaps the worst feature of social philosophies that substitute inevitabilities, materialistic in nature, for choices moral in nature because made after intelligent evaluation, is not that they get rid of choice, but that by eliminating intelligent valuation they put a premium on arbitrary choice.

I am glad to have an opportunity to say something about another question raised in Mr. Geiger's contribution. It concerns what he says about *ultimate* values. I have carried on a polemic against ultimates and finalities because I found them presented as things that are inherently absolute, like "ends-in-themselves" instead of ends-in-relationships. The reason they have been proffered as absolutes is that they have been taken out of any and all *temporal* context. A thing may be ultimate in the sense of coming last in a given temporal series, so that it is ultimate *for that series*. There are things that come last in reflective valuations and, as terminal, they are ultimate. Now Dr. Geiger is quite right in saying that for me the method of intelligent action is precisely such an ultimate value. It is the last, the final or closing, thing we come upon in inquiry into inquiry. But the place it occupies in the *temporal* manifestation of inquiry is what makes it such a value, not some property it possesses in and of itself, in the isolation of non-relatedness. It is ultimate in use and function; it does not claim to be ultimate because of an absolute "inherent nature" making it sacrosanct, a transcendent object of worship.

III. The topic of religion as presented by Dr. Schaub is not intimately connected with the subjects just discussed. But comments upon his paper seem to belong more properly here than at any other place. I shall follow Dr. Schaub's treatment in separating, for the most part, my view about religion from my larger and inclusive philosophical position, although if the latter approach had been chosen, I think something could be fruitfully said concerning my philosophic interpretation of experience in its religious aspect. As it is, Dr. Schaub finds an early article of mine prophetic of my later more explicit treatments of religion. While he mentions that the quotations he makes are from an article devoted to the question of giving religion a place in the subjects taught in our public schools he does not seem to have noted how directly and almost exclusively the passages he quotes have to do with that particular issue. An argument against the attempt to put instruction in religion into our public school curriculum (a movement that goes contrary to the whole American social and educational tradition), is not the place where I should look to find material regarding one's general attitude toward religion. Nor do I understand that Dr. Schaub is engaged in criticizing my views in that particular respect, or is himself arguing for making the teaching of religion a part of our tax-supported public school system. And yet I have some difficulty in judging just why he attaches so much importance to this particular article—written as it was so largely to explain to an English audience the difference between their and the American attitude in this matter. However, since Mr. Schaub selects it for special attention because of what he regards as its "prophetic" quality, I shall also deal with it in that aspect.

In the first place, it is true that I looked hopefully forward to a decay of the sectarian spirit that was, when I wrote, such a marked feature of the religion of the churches and to the emergence of a "broader and more catholic, and more genuinely religious spirit." I may have been unduly optimistic in entertaining these hopes; they are certainly still far from realization. But just how the fact that I had these particular hopes is a sign of an unsympathetic attitude on my part toward religion I do not see. I can hardly believe that Dr. Schaub is arguing by implication for a continuance of a narrow sectarian spirit. The alternative explanation is, I imagine, my belief that the association of religion with the *supernatural* tends by its own nature to breed the dogmatic and the divisive spirit. To this belief I plead guilty, and I do not find anything in what Mr. Schaub has to offer which contravenes what seems to be almost a commonplace of history. For, the greater the insistence by a given church body upon the supernatural, the more insistent is it bound to be upon certain tenets which must be accepted—at the peril of one's immortal soul. When Dr. Schaub quotes from me a passage about the possibility of "a religious mode of life 'which will be the fine flower of the modern spirit's achievement,'" he can hardly take that passage to be evidence of a coldly hostile attitude on my part to everything religious. So I imagine that the trouble he finds there also springs from my reference to the "modern spirit" as something which puts away the supernaturalism of the race's immaturity, and relies upon the resources of the scientific search for truth and upon a democratic way of life to generate a more humane, more liberal, and broader religious attitude.

In order that the reader may have before him the sort of thing which I was—in a spirit perhaps of too great hopefulness—"prophesying," I quote some additional remarks from the same article about the potential religious aspect of human experience when it is liberated from supernaturalism and dogmatism.

That science has the same spiritual import as supernatural-ism; that democracy translates into the same religious attitude as did feudalism; that it is only a matter of slight changes of phraseology, a development of old symbolisms into new shades of meaning—such beliefs testify to that torpor of imagination which is the uniform effect of dogmatic belief.

And again "It is the part of men to labor persistently and patiently for the clarification and development of the positive creed of life implicit in democracy and science." Again, "For all we know the integrity of mind which is loosening the hold of all these things [rites, symbols and ideas associated with dogmatic beliefs] is potentially much more religious than all it is displacing." And once more "So far as education is concerned, those who believe in religion as a natural expression of human experience must devote themselves to the development of the ideas of life which lie implicit in our still new science and our still newer democracy." I might quote other passages in the same vein. But these should suffice. I can understand why Dr. Schaub should object to the interpretation of the religious contained in these passages, for I can understand that his idea of religion may be radically different, more akin perhaps to the things to which I object in traditional religion. But he goes further than this. He finds in the article which includes such passages as those cited, signs of an attitude hostile to assigning any important significance and value to the religious phase of experience. To me, on the other hand, his interpretation is a fairly typical sign of that sectarian spirit which takes hostility to particular views about religion to be itself anti-religious.

About all I need to say accordingly about the later writings of which the passages I have quoted *are* prophetic, is that they are devoted to making explicit the religious values implicit in the spirit of science as undogmatic reverence for truth in whatever form it presents itself, and the religious values implicit in our common life, especially in the moral significance of democracy as a way of living together. Mr. Schaub prefers another kind of religion—which is his personal right. A *Common Faith* was not addressed to those who are content with traditions in which "metaphysical" is substantially identical with "supernatural." It was addressed to those who have abandoned supernaturalism, and who on that account are reproached by traditionalists for having turned their backs on everything religious. The book was an attempt to show such persons that they still have within their experience all the elements which give the religious attitude its value. The response from the persons to whom the book was especially addressed was so cordial as to more than make up for the disfavor that greeted it in other quarters.

E. Some "Metaphysical" Questions

There are certain issues—of the type usually referred to as "metaphysical"—touched upon in various criticisms; "metaphysical" in the sense in which an empirical naturalist may give that name to the more generalized statements about Nature which he finds to be justified. They are found in Mr. Parodi's article and in some of the criticisms passed by Messrs. Savery and Murphy. Before taking up the issue raised by Mr. Parodi, I want to thank him for his grasp of the main purpose of my philosophical writings: "To re-integrate human knowledge and activity in the general framework of reality and natural processes." For I doubt if another as brief a sentence can be found to express as well the problem which has most preoccupied me.

I. The special problem which Mr. Parodi's criticism raises is typical of my larger endeavor at reintegration. As stated by him, it has two sides. From one side, it is the problem of the possibility of bringing our conscious awareness into a frame of reference which also includes physical events; from the side of voluntary action, it is the problem of transition, within the same frame of reference, from conscious intent to physiological and physical movement. The first question is illustrated by the question of the relation of physical vibrations and nerve changes to sensations. Since the general problem is far too vast to be adequately considered here I shall select for discussion only the point that illustrates my position on the larger issue. Mr. Parodi says that in the sequence of physiological and nervous processes one nowhere finds "the color red, as something felt, as the sensation or the perception properly so called." This sentence suggests the difference between the problem as it presents itself to me and as it presents itself to Mr. Parodi. For in my theory, the problem is not that of the relation of the physical and external to the mental or internal. It is, as I hope some of my previous remarks have made clearer than it may have been before, the problem of the relation of immediate *qualities* to objects of science. According to my solution, the latter function as the existential causal conditions of the former, qualities being consummatory manifestations of these conditions. It is in this context, for example, that I have insisted that all qualities, even the tertiary ones and, *a fortiori,* those of color, like red, are "doings of natural conditions." If one accepts continuity as a natural category, then the problem of *how* specific transitions are made in the case of qualities is exactly the same sort of problem that is found in any case of temporal sequence where a later stage is qualitatively unlike an earlier one. The general fact that qualitative transitions occur—as, for example, in production of *water*—is something characterizing nature. It is something to be accepted rather than to be taken as posing a difficulty to be surmounted. These are problems of ascertaining the special conditions under which specific qualitative transitions take place, but not the problem of why the universe is as it is.

When I say then that Mr. Parodi states the difficulty in terms of his own philosophical premises, I mean that he takes a quality, say *red,* to be intrinsically something *felt,* a "sensation" in and of itself. My view is more realistically naïve. The *quality* occurs exactly, in principle, as any natural event, say a thunder-shower. There is no passage from the physical to the mental, from an external world to something felt or of the nature of a psychical consciousness, but from objects with one set of qualities to objects with other qualities. When, however, a quality is termed a "sensation," or is explicitly taken in connection with an act of perceiving, something additive has happened. It is now placed in a specially selected connection, that to the organism or self. Pending the outcome of an inquiry not yet completed, one may not know whether a quality, say red, belongs to *this* or *that* object in the environment,[58] nor indeed whether it may not be the product of intra-organic processes as in the case of "seeing stars" after a

---

58. It is in this connection that I identify certain forms of behavior, those denominated "psychological," as responses to the doubtful as such. Here, as in connection with Mr. Stuart's paper, they are derived, not original; secondary, not primary, occurring when an experienced *situation* becomes problematic.

blow on the head. In other words, the occurrence of qualities upon my view is a purely natural event. Scientific physical objects in their relatively quality-less character are selections of correlations between changes, in whose constitution qualities are irrelevant.

The final reference of qualities to intra-organic events is itself a reference to one kind of object *in* the natural world. Similarly, when we explain a curious superstition entertained by members of a savage tribe we do not do so, on my theory, by referring it to "consciousness," but to specifiable natural conditions—traditions and institutions being included in this case among natural conditions. According to my position the problem as it is stated by Mr. Parodi is present only when what is secondary, because arising in a definitely cognitive situation, is taken to be primary. When it is taken to be primary, all the difficulties that are found in epistemological theories—where controversy is never finally settled—present themselves: Namely, given a separate existential realm of consciousness or of the mental, how to get out of it over into a world that is "external" to it?

There is an issue closely connected with the view that qualities and individual and unrepeatable things are genuine natural existences. It is much too large to discuss here but it may be mentioned. Were it not for ambiguities in the notion of "emergence" it might be connected with that idea. If scientific laws and objects are of the kind I have said they are, the *connections* which are involved in production of qualitative objects are necessary but not the qualities themselves. There is, then, room in nature for contingency and novelty, for potentialities that are actualized under conditions so complex as to occur only in the course of processes of development that take a long time. *After* the conditions have come about and the new qualities have appeared, it is possible to form generalizations about uniformities and make predictions about the future occurrence of the qualities. But the first appearance of the qualities in question may have been utterly unpredictable. In short, according to my view of the relation between qualitative things and scientific objects the natural world is itself marked by contingencies, instead of being a closed box of tight necessities. Under specifiable conditions, these contingencies present themselves as indeterminates that need to be determined if certain life-activities are to go on. Then the kind of responsive behavior occurs that is marked by qualities which, when they are abstracted, are called sensations, images, ideas, etc., in a mentalistic sense. I do not of course offer this remark as settling the problems raised by Parodi. But I think it is clear that the problem of the relation of the "mental" to the processes of the natural world must be stated differently if that world is one of closed mechanical necessities than if it is marked by contingencies that leave room for potentialities not yet manifested. For in the former case, the terms of the problem are intrinsically opposed, whereas they are not in the latter case.

II. According to Mr. Murphy certain things I have said about the relation of experience to the world may be understood in accordance with the principle of objective relativism, so that the idea of bifurcation in nature is avoided. But, unfortunately, that strain or aspect in my doctrine he finds to be brought to nought by another and more persistent strain in my theory of knowing—producing a veritable skeleton in my philosophical closet. For

> there is an unhappy discrepancy between experience as it ought to be if its place in the natural world is to be made intelligible and experience as it must be if Dewey's epistemology is correct. In the former capacity, "experience" is the essential link between man and a world which antedates his appearance in it. In the latter, "experience" is the terminus of all knowing, in the sense that our (*sic!*) cognitive claims refer ultimately to what experience will show itself to be in a "resolved" state and nothing else. If this latter account is true, all statements about a natural environment outside of these immediate experiences become on analysis simply means of facilitating cognitive transitions to such enjoyed immediacies and the world . . . "collapses into immediacy."

The statement quoted is unfortunately not free from ambiguity. Does his reference to the fact that in *my* view knowing terminates in *experience* signify that in *his* view cognitive reference to the world (say the world antedating the appearance of human beings upon it), does not involve reference to *any* experience? Does it mean that knowledge of the world is not *in any sense* whatever an experience? These questions suggest that the problem Mr. Murphy raises as if it bore simply on my theory is one which in some way must be met by any theory whatever. If, for example,

Mr. Murphy means that knowledge of a world antedating experience is *not* in itself in any way whatever an experience of anybody, his view is certainly an extraordinary one. But if he does not mean this, he, too, must hold that knowing in such a case has its terminus in experience—namely, in an experience of the world as thus and so in time and space. If he holds the latter view, then the fact that I also hold that knowing terminates in an experience can hardly constitute a peculiarly personal skeleton. *If* then his criticism is grounded, it is not just because I hold that knowing terminates in experience, but because of the *kind* of experience in which he supposes knowing must terminate upon my theory—a view contained, I imagine, in his phrase "and nothing else." Since he offers no evidence in support of his view that the resolved situation (which is the terminal of knowledge according to my theory) cannot have as its subject-matter objects or events existing in the world independent of the knower, one hardly knows how or where to lay hold of his argument. Apparently, however, his point is somehow expressed in the clause "what experience will show itself to be in a 'resolved' state and nothing else." I am unable, however, to derive an intelligible meaning from this phrase. For if experience is, as I have said, always *of* something, namely, of the environment (though not necessarily, according to my theory, of it, in a *cognitive* mode), it is impossible to see why the environing conditions that are involved should disappear or collapse when and because they are so ordered as to constitute a terminal resolved situation. Certainly Mr. Murphy offers no reason for concluding that such a disappearance is implied in my account of the transformation, through experimental operations of inquiry, of the existential material or an indeterminate situation into the ordered objects of a resolved situation. If the problem is how from experienced materials of the *present* environment we validly infer conditions of some temporally past environment—such as that of some long bygone geological age—the problem is one which any theory whatever has to face. And it is moreover a problem to which a chapter of my *Logic* is especially devoted.

Since one can only guess at what Mr. Murphy takes to be the logical core of his criticism, it may be that it is found in reference to the fact that, according to me, the terminal experience, that of the resolved situation, is "immediate." Now as has been said earlier in this reply—and not for the first time—every experience, every existence for that matter, is immediate in its occurrence. Calling it *immediate* signifies only that it is just what it is. There is, however, a sense of *immediate* in which it is opposed to *mediate*. Now by description or truistically, the resolved situation as terminal is not mediate. But immediateness in this sense has nothing whatever to do with the subject-matter and objective reference of the resolved situation. If final conclusions or terminals of inquiry because of their final, not mediating, character, render their *subject-matter* immediate, then, according to Mr. Murphy's implied logic, *every* conclusion would, on any theory, "collapse into immediacy." As they do not on other theories, so they do not on mine.

Since there is no possible interpretation from any point of view of the passage quoted from which the conclusion that Mr. Murphy draws really follows, one has good reason for supposing that his conclusion is derived from some other source. In view of his confusion of the two senses of the instrumental already discussed, one would look in that direction for an explanation, especially because of the otherwise superfluous mention of "enjoyed immediacies." One finds in an earlier page of Mr. Murphy's essay the following passage:

> The essential fact is that where the distinction between the value of an idea as a means for discovering the truth has been confused with its value as a means for subserving interests felt on other grounds to be important, there is simply no ground left for an independent estimate of truth as such—

a statement no one can question. But as a practicing, and not just professed, contextualist I have distinguished the contexts in which ideas (in their correlation with facts of observation) serve as means for reaching knowledge as warranted assertion (or truth), and the context in which *attained* knowledge (*because* it has been attained by the foregoing process) serves as a potential means for control and enrichment of consummatory non-cognitive experiences. I confess the idea that experiences of things in the latter capacity could possibly be controlled by anything *excepting* actual conditions of the actual world had never occurred to me, since I am not a believer in magic. The fact that external environing conditions are the causes—and the only causes—of the experiences that occur is just the reason why my theory has emphasized the fact that knowledge, through the intermediary of intelligent action, is the sole means of regulating the existence in experience of values or consummatory objects. It is also the reason why, in contrast to most social and moral theories, much importance is attached to the potential functions of the conclusions reached in the natural sciences. I quote once more a typical passage:

> The final thing is appreciation and use of things of direct experience. These are *known* in as far as their constituents and their form (that of the constituents) are the result of science. *But they are also more than science.* They are natural objects experienced in relations and continuities that are summed up in rich and definite individual forms.

To be *known* natural objects and yet to be *more* than objects of sciences is hardly a way of saying that experience of a resolved situation cuts off, because of its terminal position, all links with the natural world.

III. The final "metaphysical" question upon which I shall touch has to do with a question raised by Savery—Naturalism or Materialism? I am aware that emotional causes often dictate preference for one word over another. It is then quite proper to ask whether dislike for associations with the word *materialism* have dictated my use of *naturalism* to describe my philosophic point of view. Since I hold that all the subject-matter of experience is dependent upon physical conditions, it may be asked why do I not come out frankly and use the word *materialism*? In my case, there are two main reasons. One of them is that there is involved in this view a metaphysical theory of *substance* which I do not accept; and I do not see how any view can be called materialism that does not take "matter" to be a substance and to be the *only* substance—in the traditional metaphysical sense of substance. The other reason is closely connected with this, being perhaps but a specific empirical version of what has just been said. The meaning of materialism and of matter in *philosophy* is determined by opposition to the psychical and mental as *spiritual*. When the antithetical position is completely abandoned, I fail to see what meaning "matter" and "materialism" have for philosophy. *Matter* has a definite assignable meaning in physical science. It designates something capable of being expressed in mathematical symbols which are distinguished from those defining *energy*. It is not possible to generalize the definite meaning "matter" has in this context of physical science into a philosophical view—which materialism most definitely is. This latter undertaking seems to me on an exact par with the enthusiasm displayed by a certain group whenever *energy* is regarded as an important scientific character; especially if, as is sometimes erroneously said, it is believed that science has resolved "matter," in the strictly technical sense it bears in physics, into energy. I see no inherent difference in principle between generalizing what is meant by matter in physics into materialism, and generalizing what is designated as energy in physics into spiritualistic metaphysics. Philosophy must, of course, accept what is ascertained in science as the proper *designatum* of "matter," as that which it denotatively stands for. But this acceptance instead of leading to metaphysical materialism will, if accepted at its full value, enable philosophy to free itself from associations that grew up about "matter" in the pre-scientific days when it acquired its meaning through alleged opposition to another and "higher" substance, the soul, mind, spirit or whatever.

If the term "matter" is given a philosophic interpretation, over and above its technical scientific meaning—*e.g., mass* until recently—, this meaning, I believe, should be to name a *functional* relation rather than a substance. Thus, in case there is need for a name for existential conditions in their function *as* conditions of all special forms of socio-biotic activities and values, *matter* might well be an appropriate word. But recognition that all these activities and values are existentially conditioned—and do not arise out of the blue or out of a separate substance called spirit— is far from constituting materialism in its metaphysical sense. For it is only by setting out from the activities and values in experience just as they *are* experienced that inquiry can find the clues for discovery of their conditions. Denial that the former are just what they are thus destroys the possibility of ascertaining their conditions, so that "materialism" commits suicide. It is quite possible to recognize that everything experienced, no matter how "ideal" and lofty, has its own determinate conditions without getting into that generalization beyond limits which constitutes metaphysical materialism.

As I conclude my reply, I am aware how largely controversy has bulked in it. But the plan of the volume called, and very properly, for adverse criticism as well as for favorable exposition, and it is difficult to reply to the former, where they do not appear valid, except controversially. A more pertinent criticism of my reply might be that in claiming to have been misunderstood by my critics on a number of fundamental points, I have virtually admitted lack of clearness in my previous writings. That this is true in some of the cases where misconceptions have been the ground of criticisms, I am not concerned to deny. I wish, therefore, to express my indebtedness to these critics for having made it necessary for me to reconsider not only the language I have used— words, which for the reason stated at the outset, are peculiarly treacherous in any attempt at a philosophical formulation differing from those which have attained currency—but also the ideas back of the words. In this specific respect my obligation, although naturally not my human and personal gratitude, is greater to those who have disagreed than to those whose exposition has been favorable. If it be said that in selecting the points for reply and in apportioning space I have been guided by my own interests rather than by those of my critics, I can only say that it seems reasonable to believe that one main object of this back and forth discussion is to help make clear what points *are* central to my position and what are subsidiary. Under different circumstances I might well have given attention to criticisms I have passed over— because they have seemed to me to be negotiable differences, matters of degree rather than of central principles.[59]

In any case, it is congenial to believe that conflict of ideas, as distinct from that of force, is a necessary condition of advance in understanding, and that agreements which exist only because of lack of critical contact and comparison are superficial. It was, I believe, Jane Carlyle who said that mixing things which do not go together is the Great Bad. Confusion that comes from this evil

59. This remark applies particularly to the question raised by Dr. Randall at the close of his paper. I should not want it thought that I took advantage of what is favorable in his paper to my position to ignore what is adverse.

mixture is bound to exist where criticism is not continually on the alert. Differences that proceed from clear perception of issues are a positive gain. They are conditions of further progress in indicating the direction in which thought should move. But they are also intrinsic gains since they enlarge the horizon of our vision. Although our knowledge is not *of* perspectives as its subject-matter, what is known falls into some perspective, and there is something to be learned from the perspectival arrangement of the ideas of any honest inquirer.

There is also, according to my own way of thinking, a close connection between the vital problems of philosophy and the conditions manifested in my living culture. It is for this reason I have held that, in the strictest sense, philosophy cannot solve important problems but only those that so arise from different linguistic habits that they can be straightened out by analysis. If basic problems can be settled only where they arise, namely, in the cultural conditions of our associated life; if philosophy is fundamentally a criticism which brings to light these problems and gives them the clarity that springs from definite formulation; and if after formulation philosophy can do no more than point the road *intelligent action* must take,—then the greatest service any particular philosophical theory can render is to sharpen and deepen the sense of these problems. Criticism by means of give-and-take of discussion is an indispensable agency in effecting this clarification. Discussion is communication, and it is by communication that ideas are shared and become a common possession.

Finally, in connection with the relation of philosophy and culture, we may felicitate ourselves that we live where free discussion and free criticism are still values which are not denied us by some power reaching out for a monopoly of cultural and spiritual life. The inability of human beings in so many parts of the world to engage in free exchange of ideas should make us aware, by force of contrast, of the privilege we still enjoy and of our duty of defending and extending it. It should make us aware that free thought itself, free inquiry, is crippled and finally paralyzed by suppression of free communication. Such communication includes the right and responsibility of submitting every idea and every belief to severest criticism. It is less important that we all believe alike than that we all alike inquire freely and put at the disposal of one another such glimpses as we may obtain of the truth for which we are in search. If there is one thing more than another which my participation in the discussions composing this volume has impressed upon me, it is the extent and depth of my indebtedness to ideas which others have expressed;—not only my teachers, students, colleagues and present fellow workers but the long succession of thinkers whose names are enrolled as the bearers of the ceaseless enterprise which is philosophy.

I Believe

My contribution to the first series of essays in *Living Philosophies* put forward the idea of faith in the possibilities of experience as the heart of my own philosophy. In the course of that contribution I said, "Individuals will always be the centre and the consummation of experience, but what the individual actually *is* in his life-experience depends upon the nature and movement of associated life." I have not changed my faith in experience nor my belief that individuality is its centre and consummation. But there has been a change in emphasis. I should now wish to emphasize more than I formerly did that individuals are the finally decisive factors of the nature and movement of associated life.

The cause of this shift of emphasis is the events of the intervening years. The rise of dictatorships and totalitarian states and the decline of democracy have been accompanied with loud proclamation of the idea that only the state, the political organization of society, can give security to individuals. In return for the security thus obtained, it is asserted even more loudly (and with much greater practical effect) that individuals owe everything to the state.

This fundamental challenge compels all who believe in liberty and democracy to rethink the whole question of the relation of individual choice, belief, and action to institutions, to reflect on the kind of social changes that will make individuals in actuality the centres and the possessors of worth-while experience. In rethinking this issue in the light of the rise of totalitarian states, I am led to emphasize the idea that only the voluntary initiative

[First published in *I Believe: The Personal Philosophies of Certain Eminent Men and Women of Our Time*, ed. Clifton Fadiman (New York: Simon and Schuster, 1939), pp. 347–54.]

and voluntary cooperation of individuals can produce social institutions that will protect the liberties necessary for achieving
development of genuine individuality.

This change of emphasis does not in any way minimize the belief that the ability of individuals to develop genuine individuality is intimately connected with the social conditions under
which they associate with one another. But it attaches fundamental importance to the activities of individuals in determining
the social conditions under which they live. It has been shown in
the last few years that democratic *institutions* are no guarantee
for the existence of democratic individuals. The alternative is that
individuals who prize their own liberties and who prize the liberties of other individuals, individuals who are democratic in
thought and action, are the sole final warrant for the existence
and endurance of democratic institutions.

The belief that the voluntary activities of individuals in voluntary association with one another is the only basis of democratic
institutions does not mean a return to the older philosophy of
individualism. That philosophy thought of the individual after
the analogy of older physical science. He was taken to be a centre
without a field. His relations to other individuals were as mechanical and external as those of Newtonian atoms to one another. Liberty was supposed to be automatically acquired by
abolition of restraints and constraints; all the individual needed
was to be let alone.

The negative and empty character of this individualism had
consequences which produced a reaction toward an equally arbitrary and one-sided collectivism. This reaction is identical with
the rise of the new form of political despotism. The decline of
democracy and the rise of authoritarian states which claim they
can do for individuals what the latter cannot by any possibility
do for themselves are the two sides of one and the same indivis-
ible picture.

Political collectivism is now marked in all highly industrialized
countries, even when it does not reach the extreme of the totalitarian state. It is the social consequence of the development of
private capitalistic collectivism in industry and finance. For this
reason those who look backward to restoration of the latter system are doomed to fight a losing battle. For the tendency toward
state socialism and state capitalism is the product of the eco-

nomic collectivism of concentrated capital and labor that was produced by mass production and mass distribution. The inherent identity of the two forms of collectivism is disguised by the present angry and clamorous controversy waged between representatives of private and public collectivism, both claiming to speak, moreover, in the interest of the individual, one for his initiative, the other for his security.

The strict reciprocity that exists between the two collectivisms is also covered from view because they are promoted in the respective interests of different social groups. Roughly speaking, the "haves" stand for private collectivism and the "have nots" for state collectivism. The bitter struggle waged between them in the political arena conceals from recognition the fact that both favor some sort of collectivism and represent complementary aspects of the same total picture.

Between the struggles of the two parties, both purporting to serve the cause of ultimate individual freedom, the individual has in fact little show and little opportunity. Bewildered and temporarily lost anyway, the din of the contending parties increases his bewilderment. Everything is so big that he wants to ally himself with bigness, and he is told that he must make his choice between big industry and finance and the big national political state. For a long time, what political agencies did and did not do in legislation and in the courts favored the growth of private capitalistic collectivism. By way of equalizing conditions, I do not doubt that for some time to come political activity will move in the direction of support of underprivileged groups who have been oppressed and made insecure by the growth of concentrated industry and finance. The imminent danger, as events of recent years demonstrate, is that political activity will attempt to retrieve the balance by moving in the direction of state socialism.

Indeed, many persons will ask how it is possible for political action to restore the balance except by direct control over and even ownership of big industrial and financial enterprises. The answer in general is that political activity can, first and foremost, engage in aggressive maintenance of the civil liberties of free speech, free publication and intercommunication, and free assemblage. In the second place, the government can do much to encourage and promote in a positive way the growth of a great variety of voluntary cooperative undertakings.

This promotion involves abolition or drastic modification of a good many institutions that now have political support, since they stand in the way of effective voluntary association for social ends. There are tariffs and other monopoly-furthering devices that keep back individual initiative and voluntary cooperation. There is our system of land tenure and taxation that puts a premium on the holding of land—including all natural resources—for the sake of private profit in a way that effectively prevents individuals from access to the instruments of individual freedom. There is the political protection given to return on long-term capital investments which are not now accompanied by any productive work, and which are, therefore, a direct tax levied on the productive work of others: an almost incalculable restriction, in its total effect, upon individual freedom.

The intrinsic likeness of political and private collectivism is shown in the fact that the government has had recourse to promotion of a regime of scarcity instead of increased productivity. It is evident on its face that enforced restriction of productivity, whether enforced in the name of private profit or of public relief, can have only a disastrous effect, directly and indirectly, upon individual freedom. But given existing conditions, it is the sole alternative to governmental activity that would abolish such limitations upon voluntary action as have been mentioned, a list that would easily be made more specific and more extensive.

Moreover, the principle of confining political action to policies that provide the conditions for promoting the voluntary association of free individuals does not limit governmental action to negative measures. There are, for example, such political activities as are now represented by provision of public highways, public schools, protection from fire, etc., etc., supported by taxation. This type of activity can doubtless be extended in a way which will release individual liberties instead of restricting them. The principle laid down does not deter political activity from engaging in constructive measures. But it does lay down a criterion by which every political proposal shall be judged: Does it tend definitely in the direction of increase of voluntary, free choice and activity on the part of individuals?

The danger at present, as I have already said, is that in order to get away from the evils of private economic collectivism we shall plunge into political economic collectivism. The danger is so great that the course that has been suggested will be regarded as an unrealistic voice crying in the wilderness. It would be unrealistic to make light of the present drive in the direction of state socialism. But it is even more unrealistic to overlook the dangers involved in taking the latter course. For the events of recent years have demonstrated that state capitalism leads toward the totalitarian state whether of the Russian or the Fascist variety.

We now have demonstrations of the consequences of two social movements. Earlier events proved that private economic collectivism produced social anarchy, mitigated by the control exercised by an oligarchic group. Recent events have shown that state socialism or public collectivism leads to suppression of everything that individuality stands for. It is not too late for us in this country to learn the lessons taught by these two great historic movements. The way is open for a movement which will provide the fullest opportunity for cooperative voluntary endeavor. In this movement political activity will have a part, but a subordinate one. It will be confined to providing the conditions, both negative and positive, that favor the voluntary activity of individuals.

There is, however, a socialism which is not state socialism. It may be called functional socialism. Its nature may be illustrated by the movement for socialization of medicine. I think this socialization is bound to come anyway. But it may come about in two very different ways. It may come into existence as a state measure, under political control; or it may come about as the result of the efforts of the medical profession made aware of its social function and its responsibilities. I cannot develop the significance of the illustration. But as an illustration, its significance applies to all occupational groups; that is, to all groups that are engaged in any form of socially useful, productive, activity.

The technocrats of recent memory had a glimpse of the potentialities inherent in self-directed activities of autonomous groups performing necessary social functions. But they ruined their vision when they fell into the pit dug by Wells and Shaw, that of rule from above by an elite of experts—although according to technocracy engineers were to be the samurai. The N.I.R.A. had a glimpse of self-governing industrial groups. But, quite apart from its conflict with the existing legal system, the plan loaded the dice in favor of the existing system of control of industry—with a few sops thrown in to "labor." At best it could not have worked out in the direction of freely functioning occupational groups. The Marxists professed the idea, but they held it as an ultimate goal to be realized through seizure of political power by a single class, the proletariat. The withering away of the state which was supposed to take place is not in evidence. On the contrary, seizure of political power as the means to the ultimate end of free individuals organized in functional occupational groups has led to the production of one more autocratic political state.

The dialectic that was supposed to work in solving the contradiction between increase of political power and its abolition is conspicuous by its absence—and inherently so. The Fascists also proclaim the idea of a corporate state. But again there is reliance upon uncontrolled and irresponsible political power. Instead of a corporate society of functional groups there is complete suppression of every formal voluntary association of individuals.

Before concluding that in America adoption of the method of voluntary effort in voluntary associations of individuals with one another is hopeless, one should observe the course of history. For if history teaches anything it is that judgments regarding the future have been predicated upon the basis of the tendencies that are most conspicuous at the time, while in fact the great social changes which have produced new social institutions have been the cumulative effect of flank movements that were not obvious at the time of their origin.

During the height of expanding competitive industrialism, for example, it was freely predicted that its effect would be a future society of free individuals and of free nations so interdependent that lasting peace would be achieved—*vide* Herbert Spencer. Now that the actual result has been the opposite, it is prophesied on the basis of the tendencies that are now most prominent that increased control of industrial activity by the state will usher in an era of abundance and security. Nevertheless those who can escape the hypnotic influence exercised by the immediate contemporary scene are aware that movements going on in the interstices of the existing order are those which will in fact shape the future. As a friend of mine puts it, the last thing the lord of the feudal castle would have imagined was that the future of society was with the forces that were represented by the humble trader who set up his post under the walls of his castle.

I am not optimistic enough to believe that voluntary associations of individuals, which are even now building up within the cracks of a crumbling social order, will speedily reverse the tendency toward political collectivism. But I am confident that the ultimate way out of the present social dead end lies with the movement these associations are initiating. Individuals who have not lost faith in themselves and in other individuals will increasingly ally themselves with these groups. Sooner or later they will construct the way out of present confusion and conflict. The sooner it is done the shorter will be the time of chaos and catastrophe.

Time and Individuality

The Greeks had a saying "Count no man happy till after his death." The adage was a way of calling attention to the uncertainties of life. No one knows what a year or even a day may bring forth. The healthy become ill; the rich poor; the mighty are cast down; fame changes to obloquy. Men live at the mercy of forces they cannot control. Belief in fortune and luck, good or evil, is one of the most widespread and persistent of human beliefs. Chance has been deified by many peoples. Fate has been set up as an overlord to whom even the Gods must bow. Belief in a Goddess of Luck is in ill repute among pious folk but their belief in providence is a tribute to the fact no individual controls his own destiny.

The uncertainty of life and one's final lot has always been associated with mutability, while unforeseen and uncontrollable change has been linked with time. Time is the tooth that gnaws; it is the destroyer; we are born only to die and every day brings us one day nearer death. This attitude is not confined to the ignorant and vulgar. It is the root of what is sometimes called the instinctive belief in immortality. Everything perishes in time but men are unable to believe that perishing is the last word. For centuries poets made the uncertainty which time brings with it the theme of their discourse—read Shakespeare's sonnets. Nothing stays; life is fleeting and all earthly things are transitory.

It was not then for metaphysical reasons that classic philosophy maintained that change, and consequently time, are marks of inferior reality, holding that true and ultimate reality is immutable and eternal. Human reasons, all too human, have given birth to the idea that over and beyond the lower realm of things

[First published in *Time and Its Mysteries*, series 2 (New York: New York University Press, 1940), pp. 85–109, from a lecture given on the James Arthur Foundation at New York University on 21 April 1938.]

that shift like the sands on the seashore there is the kingdom of the unchanging, of the complete, the perfect. The grounds for the belief are couched in the technical language of philosophy, but the cause for the grounds is the heart's desire for surcease from change, struggle, and uncertainty. The eternal and immutable is the consummation of mortal man's quest for certainty.

It is not strange then that philosophies which have been at odds on every other point have been one in the conviction that the ultimately real is fixed and unchanging, even though they have been as far apart as the poles in their ideas of its constitution. The idealist has found it in a realm of rational ideas; the materialist in the laws of matter. The mechanist pins his faith to eternal atoms and to unmoved and unmoving space. The teleologist finds that all change is subservient to fixed ends and final goals, which are the one steadfast thing in the universe, conferring upon changing things whatever meaning and value they possess. The typical realist attributes to unchanging essences a greater degree of reality than belongs to existences; the modern mathematical realist finds the stability his heart desires in the immunity of the realm of possibilities from vicissitude. Although classic rationalism looked askance at experience and empirical things because of their continual subjection to alteration, yet strangely enough traditional sensational empiricism relegated time to a secondary role. Sensations appeared and disappeared but in their own nature they were as fixed as were Newtonian atoms—of which indeed they were mental copies. Ideas were but weakened copies of sensory impressions and had no inherent forward power and application. The passage of time dimmed their vividness and caused their decay. Because of their subjection to the tooth of time, they were denied productive force.

In the late eighteenth and the greater part of the nineteenth centuries appeared the first marked cultural shift in the attitude taken toward change. Under the names of indefinite perfectability, progress, and evolution, the movement of things in the universe itself and of the universe as a whole began to take on a beneficent instead of a hateful aspect. Not every change was regarded as a sign of advance but the general trend of change, cosmic and social, was thought to be toward the better. Aside from the Christian idea of a millennium of good and bliss to be finally wrought by supernatural means, the Golden Age for the first time in history was placed in the future instead of at the beginning, and change and time were assigned a benevolent role.

Even if the new optimism was not adequately grounded, there were sufficient causes for its occurrence as there are for all great changes in intellectual climate. The rise of new science in the seventeenth century laid hold upon general culture in the next century. Its popular effect was not great, but its influence upon the intellectual elite, even upon those who were not themselves engaged in scientific inquiry, was prodigious. The enlightenment, the *éclaircissement,* the *Aufklärung*—names which in the three most advanced countries of Europe testified to the widespread belief that at last light had dawned, that dissipation of the darkness of ignorance, superstition, and bigotry was at hand, and the triumph of reason was assured—for reason was the counterpart in man of the laws of nature which science was disclosing. The reign of law in the natural world was to be followed by the reign of law in human affairs. A vista of the indefinite perfectability of man was opened. It played a large part in that optimistic theory of automatic evolution which later found its classic formulation in the philosophy of Herbert Spencer. The faith may have been pathetic but it has its own nobility.

At last, time was thought to be working on the side of the good instead of as a destructive agent. Things were moving to an event which was divine, even if far off.

This new philosophy, however, was far from giving the temporal an inherent position and function in the constitution of things. Change was working on the side of man but only because of *fixed* laws which governed the changes that take place. There was hope in change just because the laws that govern it do not change. The locus of the immutable was shifted to scientific natural law, but the faith and hope of philosophers and intellectuals were still tied to the unchanging. The belief that "evolution" is identical with progress was based upon trust in laws which, being fixed, worked automatically toward the final end of freedom, justice, and brotherhood, the natural consequences of the reign of reason.

Not till the late nineteenth century was the doctrine of the subordination of time and change seriously challenged. Bergson and William James, animated by different motives and proceeding by different methods, then installed change at the very heart of things. Bergson took his stand on the primacy of life and consciousness, which are notoriously in a state of flux. He assimilated that which is completely real in the natural world to them, conceiving the static as that which life leaves behind as a deposit as it moves on. From this point of view he criticized mechanistic and teleological theories on the ground that both are guilty of the same error, although from opposite points. Fixed laws which govern change and fixed ends toward which changes tend are both the products of a backward look, one that ignores the forward movement of life. They apply only to that which life has produced and has then left behind in its ongoing vital creative course, a course whose behavior and outcome are unpredictable both mechanically and from the standpoint of ends. The intellect is at home in that which is fixed only because it is done and over with, for intellect is itself just as much a deposit of *past* life as is the matter to which it is congenial. Intuition alone articulates in the forward thrust of life and alone lays hold of reality.

The animating purpose of James was, on the other hand, primarily moral and artistic. It is expressed, in his phrase, "block universe," employed as a term of adverse criticism. Mechanism and idealism were abhorrent to him because they both hold to a closed universe in which there is no room for novelty and adventure. Both sacrifice individuality and all the values, moral and aesthetic, which hang upon individuality, for according to absolute idealism, as to mechanistic materialism, the individual is simply a part determined by the whole of which he is a part. Only a philosophy of pluralism, of genuine indetermination, and of change which is real and intrinsic gives significance to individuality. It alone justifies struggle in creative activity and gives opportunity for the emergency of the genuinely new.

It was reserved, however, for the present century to give birth to the out-and-out assertion in systematic form that reality *is* process, and that laws as well as things develop in the processes of unceasing change. The modern Heraclitean is Alfred North Whitehead, but he is Heraclitus with a change. The doctrine of the latter, while it held that all things flow like a river and that change is so continuous that a man cannot step into the same river even once (since it changes as he steps), nevertheless also held that there is a fixed order which controls the ebb and flow of the universal tide.

My theme, however, is not historical, nor is it to argue in behalf of any one of the various doctrines regarding time that have been advanced. The purpose of the history just roughly sketched is to indicate that the nature of time and change has now become in its own right a philosophical problem of the first importance. It is of time as a *problem* that I wish to speak. The aspect of the problem that will be considered is the connection of time with individuality, as the latter is exemplified in the living organism and especially in human beings.

Take the account of the life of any person, whether the account is a biography or an autobiography. The story begins with birth, a temporal incident; it extends to include the temporal existence of parents and ancestry. It does not end with death, for it takes in the influence upon subsequent events of the words and deeds of the one whose life is told. Everything recorded is an historical event; it is something temporal. The individual whose life history is told, be it Socrates or Nero, St. Francis or Abraham Lincoln, is an extensive event; or, if you prefer, it is a course of events each of which takes up into itself something of what went before and leads on to that which comes after. The skill, the art, of the biographer is displayed in his ability to discover and portray the subtle ways, hidden often from the individual himself, in which one event grows out of those which preceded and enters into those which follow. The human individual is himself a history, a career, and for this reason his biography can be related only as a temporal event. That which comes later explains the earlier quite as truly as the earlier explains the later. Take the individual Abraham Lincoln at one year, at five years, at ten years, at thirty years of age, and imagine everything later wiped out, no matter how minutely his life is recorded up to the date set. It is plain beyond the need of words that we then have not his biography but only a fragment of it, while the significance of that fragment is undisclosed. For he did not just exist in a time which externally surrounded him, but time was the heart of his existence.

Temporal seriality is the very essence, then, of the human individual. It is impossible for a biographer in writing, say the story of the first thirty years of the life of Lincoln, not to bear in mind his later career. Lincoln as an individual *is* a history; any particular event cut off from that history ceases to be a part of his life as an individual. As Lincoln is a particular development in time, so is every other human individual. Individuality is the uniqueness of the history, of the career, not something given once for all at the beginning which then proceeds to unroll as a ball of yarn may be unwound. Lincoln made history. But it is just as true that he made himself as an individual in the history he made.

I have been speaking about human individuality. Now an important part of the problem of time is that what is true of the human individual does not seem to be true of physical individuals. The common saying "as like as two peas" is a virtual denial to one kind of vegetable life of the kind of individuality that marks human beings. It is hard to conceive of the individuality of a given pea in terms of a unique history or career; such individuality as it appears to possess seems to be due in part to spatial separateness and in part to peculiarities that are externally caused. The same thing holds true of lower forms of animal life. Most persons would resent denial of some sort of unique individuality to their own dogs, but would be slow to attribute it to worms, clams, and bees. Indeed, it seems to be an exclusive prerogative of the romantic novelist to find anything in the way of a unique career in animal lives in general.

When we come to inanimate elements, the prevailing view has been that time and sequential change are entirely foreign to their nature. According to this view they do not have careers; they simply change their relations in space. We have only to think of the classic conception of atoms. The Newtonian atom, for example, moved and was moved, thus changing its position in space, but it was unchangeable in its own being. What it was at the beginning or without any beginning it is always and forever. Owing to the impact of other things it changes its direction and velocity of motion so that it comes closer and further away from other things. But all this was believed to be external to its own substantial being. It had no development, no history, because it had no potentialities. In itself it was like a God, the same yesterday, today, and forever. Time did not enter into its being either to corrode or to develop it. Nevertheless, as an ultimate element it was supposed to have some sort of individuality, to be itself and not something else. Time, in physical science, has been simply a measure of motion in space.

Now, this apparently complete unlikeness in kind between the human and the physical individual is a part of the problem of time. Some philosophers have been content to note the difference and to make it the ground for affirming a sheer dualism between man and other things, a ground for assigning to man a spiritual being in contrast with material things. Others, fewer in numbers, have sought to explain away the seeming disparity, holding that the apparent uniqueness of human individuality is specious, being in fact the effect of the vast number of physical molecules, themselves complex, which make up his being, so that what looks like genuine temporal change or development is really but a function of the number and complexity of changes of constituent fixed elements. Of late, there have been a few daring souls who have held that temporal quality and historical career are a mark of everything, including atomic elements, to which individuality may be attributed.

I shall mention some of the reasons from the side of physical science that have led to this third idea. The first reason is the growing recognition that scientific objects are purely relational and have nothing to do with the intrinsic qualities of individual things and nothing to say about them. The meaning of this statement appears most clearly in the case of scientific laws. It is now a commonplace that a physical law states a correlation of changes or of ways and manners of change. The law of gravitation, for example, states a relation which holds between bodies with respect to distance and mass. It needs no argument to show that distance is a relation. Mass was long regarded as an inherent property of ultimate and individual elements. But even the Newtonian conception was obliged to recognize that mass could be defined only in terms of inertia and that inertia could be defined only in terms, on the one hand, of the resistance it offered to the impact of other bodies, and, on the other hand, of its capacity to exercise impact upon them, impact being measured in terms of motion with respect to acceleration. The idea that mass is an inherent property which caused inertia and momentum was simply a holdover from an old metaphysical idea of force. As far as the findings of science are concerned, independent of the intrusion of metaphysical ideas, mass is inertia-momentum and these are strictly measures and relations. The discovery that mass changes with velocity, a discovery made when minute bodies came under consideration, finally forced surrender of the notion that mass is a fixed and inalienable possession of ultimate elements or individuals, so that time is now considered to be their fourth dimension.

It may be remarked incidentally that the recognition of the relational character of scientific objects completely eliminates an old metaphysical issue. One of the outstanding problems created by the rise of modern science was due to the fact that scientific definitions and descriptions are framed in terms in which qualities play no part. Qualities were wholly superfluous. As long as the idea persisted (an inheritance from Greek metaphysical science) that the business of knowledge is to penetrate into the inner being of objects, the existence of qualities like colors, sounds, etc., was embarrassing. The usual way of dealing with them is to declare that they are merely subjective, existing only in the consciousness of individual knowers. Given the old idea that the purpose of knowledge (represented at its best in science) is to penetrate into the heart of reality and reveal its "true" nature, the conclusion was a logical one. The discovery that the objects of scientific knowledge are purely relational shows that the problem is an artificial one. It was "solved" by the discovery that it needed no solution, since fulfillment of the function and business of science compels disregard of qualities. Using the older language, it was seen that so-called primary qualities are no more inherent properties of ultimate objects than are so-called secondary qualities of odors, sounds, and colors, since the former are also strictly relational; or, as Locke stated in his moments of clear insight, are "retainers" of objects in their connections with other things. The discovery of the nonscientific because of the empirically unverifiable and unnecessary character of absolute space, absolute motion, and absolute time gave the final *coup de grâce* to the traditional idea that solidity, mass, size, etc., are inherent possessions of ultimate individuals.

The revolution in scientific ideas just mentioned is primarily logical. It is due to recognition that the very method of physical science, with its primary standard units of mass, space, and time, is concerned with measurement of relations of change, not with individuals as such. This acknowledgment brought with it a further idea which, in spite of the resistance made to it by adherents of older metaphysical views, is making constant headway. This idea is that laws which purport to be statements of what actually occurs are statistical in character as distinct from so-called dynamic laws that are abstract and mathematical, and disguised definitions. Recognition of the statistical nature of physical laws was first effected in the case of gases when it became evident that generalizations regarding the behavior of swarms of molecules were not descriptions or predictions of the behavior of any individual particle. A single molecule is not and cannot be a gas. It is consequently absurd to suppose that the scientific law is about the elementary constituents of a gas. It is a statement of what happens when a very large number of such constituents interact with one another under certain conditions.

Statistical statements are of the nature of probability formulations. No insurance company makes any prediction as to what will happen to any given person in respect to death, or to any building with respect to destruction by fire. Insurance is conducted upon the basis of observation that out of a large number of persons of a given age such and such a proportionate number will probably live one year more, another proportionate number two years, and so on, while premiums are adjusted on the basis of these probability estimates. The validity of the estimates depends, as in the case of a swarm of molecules, upon the existence of a sufficiently large number of individuals, a knowledge which is a matter of the relative frequency of events of a certain kind to the total number of events which occur. No statement is made about what will take place in the case of an *individual*. The application to scientific formulations of the principle of probability statistically determined is thus a logical corollary of the principle already stated, that the subject matter of scientific findings is relational, not individual. It is for this reason that it is safe to predict the ultimate triumph of the statistical doctrine.

The third scientific consideration is found in Heisenberg's principle of uncertainty or indeterminacy, which may be regarded as a generalization of the ideas already stated. In form, this principle seems to be limited in its application. Classical science was based upon the belief that it is possible to formulate both the position and the velocity at one time of any given particle. It followed that knowledge of the position and velocity of a given number of particles would enable the future behavior of the whole collection to be accurately predicted. The principle of Heisenberg is that given the determination of position, its velocity can be stated only as of a certain order of probability, while if its velocity is determined the correlative factor of position can be stated only as of a certain order of probability. Both cannot be determined at once, from which it follows necessarily that the future of the whole collection cannot possibly be foretold except in terms of some order of probability.

Because of the fundamental place of the conceptions of position and velocity in physical science the principle is not limited in scope but is of the broadest possible significance.

Given the classic conception, Laplace stated its logical outcome when he said "we may conceive the present state of the universe as the effect of its past and the cause of its future. An intellect who at any given instant knew all the forces of animate nature and the mutual positions of the beings who compose it . . . could condense into a single formula the movement both of the greatest body in the universe and of its lightest atom. Nothing would be uncertain to such an intellect, for the future, even as the past would be ever present before his eyes." No more sweeping statement of the complete irrelevancy of time to the physical world and of the complete unreality for individuals of time could well be uttered. But the principle of indeterminacy annihilates the premises from which the conclusion follows. The principle is thus a way of acknowledging the pertinency of real time to physical beings. The utmost possible regarding an individual is a statement as to some order of probability about the future. Heisenberg's principle has been seized upon as a basis for wild statements to the effect that the doctrine of arbitrary free will and totally uncaused activity are now scientifically substantiated. Its actual force and significance is generalization of the idea that the individual is a temporal career whose future cannot be *logically* deduced from its past.

As long as scientific knowledge was supposed to be concerned with individuals in their own intrinsic nature, there was no way to bridge the gap between the career of human individuals and that of physical individuals, save by holding that the seeming fundamental place of development and hence of time in the life histories of the former is only seeming or specious. The unescapable conclusion is that as human individuality can be understood only in terms of time as fundamental reality, so for physical individuals time is not simply a measure of predetermined changes in mutual positions, but is something that enters into their being. Laws do not "govern" the activity of individuals. They are a formulation of the frequency-distributions of the behavior of large numbers of individuals engaged in interactions with one another.

This statement does not mean that physical and human individuality are identical, nor that the things which appear to us to be nonliving have the distinguishing characteristic of organisms. The difference between the inanimate and the animate is not so easily wiped out. But it does show that there is no fixed gap between them. The conclusion which most naturally follows, without indulging in premature speculations, is that the principle of a developing career applies to all things in nature, as well as to human beings—that they are born, undergo qualitative changes, and finally die, giving place to other individuals. The idea of development applied to nature involves differences of forms and qualities as surely as it rules out absolute breaches of continuity. The differences between the amoeba and the human organism are genuinely there even if we accept the idea of organic evolution of species. Indeed, to deny the reality of the differences and their immense significance would be to deny the very idea of development. To wipe out differences because of denial of complete breaks and the need for intervention of some outside power is just as surely a way to deny development as is assertion of gaps which can be bridged only by the intervention of some supernatural force. It is then in terms of development, or if one prefers the more grandiose term, evolution, that I shall further discuss the problem of time.

The issue involved is perhaps the most fundamental one in philosophy at the present time. Are the changes which go on in the world simply external redistributions, rearrangements in space of what previously existed, or are they genuine qualitative changes such as apparently take place in the physiological development of an organism, from the union of ovum and sperm to maturity, and as apparently take place in the personal life career of individuals? When the question is raised, certain misapprehensions must be first guarded against. Development and evolution have historically been eulogistically interpreted. They have been thought of as necessarily proceeding from the lower to the higher, from the relatively worse to the relatively better. But this property was read in from outside moral and theological preoccupations. The real issue is that stated above: Is what happens simply a spatial rearrangement of what existed previously or does it involve something qualitatively new? From this point of view, cancer is as genuinely a physiological development as is growth in vigor; criminals as well as heroes are a social development; the emergence of totalitarian states is a social evolution out of constitutional states independently of whether we like or approve them.

If we accept the intrinsic connection of time with individuality, they are not mere redistributions of what existed before.

Since it is a *problem* I am presenting, I shall assume that genuine transformations occur, and consider its implications. First and negatively, the idea (which is often identified with the essential meaning of evolution) is excluded that development is a process of unfolding what was previously implicit or latent. Positively it is implied that potentiality is a category of existence, for development cannot occur unless an individual has powers or capacities that are not actualized at a given time. But it also means that these powers are not unfolded from within, but are called out through interaction with other things. While it is necessary to revive the category of potentiality as a characteristic of individuality, it has to be revived in a different form from that of its classic Aristotelian formulation. According to that view, potentialities are connected with a *fixed* end which the individual endeavors by its own nature or essence to actualize, although its success in actualization depended upon the cooperation of external things and hence might be thwarted by the "accidents" of its surroundings—as not every acorn becomes a tree and few if any acorns become the typical oak.

When the idea that development is due to some indwelling end which tends to control the series of changes passed through is abandoned, potentialities must be thought of in terms of consequences of interactions with other things. Hence potentialities cannot be *known* till *after* the interactions have occurred. There are at a given time unactualized potentialities in an individual because and in as far as there are in existence other things with which it has not as yet interacted. Potentialities of milk are known today, for example, that were not known a generation ago, because milk has been brought into interaction with things other than organisms, and hence now has other than furnishing nutriment consequence. It is now predicted that in the future human beings will be wearing clothes made of glass and that the clothes will be cleaned by throwing them into a hot furnace. Whether this particular prediction is fulfilled or not makes no difference to its value as an illustration. Every new scientific discovery leads to some mode of technology that did not previously exist. As things are brought by new procedures into new contacts and new interactions, new consequences are produced and the power to produce these new consequences is a recognized potentiality of the thing in question. The idea that potentialities are inherent and fixed by relation to a predetermined end was a product of a highly restricted state of technology. Because of this restriction, the only potentialities recognized were those consequences which were customary in the given state of culture and were accordingly taken to be "natural." When the only possible use of milk was as an article of food, it was "natural" to suppose that it had an inherent tendency to serve that particular end. With the use of milk as a plastic, and with no one able to tell what future consequences may be produced by new techniques which bring it into new interactions, the only reasonable conclusion is that potentialities are not fixed and intrinsic, but are a matter of an indefinite range of interactions in which an individual may engage.

Return for a moment to the human individual. It is impossible to think of the historical career, which is the special individuality constituting Abraham Lincoln, apart from the particular conditions in which he lived. He did not create, for example, the conditions that formed the issues of States' rights and of slavery, the issues that influenced his development. What his being as an individual would have been without these interacting conditions it is idle to speculate upon. The conditions did not form him from without as wax is supposed to be shaped by external pressure. There is no such thing as interaction that is merely a one-way movement. There were many other persons living under much the same conditions whose careers were very different, because conditions acted upon them and were acted upon by them in different ways. Hence there is no account possible of Lincoln's life that does not portray him interacting day by day with special conditions, with his parents, his wife and children, his neighbors, his economic conditions, his school facilities, the incidents of his profession as a lawyer, and so on. The career which is his unique individuality is the series of interactions in which he was created to be what he was by the ways in which he responded to the occasions with which he was presented. One cannot leave out either conditions *as opportunities* nor yet unique ways of responding to them. An occasion is an opportunity only when it is an evocation of a specific event, while a response is not a necessary effect of a cause but is a way of using an occasion to render it a constituent of an ongoing unique history.

Individuality conceived as a temporal development involves uncertainty, indeterminacy, or contingency. Individuality is the source of whatever is unpredictable in the world. The indeterminate is not change in the sense of violation of law, for laws state probable correlations of change and these probabilities exist no matter what the source of change may be. When a change occurs, *after* it has occurred it belongs to the observable world and is connected with other changes. The nomination of Lincoln for the presidency, his election, his Emancipation Proclamation, his assassination, after they took place can be shown to be related to other events; they can also be shown to have a certain connection with Lincoln's own past. But there was nothing in Lincoln's own life to cause by itself the conjunction of circumstances which brought about any one of these events. As far as he as an individual was concerned, the events were contingent, and as far as the conjunction of circumstances was concerned, his behavior at any given time in response to them was also contingent, or if you please fortuitous.

At critical junctures, his response could not be predicted either from his own past or from the nature of the circumstances, except as a probability. To say this is not arbitrarily to introduce mere chance into the world. It is to say that genuine individuality exists; that individuality is pregnant with new developments; that time is real. If we knew enough about Shakespeare's life we could doubtless show *after Hamlet* was produced how it is connected with other things. We could link it with sources; we could connect its mood with specific experiences of its author, and so on. But no one with the fullest knowledge of Shakespeare's past could have predicted the drama as it stands. If they could have done so, they would have been able to write it. Not even Shakespeare himself could have told in advance just what he was going to say— not if he was an individual, not a nodal point in the spatial redistribution of what already existed.

The mystery of time is thus the mystery of the existence of real individuals. It is a mystery because it is a mystery that anything which exists is just what it is. We are given to forgetting, with our insistence upon causation and upon the necessity of things happening as they do happen, that things exist as just what they qualitatively are. We can account for a change by relating it to other changes, but existences we have to accept for just what they are. Given a butterfly or an earthquake as an event, as a change, we can at least in theory find out and state its connection with other changes. But the individual butterfly or earthquake remains just the unique existence which it is. We forget in explaining its occurrence that it is only the *occurrence* that is explained, not the thing itself. We forget that in explaining the occurrence we are compelled to fall back on other individual things that have just the unique qualities they do have. Go as far back as we please in accounting for present conditions and we still come upon the mystery of things being just what they are.

Their occurrence, their manifestation, may be accounted for in terms of other occurrences, but their own quality of existence is final and opaque. The mystery is that the world is as it is—a mystery that is the source of all joy and all sorrow, of all hope and fear, and the source of development both creative and degenerative. The contingency of all into which time enters is the source of pathos, comedy, and tragedy. Genuine time, if it exists as anything else except the measure of motions in space, is all one with the existence of individuals as individuals, with the creative, with the occurrence of unpredictable novelties. Everything that can be said contrary to this conclusion is but a reminder that an individual may lose his individuality, for individuals become imprisoned in routine and fall to the level of mechanisms. Genuine time then ceases to be an integral element in their being. Our behavior becomes predictable because it is but an external rearrangement of what went before.

In conclusion, I would like to point out two considerations that seem to me to follow, two morals, if you wish to give them that name. I said earlier that the traditional idea of progress and evolution was based upon belief that the fixed structure of the universe is such as automatically brings it about. This optimistic and fatalistic idea is now at a discount. It is easy in the present state of the world to deny all validity whatever to the idea of progress, since so much of the human world seems bent on demonstrating the truth of the old theological doctrine of the fall of man. But the real conclusion is that, while progress is not inevitable, it is up to men as individuals to bring it about. Change is going to occur anyway, and the problem is the control of change in a given direction. The direction, the quality of change, is a matter of individuality. Surrender of individuality by the many to some one who is taken to be a superindividual explains the retrograde movement of society. Dictatorships and totalitarian states, and belief in the inevitability of this or that result coming to pass are, strange as it may sound, ways of denying the reality of time and the creativeness of the individual. Freedom of thought and of expression are not mere rights to be claimed. They have their roots deep in the existence of individuals as developing careers in time. Their denial and abrogation is an abdication of individuality and a virtual rejection of time as opportunity.

The ground of democratic ideas and practices is faith in the potentialities of individuals, faith in the capacity for positive developments if proper conditions are provided. The weakness of the philosophy originally advanced to justify the democratic movement was that it took individuality to be something given ready-made; that is, in abstraction from time, instead of as a power to develop.

The other conclusion is that art is the complement of science. Science as I have said is concerned wholly with relations, not with individuals. Art, on the other hand, is not only the disclosure of the individuality of the artist but is also a manifestation of individuality as creative of the future, in an unprecedented response to conditions as they were in the past. Some artists in their vision of might be but is not have been conscious rebels. But conscious protest and revolt is not the form which the labor of the artist in creation of the future must necessarily take. Discontent with things as they are is normally the expression of vision of what may be and is not, art in being the manifestation of individuality is this prophetic vision. To regiment artists, to make them servants of some particular cause does violence to the very springs of artistic creation. But it does more than that. It betrays the very cause of a better future it would serve, for in its subjection of the individuality of the artist it annihilates the source of that which is genuinely new. Were the regimentation successful, it would cause the future to be but a rearrangement of the past.

The artist in realizing his own individuality reveals potentialities hitherto unrealized. This revelation is the inspiration of other individuals to make the potentialities real, for it is not sheer revolt against things as they are which stirs human endeavor to its depths, but vision of what might be and is not. Subordination of the artists to any special cause no matter how worthy does violence not only to the artist but to the living source of a new and better future. Art is not the possession of the few who are recognized writers, painters, musicians; it is the authentic expression of any and all individuality. Those who have the gift of creative expression in unusually large measure disclose the meaning of the individuality of others to those others. In participating in the work of art, they become artists in their activity. They learn to know and honor individuality in whatever form it appears. The fountains of creative activity are discovered and released. The free individuality which is the source of art is also the final source of creative development in time.

My Philosophy of Law

When the question of the nature of law is examined in the light of the doctrines of various schools and the controversies between them, it is found to break up into at least three distinct yet related questions. The three issues concern the *source* of law, its *end,* and its *application,* including under this last head questions of the methods by which law is and can be made effective.

The problems involved in the discussions about law that can be called philosophical seem to arise from the need for having some principles which can be employed to justify and/or criticize existing legal rules and practices. This need and motive are perhaps most clearly manifested in those philosophies which made an explicit distinction between what they called positive law on one side and the law of nature on the other hand, the latter being employed as the end positive laws ought to realize and the standard to which they should conform. This particular formulation is at present in vogue only in the school of thought that remains faithful to the general line of ideas formulated in the Middle Ages and that continued to influence continental writers on law through the seventeenth century. But the distinction between what happens to exist at a given time and what might and should be, and the need for such a conception of the latter as will provide "principles" for organizing, justifying, and/or disapproving and reforming some aspects of what exists seem to be back of all movements that fall in the field of legal philosophy.

From this point of view, discussion of the source and the end of law can be brought under a single head, that of the *standard* or criterion by which to evaluate existing legal regulations and practices. The question of what law *is* then reduces itself to a

[First published in *My Philosophy of Law: Credos of Sixteen American Scholars,* under the direction of the Julius Rosenthal Foundation, Northwestern University (Boston: Boston Law Book Co., 1941), pp. 73–85.]

question of what it is believed regulations and practices *should be*. According to traditions that are highly influential, determination of the end and standard is intimately bound up with determination of an *ultimate* source—as is obvious when the Will or Reason of God, or the ultimate and intrinsic Law of Nature, is held to be the source of law. What lies back of this identification of source with end and standard is the belief that unless a source higher and more fixed than that of experience can be found, there is no sure ground for any genuinely philosophic valuation of law as it actually exists. This appeal to a source is not, then, the same as appeal to origin in time, since that last procedure links the matter up with experience, and with all the defects that the classic tradition attaches to whatever is experiential.

These preliminary remarks have a double purpose. On one hand, they are designed to express the belief that there is a genuine and important matter involved in the discussions called "legal philosophy"; the question, namely, of the ground upon which existing legal affairs, including rules of law, the work of legislation, judicial decisions, and administrative practices, can be legitimately and profitably evaluated. The other point is that as matter of fact legal philosophies have reflected and are sure to continue to reflect movements of the period in which they are produced, and hence cannot be separated from what these movements stand for.

This last remark is a sweeping one. To many persons, it will seem to beg all the important questions with which legal philosophy is concerned. However, upon the side of past systems, it signifies that they have to be viewed in connection with actual cultural and social movements of the periods in which they appeared. The view also holds that the real significance of those philosophies is increased when they are viewed as manifestations of efforts put forth practically. For upon an exclusively intellectual basis, the various legal philosophies are in such conflict with one another as to indicate that all alike are attempting the impossible. On the view here suggested, they have all the importance that is possessed by the movements they reflect; their conflicts are proofs of a certain vital genuineness. On the same score, if different contributions to this volume represent incompatible positions, it is because they express different attitudes toward practical questions of what should be done and how best to do it.

At all events, what I myself have to say is put forth in this spirit. Fundamentally, a program for action to be tested in action is set forth, not something that can be judged (beyond assertions of fact and matters of logical consistency) on a purely intellectual basis.

The standpoint taken is that law is through and through a social phenomenon; social in origin, in purpose or end, and in application. Now one cannot utter or write the word "social" without being aware of all the ambiguities and controversies that attend the meaning of the words *society* and *social*. Here what was just said may be objected to on the ground that it tries to explain what is obscure, namely the nature of law, by reference to something still more obscure, namely, society. For the purpose of the present topic, however, it is needful to make only two statements regarding what is denoted by "social." It is postulated that whatever else social means it applies, first, to human *activities*, and secondly to these activities, as forms of behavior, as *inter*-activities. By saying that social facts, or phenomena, are activities, it is meant, negatively, that they are *not* facts of the kind indicated when "fact" is taken to mean something done, finished, and over with; and positively that they are processes, things going *on*. Even in the case of past events, when social facts are under consideration, it is important to recognize that they represent slices of time having a dimension long enough to cover initial conditions and a later stage of issue or outcome, the latter being in its turn an *on*going. With reference to law, this position signifies that law must be viewed both as intervening in the complex of other activities, and as itself a social process, not something that can be said to be done or to happen at a certain date. The first part of the foregoing statement means that "law" cannot be set up as if it were a separate entity, but can be discussed only in terms of the social conditions in which it arises and of what it concretely does there. It is this fact which renders the use of the word "law" as a single general term rather dangerous, making it needful to state explicitly that the word is used as a summary term to save repeating legal rules, legislative and administrative activities (as far as the latter influence the course of human activities), judicial decisions, etc.

The second part of the statement involves the conclusion that what is called *application* is not something that happens *after* a rule or law or statute is laid down but is a necessary part of them; such a necessary part indeed that in given cases we can judge what the law *is* as matter of fact only by telling how it operates, and what are its effects in and upon the human activities that are going on. For special purposes, the signification of "applicability" may be restricted much more technically. But from the standpoint that can be called philosophical, application must be taken broadly. A given legal arrangement *is* what it *does,* and what it does lies in the field of modifying and/or maintaining human activities as going concerns. Without application there are scraps of paper or voices in the air but nothing that can be called law.

It might seem as if what is conveyed by saying that social activities are *inter*-activities were already included in the word "*social,*" since social means association. By calling especial attention to this trait, however, we indicate that there is a *de facto,* though not necessarily *de jure* or moral, reciprocity in every fact of social behavior. A *trans*-action does not just go across in a one-way direction, but is a two-way process. There is reaction as well as action. While it is convenient to view some human beings as agents and others as patients (recipients), the distinction is purely relative; there is no receptivity that is not also a re-*action* or response, and there is no agency that does not also involve an element of receptivity. The emphasis upon agreement, contract, consensus, in various political and legal philosophies is in effect a recognition of this aspect of social phenomena, although a rather over-idealized expression of it.

Social processes have conditions which are stable and enduring as compared with the multitudes of special actions composing the process. Human beings form habits as surely as they perform special deeds, and habits, when embodied in interactivities, are customs. These customs are, upon the view here taken, the *source* of law. We may use the analogy, or if one prefers, the metaphor, of a river valley, a stream, and banks. The valley in its relation to surrounding country, or as the "lie of the land," is the primary fact. The stream may be compared to the social process, and its various waves, wavelets, eddies, etc., to the special acts which make up a social process. The banks are stable, enduring conditions, which limit and also direct the course taken by the stream, comparable to customs. But the permanence and fixity of the banks, as compared with the elements of the passing stream, is relative, not absolute. Given the lie of the land, the stream is an energy which carves its way from higher to lower levels and thereby, when viewed as a long run (in time as well as in space) process, it forms and reforms its own banks. Social customs, including traditions, institutions, etc., are stable and enduring as compared with special deeds and with the serial arrangement of these acts which forms a process. But they, and therefore the legal regulations which are their precipitated formulations, are only relatively fixed. They undergo, sooner or later, more slowly or more rapidly, the attrition of ongoing processes. For while they constitute the *structure* of the processes that go *on*, they are the structure *of* the processes in the sense that they arise and take shape within the processes, and are not forced upon the processes from without.

Habit and custom introduce factors into the constitution of human activities which were not taken account of by earlier philosophers who called themselves empirical; factors which, when they are taken account of, profoundly modify the demand for an origin and source of law outside of time, and for a standard or norm that is outside of and independent of experience. As for the first point, earlier empirical philosophers in their revolt against universals and principles that were alleged to be immutable and eternal, beyond criticism and beyond alteration, often pulverized experience, and reduced all general and enduring factors in it to the general names they bore. Every habit and every custom is, however, general within certain limits. It arises out of interaction of environing conditions, which change slowly, with needs and interests of human beings which also endure with but slight change throughout considerable periods of time. Limitation of space does not permit an adequate statement of the nature of the connections that exist between habits and rules of law. But it is clear without extended argument that explicit enactment of a custom into law, however the enactment takes place, reinforces and often extends the relatively enduring and stable character of custom, thus modifying its general character.

It is possible that the bearing of the generality of custom and law, as structural conditions of social activities, upon mooted problems of legal philosophical doctrine is not readily apparent. The point is that recognition of this aspect of social phenomena makes it unnecessary to appeal, on *practical* grounds, to an outside source. As a matter of pure metaphysical theory, a person may continue to have a very low opinion of time and of things affected by temporal conditions. But from any practical standpoint, recognition of the relatively slow rate of change on the part of certain constituents of social action is capable of accomplishing every useful, every *practically* needed, office that has led in the past and in other cultural climes to setting up external sources such as the Will or Reason of God, the Law of Nature in medieval theory and in philosophers like Grotius and his successors, the General Will of Rousseau, and the Practical Reason of Kant.

What has been said does not apply to the doctrine that *sovereignty* is the source of law. Sovereignty is used to denote something which is at least of the nature of a social fact, something existing *within* social activities and relations and not outside of them. Unless I am mistaken, the fact that this view which once highly commended itself to students of politics and of jurisprudence no longer exercises any great appeal indicates why a brief statement about it will suffice. For (unless again I am much mistaken) the view already wears a certain antiquarian air, so that it is hard even in imagination to see why once it had such a vogue. Seen in perspective, this doctrine owed its force to two things. It got away from making law depend upon outside metaphysical sources; it instituted in their place reliance upon conditions and agencies to which some verifiable empirical meaning could be given. In the second place, sovereignty is a *political* term, and the vogue of the doctrine coincided with that immense outburst of legislative activity which took place in the field conventionally labeled "political." The Austinian theory of the source of law may be said to constitute a rationalized approbation of a movement to bring legal rules and arrangements within the scope of deliberate purposive action, at the expense of the comparatively unplanned results of customs interpreted in judicial decisions. The doctrine has lost much of its original appeal because development of the social sciences, viz., of history, anthropology, sociology, and psychology, has tended to make sovereignty at best an expression of the working of a vast multitude of social forces, and at worst a pure abstraction. The sovereignty doctrine of the source of law thus represents a transition from acceptance of "sources" outside of social actions into one within them, but a transition which fastened on only one social factor and froze that one in isolation. When it was discovered that social customs, and to some extent social interests, lord it over any specific set of persons who can be picked out and called "sovereign," the doctrine declined. The growing tendency to interpret political activities in connection with economic factors acted, of course, in the same direction.

So far the topic of end and standard has not received attention. It may be urged that if the account that has been given of the experiential source of law is accepted, it only strengthens the case for an end and standard that lie outside of actual social activities. For, it is argued, the fact that such and such customs and laws have grown up is no sign that they *should* exist; it furnishes no test for their value. In short, we come here upon the large problem of "value in relation to fact," and upon the conclusion, held by many that they are so separate that standards for judging the value of what exists must have *their* source as standards outside of any possible empirical field.

With reference to this issue, recognition of the ongoing character of social facts as continuing activities is of fundamental importance. If what are taken to be social facts are chopped off by being regarded as closed and completely ended, then there is much to be said on theoretical grounds for the view that the standard for evaluating them must lie outside the field of actual existences. But if they are ongoing, they have consequences; and consideration of consequences may provide ground upon which it is decided whether they be maintained intact or be changed.

When it is stated that there is much to be said *theoretically* for the view that an outside end and standard are needed if social facts are not taken as going concerns, it is not meant that much can be said in favor of the applicability of such standards to actual social conditions, with which, by definition, they have nothing to do. It is undeniable that different standards, so different as to conflict with one another, have been held and used at different places and times in the past. Their conflict is sufficient evidence that they were not derived from any *a priori* absolute standard. Denial of the possibility of extracting a standard from actual social activities is thus in effect a denial that an absolute standard, even if it exists, ever had any influence or effect. *For what reason is there for thinking that the standards now put forth by those who appeal to a non-empirical absolute end, will have a different fortune from those put forward in the past?*

The usual way of meeting difficulties of this type is to admit that a distinction must be made between *form,* which is absolute, and its contents or filling, which are historical and relative. The admission is fatal to everything which the doctrine of absolute ends was framed to meet. For according to the admission, all concrete valuations must be based upon what is admitted to be experiential and temporal.

On the view here presented, the standard is found in consequences, in the *function* of what goes on socially. If this view were generally held, there would be assurance of introduction on a large scale of the rational factor into concrete evaluations of legal arrangements. For it demands that intelligence, employing the best scientific methods and materials available, be used, to investigate, in terms of the context of actual situations, the consequences of legal rules and of proposed legal decisions and acts of legislation. The present tendency, hardly more as yet than in a state of inception, to discuss legal matters in their concrete social setting, and not in the comparative vacuum of their relations to one another, would get the reinforcement of a consistent legal theory. Moreover, when it is systematically acknowledged in practice that social facts are going concerns and that all legal matters have their place *within* these ongoing concerns, there will be a much stronger likelihood than at present that new knowledge will be acquired of a kind which can be brought to bear upon the never-ending process of improving standards of judgment.

The Philosophy of Whitehead

I

It was long the fashion for philosophers to base their doctrines upon what each one happened to regard as "first principles," the latter being "premises" in their capacity of coming logically first. When the principles were regarded, under the influence of Aristotelianism, as axioms or self-evident truths, apart from which there was no demonstration of other truths (and without demonstration no "science"), they seemed to descend directly via pure intellect, out of the ether of reason, situated next to God or perhaps in his own intrinsic abode. Even if there were some special occasion in virtue of which they were humanly noted, there was nothing beyond them or outside of them from which, as truths, they arose or upon which they depended. One might as well suppose that the stars, and not simply the view of them, were dependent upon the ladder by which one, perhaps, mounted to see them as to give attention to the setting in which "principles" were formulated. When the latter were called postulates, in place of premises, there was gain in candor and in knowledge by philosophers of what they were about. But the change did not of itself ensure recognition and statement of the background out of which postulates arise and which determines the function they perform.

It cannot be said, even yet, that explicit attention is given as a matter of course to the background which sets the special problems with which a given philosopher is occupied. This failure is partly due to the persistence of the tradition according to which it derogates from the purity of philosophy to doubt its immacu-

[First published in *The Philosophy of Alfred North Whitehead*, Library of Living Philosophers, ed. Paul Arthur Schilpp (Evanston and Chicago: Northwestern University, 1941), 3:643–61.]

late conception. But it is also due, I think, to the fact that a philosophic thinker is much more explicitly aware of what lies ahead and of being urged forward than of the background from which he derives his push. And, as I write these words, I am painfully aware of the inadequacy of the word "background" to convey what I have in mind—the words "place" or "point of departure" being even more inadequate, if they suggest anything narrower than the home and regional environment from which a traveller sets out.

Whitehead, it seems to me, has come closer than most philosophers have done to stating the nature of the region from which he sets out. It is for that reason I have engaged in these introductory remarks. I am thinking especially of a passage in which, after saying that philosophy "can deal only with things in some sense experienced," he goes on to say,

> The living organ of experience is the living body as a whole. Every instability of any part of it—be it chemical, physical, or molar—imposes an activity of readjustment throughout the whole organism. In the course of such physical activities human experience has its origin. The plausible interpretation of such experience is that it is one of the natural activities involved in the functioning of such a high-grade organism. *The actualities of nature must be . . . explanatory of this fact. . . .*
>
> Such experience seems to be more particularly related to the activities of the brain. But . . . we cannot determine with what molecules the brain begins and the rest of the body ends. Further, we cannot tell with what molecules the body ends and the external world begins. The truth is that the brain is continuous with the body, and the body is continuous with the rest of the natural world. Human experience is an act of self-origination including the whole of nature, limited to the *perspective* of a focal region, located within the body, but not necessarily persisting in any fixed coördination with a definite part of the brain.[1]

1. *Adventures of Ideas*, 289–90. (Italics not in original text.) The fact that my further references and quotations are limited to this particular book of Whitehead's is partially due to the limitations under which this essay is written. But in view of the simplicity and completeness with which the gist of Whitehead's doctrines is set forth in this book, I do not regard this limitation as of especial importance in respect to my interpretation and criticism.

If I had a right to assume on the part of the reader acquaintance with my own writings on the topic of the reciprocal connections of nature and experience, and the bearing of these connections upon the problems and task of philosophy, I would add that it will also be obvious why I cite this particular passage. For what I have called the background and point of departure seems to be the same for both of us, no matter what deviations may occur later. And such a community of backgrounds is so rare that I make no apology for dwelling upon it at the outset. In any case, the reader is entitled to the warning that my belief in the fundamental significance of the ideas set forth in the passage quoted controls what I have to say about the tenor of Whitehead's philosophy. If I am wrong in attributing central importance to the ideas that experience is a manifestation of the energies of the organism; that these energies are in such intimate continuity with the rest of nature that the traits of experience provide clews for forming "generalized descriptions" of nature—the especial business of philosophy according to Whitehead—and that what is discovered about the rest of nature (constituting the conclusions of the natural sciences) provides the organs for analyzing and understanding what is otherwise obscure and ambiguous in experiences directly had—if, I say, I am wrong in this view, then there will be no particular point to what I have further to say.

Whitehead is of course well aware that "experience" has often been restricted, both by those who called themselves empiricists and by their opponents, to certain arbitrarily selected activities of the organism to which a privileged role is assigned. For experience has, notoriously, been limited to the activities of sense-organs—or rather to their products, called sensations, or, better, sensa. In the light of the history of culture, one can find reasons for this peculiar arbitrary selection. But, viewing the matter impartially, the limitation can only be regarded as one of the most extraordinary and uncalled for errors human belief has ever indulged in—especially since, if one really began there and stuck, in the conclusion, solely to what the beginning justifies, one would never know even that he had sense-organs or that the sense-organs are organs of a creature engaged in living in an environment partly friendly and partly hostile to its activities. Whitehead expressly repudiates this restriction:

We must appeal to evidence relating to every variety of occasion. Nothing can be omitted, experience drunk and experience sober, experience sleeping and experience waking, experience drowsy and experience wide-awake, experience self-conscious and experience self-forgetful, experience intellectual and experience physical, experience religious and experience sceptical, experience anxious and experience carefree, experience anticipatory and experience retrospective, experience happy and experience grieving, experience dominated by emotion and experience under self-restraint, experience in the light and experience in the dark, experience normal and experience abnormal.[2]

Those who profess belief in empirical philosophy can hardly be other than grateful for emancipation from chains which, after all, were self-imposed. Artists, poets, prophets may be drawn to a philosophy that sees "experience" to be rich beyond the possibility of exhaustion and subtle beyond the reach of human wit.

II

I am not sure that the denial of "the bifurcation of nature" found in Whitehead's earlier writings was connected, consciously, with the enlarged and deepened idea about experience which is expressed in the passages quoted from his later writings. I imagine the denial had its source in Whitehead's reflections upon the new science; a mathematical strain dominates his cosmological account. But I have no doubt the denial has its completion in the express sense that physical nature must be such as to account for the specialized peculiarities of human experience, while the latter provides clews to be used in expanding to their full significance that which physical science discovers. "Neutral monists" have denied the existence of a gulf between physical and "mental" experience. Indeed, thoroughgoing materialism and spiritual idealism have at all times denied its existence. But as long as Newtonian physics was the accepted authority about the constitution of nature in its physical aspects, such theories seemed forced. Dualism was not so much an inferential conclusion as it was a frank recognition of the difference between the

2. *Op. cit.*, 290f.

traits marking the objects of (Newtonian) physics and the undeniable features of immediate experience. The genius of Whitehead is exhibited in the earliness of his perception that the new mathematical physics did away with the supposedly scientific foundations, upon the physical side, which gave obvious point to the separation. Given this initial move, continued reflection could hardly do other than develop a less abstract, a more vital, sense of the essential community of the less and the more specialized occasions of experience.

In any case we have such a passage as the following: "All final individual actualities have the metaphysical character of occasions of experience"; a passage to be read and understood in connection with the thesis that, granted this view, "the direct evidence as to the connectedness of one's immediate present occasion of experience with one's immediately past occasions can be validly used to suggest categories applying to the connectedness of all *occasions in nature*." [3] If the meaning assigned to this sentence is not entirely clear, the following sentence should render it definite: "An occasion of experience which includes a human mentality is an extreme instance, at one end of the scale, of those happenings which constitute nature" [4]—a sentence which shows, I believe, the sense in which propositions like the following are to be understood: "It is a false dichotomy to think of Nature *and* Man. Mankind is that factor *in* Nature which exhibits in its most intense form the plasticity of nature." [5]

This doctrine that all actual existences are to be treated as "occasions of experience" carries and elaborates, it seems to me, the significance contained in the propositions I quoted earlier about the depth and width of scope of experience. The idea that the immediate traits of distinctively human experience are highly specialized cases of what actually goes on in every actualized event of nature does infinitely more than merely deny the existence of an impassable gulf between physical and psychological subject-matter. It authorizes us, as philosophers engaged in forming highly generalized descriptions of nature, to use the traits of immediate experience as clews for interpreting our observations of non-human and non-animate nature. It also authorizes us to carry over the main conclusions of physical science

3. *Op. cit.*, 284. (Italics not in original text.)
4. *Op. cit.*, 237.
5. *Op. cit.*, 99.

into explanation and description of mysterious and inexplicable traits of experience marked by "consciousness." It enables us to do so without engaging in the dogmatic mechanistic materialism that inevitably resulted when Newtonian physics was used to account for what is distinctive in human experience. That which on the negative side is simply an elimination of the grounds of the metaphysical dualism of physical and mental, material and ideal, object and subject, opens the road to free observation of whatever experience of any kind discloses and points toward:—free, that is, from a rigid frame of preconceptions.

For the generalization of "experience" which is involved in calling every actual existence by the name "occasion of experience" has a two-fold consequence, each aspect of this dual consequence being complementary to the other. The traits of human experience can be used to direct observation of the generalized traits of all nature. For they are intensified manifestations, specialized developments, of conditions and factors found everywhere in nature. On the other hand, all the generalizations to which physical science leads are resources available for analysis and descriptive interpretation of all the phenomena of human life, personal and "social." It is my impression that in his earlier writings Whitehead started preferably from the physical side, and then moved on to a doctrine of nature "in general" without much explicit attention to what may be called experience from the psychological point of view, while in his later writings he supplements and extends the conclusions thus reached by adoption of a reverse movement:—that from specialized human experience through physical experience to a comprehensive doctrine of Nature. The "events" of his earlier treatises thus become the "occasions of experience" of later writings. But whether or not this impression is well-founded is of slight importance compared with the fact that Whitehead proceeds systematically upon the ground indicated in the following passage: "The world within experience is identical with the world beyond experience, the occasion of experience is within the world and the world is within the occasion. The categories have to elucidate this paradox of the connectedness of things:—the many things, the one world without and within."[6]

In putting forward this particular mode of approach to inter-

6. *Op. cit.*, 293.

pretation of Whitehead's philosophy, I am doubtless deliberately emphasizing the things with which my own way of philosophical thinking most agrees. I would not deny that Whitehead's philosophy is so comprehensive that there are other ways of approach that other commentators and critics may find more significant than the one I have taken. None the less it cannot be denied that the path I have chosen is explicitly indicated (with increasing plainness) in Whitehead's own writings, so that what I say is legitimate if not inclusive. And if it is legitimate then I am entitled to my personal, and perhaps private, view that the consistency and sensitivity with which Whitehead follows the method thereby determined is the source of the originality and fecundity of his writings. For I believe that only by means of a view of the same general nature as is involved in this position can philosophy escape the road it has been following, a road which demonstrably has led to a dead end, where virtuosity of academic technique may flourish, but which cannot save philosophy from the sterility that is the Dead Sea fruit of academicism.

III

The passage already quoted to the effect that experiences involving human mentality are but extreme instances of the happenings constitutive of nature, is directly followed by the sentences:

> Any doctrine that refuses to place human experience outside nature, must find in the description of experience factors which enter also into the description of less specialized natural occurrences. If there be no such factors, then the doctrine of human experience as a fact within nature is mere bluff, founded upon vague phrases whose sole merit is a comforting familiarity. We should either admit dualism, at least as a provisional doctrine, or we should point out the identical elements connecting human experience with physical science.[7]

That my interpretation is justly to the charge of oversimplifying the philosophy of Whitehead is true in the sense in which it is an oversimplification to exhibit the skeleton of an or-

7. *Op. cit.*, 237.

ganism without reference to flesh, blood, and the muscles with which it performs its actions. But I do not claim to be here concerned with anything but the skeleton of Whitehead's system, and even so only with its backbone. Any reader of his writings who keeps an open mind does not have to be reminded of the profound suggestiveness that marks the pages of such a book as *Science and the Modern World* and *Adventures of Ideas,* and of the extraordinarily wide field to which these suggestions refer. My particular theme compels me to be content with only this indefinite reference to everything in his books that does not have to do with what I take to be the general structural condition of his thinking. Accordingly, I now pass to consideration of the treatment given two historic problems of philosophy, confining myself in respect to them to matters that exemplify the principle of procedure I have taken to constitute the originality of Whitehead's thought, and that mark the direction in which he has made a contribution to subsequent philosophizing the surest to grow in scope and fruitfulness.

IV

In speaking of Whitehead's doctrine of the identity of elements in human and physical subject-matter of experience, I quoted a sentence in which the general view took on a special concrete form. The sentence was to the effect that the connectedness of present conscious experience with experience immediately past "can be validly used to suggest categories applying to the connectedness of all occasions in nature." I propose to apply this statement to an account of what follows with respect to the problem of the subject-object relation, and the problem of the discrete-continuous, or individuality and relativity. That is to say, I wish to give in condensed form an outline of how Whitehead, starting from the *prima facie* fact that every temporally present immediate experience contains within itself elements of what is passing (which will soon *be* the past) and what is coming (which will be itself the immediately present as soon as the passing has become the past), goes on to derive from the fact an explanation both of the subject-object relation and the individuality-continuity relation, as universal traits of all the actualities of Nature.

The fact as to human experience is stated as follows: "Each moment of experience confesses itself to be a transition between two worlds, the immediate past and the immediate future. This is the persistent delivery of common-sense. Also this immediate future is immanent in the present with some degree of structural definition." In a previous passage, after speaking of "the immanence of past occasions in the occasions which are future, relatively to them," he goes on to say:

> It is evident that the future certainly is something for the present. The most familiar habits of mankind witness to this fact. Legal contracts, social understandings of every type, ambitions, anxieties, railway time-tables, are futile gestures of consciousness apart from the fact that the present bears in its own realized constitution relationships to a future beyond itself. Cut away the future and the present collapses, emptied of its proper content. Immediate existence requires the insertion of the future in the crannies of the present.[8]

The immanence of the immediately past in the immediately present is with equal assurance a direct fact of observation. Otherwise we should be always starting anew and never getting anywhere. Life would be unceasing interruptions with nothing to interrupt. As Whitehead acutely remarks, Hume was forced, in order to procure even a semblance of plausibility, to balance his extreme atomization with recognition of cumulative continuity in the force he attributes to habit and to anticipation. Without the presence of the past in the immediate present there would be no keeping track of what we are doing (including thinking), and no power of selecting and adapting means to effectuation of the plans which are the future in the present. We should not even be aware, I add on my own account, that what is called "consciousness" is in flux, unless the past somehow lingered in the present so that we are aware of change and contrast.

The influence of the new physics, with its theories of space-time, relativity, vectors and world-lines, paths of energy, differentiates the identification of actual entities with processes, asserted by Whitehead to exist, from everything of the kind traditionally ascribed to the Heraclitean river:—a point, it seems to me, not always taken into consideration by critics of his position. For in-

8. *Op. cit.*, 246.

stead of our not being able to step into the same river twice, we can step in twice—and many times, as we do whenever we make statements about an *object*—because the river or process exhibits temporal immanences. But even if the new physics was the original source of the idea, it does not seem probable that the idea of "prehension" would have acquired the broad sweep now marking it without explicit observation of the facts of immediate experience. The interpretation given by Whitehead of the subject-object structure is a fundamental instance of the peculiar kind of "prehension" which is seen in the presence of past and future in every immediately present experience.

For he agrees with the view of (modern) philosophy that the relation of subject-object "is the fundamental structural pattern of experience . . . but not in the sense in which subject-object is identified with knower-known." The ground of his dissent from this identification (which has so controlled modern epistemology as to make it impossible for any one view to win general acceptance over against other views) is suggested in the sentence after the one just quoted: "I contend that the notion of mere knowledge is a high abstraction, and that conscious discrimination itself is a variable factor only present in the more elaborate examples of occasions of experience."[9] However, the next sentence reads, "The basis of experience is emotional," and the context indicates that Whitehead is chiefly interested in showing that the fundamental connection of actual occasions is that of taking over "affective tone," or a connection in which things have "concern" one for another. Although this aspect of his doctrine tends to dominate his interpretation of that temporal immanence which is manifested in determination of a present experience by retention and anticipation, nevertheless the latter is so involved in Whitehead's account of the "subject-object" structure, that I confine my account to this point, reserving what I have to say about its subordination to a superior emphasis upon emotion and affection till later. Anticipating here the gist of my later critical remarks, I would say his emphasis upon the emotional seems to be the result of the failure to adopt and carry through consistently his interpretation in terms of *active energies*. For this procedure would have resulted in a *functional* interpretation of "identical ele-

9. *Op. cit.*, 225f.

ments," while as it is, Whitehead seems to fall back upon identity of *contents*.

The chapter in which the subject-object structure of experience is discussed is clothed in language not readily understandable when it is taken in isolation from the system which gives words their technical meanings. However, I shall quote a passage and then venture upon an interpretation through a paraphrase.

> An occasion of experience is an activity, analysable into modes of functioning which jointly constitute its process of becoming. Each mode [of experience] is analysable into the total experience as [an] active subject, and into the thing or object with which the special activity is concerned. . . . An object is anything performing this function of a datum provoking some special activity of the occasion in question. Thus subject and object are relative terms. An occasion is a subject in respect to its special activity concerning an object; and anything is an object in respect to its provocation of some special activity within a subject.[10]

Any difficulties that attend grasp of the meaning of this passage will be mitigated, if not dissipated, I think, if one bears in mind a certain duality of relationship. We begin with the fact that every occasion or actual existence is a temporal process. When we observe, without preconception, the nature of the becoming which forms the process, we see that it is aroused or provoked by some other actual and active occasion. In so far, the latter is object, and the process is subject, which started but which is carried forward to *special* or distinctive activity only by the stimulation it receives from another process. A process as subject does not merely undergo or experience the object. Its own actualization, as the single special process it is, is conditioned upon the nature of the provocation it receives.

If the account stopped at this point, it would, however, be defective. For the process which in the account just given forms the subject, and which is so to speak on the receiving end, is also an active factor in evoking the special activities of other things. In other words, occasions that are objects with respect to being

10. *Op. cit.*, 226f. This passage taken by itself would justify interpretation of Whitehead's doctrine in terms of a connection of active energies, or what I just called the functional interpretation.

things already given, and hence can function to provoke the special activities that determine other processes as subjects, are themselves subjects, having their own qualitative immediacy of being with respect to some other processes or given objects. Indeed, a process may achieve its own special forms of activity, and become thereby a subject in the full sense of the term, in the very interaction in which it operates as object in reference to some other process as subject. Reciprocally, it is true that the process which, from the standpoint first mentioned, is subject, becomes, as the process which it is moves forward, that which provokes the distinctive energies of other processes;—it takes on, that is to say, the function that defines an object. These considerations provide what I call the "duplicity"—though not a rigid dualism—in the subject-object structure. It follows that the subject-object relation in cases of deliberate or conscious knowledge is a specialized case of this general form of interconnectedness of the energies constituting processes as actual entities.

In discussing the subject-object relation we have, of necessity, trenched upon considerations which are pertinent to determination of the meaning of the discrete-continuous, individual-associational, relation. Indeed, at times I am not sure but that it was the problem in this latter form that was the primary factor in initiation of the distinctive elements in Whitehead's system. In any event, the need for reconstructing the doctrine of independent Newtonian atoms, which was forced by the doctrine of relativity as well as by that of quanta, brought the problem of atomicity-continuity into the foreground. Hence we have the intimate connection of this problem with the subject-object problem, a closeness that is contained in the passage in which it is said that "subject" is a name for "an actual entity in its immediacy of self-attainment when it stands out for itself alone. . . ."[11] It constitutes atomicity in physical occasions as it determines what we call individuality in human occasions. As in the latter we find both "distinguishable individualities" and continuity in the form of "personal identity," so in the former "we should expect a doctrine of quanta, where the individualities of the occasions are relevant, and a doctrine of continuity where the conformal transference of subjective form is the dominating fact."[12]

11. *Op. cit.*, 227.
12. *Op. cit.*, 239.

The meaning of the last clause of the sentence just quoted may not be readily understandable apart from reference to the places in which the phrase "conformal transference" is explained. For the purpose of the present theme, however, it may suffice to identify its meaning in terms of the immanence of the past in the present, thereby involving the way in which the present, in spite of its relative novelty as present, is subordinated to what the past inserts in it. The meaning could then be paraphrased as follows: The process of self-attainment is durational and, in its dependence upon given "objects," extensional. It is not so much a name for the process as a whole as for its "decisive moment." Although in a certain sense "self-originating," it is not literally self-achieving, since the latter is a matter of connectedness. When the special activities are relatively complete, the subject (a functional term, be it recalled) takes on that function which defines an object, and thereby it gives direction to other occasions which, like itself, would remain aborted potentialities unless given direction from what, in a certain sense, is external and "objective." The self-attainment of qualitative immediacy and finality (of individuality) is then a phase, though a decisive and outstanding one, of a process having continuity. Or, in Whitehead's own words, "The individual immediacy of an occasion is the final unity of subjective form, which is the occasion as an absolute reality. This immediacy is its moment of *sheer individuality, bounded on either side by essential relativity.*" [13]

V

I recall the fact that my discussion is limited to statement of what I take to be that which provides the most direct clew for entering into the system of Whitehead, so that the special points brought up are by way of illustrating the central theme. The new philosophical departure initiated by deep reflection upon the general significance of the new physics in its contrast with Newtonian cosmology was, as I have said, carried through by taking human experience to be a specialization of the traits of nature thus disclosed. When so taken, it was possible, indeed, was necessary, to turn around and use the specialized traits in in-

13. *Op. cit.*, 227. (Italics not in original text.)

terpretation of physical occasions. This procedure is the source, in my opinion, of the immense provocative and directive power of Whitehead's thought in the present critical juncture of philosophy. This opinion is the reason I limit my discussion to it, omitting reference to the multitude of special themes upon which Whitehead has shed abundant light. I turn now to certain matters in which Mr. Whitehead's treatment has aroused queries and uncertain misgivings. I begin with the following question: What, after all, does he take the task and office of philosophy to be? If, in discussing this question, I quote passages which seem to indicate two different views about this matter, it is not for the cheap purpose of pointing out inconsistencies—which in any case may be verbal rather than actual. It is for the sake of the possible bearing of what can be looked upon as two different strains upon an issue that is discussed later.

What may be called the official view of philosophy is set forth in a passage in which, after saying that the business of philosophy is to frame "descriptive generalization" (a statement in itself neutral to the problem I am raising), he goes on to say that the generalizations should be such as to form "a *coherent, logical, necessary system of general ideas* in terms of which every element of our experience can be interpreted. Here 'interpretation' means that *each element shall have* the character of a particular instance of the general scheme." [14] The italicized words of this passage suggest the kind of structure exhibited in pure mathematics. It seems to go much further than the mere statement—to which no exception can be taken—that the different portions of any philosophical scheme must hang together. For it makes, if I understand it aright, an assertion about what the constituents of nature itself *must* be in and of themselves. This conception of the nature and office of philosophy is in line with the classic tradition, according to which philosophy is that branch of theory which tells, in the theoretical form appropriate to knowledge as knowledge, the story of the ultimate metaphysical or ontological structure of the universe. In connection with Whitehead's frequent recurrence to the "Seven Notions" of Plato,[15] he expressly states that all philosophy is in fact "an endeavour to obtain a co-

14. *Op. cit.*, 285; cited there from p. 4 of the author's *Process and Reality*. (Italics not in original text.)
15. *Op. cit.*, 171–2, 188, 203, 241–2, 354, 366.

herent system out of some modification of these notions" (p. 354). Again, it is expressly said that "The order of nature expresses the characters of the real things which jointly compose the *existences* to be found in nature. When we understand the *essences* of these things, we *thereby know* their mutual relations to each other."[16]

Assignment of ontological priority to general characters and essences, and subordination to them of the existences actually observed in nature accords, to all appearances, not simply with the Platonic point of view, but with the assimilation of the proper subject-matter of philosophy (the constitution of nature) to that of mathematical theory. Hence it is legitimate to quote in this connection the following passage:

> The general science of mathematics is concerned with the investigation of patterns of connectedness in abstraction from the particular relata and the particular modes of connection. . . . The essential connectedness of things can never be safely omitted. This is the doctrine of the thoroughgoing relativity which infects the universe and which makes the totality of things as it were a Receptacle uniting all that happens.[17]

Such passages seem to be intended to convey the meaning implied in the expression that it is the business of philosophy to frame a system in which "each element shall have the character of a particular instance of a general scheme." Thereby they seem to warrant the conclusion that the phrase saying that general characters or *essences* constitute natural *existences* is to be taken literally. Deficiency of my own intellectual grasp may be the cause of my belief that this entire strain of thought substitutes abstract logical connectedness for the concrete existential *temporal* connectedness upon which I have based my interpretation of Whitehead's system. It is enough, in any case, to make me wonder whether I am on the right track when I make that interpretation.

Yet there are passages that give a freer and perhaps looser view of the office of philosophy, passages in which it is affirmed that the "gifts of philosophy" are "insight and foresight, and a sense of the worth of life, in short, that sense of *importance which nerves all civilized effort* . . . ," a passage which ends by saying

16. *Op. cit.*, 142. (Italics not in the original text.)
17. *Op. cit.*, 197.

that "Philosophy is an attempt to clarify those fundamental beliefs [connected with fears, hopes, judgment of what is worth
while] which finally determine the emphasis of attention that is
the base of character." [18]

A philosophy of experience that is thoroughgoing and systematic in its treatment of experience will, it seems to me, treat philosophy itself as a form of experience. It will realize that this
statement is true not only of the philosophies put forward by
others but of the philosophy one is now and here engaged in putting forth. It will realize that philosophies, itself included, are
not outside intellectual reports upon subject-matters of experience that are complete and finished in themselves, but that that
philosophy is an experimental effort at purification, continua-
tion and extension of those elements of things already experienced that commend themselves to critical judgment as worthy,
while it operates upon the basis of knowledge as wide and accurate as possible. It will necessarily look to what is known for
clews and for means of testing. But it will not take itself to be a
kind of knowledge. It will not be concerned with just reporting
and "explaining" in a coherent way the things that are valid in
past experiences. It will concern itself with the conditions under
which they have arisen for the sake of being better able to form
plans by which they may be reinforced and expanded. It will be
in so far a genetic account of experience. When a new mode and
object of experience is anticipated or actually brought into being
it will ask, without ceasing, after its *consequences*. It will be a
functional account of experience. Report, even in the most systematic fashion, of subject-matters and contents, of even the
most "universal" and "essential" characters will be subordinated
to determination of what will follow in consequence of them:—
as a result, namely, of the way in which existential incarnations
operate for good and for evil.

I may appear to have abandoned the philosophy of Whitehead
to set forth my own idea of what philosophy is. But what I am
actually trying to do is to state my uncertainty, when all is said
and done, of just what course is followed by Mr. Whitehead. Of
one thing I am quite sure. He has opened an immensely fruitful

18. *Op. cit.*, 125. (Italics not in original text.) Cf. what is said on pp. 203–4 of
    op. cit.

new path for subsequent philosophy to follow, and has accomplished this task by wedding observable facts of physical experience to observable facts of human experience. The result is an almost incomparable suggestiveness on all sorts of topics—in case a mind is not closed to suggestion from a new source. But I am not sure that he does not frequently block and divert his own movements on the road he is opening by subjecting his conclusions to a combination of considerations too exclusively derived from a combination of mathematics with excessive piety toward those historic philosophers from whom he has derived valuable suggestions.

I have little sympathy with most of the criticisms that are passed upon Mr. Whitehead on the score of the terminology he uses. I find myself in complete agreement with what he has said about the limitations the inherited state of language places upon development of new ideas. And I fail to see how anyone who has struggled to get beyond restatement, in slightly changed verbal form, of old ideas can fail to sympathize with Whitehead's struggles to find words to convey ideas which have not been previously fixed in conventional modes of expression. Consequently, if I mention by way of adverse criticism his use of a mentalistic vocabulary, illustrated by such words as emotion, enjoyment, etc., etc., in his description of what are usually called physical phenomena, it is only because that usage seems to me to arise from that aspect of his philosophy in which cognitive report of existing subject-matter gets the better of a *genetic-functional* account made in behalf of possibilities of experience not yet adequately realized.

It is one thing, marking to my mind a great advance, to see and say that there must be something homologous in the material of physical science and that of feeling, ideas, emotion and enjoyment as they occur in human experience. But for the purpose of discovery of better possibilities and the criticism of what exists all that is needed in the way of homology is correspondence of *functions*. Insistence upon identity of content tends, I believe, to obscuration of what is philosophically important. One can thoroughly agree with Whitehead when for example he says: "The mere phrase that 'physical science is an abstraction,' is a confession of philosophic failure. It is the business of rational thought to describe the more concrete fact from which that abstraction is derivable." But one may unite such agreement with deep regret that a previous sentence reads: "The notion of physical energy, which is at the base of physics, must then be conceived as an abstraction from the complex energy, *emotional and purposeful,* inherent in the subjective form of the *final* synthesis in which each occasion completes itself."[19] That the statement does not appear to be in harmony with his own theory according to which attainment of a subjective form is not final but marks a selected moment in an ongoing process may be only a technical matter. But in what the passage stands for, it appears to repeat that conversion of moral idealism, the idealism of action, into ontological idealism or "spiritualism," a conversion which the history of thought demonstrates to be the fatal weakness of the whole movement initiated by Plato and Aristotle. It is doubtless true, as Mr. Whitehead has said, that the reaction against dogmatic and imposed systematizations marking so many historic philosophies, has led other thinkers to undue neglect of the kind of system that is important. But the abstract formalization that defines systematization upon the model provided by mathematics does not shut out the possibility of that kind of system in which what is known about Nature, physical and human, is brought to bear upon intelligent *criticism* of what exists (and hence is capable of being *known*) and upon construction of alternatives, of possibilities, which the play of free critical intelligence indicates to be better worth while. The substance of Whitehead's system I find to be of the latter sort; its formal statements seem to me often to lean in the former direction.

19. *Op. cit.,* 239. (Italics not in original text.)

Nature in Experience

The topic announced for this session is capable of two interpretations. When it was communicated to me I took it to mean that the subject for discussion was the relation between the theory of experience and the theory of nature. When the two papers we have just heard were sent to me I found that impression borne out in part. But it also became clear that the topic could be interpreted broadly so that anything I have written concerning either nature or experience is open for consideration. I had then to decide how should I plan my reply. I have adopted the first of the two versions. It has the advantage of enabling me to centralize what I have to say, since I should otherwise have to disperse what I have to say over a large variety of topics. It has the disadvantage that it may seem to show lack of respect for some quite important criticisms that are passed over, and perhaps that of accepting as sound the interpretations upon which the criticisms rest.

In this dilemma the finally decisive consideration was that the course which enables me to introduce more unity and organization serves also to focus attention upon a problem which is so central in philosophy that it must be met and dealt with by all schools. The theme of the Carus Lectures, to which we are having the pleasure of listening, brings to our attention the importance of the category of perspectives, and this matter of perspectives is basic in the issue of the connection between nature and experience. I find that with respect to the hanging together of various problems and various hypotheses in a perspective de-

[First published in *Philosophical Review* 49 (March 1940): 244–58, from an address at the American Philosophical Association symposium on Dewey's Concepts of Experience and Nature, at Columbia University on 28 December 1939, in honor of his eightieth birthday. For Morris R. Cohen's and William Ernest Hocking's addresses to which this is a reply, see this volume, Appendixes 1 and 2.]

termined by a definite point of view, I have a system. In so far I have to retract disparaging remarks I have made in the past about the need for system in philosophy.

The peculiar importance in philosophy of a point of view and of the perspective it institutes is enhanced by the fact that a fairly large number of alternative points of view have been worked out in the history of philosophy in terms of the ways in which the world looks from them; that is to say, in terms of the leading categories by which the things of the world are to be understood. The significations attached to words and ideas which recur in practically every system tend to become fixed till it seems as if no choice were left, save to give the names (and the problems to which they relate) the import sanctioned by some one or other past philosophic point of view. In the degree in which a philosophy involves a shift from older points of view and from what is seen in their perspectives, both its author and those to whom he addresses himself find themselves in difficulties. The former has to use words that have meanings fixed under conditions of more or less alien points of view and the latter have to engage in some kind of imaginative translation.

The bearing of this general remark upon the present theme has to do first of all with the word "experience" and the allied word "empiricism." There is a long tradition of empiricism in the story of philosophy; upon the whole the tradition is particularistic and nominalistic, if not overtly sensationalistic, in its logic and ontology. When empiricism has escaped from the limits thereby set it has, upon the whole, been through making human experience the broken but still usable ladder of ascent to an absolute experience, and there has been a flight to some form of cosmic idealism. Presentation of a view of experience which puts experience in connection with nature, with the cosmos, but which would nevertheless frame its view of experience on the ground of conclusions reached in the natural sciences, has trouble in finding ways of expressing itself which do not seem to lead into one or the other of these historically sanctioned alternative perspectives.

There is a circularity in the position taken regarding the connection of experience and nature. Upon one side, analysis and interpretation of nature is made dependent upon the conclusions of the natural sciences, especially upon biology, but upon a biology that is itself dependent upon physics and chemistry. But when I say "dependent" I mean that the intellectual instrumentalities, the organs, for understanding the new and distinctive material of experienced objects are provided by the natural sciences. I do *not* mean that the material of experienced things *qua* experienced must be translated into the terms of the material of the physical sciences; that view leads to a naturalism which denies distinctive significance to experience, thereby ending in the identification of naturalism with mechanistic materialism.

The other aspect of the circle is found in the fact that it is held that experience itself, even ordinary gross macroscopic experience, contains the materials and the processes and operations which, when they are rightly laid hold of and used, lead to the methods and conclusions of the natural sciences; namely, to the very conclusions that provide the means for forming a theory of experience. That this circle exists is not so much admitted as claimed. It is also claimed that the circle is not vicious; for instead of being logical it is existential and historic. That is to say, if we look at human history and especially at the historic development of the natural sciences, we find progress made from a crude experience in which beliefs about nature and natural events were very different from those now scientifically authorized. At the same time we find the latter now enable us to frame a theory of experience by which we can tell *how* this development out of gross experience into the highly refined conclusions of science has taken place.

I come now to certain topics and criticism to be dealt with on the basis of the idea of this circular relation. The most inclusive criticism of my friend Morris Cohen is suggested, I think, by the word "anthropocentric" in the title of his paper; it is expressed in the saying that my absorption in human experience prevents me from formulating any adequate theory of non-human or physical nature. In short, it is held that the fact—which is not denied to be a fact—that experience involves a human element limits a philosophy that makes experience primary to human affairs as its sole material; hence it does not admit of propositions about such things as, say, the origin of life on earth or the events of geological ages preceding the advent of man and hence, of necessity, human experience.

Now there is a problem here which every empirical philosophy must meet; it can evade the challenge only to its own damage. Yet the problem is not confined to empiricism; the existence of experience is a fact, and it is fact that the organs of experience, the body, the nervous system, hands and eyes, muscles and senses, are means by which we have access to the non-human world. It would seem then as if the philosophy which denies that it is possible for experienced things and processes to form a road into the natural world must be controlled by an underlying postulate that there is a breach of continuity between nature and man and hence between nature and human experience. At all events, a fundamental question is raised. Is experience itself natural, a doing or manifestation of nature? Or is it in some genuine sense extranatural, sub-natural or supernatural, something superimposed and alien? At all events, this is the setting in which I shall place and interpret some of the more basic criticisms passed upon my views.

(1) There are traits, qualities, and relations found in things experienced, in the things that are typically and emphatically matters of human experience, which do not appear in the objects of physical science; namely, such things as immediate qualities, values, ends. Are such things inherently relevant and important for a philosophical theory of nature? I have held that philosophical empiricism must take the position that they are intrinsically pertinent. I have written (and Cohen has quoted): "It is as much a part of the real being of atoms that they give rise in time, under increasing complications of relationships, to qualities of blue and sweet, pain and beauty, as that they have, at a certain cross-section of time, extension, mass or weight." Now whether this statement is correct or false, it is simply an illustration of what any theory must hold which sees things in the perspective determined by the continuity of experience with nature.[1]

I also write that domination of man by desire and reverie is as pertinent to a philosophical theory of nature as is mathematical physics. The point of this statement is also truistic, given the point of view of the continuity of experience with nature. It certainly is not countered by the statement that "For the under-

---

1. "Giving rise to" implies no particular theory as to causal determination, and the word "atom" is used illustratively. The point made would be the same if at some time in the future natural science abandoned the atomic theory and put something else in the place of atoms.

standing of the general processes of nature throughout time and space, the existence of human reverie and desire is surely not as illuminating as are considerations of mathematical physics." For the whole point of the passage is that qualities of experienced things that are not the least bit illuminating for the understanding of nature in physical science are as important for a philosophy of nature as the thing most illuminating, namely mathematical physics—a view, as I have said, which any theory making experience continuous with nature is bound to hold.

This point gains more general philosophical significance because of the fact that qualities and values, which are not traits of the objects of natural science as these are now ascertained to be, were once completely fused with the material of what was taken to be science. The whole classic cosmology or theory of nature is framed in this sense. It is the progress of natural science itself that has destroyed this cosmology. As the history of modern philosophy proves, this destruction brought about that crisis which is represented by the bifurcation expressed in the dualistic opposition of subjective and objective, mind and matter, experience and nature. The problem involved is one which all philosophies alike must face. Any one view, such as the one I have set forth, can be intelligently criticized only from the standpoint of some alternative theory, while theories of bifurcation have their own difficulties and troubles, as the history of modern thought abundantly proves.[2] Affirmation of the continuity of experience with nature has its difficulties. But they are not grasped nor the theory refuted by translating what it says into terms of a theory which assumes that the presence of the human factor in experience precludes getting from experience to the non-human or physical.

(2) The passage which has been cited about the "real being" of the atom contains an explicit contrast between nature as judged

2. While Cohen, it seems to me, has somewhat overstated my opposition to Greek and medieval philosophy, it is just the fact of the enormous change that has taken place in the method and conclusions of natural science which is the ground of my insistence upon need for a radical change in the theory of nature and of knowledge. Upon this point, it seems to me that it is rather Cohen than myself who fails to attach sufficient importance to physical science in its relation to philosophy. Piety to classic thought is an admirable trait; but a revolution in the physical constituents of nature demands considerable change in cosmological theory, as change in the method of inquiry demands reconstruction *in* (though not *of*) logic.

in a short-time span or "cross-section" and in a long temporal span—one long enough to cover the emergence of human beings and their experiences. In order to be understood, what I have said about genesis and function, about antecedents and consequences, has to be placed in the perspective suggested by this emphasis upon the need of formulating a theory of nature and of the connections of man *in* (not *to*) nature on the basis of a temporal continuum.

What is basically involved is that some changes, those for example which terminate in the things of human experience, form a *history*, or a set of changes marked by development or growth. The dichotomy of the old discussion as to whether antecedents or ends are of primary importance in forming a theory of nature is done away with when growth, development, history is taken to be primary. Genesis and ends are of equal importance, but their import is that of terms or boundaries which delimit a history, thereby rendering it capable of description. The sentence before the one about the atom, reads, for example, as follows: "For knowledge, 'cause' and 'effect' have a partial and truncated being"; the paragraph as a whole is devoted to criticizing the notion that causal conditions have a "reality" superior to that of outcomes or effects. It is argued that the prevalent view which attributes superior rank to them results from hypostatizing a *function*: the function of causal conditions as means of control (ultimately, the *sole* means of control) is converted into a direct ontological property. Moreover, the chapter of which the paragraph is a part is devoted to showing that while Existence as process and as history involves "ends," the change from ancient to modern science compels us to interpret ends relatively and pluralistically, because as limits of specifiable histories.

Of the many special points which follow from this basic element in my theory of the connection of experience with nature— as itself an historical outcome or "end," I shall here deal with only one. In what I have said about meanings my critic finds an undue importance attached to consequences; in what I say (in a discussion devoted to a special problem) about the background of Greek philosophy he finds an equally one-sided importance attached to genesis. That in discussion of one particular history the emphasis with respect to a particular problem falls upon results, and in another history discussed in respect to another particular problem, emphasis falls upon antecedents, involves no inconsistency. With respect to consequences in their connection with meaning and verification I have repeatedly and explicitly insisted upon the fact that there is no way of telling what the consequences are save by discovery of antecedents, so that the latter are necessary and yet are subordinate in function.[3]

(3) Another aspect of the perspective determined by the point of view expressed in the continuity of nature and experience concerns the relation of theory and practical ends, particularly of physical science and morals. It is about this point, unless I am mistaken, that the fundamental criticisms of Cohen cluster, since the passages upon which the criticisms are based are interpreted in another perspective than that in which they are stated. The fact that I have, quite consistently and persistently, as far as I am aware, insisted that inquiry should follow the lead of its subject-matter[4] and not be subordinated to any end or motive having an external source, is less important than the fact that any other view would be contradictory to my main theses regarding (i) the place of the natural sciences in the formation of the ends and values of practical life, and (ii) the importance of the experimental method of the natural sciences as the model for the sciences involving human practice, or the social and moral disciplines.

The view I have put forward about the nature of that to which the adjective "physical" applies is that, while it is arrived at by following out clews given in directly experimental matter, it constitutes the *conditions* upon which all the qualities and terminal values, the consummations, of experience, depend. Hence those things which are physical are the sole means that exist for con-

3. My use of the compound word "genetic-functional" to describe what I regard as the proper method of philosophy is, then, directly linked to the position taken regarding the temporal continuum.

4. I would call attention to one passage, found on pp. 67–68 of *The Quest for Certainty* (cf. p. 228) [*Later Works* 4:55, 182]. The text states the nature of the ambiguity in the word "theoretical" which is the source of misunderstanding, the confusion of the attitude of the *inquirer* with the nature of the *subject-matter* inquired into. It is explicitly said that the former must be theoretical and cognitive, purged of personal desire and preference, marked by willingness to subordinate them to the lead of subject-matter. But it is also said that only inquiry itself can determine whether or not *subject-matter* contains practical conditions and qualities. To argue from the strictly theoretical character of the motives of the inquirer, from the necessity for "disinterested curiosity," to the nature of that investigated is a kind of "anthropocentrism" of which I should not wish to be guilty.

trol of values and qualities. To read anything extraneous into them, to tamper in any way with the integrity of the inquiry of which they are the product, would thus be to nullify the very function in terms of which the *physical* as such is defined. I have even gone so far as to ascribe the backwardness of the human, the practical, sciences in part to the long period of backwardness of the physical sciences themselves and in part to the refusal of moralists and social scientists to utilize the physical, especially the biological, material that is at their disposal.

(4) These considerations bring me to my view regarding the nature and function of philosophy, a point which I think will be found crucial for the interpretation, and hence the criticism, of the passages upon which Cohen bases his view that I have pretty systematically subordinated inquiry, reflection, and science to extraneous practical ends. For speaking of *philosophy* (not of science) I have constantly insisted that since it contains value-considerations within itself, indispensable to its existence as philosophy—in distinction from science—it has a "practical," that is a *moral* function, and I have held that since this element is inherent, the failure of philosophies to recognize and make explicit its presence introduces undesirable properties into them, leading them on one side to make claims of being purely cognitive, which bring them into rivalry with science, and on the other side to neglect of the field in which they may be genuinely significant, that of possible guidance of human activity in the field of values.

The following passage is fairly typical of what I have said: "What would be its [philosophy's] office if it ceased to deal with the problem of reality and knowledge at large? In effect, its function would be to facilitate the fruitful interaction of our cognitive beliefs, our beliefs resting upon the most dependable methods of inquiry, with our practical beliefs about the values, the ends and purposes, that should control human action in the things of large and liberal human import." [5] Now whether this view of the nature of philosophic as distinct from distinctively scientific inquiry is correct or incorrect, the following points are so involved that the view cannot be understood without taking them into account: (i) It is one aspect of the general position of the experiential continuum constituted by the interaction of different modes

5. *The Quest for Certainty*, 36–37 [*Later Works* 4:29].

of experienced things, in this case of the scientific and the moral; (ii) it gives philosophy a subject-matter distinct from the subject-matter of science and yet inherently connected with the latter, namely, the bearing of the conclusions reached in science ("the most dependable methods of inquiry") upon the value-factors involved in human action; (iii) there is no subordination of the results of knowledge to any preconceived scheme of values or pre-determined practical ends (such as fixes the usual meaning of "reform"), but rather emphasis upon the reconstruction of existing ends and values in behalf of more generous and liberal human activities.

Now whether this view of philosophy is right or wrong (and my critic says nothing about what he takes to be the subject-matter and function of philosophy in connection with, or distinction from, that of science), if what is said about philosophy is taken to be said about science or about reflection in general, the meanings which result will be justly exposed to all the criticisms passed upon them.[6] It is perhaps significant that Cohen himself virtually recognizes the presence of the human and moral factor in philosophy as distinct from science. For the "resignation" which he finds to be the lesson taught by a just theory of nature is surely a human and moral factor; it remains such even if I have over-emphasized the traits of courage and active responsibility, as I may have done in view of the fact that resignation and the purely consolatory office of philosophy have received more than enough emphasis in the historical tradition. But I have also pointed out that the classic or catholic version of that tradition recognizes that this lesson of passive resignation is not final; that

6. It often happens in addition that what is said about a particular type of philo-sophic system, in a context which qualifies what is said, is taken by Cohen absolutely, without qualification. For example, if the reader will consult the passage (*The Influence of Darwin*, 298–299 [*Early Works* 5:21]) containing the words "luxury," "nuisance," etc., it will be seen that instead of referring to philosophy in general or even to a particular historical school or schools—much less to impartial inquiry—it is qualified by a succession of "ifs." And the passage which says (*Creative Intelligence*, 60 [*Middle Works* 10:42]) that phi-losophy is of account only if it affords guidance to action, occurs in a para-graph dealing with the grounds for the difference between the popular and the professional reception of "pragmatism," not in a statement of my own view, although the idea that philosophy is love of wisdom as distinct from love of knowledge and that "philosophy is the guide of life" is not peculiarly new nor peculiarly a product of pragmatism.

it has to be supplemented by a divine institution which undertakes the positive function of guidance, and that in so far the practical logic of the situation is with the Church rather than with traditional philosophy which is minus institutional support and aid. As far as I am concerned the issue is between a theory of experience in nature which renders experienced things and operations impotent, and a theory which would search for and utilize the *things in experience* that are capable of progressively providing the needed support and guidance.[7] Finally, while I am grateful and deeply appreciative of Cohen's approval of my personal liberalism, I must add not only that this liberalism is definitely rooted in the very philosophy to which he takes exception, but that any theory of activity in social and moral matters, liberal or otherwise, which is not grounded in a comprehensive philosophy seems to me to be only a projection of arbitrary personal preference.

I come now, rather belatedly, to the criticisms of my other friendly critic, Ernest Hocking. If I grasp aright the point of view from which his criticisms are made, it does not involve the postulate of separation of experience from nature that is found in Cohen's criticisms, but rather a point of departure similar to mine. In that respect, Cohen's paper involves a criticism of Hocking as well as of me, and reciprocally. The trouble with my views lies, then, according to Hocking, in the account I have given of experience, primarily in my failure to give its due place and weight to thought in relation to knowledge and to the world of reality. I am grateful to Hocking for his explicit recognition of the place given in my theory of knowledge to thought and theory, to his recognition that in my theory "the scientific process is intellectualized to the last limit." His conclusion that, since I have done this, I am logically bound to go farther and take the position that "the more thought, the more reality," thus has a relevancy to my position not possessed by criticisms based upon the notion that I have adopted the depreciatory view of thought, theory, and abstraction characteristic of traditional nominalistic empiricism.

---

7. Since readers cannot be expected to look up all quotations made from my writings, I will say that the sentence about the capacity of man to shape his own destiny is part of a passage about the atmosphere of the eighteenth-century thought which put forth the doctrine of the indefinite perfectibility of man. My own view is much more qualified.

(1) However, in criticizing sensational and particularistic empiricism and in insisting upon the indispensable role of thought and theory in the determination of scientific objects, I have not gone so far as to deny the really indispensable role of observed material and the processes of observation. On the contrary, I have criticized traditional rationalism, not indeed for pointing out the necessary operational presence of thought, but for its failure to recognize the essential role of observation to bring into existence that material by which objects of thought are tested and validated—or the contrary—so as to be given something more than a hypothetical status. I quote from Hocking the following passage, speaking of such things as atoms and electrons: "Dewey will not say that I observe them, but only that I think them. I agree. But is the atom then less real than the chair?" My view more completely stated is that *at present* atom and electron are objects of thought *rather* than of observation. But, instead of denying the necessity of observed material, or even the possibility of observation of objects that are atomic in the scientific sense, I have held that the theoretical value of the atom consists in its ability, as a hypothesis or *thought,* to direct observations experimentally and to coordinate their results. The mere observation of something which if it were observed by a physicist would be an atom is not, however, observation of an atom as a *scientific object* unless and only in so far as it meets the requirements of definition which has been attained by a set of systematic inferences, that is, of the function to which the name thought is given. The place of differential equations in the formulation of the atom as a scientific theoretical and hypothetical object is undeniable. But the equations as far as atoms as *existences* are concerned (in distinction from their function in facilitating and directing further inferences) state conditions to be satisfied by any observed material if it is to be warrantably asserted to *be* atomic.

(2) The formulation of the conditions to be satisfied takes a form which prescribes operations that are to be performed in instituting and interpreting observations. This fact leads to consideration of what Hocking says about operations. *If* thought and its object *as* object of thought were as complete and final apart from any connection with observed things as Hocking assumes them to be, then the operational view of scientific objects would indeed hang idly and unsupported in the void. To place, as Hock-

ing does, interest in the entities of differential equations in opposition to interest in operations is to overlook, it seems to me, the fundamental thesis of operationalism; namely that these entities, as far as physics, including mathematical physics, is concerned, *are* formulations of operations to be performed in obtaining specified observed materials and determining whether or not that material answers to or satisfies certain conditions imposed upon it if it is to merit the name of a certain scientific object, atom, electron, or whatever. As I have frequently said, a given scientific person may occupy himself exclusively with the mathematical aspect of the matter, and do so fruitfully as far as the historic development of a science is concerned. But this fact taken by itself is not decisive about the actual place and function of the mathematical material.

(3) I come now to another criticism of Hocking's, connected with the "reality" part of his saying "the more thought, the more reality." My criticism of Hocking's criticism has up to this point concerned only the first part of his sentence. It amounts to saying that while he has not disrupted the continuity of experience with nature, he has, to my mind, broken off one aspect of experience, namely thought, from another aspect, that of perception. Further consequences of this artificial breach seem to me to be found in what he says about "reality." It is quite true, as he says, that one meaning of reality is the "independent being upon which other things depend"; and he finds this independent being in "the content of true judgment," a saying which seems to me to express in an almost flagrantly emphatic way the isolation of one mode of experience and its material from other modes and *their* things. For he goes on to say that Nature, as the content of true judgment or the object of perfect thought in its capacity of measure of knowledge, is the independent reality of which experience is the dependent derivative.

Now reality is, I fear, more than a double-barrelled word. Its ambiguity and slipperiness extend beyond the two significations which Hocking mentions in such a way as to affect the interpretation of "independence" and "dependence" in the view taken by him. For there is a definitely pragmatic meaning of "dependence" and "derivation," which affects the meaning of that most dangerous of all philosophical words, "reality." The objects of knowledge, when once attained, exercise, as I have already said, the function of *control* over other materials. Hence the latter in so far depend for their status and value upon the object of knowledge. The idea of the ether was dropped when it ceased to exercise any office of control over investigations. The idea of quanta has increased its role because of its efficacy and fertility in control of inquiries. But this interpretation of dependence is strictly functional. Instead of first isolating the object of knowledge or judgment and then setting it up in its isolation as a measure of the "reality" of other things, it connects the scientific object, genetically and functionally, with other things without casting the invidious shadow of a lesser degree of reality upon the latter.

(4) This consideration brings me to the fourth point in Hocking's paper upon which I shall comment. It is of course true that I have emphasized the temporal continuity of inquiry, and in consequence the dependence of conclusions reached at a given time upon the methods and results of previous investigations, and their subjection to modification in subsequent inquiries. But, as far as I can see, the idea that this view indefinitely defers possession and enjoyment of stable objects to the end of an infinite progression applies rather to Hocking's position than to mine. That is, if I held that thought is the only valid approach to "reality" and that the latter is the content of a perfect judgment, I should be troubled by the question of the worth, from the standpoint of reality, of all my present conclusions.

But I do not see that the question arises within the perspective of my own point of view. For in the latter, instead of there being isolation of the material of knowledge, there is its continual interaction with the things of other forms of experience, and the worth (or "reality") of the former is to be judged on the basis of the control exercised by it over the things of non-cognitive experiences and the increment of enriched meaning supplied to them. Even from the standpoint of knowledge by itself, inquiry produces such cumulative verification and stability that the prospect of future modification is an *added* value, just as in all other affairs of life those accomplishments that open up new prospects and new possibilities are enhanced, not depressed, by their power in this respect. But what is even more important is that, from the standpoint of the continuous interaction of the things of different modes of experience, the final test of the value of "contents of judgment" now attained is found not in their relation to the content of some final judgment, to be reached at the close of an infinite progression, but in what is done in the living present, what is done in giving enriched meaning to other things and in increasing our control over them.

In recurring to what I said at the outset about my choice of a theme, I wish to repeat that the limitation of my reply to criticisms passed upon my views only so far as they bear upon the problem of the connection of experience with nature is not intended to be evasive, nor does it evince lack of respect for criticisms I have not touched upon. I have not in the past been as unobservant or inattentive of criticisms as my good friend Ernest Hocking has humorously suggested. On the contrary, if my views have progressed either in clarity or in range, as I hope they have done, it is mainly because of what my critics have said and the thought I have given their criticisms. Given a point of view that determines a perspective and the nature and arrangement of things seen in that perspective, the point of view is, I suppose, the last thing to be seen. In fact it is never capable of being seen unless there is some change from the old point of view.

Criticisms are the means by which one is enabled to take, at least in imagination, a new point of view, and thus to re-see, literally to review and revise, what fell within one's earlier perspective. If I have succeeded today in making my views clearer to others than I have managed to do in my previous writings, it is because my critics have made their import clearer to myself. For that I am grateful to them, as I am deeply appreciative of the honor the Association and my friends Morris Cohen and Ernest Hocking have done me in giving time and thought to my writings.

The Vanishing Subject in the
Psychology of James

There is a double strain in the *Principles of Psychology* by William James. One strain is official acceptance of epistemological dualism. According to this view, the science of psychology centres about a *subject* which is "mental" just as physics centres about an *object* which is material. But James's analysis of special topics tends, on the contrary, to reduction of the subject to a vanishing point, save as "subject" is identified with the organism, the latter, moreover, having no existence save in interaction with environing conditions. According to the latter strain, subject and object do not stand for separate orders or kinds of existence but at most for certain distinctions made for a definite purpose *within* experience.

The first view is explicitly set forth by James in the following words:

> *The psychologist's attitude toward cognition* will be so important in the sequel that we must not leave it till it is made perfectly clear. *It is a thoroughgoing dualism.* It supposes two elements, mind knowing and thing known, and treats them as irreducible. . . . They just stand face to face in a common world, and one simply knows, or is known unto, its counterpart. This singular relation is not to be expressed in any lower terms, or translated into any more intelligible name. . . . Even in mere sense-impression the duplication of the object by an inner construction must take place. . . . The dualism of Object and Subject and their pre-established harmony are what the psychologist as such must assume, whatever ulterior monistic philosophy he may, as an individual who has the right also to be a metaphysician, have in reserve.[1]

1. *The Principles of Psychology,* Vol. I, pp. 218–220, passim. Italics in original text. Referred to hereafter as *Psychology.*

[First published in *Journal of Philosophy* 37 (24 October 1940): 589–99.]

The *Psychology* was published in 1890. Much of the book was written some years before. The material of the important chapter on the "Stream of Consciousness," which verbally is probably the most subjectivistic part of the whole book, was published in *Mind* in 1884.[2] In 1904 in his article "Does 'Consciousness' Exist?" he says of the "consciousness," which the passage quoted takes as the basis and source of the material of his *Psychology,* that it is "mere echo, the faint rumor left behind by the disappearing 'soul' upon the air of philosophy." And what is especially significant for the present theme, the tendency of the separate subject as knower to disappear even in the *Psychology,* he adds "for twenty years past I have mistrusted 'consciousness' as an entity; for seven or eight years past I have suggested its nonexistence to my students."[3] "Twenty years" takes his distrust well back of the date at which his *Psychology* appeared. A moderate amount of psycho-analysis might lead one to infer that the explicitness with which he states that the assumption of dualism is necessary for the psychologist means that he entertained doubt about the *ultimate* soundness of the dualistic position.

That he did not go further than he did go in his *Psychology* is not surprising in view of the state of the subject at the time he wrote. In view especially of the fact that he attacked both of the only two trends which then existed in psychology, namely, associationalist and "rational" psychology, one can understand why he hesitated to carry his scepticism to an even more radical extreme. For the only alternative to these two views that existed at that time was a dogmatic materialism with its "automaton" theory of psychological phenomena. In spite of the tenderness of James on the topic of the *soul* he wrote that there was no scientific need whatever for a substantial soul or permanent mind; he went so far as to give a strictly empirical account of personal identity.[4]

---

2. I say "verbally" because it is quite possible to translate "stream of consciousness" into "course of experience" and retain the substance of the chapter.

3. Essay reprinted in *Essays in Radical Empiricism,* p. 2 and p. 3.

4. For his tenderness see the *Principles of Psychology,* Vol. I, p. 181, where he says "The fact is that one cannot afford to despise any of these great traditional objects of belief." As to the substantial soul and permanent mind, see Vol. I, p. 346, where he says "As *psychologists,* we need not be metaphysical at all. The phenomena are enough, the passing Thought itself is the only *verifiable* thinker, and its empirical connection with the brain-process is the ultimate known law." As to personal identity, as evidence for a permanent substantial

His reduction of the "subject" to a "passing Thought" is itself sufficient proof of the way he whittled down the knowing subject. And it is worth special note that in one passage, written in direct connection with his discussion of the Self, he goes so far as to express a doubt about the existence of even a separate "thought" or mental state of any kind as the knower, saying that it might be held that "the existence of this thinker would be given to us rather as logical postulate than as that direct inner perception of spiritual activity which we naturally believe ourselves to have."[5] However, he dismisses this conclusion, although it is a direct result of his actual analysis, as "speculative" and says that speculations "contradict the fundamental assumption of *every* philosophic school. Spiritualists, transcendentalists, and empiricists alike admit in us a continual direct perception of the thinking activity in the concrete. However they may otherwise disagree, they vie with each other in the cordiality of their recognition of our *thoughts* as the one sort of existence which skepticism cannot touch" (pp. 304–305). But he adds in a footnote a remark that is especially significant in view of the article of 1904 to which reference has been made. For he says that there is one exception to the statement about all philosophical schools, namely, the important article of M. Souriau, the conclusion of which is "que la conscience n'existe pas." That James's own denial of the existence of consciousness involves a complete repudiation of the dualism earlier officially professed is obvious from the following words of his later essay in which he says what is denied is an "aboriginal stuff or quality of being, contrasted with that out of which material objects are made, out of which our thoughts of them are made."

Before taking up in detail the whittling down of the mental or psychical subject as it occurs in the *Psychology*, I shall say something about the position which, if it had been developed positively and in detail, would have rendered unnecessary from the start any reference even to the "passing thought" as that which remains from the old substantial subject. This position is sug-

---

subject or self, he was influenced by the recently discovered facts of split personality and wrote (Vol. I, p. 350), "The definitively closed nature of our personal consciousness is probably an average statistical resultant of many conditions, but not an elementary force or fact."

5. *Principles of Psychology*, Vol. I, p. 304.

gested in the passage already quoted in which James refers to the brain process as "the ultimate known law." James came to the study of psychology from a grounding in physiology in connection with a preparatory medical education. His naturalistic strain, as far as constructively stated, and its conflict with the professed epistemological dualism, was derived from this source. If it had been consistently developed it would have resulted in a biological behavioristic account of psychological phenomena. In his first expression of opposition to both the "rational" and the "associational" psychologies, he says that certain deficiencies in both of them proceed from their inability to take into account obvious physiological facts which demand recognition of the organism and the nervous system. He goes on to say that the Spencerian formula according to which biological and psychological phenomena are one in essence, both being adjustments of "inner" to "outer" relations, while very vague, is immensely more fertile than the old-fashioned rational psychology "because it takes into account the fact that minds inhabit environments which act on them and on which they in turn react."[6] On this side, James's fundamental doctrine is that psychological phenomena (called by him the *mental life*) are intermediate between impressions received from the environment and the responsive adjustments the organism makes to the environment. If what is involved in this view had been consistently maintained, the dualism that existed in Spencer's two sets of "inner" and "outer" relations would have been overcome, and organisms or personal beings, not "minds," would have been said to "inhabit the environment." The behavioral position is maintained when James says that "pursuance of future ends and choice of means for their attainment are the mark and criterion of presence of mentality in a phenomenon," since the passage suggests that the whole meaning of *mentality* consists in objectively observable facts of the kind mentioned. But as the matter is finally left it may be doubted whether James intended to go further than to say that this pursuance and choice is the external sign of something called "mental" operating behind. For he limits the scope of the statement by saying that the view just stated would be adopted as the mark and criterion by which to circumscribe the subject-matter of this

6. *Principles of Psychology,* Vol. I, p. 6.

work *as far as action enters in*.[7] The clause I have italicized indicates that he held to the existence of phenomena so "mental" in nature that action (behavior) does not enter into them. At the same time, the position of James is free from that defect of the latter "behaviorism" which locates behavior, and hence psychological phenomena, *inside* the organism. For he says that the function of the nervous system "is to bring each part into harmonious co-operation with every other" part so as to make possible acts which are of service in connection with the sensory impressions proceeding from the environment.[8]

Since the biological approach does not control subsequent analyses to the extent that the introductory chapters would by themselves have led one to expect, it is worth while to note instances in which it is definitely influential. The chief cases are the treatment of habit and the effect of practice. The former, treated as a biological factor having its basis in the constitution of matter, is said to be the "cause" of "association of ideas," and hence of retention and recollection, and also of imagination.[9] Even more significant in its implications (which, however, are not developed) is his statement that "attention and effort . . . seem in some degree subject to the law of habit, which is a material law."[10] The operation of practice, understood in terms of motor activities, is made central in discrimination. "Where . . . a distinction has no practical interest, where we gain nothing by analyzing a feature from out of the compound total of which it forms a part, we contract a habit of leaving it unnoticed."[11] He makes a great deal of Helmholtz's view that we notice "sensations" not *per se* but as "far as they enable us to judge rightly of the world about us; and our practice in discriminating between them usually goes only just far enough to meet this end" (p. 517). The ambiguity, noted later, between "sensation" as a strictly physiological process in the afferent structures and as a perceived quality of an object, influences James's treatment, since he seems to assume that the "sensation" is there all the time but is sometimes noted and sometimes not—a position all the more surprising because

7. *Principles of Psychology*, Vol. I, pp. 8 and 11.
8. *Ibid.*, p. 12.
9. *Ibid.*, pp. 566 and 653, and Vol. II, p. 44.
10. Vol. I, p. 126.
11. *Ibid.*, pp. 515–516.

of his elaborate criticism of the doctrine of "unconscious mental states." He uses such expressions as the following: "Helmholtz's law is that we leave all impressions unnoticed which are valueless to us as signs by which to *discriminate things*. At most such impressions fuse with their consorts into an aggregate effect." Only the influence of an inveterate dualism could lead James to call sensory processes "impressions."

The later pragmatism of James is implicit in what he says about reflective thinking or reasoning. "My thinking is first and last and always for the sake of doing, and I can only do one thing at a time." There are no "truer ways of conceiving [understanding or interpreting]" things than any others; there are "only more important ways; more frequently serviceable ways." [12] Finally, in contrast with the current theory of perception, James gives an account which is definitely biological and behavioral.

> We certainly ought not to say what usually is said by psychologists, and treat the perception as a sum of distinct psychic entities, the present sensation namely, *plus* a lot of images from the past, all "integrated" together in a way impossible to describe.

The simple and natural description is

> that the process aroused in the sense-organ has shot into various paths which habit has already organized in the hemispheres, and that instead of our having the sort of consciousness [perception] which would be correlated with the simple sensorial process, we have that which is correlated with this more complex process. [13]

When we ask why James did not develop his treatment in the direction indicated by these considerations, we come back to the influence exercised by the surviving metaphysical dualism. For as long as this dualism is postulated, the connection the nervous

12. Vol. II, pp. 333–336. On page 335 we read the following: "The essence of a thing is that one of its properties which is so *important for my interests* that in comparison with it I may neglect the rest." The important role of "interest" in the entire scheme of James's account of psychological phenomena is a well-known fact. Officially he assumes interest to be mentalistic. What he actually says about it is most readily understood in terms of the selections effected by motor factors in behavior.
13. *Ibid.*, Vol. II, pp. 80 and 79; cf. pp. 103–104.

system, including the brain, indubitably has with psychological phenomena is a "mystery," and the more detailed and complete the evidence for the connection the more the mystery deepens. The influence of the dualism is so strong that James does not follow out the implication of his hypothesis that the brain—and nervous system generally—functions as an organ in the behavior constituted by interaction of organism and environment. Consequently, instead of applying the idea to the description of each one of the diversity of observed psychological occurrences, showing how it links up in detail with the general doctrine of the function of the nervous system as an instrumentality of effective interaction of organism and environment, he goes so far as to express adherence to the most miraculous of all the theories about the "mystery," namely, the parallelism or pre-established harmony of physical and psychical.

There is indeed a problem. But it can be broken down into a large number of things to be investigated. It is not a wholesale metaphysical problem, but a special problem like that of any scientific inquiry: namely, the problem of discovering the conditions of the occurrence of an observed phenomenon. Certain experienced situations occur, some of them mainly emotive or affectional in quality; others that of knowledge of this or that thing. The question of how these experienced situations come into existence is important because knowledge of conditions is always a prerequisite of control. Knowledge of organic conditions is part of the knowledge required if having of desired experiences and not having of unwanted experiences is to come under our control, knowledge of environing conditions being, of course, the other part. Knowledge of processes in the nervous system and brain is an important, although far from exclusive, part of the required knowledge of organic conditions. But in principle there is no difference between discovering the cerebral conditions involved in a hallucinatory or a veridical perception and the chemical conditions involved in occurrence of water. The difference is one of greater complexity. But our comparative ignorance of concrete conditions in the case of situations, as matters of experience, does not make a "mystery" out of them.

I now come to discussion of some psychological matters where James admits that the duplication in an "inner construction" of what is experienced is no part of the fact which is observed, but is a later theoretical interpretation. In the passage about dualism, quoted at the outset, James says that this duplication is demanded even in the case of "mere sense impression." In his chapter on sensation James says:

> A *pure sensation is an abstraction;* and when we adults talk of our "sensations" we mean one of two things: either certain *objects,* namely, simple *qualities* or *attributes,* like *hard, hot, pain;* or else those of our thoughts in which acquaintance with these objects is least combined with knowledge about the relations of them to other things.[14]

The latter part of this sentence retains the reference to the inner "thought" as that which knows its outer counterpart. But James's sense for empirical fact caused him to recognize that in the actual experience of qualities as objects no reduplication in inner sensations is to be found. For immediately afterward he says:

> *The first sensation which an infant gets is for him the Universe.* . . . The infant encounters an object in which (though it be given in a pure sensation) all the "categories of the understanding" are contained. . . . Here the young knower [the infant, not a mental state] meets and greets his world. (P. 8.)

This position about sensory qualities is the one in line with the objective stand he takes whenever guided by evidence into the particular issue with which he is dealing.[15] The following passages are representative:

> Take the example of an altogether unprecedented experience, such as a new taste in the throat. Is it a subjective quality of feeling, or an objective quality felt? You do not even ask the question at this point. It is simply *that taste.* But if a doctor hears you describe it, and says: "Ha! now you know what *heartburn* is," then it becomes a quality already existent *extra mentem tuam* which you in turn have come upon and learned. The first spaces, times, things, qualities, experienced

14. *Principles of Psychology,* Vol. II, p. 3.
15. There is nothing intrinsically *sensory* about *red, hot, pain.* They are so named because experience has shown the importance of the organic apparatus by which they are mediated. That color is visual and sound auditory is an item of knowledge gained through study of the conditions of the *occurrence* of the quality; it is no part of the quality.

by the child probably appear, like the first heartburn, in this absolute way, as simple *beings,* neither in nor out of thought.[16]

This view is probably the germ of his later theory of "neutral entities." The direct empirical meaning of *neutral* in this connection would seem to be that of indifference to the distinction between subjective and objective, this distinction arising when the proper guidance of behavior requires that we be able to tell whether a given sound or color is a sign of an environing object or of some process within the organism. Unfortunately his later writings seem at times to give the impression that these entities are a kind of stuff out of which both the subjective and objective are made—instead of the distinction being a question of the kind of object to which a quality is *referred.* If the latter position is taken then one of the problems of the psychologist is to determine the conditions under which a given *reference* occurs, the question of proper reference being the same *kind* of question that comes up when we inquire whether a given sound is produced by gunshot or by backfiring of an automobile.

Again, James says that "experience, from the very first, presents us with concreted objects, vaguely continuous with the rest of the world which envelops them in space and time, and potentially divisible into inward elements and parts." This passage is meant to apply to primitive as well as to highly elaborated experience of objects. For in the same context he speaks of "sensible totals . . . subdivided by discriminative attention." [17] In another place he writes "No one ever had a simple sensation by itself. Consciousness [experience], from our natal day, is a teeming multiplicity of objects and relations and what we call simple sensations [qualities] are results of discriminative attention, pushed often to a very high degree." [18] Surely such passages as these indicate what is intended when it is said that the child's first sensation (experience) is for him the Universe, and that the "Universe which he later comes to know is nothing but an amplification and an implication of that first simple germ." [19] To hold that there is at the same time inner reduplication in thought or feeling is a

16. Vol. I, p. 272.
17. Vol. I, p. 487.
18. Vol. I, p. 224.
19. Vol. II, p. 8.

case of what James elsewhere calls the psychologist's fallacy, reading into the original experience an inferential conclusion which the psychologist arrives at in his special investigations—in this case a wrong inferential result.

I now come to the central case in which the issue is clinched—the account given by James of the nature of the self and our consciousness of it, in which the "subject" of dualistic epistemology disappears and its place is taken by an empirical and behavioral self. In speaking of the nature of "self-love" or egoism, he wrote:

> *The words* ME, *then, and* SELF, *so far as they arouse feeling and connote emotional worth, are* OBJECTIVE *designations, meaning* ALL THE THINGS *which have the power to produce in a stream of consciousness excitement of a certain peculiar sort.*[20]

This position is developed in detail in connection with the bodily or material and the social selves which he has mentioned earlier. The general or theoretical position is that

> To have a self that I can *care for,* nature must first present me with some *object* interesting enough to make me instinctively wish to appropriate it for its *own* sake.

> What happens to them [our bodies] excites in us emotions and tendencies to action more energetic and habitual than any which are excited by other portions of the "field."

> My *social* self-love, my interest in the images other men have framed of me, is also an interest in a set of objects external to my thought.[21]

James, however, had postulated what he calls a "spiritual" self in addition to material and social selves. It might then well seem

20. *Ibid.,* Vol. I, p. 319. The dualism is verbally retained in the mention of the "stream of consciousness." But aside from the fact that no difference is made in the argument when we substitute the words "the ongoing course of experienced things," the self or person is here expressly defined in objective terms, the small capitals being in the original text.

21. Vol. I, pp. 319–321. Cf. the following: "The fact remains . . . that certain special sorts of thing tend primordially to possess this interest, and form the *natural* me. But all these things are *objects*" (p. 325). The discussion of the special topic of egoism is an amplification of the earlier statement that a man's self is "*the sum total of all that he* CAN *call his,*" all the objects he appropriates through the medium of a positive interest (Vol. I, p. 291).

as if this psychical self, consisting of acts of choosing, consenting, refusing, and emotions like fearing, hoping, etc., remained *the* inner self, as an inexpugnable object of direct observation. But in fact it is in dealing with this aspect of the self that James puts forth his most explicit and detailed biological interpretation. For he says all that he can directly and empirically observe shows that this "'Self of selves,' when carefully examined, is found to consist mainly of the collection of these peculiar motions in the head or between the head and the throat."[22] In the context "these peculiar motions" are said to be "a fluctuating play of pressures, convergences, divergences, and accommodations in my eyeballs," and "the opening and closing of the glottis," with "contractions in the jaw-muscles" and the chest. These bodily movements, which are all that is directly experienced as the innermost centre, the "sanctuary within the citadel" of the self, are expressions of "a constant play of furtherances and hindrances, of checks and releases, of tendencies that run with desire and that run the other way." The theoretical interpretation is expressly stated in the following words:

> The nuclear part of the Self . . . would be a collection of activities physiologically in no essential way different from the overt acts themselves. If we divide all possible physiological acts into *adjustments* and *executions,* the nuclear self would be the adjustments collectively considered; and the less intimate, more shifting self, so far as it was active, would be the executions. (*Ibid.,* p. 302.)

He then says, since the adjustment activities are "entirely unimportant and uninteresting except through their uses in furthering or inhibiting the presence of various things, and actions," it is not surprising they are commonly overlooked. But the fact that adjustment activities are involved in all interactions with environing conditions, save in the acts that are most routine and "automatic," confers upon them a certain special position, for "they are the permanent core of turnings-towards and turnings-from, of yieldings and arrests, which naturally seem central and interior."[23]

What is further said about personal identity is consistent with

22. Vol. I, p. 301.
23. Vol. I, p. 302.

this behavioral interpretation. The appropriateness of the passing thought are "less to *itself* than to the most intimately felt *part of its present Object, the body, and the central adjustments,* which accompany the act of thinking, in the head." [24] Furthermore, the belief in the sameness of the self arises on empirical grounds in the same way as belief in the sameness of any object whatever, "*the sense of our own personal identity*" being "*exactly like anyone of our other perceptions of sameness among phenomena.*" [25] Nevertheless the dualism reappears, for he still assumes that a "passing thought" must be there as the knowing subject. Hence, after recurring to his doctrine that "'perishing' pulses of thought" are what know, he makes what on the face of it looks like an extraordinary compromise between the "pulse of thought" as *I* and the "empirical person" as *Me*.[26]

Were it important to do so, more evidence could be cited for the proposition that there are two incompatible strains in the Jamesian psychology, and that the conflict between them is most marked in the case of the self. But there is also evidence that on the side of the empirical strain there are the elements needed for a behavioral theory of the self. What he finally said in 1904, after he had thrown over his knowing Thought or Consciousness as a mere echo of a departed soul, was, after all, but an expression of ideas put forth in his *Psychology,* freed from hesitation and ambiguity. There is "the elementary activity involved in the mere *that* of experience, . . . and the farther specification of this *something* into two *whats,* an activity felt as 'ours' and an activity ascribed to objects." The former, he goes on to say, is

> part . . . of the world experienced. The world experienced . . . comes at all times with our body as its centre, centre of vision, centre of action, centre of interest. . . . The body is the storm centre, the origin of co-ordinates, the constant place of stress in all that experience-train. . . . The word "I," then, is primarily a noun of position, just like "this" and "here." [27]

But, as I have already intimated, he never reworked his *Psychology* so that all phases and aspects of psychological phenom-

24. Vol. I, p. 341.
25. Vol. I, p. 334.
26. Vol. I, p. 371.
27. *Essays in Radical Empiricism,* pp. 169–170n.

ena were observed and reported from this point of view. In consequence psychological theory is still the bulwark for all doctrines that assume independent and separate "mind" and "world" set over against each other. The idea originally came into psychology from philosophy. But now it is advanced by philosophers as having the warrant of psychology and hence possessed of the authority of one of the positive sciences. Philosophy will not be emancipated to perform its own task and function until psychology is purged, as a whole and in all its special topics, of the last remnant of the traditional dualism. And the purge requires more than a statement nominally made in terms of the living organism but in fact simply carrying over to the body distinctions that originated when there was a current belief in mind (or in consciousness) as a distinctive entity. This importation occurs whenever the phenomena are described in terms of the organism exclusively instead of as aspects and functions of the interactivity of organism and environment.

Propositions, Warranted Assertibility, and Truth

I propose in what follows to restate some features of the theories I have previously advanced on the topics mentioned above. I shall shape this restatement on the basis of ascriptions and criticisms of my views found in Mr. Russell's *An Inquiry into Meaning and Truth*. I am in full agreement with his statement that "there is an important difference between his views and mine, which will not be elicited unless we can understand each other."[1] Indeed, I think the statement might read "We can not understand each other unless important differences between us are brought out and borne in mind." I shall then put my emphasis upon what I take to be such differences, especially in relation to the nature of propositions; operations; the respective force of antecedents and consequences; tests or "verifiers"; and experience, the latter being, perhaps, the most important of all differences because it probably underlies the others. I shall draw contrasts which, in the interest of mutual understanding, need to be drawn for the purpose of making my own views clearer than I have managed previously to do. In drawing them I shall be compelled to ascribe certain views to Mr. Russell, without, I hope, attributing to him views he does not in fact hold.

I

Mr. Russell refers to my theory as one which "substitutes 'warranted assertibility' for 'truth.'"[2] Under certain con-

1. *Op. cit.*, p. 401.
2. *Op. cit.*, p. 362. This interpretation is repeated on p. 401, using the words "should take the place of" instead of "substitutes."

[First published in *Journal of Philosophy* 38 (27 March 1941): 169–86.]

ditions, I should have no cause to object to this reference. But the conditions are absent; and it is possible that this view of "substitution" as distinct from and even opposed to *definition,* plays an important role in generating what I take to be misconceptions of my theory in some important specific matters. Hence, I begin by saying that my analysis of "warranted assertibility" is offered as a *definition* of the nature of knowledge in the honorific sense according to which only *true* beliefs are knowledge. The place at which there is pertinency in the idea of "substitution" has to do with *words.* As I wrote in my *Logic: The Theory of Inquiry,* "What has been said helps explain why the term 'warranted assertibility' is preferred to the terms *belief* and *knowledge.* It is free from the ambiguity of the latter terms."[3] But there is involved the extended analysis, given later, of the nature of assertion and of warrant.

This point might be in itself of no especial importance. But it is important in its bearing upon interpretation of other things which I have said and which are commented upon by Mr. Russell. For example, Mr. Russell says, "One important difference between us arises, I think, from the fact that Dr. Dewey is mainly concerned with theories and hypotheses, whereas I am mainly concerned with assertions about particular matters of fact."[4] My position is that something of the order of a theory or hypothesis, a meaning entertained as a *possible significance* in some actual case, is demanded, if there is to be *warranted* assertibility in the case of a particular matter of fact. This position undoubtedly gives an importance to ideas (theories, hypotheses) they do not have upon Mr. Russell's view. But it is not a position that can be put in opposition to assertions about matters of particular fact, since, in terms of my view, it states the *conditions* under which we reach warranted assertibility about particular matters of fact.[5]

There is nothing peculiarly "pragmatic" about this part of my

3. *Logic,* p. 9 [*Later Works* 12:16]. Perhaps in the interest of clearness, the word "term" should have been italicized. The ambiguities in question are discussed in previous pages. In the case of *belief,* the main ambiguity is between it as a state of mind and as *what* is believed—subject-matter. In the case of *knowledge,* it concerns the difference between knowledge as an outcome of "competent and controlled inquiry" and knowledge supposed to "have a meaning of its own apart from connection with, and reference to, inquiry."
4. *Op. cit.,* p. 408.
5. As will appear later, the matter is inherently connected with the proper interpretation of *consequences* on my theory, and also with the very fundamental matter of *operations,* which Mr. Russell only barely alludes to.

view, which holds that the presence of an *idea*—defined as a possible significance of an existent something—is required for any assertion entitled to rank as knowledge or as true; the insistence, however, that the "presence" be by way of an existential operation demarcates it from most other such theories. I may indicate some of my reasons for taking this position by mentioning some difficulties in the contrasting view of Mr. Russell that there are propositions known in virtue of their own immediate direct presence, as in the case of "There is red," or, as Mr. Russell prefers to say, "Redness-here."

(i) I do not understand how "here" has a self-contained and self-assured meaning. It seems to me that it is void of any trace of meaning save as discriminated from *there*, while *there* seems to me to be plural; a matter of manifold *theres*. These discriminations involve, I believe, determinations going beyond anything directly given or capable of being directly present. I would even say, with no attempt here to justify the saying, that a theory involving determination or definition of what is called "Space" is involved in the allegedly simple "redness-here." Indeed, I would add that since any adequate statement of the matter of particular fact referred to is "redness-here-now," a scientific theory of *space-time* is involved in a fully warranted assertion about "redness-here-now."

(ii) If I understand Mr. Russell aright, he holds that the ultimacy and purity of basic propositions is connected with (possibly is guaranteed by) the fact that subject-matters like "redness-here" are of the nature of perceptual experiences, in which perceptual material is reduced to a direct *sensible* presence, or a *sensum*. For example, he writes: "We can, however, in theory, distinguish two cases in relation to a judgment such as 'that is red'; one, when it is caused by what it asserts, and the other, when words or images enter into its causation. In the former case, it must be true; in the latter it may be false." However, Mr. Russell goes on to ask: "What can be meant when we say a percept 'causes' a word or sentence? On the face of it, we have to suppose a considerable process in the brain, connecting visual centres with motor centres; the causation, therefore, is by no means direct."[6] It would, then, seem as if upon Mr. Russell's own view a quite

6. *Op. cit.*, p. 200.

elaborate physiological theory intervenes in any given case as condition of assurance that "redness-here" is a true assertion. And I hope it will not appear unduly finicky if I add that a theory regarding causation also seems to be intimately involved.

Putting the matter on somewhat simpler and perhaps less debatable ground, I would inquire whether what is designated by such words as "sensible presence" and "sensa" is inherently involved in Mr. Russell's view. It would seem as if some such reference were necessary in order to discriminate "*redness-here*" from such propositions as "*this ribbon is red*," and possibly from such propositions as "*hippogriff-here*." If reference to a sensum *is* required, then it would seem as if there must also be reference to the bodily sensory apparatus in virtue of whose mediation a given quality is determined to be a *sensum*. It hardly seems probable to me that such knowledge is any part of the datum as directly "here"; indeed, it seems highly probable that there was a long period in history when human beings did not institute connection between colors and visual apparatus, or between sounds and auditory apparatus; or at least that such connection as was made was inferred from what happened when men shut their eyes and stopped up their ears.

The probability that the belief in certain qualities as "sensible" is an inferential matter is increased by the fact that Mr. Russell himself makes no reference to the presence of the bodily *motor* element which is assuredly involved in "redness-here";—an omission of considerable importance for the difference between our views, as will appear later. In view of such considerations as these, any view which holds that all complex propositions depend for their status *as knowledge* upon prior atomic propositions, of the nature described by Mr. Russell, seems to me the most adequate foundation yet provided for complete scepticism.

The position which I take, namely, that all knowledge, or warranted assertion, depends upon inquiry and that inquiry is, truistically, connected with what is questionable (and questioned) involves a sceptical element, or what Peirce called "fallibilism." But it also provides for *probability,* and for determination of degrees of probability in rejecting all intrinsically dogmatic statements, where "dogmatic" applies to *any* statement asserted to possess inherent self-evident truth. That the only alternative to ascribing to some propositions self-sufficient, self-possessed, and self-evident truth is a theory which finds the test and mark of truth in *consequences* of some sort is, I hope, an acceptable view. At all events, it is a position to be kept in mind in assessing my views.

II

In an earlier passage Mr. Russell ascribes certain views to "instrumentalists" and points out certain errors which undoubtedly (and rather obviously) exist in those views—as *he* conceives and states them. My name and especial view are not mentioned in this earlier passage. But, aside from the fact that I have called my view of propositions "instrumental" (in the particular technical sense in which I define propositions), comment on the passage may assist in clarifying what my views genuinely are. The passage reads:

> There are some schools of philosophy—notably the Hegelians and the instrumentalists—which deny the distinction between data and inference altogether. They maintain that in all our knowledge there is an inferential element, that knowledge is an organic whole, and that the test of truth is coherence rather than conformity with "fact." I do not deny an element of truth in this view, but I think that, if taken as a whole truth, it renders the part played by perception in knowledge inexplicable. It is surely obvious that every perceptive experience, if I choose to notice it, affords me either new knowledge which I could not previously have inferred, or, at least, as in the case of eclipses, greater certainty than I could have previously obtained by means of inference. To this the instrumentalist replies that any statement of the new knowledge obtained from perception is always an interpretation based upon accepted theories, and may need subsequent correction if these theories turn out to be unsuitable.[7]

7. *Op. cit.*, p. 154. To clear the ground for discussion of the views advanced in the passage quoted in the text, and as a means of shortening my comments, I append a few categorical statements, which can be substantiated by many references to "instrumentalist" writings. Instrumentalists do *not* believe that "knowledge is an organic whole"; in fact, the idea is meaningless upon their view. They do *not* believe the test of truth is coherence; in the operational sense, stated later in this paper, they hold a correspondence view.

I begin with the ascription to instrumentalists of the idea that "in all our knowledge, there is an inferential element." This statement is, from the standpoint of my view, ambiguous; in one of its meanings, it is incorrect. It is necessary, then, to make a distinction. If it means (as it is apparently intended to mean) that an element due to inference appears *in propria persona*, so to speak, it is incorrect. For according to my view (if I may take it as a sample of the instrumentalists' view), while to infer something is necessary if a warranted assertion is to be arrived at, this inferred somewhat never appears *as such* in the latter; that is, in knowledge. The inferred material has to be checked and tested. The means of testing, required to give an inferential element any claim whatsoever to be *knowledge* instead of conjecture, are the data provided by observation—and *only* by observation. Moreover, as is stated frequently in my *Logic: The Theory of Inquiry*, it is necessary that data (provided by observation) be *new*, or different from those which first suggested the inferential element, if they are to have any value with respect to attaining knowledge. It is important that they be had under as many different conditions as possible so that data due to *differential* origins may supplement one another. The necessity of both the distinction and the cooperation of inferential and observational subject-matters is, on my theory, the product of an analysis of scientific inquiry; this necessity is, as will be shown in more detail later, the heart of my whole theory that knowledge is warranted assertion.

It should now be clear that the instrumentalist would not dream of making the kind of "reply" attributed to him. Instead of holding that "*accepted* theories" are always the basis for interpretation of what is newly obtained in perceptual experience, he has not been behind others in pointing out that such a mode of interpretation is a common and serious source of wrong conclusions; of dogmatism and of consequent arrest of advance in knowledge. In my *Logic*, I have explicitly pointed out that one chief reason why the introduction of experimental methods meant such a great, such a revolutionary, change in natural science, is that they provide data which are new not only in detail but in *kind*. Hence their introduction compelled new kinds of inference to new kinds of subject-matters, and the formation of new types of theories—in addition to providing more exact means of testing old theories. Upon the basis of the view ascribed to instrumentalists, I should suppose it would have been simpler and more effective to point out the contradiction involved in holding, on one side, that the instrumentalist has no way of discovering "need for further correction" in accepted theories, while holding, on the other side, that all accepted theories are, or may be, "unsuitable." Is there not flat contradiction between the idea that "any statement of new knowledge obtained by perception is always an interpretation based upon accepted theories," and the view that it may need subsequent correction if these theories prove "unsuitable"? How in the world, upon the ground of the first part of the supposed "reply" of the instrumentalist, could any theory once "accepted" ever be shown to be unsuitable?

I am obliged, unfortunately, to form a certain hypothesis as to how and why, in view of the numerous and oft-repeated statements in my *Logic* of the *necessity* for distinguishing between inferential elements and observational data (necessary since otherwise there is no approach to warranted assertibility), it could occur to anyone that I denied the distinction. The best guess I can make is that my statements about the necessity of hard data, due to experimental observation and freed from all inferential constituents, were not taken seriously because it was supposed that upon my theory these data themselves represent, or present, *cases of knowledge,* so that there must be on my theory an inferential element also in them. Whether or not this is the source of the alleged denial thought up by Mr. Russell, it may be used to indicate a highly significant difference between our two views. For Mr. Russell holds, if I understand him, that propositions about these data are in some cases instances of knowledge, and indeed that such cases provide, as basic propositions, the models upon which a theory of truth should be formed. In my view, they are not cases of *knowledge,* although propositional formulation of them is a *necessary* (but not sufficient) condition of knowledge.

I can understand that my actual view may seem even more objectionable to a critic than the one that has been wrongly ascribed to me. None the less, in the interest of understanding and as a ground of pertinent criticism, it is indispensable that this position, and what it involves, be recognized as fundamental in my theory. It brings me to what is meant, in my theory, by the instrumental character of a proposition. I shall, then, postpone consideration of the ascription to me of the view that propositions are true if they are instruments or tools of successful action till I have stated just what, on my theory, a proposition is. The view imputed to me is that "Inquiry uses 'assertions' as its tools, and assertions are 'warranted' in so far as they produce the desired result."[8] I put in contrast with this conception the following statement of my view:

> Judgment may be identified as the settled outcome of inquiry. It is concerned with the concluding objects that emerge from inquiry in their status of being *conclusive*. Judgment in this sense is distinguished from *propositions*. The content of the latter is intermediate and representative and is carried by symbols; while judgment, as finally made, has *direct* existential import. The terms *affirmation* and *assertion* are employed in current speech interchangeably. But there is a difference, which should have linguistic recognition, between the logical status of intermediate subject-matters that are taken for use in connection *with what they lead to as means,* and subject-matter which has been prepared to be final. I shall use *assertion* to designate the latter logical status and *affirmation* to name the former. . . . However, the important matter is not the words, but the logical properties characteristic of different subject-matters.[9]

Propositions, then, on this view, are what are affirmed but not asserted. They are means, instrumentalities, since they are the operational agencies by which *beliefs* that have adequate grounds for acceptance are reached as *end* of inquiry. As I have intimated, this view may seem even more objectionable than is the one attributed to me, i.e., the one which is not mine. But in any case the difference between the instrumentality of a *proposition* as means of attaining a grounded *belief* and the instrumentality of a *belief* as means of reaching certain "*desired* results," should be fairly obvious, independently of acceptance or rejection of my view.

8. *Op. cit.,* pp. 401–402.
9. *Logic: The Theory of Inquiry,* p. 120 [*Later Works* 12:123] (not all italics in original). The word "logical," as it occurs in this passage, is, of course, to be understood in the sense given that term in previous chapters of the volume; a signification that is determined by connection with operations of inquiry which are undertaken because of the existence of a problem, and which are controlled by the conditions of that problem—since the "goal" is to resolve the problem which evokes inquiry.

Unless a critic is willing to entertain, in however hypothetical a fashion, the view (i) that *knowledge* (in its honorific sense) is in every case connected with inquiry; (ii) that the conclusion or end of inquiry has to be demarcated from the intermediate means by which inquiry goes forward to a warranted or justified conclusion; that (iii) the intermediate means are formulated in discourse, i.e., as propositions, and that as means they have the properties appropriate to means (viz., relevancy and efficacy— including economy), I know of no way to make my view intelligible. If the view is entertained, even in the most speculative conjectural fashion, it will, I think, be clear that according to it, truth and falsity are properties only of that subject-matter which is the *end,* the close, of the inquiry by means of which it is reached. The distinction between true and false conclusions is determined by the character of the operational procedures through which propositions about data and propositions about inferential elements (meanings, ideas, hypotheses) are instituted. At all events, I can not imagine that one who says that such things as hammers, looms, chemical processes like dyeing, reduction of ores, when used as means, are marked by properties of fitness and efficacy (and the opposite) rather than by the properties of truth-falsity, will be thought to be saying anything that is not commonplace.

III

My view of the nature of propositions, as distinct from that held by Mr. Russell, may be further illustrated by commenting upon the passage in which, referring to my view concerning changes in the matter of hypotheses during the course of inquiry, he writes: "I should say that inquiry begins, as a rule, with an assertion that is vague and complex, but replaces it, when it can, by a number of separate assertions each of which is less vague and less complex than the original assertion." [10] I remark in passing that previous observations of this kind by Mr. Russell were what led me so to misapprehend his views as to impute to him the assumption "that *propositions* are the subject-matter of in-

10. *Op. cit.*, p. 403.

quiry"; an impression, which, if it were not for his present explicit disclaimer, would be strengthened by reading, "When we embark upon an inquiry we assume that *the propositions about which we are inquiring* are either true or false." [11] Without repeating the ascription repudiated by Mr. Russell, I would say that upon my view "propositions are *not* that about which we are inquiring," and that as far as we do find it necessary or advisable to inquire about them (as is almost bound to happen in the course of an inquiry), it is not their truth and falsity about which we inquire, but the relevancy and efficacy of their subject-matter with respect to the problem in hand. I also remark, in passing, that Mr. Russell's statement appears to surrender the strict two-value theory of propositions in admitting that they may have the properties of being vague-definite; complex-simple. I suppose, however, that Mr. Russell's reply would be that on his view these latter qualities are derivative; that the first proposition is vague and complex because it is a mixture of some (possibly) true and some (possibly) false propositions. While dialectically this reply covers the case, it does not seem to agree with what happens in any actual case of analysis of a proposition into simpler and more definite ones. For this analysis always involves modification or transformation of the terms (meanings) found in the original proposition, and not its division into some true and some false propositions that from the start were its constituents although in a mixture.

Coming to the main point at issue, I hold that the first propositions we make as means of resolving a problem of any marked degree of difficulty are indeed likely to be too vague and coarse to be effective, just as in the story of invention of other instrumentalities, the first forms are relatively clumsy, uneconomical, and ineffective. They have then, as means, to be replaced by others which are more effective. Propositions are vague when, for example, they do not delimit the problem sufficiently to indicate what kind of a solution is relevant. It is hardly necessary to say that when we don't know the conditions constituting a problem we are trying to solve, our efforts at solution at best will be fumbling and are likely to be wild. Data serve as tests of any idea or hypothesis that suggests itself, and in this capacity also their

11. *Op. cit.*, p. 361. My italics.

definiteness is required. But, upon my view, the degree and the quality of definiteness and of simplicity, or elementariness, required, are determined by the problem that evokes and controls inquiry. However the case may stand in epistemology (as a problem based upon a prior assumption that knowledge is and must be a relation between a knowing subject and an object), upon the basis of a view that takes knowing (inquiry) as it finds it, the idea that simplicity and elementariness are *inherent* properties of propositions (apart from their place and function in inquiry) has no meaning. If I understand Mr. Russell's view, his test for the simple and definite nature of a proposition applies indifferently to all propositions and hence has no indicative or probative force with respect to any proposition in particular.

Accepting, then, Mr. Russell's statement that his "problem has been, throughout, the relation between events and propositions," and regretting that I ascribed to him the view that "propositions are the subject-matter of inquiry," I would point out what seems to be a certain indeterminateness in his view of the relation between events and propositions, and the consequent need of introducing a distinction: *viz.*, the distinction between the problem of the relation of events and propositions *in general,* and the problem of the relation of a *particular* proposition to the *particular* event to which it purports to refer. I can understand that Mr. Russell holds that certain propositions, of a specified kind, are such direct effects of certain events, and of nothing else, that they "must be true." But this view does not, as I see the matter, answer the question of how we know that *in a given case* this direct relationship actually exists. It does not seem to me that his theory gets beyond specifying the kind of case *in general* in which the relation between an event, as causal antecedent, and a proposition, as effect, is such as to confer upon instances of the latter the property of being true. But I can not see that we get anywhere until we have means of telling *which* propositions in particular *are* instances of the kind in question.

In the case, previously cited, of *redness-here,* Mr. Russell asserts, as I understand him, that it is true when it is caused by a simple, atomic event. But how do we know in a given case whether it is so caused? Or if he holds that it *must* be true because it *is* caused by such an event, which is then its sufficient verifier, I am compelled to ask how such is known to be the case.

These comments are intended to indicate both that I hold a "correspondence" theory of truth, and the sense in which I hold it;—a sense which seems to me free from a fundamental difficulty that Mr. Russell's view of truth can not get over or around. The event *to be* known is that which operates, on his view, as cause of the proposition while it is also its verifier; although the proposition is the sole means of knowing the event! Such a view, like any strictly epistemological view, seems to me to assume a mysterious and unverifiable doctrine of pre-established harmony. How an event can be (i) what-is-to-be-known, and hence by description is unknown, and (ii) what is capable of being *known* only through the medium of a proposition, which, in turn (iii) in order to be a case of knowledge or be true, must correspond to the to-be-known, is to me *the* epistemological miracle. For the doctrine states that a proposition is true when it conforms to that which is not known save through itself.

In contrast with this view, my own view takes correspondence in the operational sense it bears in all cases except the unique epistemological case of an alleged relation between a "subject" and an "object"; the meaning, namely, of *answering,* as a key answers to conditions imposed by a lock, or as two correspondents "answer" each other; or, in general, as a reply is an adequate answer to a question or a criticism—as, in short, a *solution* answers the requirements of a *problem*. On this view, both partners in "correspondence" are open and above board, instead of one of them being forever out of experience and the other in it by way of a "percept" or whatever. Wondering at how something in experience could be asserted to correspond to something by definition outside experience, which it is, upon the basis of epistemological doctrine, the sole means of "knowing," is what originally made me suspicious of the whole epistemological industry.[12]

12. In noting that my view of truth involves dependence upon consequences (as his depends upon antecedents, not, however, themselves in experience), and in noting that a causal law is involved, Mr. Russell concludes: "These causal laws, if they are to serve their purpose, must be 'true' in the very sense that Dr. Dewey would abolish" (*op. cit.*, p. 408). It hardly seems unreasonable on my part to expect that my general theory of truth be applied to particular cases, that of the truth of causal laws included. If it was unreasonable to *expect* that it would be so understood, I am glad to take this opportunity to say that such is the case. I do not hold in this case a view I have elsewhere "abolished." I *apply* the general view I advance elsewhere. There are few matters with respect to which there has been as much experience and as much testing

In the sense of correspondence as operational and behavioral (the meaning which has definite parallels in ordinary experience), I hold that my *type* of theory is the only one entitled to be called a correspondence theory of truth.

IV

I should be happy to believe that what has been said is sufficiently definite and clear as to the nature and function of "consequences," so that it is not necessary to say anything more on the subject. But there are criticisms of Mr. Russell's that I might seem to be evading were I to say nothing specifically about them. He asserts that he has several times asked me what the goal of inquiry is upon my theory, and has seen no answer to the question.[13] There seems to be some reason for inferring that this matter is connected with the belief that I am engaged in *substituting* something else for "truth," so that truth, as he interprets my position, not being the goal, I am bound to provide some other goal. A person turning to the Index of my *Logic: The Theory of Inquiry* will find the following heading: "Assertibility, warranted, as end of inquiry." Some fourteen passages of the text are referred to. Unless there is a difference which escapes me between "end" and "goal," the following passage would seem to give the answer which Mr. Russell has missed:

> Moreover, inference, even in its connection with test, is not logically final and complete. The heart of the entire theory developed in this work is that the resolution of an indeterminate situation is the end, in the sense in which "end" means *end-in-view* and in the sense in which it means *close*.[14]

---

as in the matter of the connection of means and consequences, since that connection is involved in all the details of every occupation, art, and undertaking. That warranted assertibility is a matter of probability in the case of causal connections is a trait it shares with other instances of warranted assertibility; while, apparently, Mr. Russell would deny the name of knowledge, in its fullest sense, to anything that is not certain to the point of infallibility, or which does not ultimately rest upon some absolute certainty.

13. *Op. cit.*, p. 404.
14. *Logic: The Theory of Inquiry*, pp. 157–158 [*Later Works* 12:160].

The implication of the passage, if not in its isolation then in its context, is that inquiry begins in an *indeterminate* situation, and not only begins in it but is controlled by its specific qualitative nature.[15] Inquiry, as the set of operations by which the situation is resolved (settled, or rendered determinate) has to discover and formulate the conditions that describe the problem in hand. For *they* are the conditions to be "satisfied" and the determinants of "success." Since these conditions are existential, they can be determined only by observational operations; the operational character of observation being clearly exhibited in the experimental character of all scientific determination of data. (Upon a nonscientific level of inquiry, it is exhibited in the fact that we *look* and see; *listen* and hear; or, in general terms, that a motor-muscular, as well as sensory, factor is involved in any perceptual experience.) The conditions discovered, accordingly, in and by operational observation, constitute the *conditions of the problem* with which further inquiry is engaged; for data, on this view, are always data of some specific problem and hence are not given ready-made to an inquiry but are determined in and by it. (The point previously stated, that propositions about data are not cases of knowledge but means of attaining it, is so obviously an integral part of this view that I say nothing further about it in this connection.) As the problem progressively assumes definite shape by means of repeated acts of observation, possible solutions suggest themselves. These possible solutions are, truistically (in terms of the theory), *possible* meanings of the data determined in observation. The process of reasoning is an elaboration of them. When they are checked by reference to observed materials, they constitute the subject-matter of *inferential* propositions. The latter are means of attaining the goal of knowledge as warranted assertion, not instances or examples of knowledge. They are also operational in nature since they institute new experimental observations whose subject-matter provides both tests for old hypotheses and starting-points for new ones or at least for modi-

15. *Logic,* p. 105 [*Later Works* 12:109]. "It is a unique doubtfulness" that not only evokes the particular inquiry, but as explicitly stated "exercises control" over it. To avoid needless misunderstanding, I quote also the following passage: "No situation which is *completely* indeterminate can possibly be converted into a problem having definite constituents" (*Ibid.,* p. 108 [*Later Works* 12:112]).

fying solutions previously entertained. And so on until a determinate situation is instituted.

If this condensed statement is taken in its own terms and not
by first interpreting its meaning in terms of some theory it doesn't
logically permit, I think it will render unnecessary further comment on the notion Mr. Russell has ascribed to me: the notion,
namely, that "a belief is 'warranted,' if as a tool, it is useful in
some activity, i.e., if it is a cause of satisfaction of desire," and
that "the only essential result of successful inquiry is successful
action." [16]

In the interest of mutual understanding, I shall now make
some comments on a passage which, if I interpret it aright, sets
forth the nature of Mr. Russell's wrong idea of my view, and
which also, by implication, suggests the nature of the genuine
difference between our views:

> If there are such occurrences as "believings," which seems
> undeniable, the question is: Can they be divided into two
> classes, the "true" and the "false"? Or, if not, can they be so
> analysed that their constituents can be divided into these two
> classes? If either of these questions is answered in the affir-
> mative, is the distinction between "true" and "false" to be
> found in the success or failure of the effects of believings, or
> is it to be found in some other relation which they may have
> to relevant occurrences? [17]

On the basis of other passages, such as have been quoted, I am
warranted in supposing that there is ascribed to me the view that
"the distinction between 'true' and 'false' is to be found in the
success or failure of the effects of believings." After what I have
already said, I hope it suffices to point out that the question of
truth-falsity is *not*, on my view, a matter of the effects of *believing*, for my whole theory is determined by the attempt to state
what conditions and operations of inquiry *warrant* a "believing," or justify its assertion as true; that propositions, as such,
are so far from being cases of believings that they are means of
attaining a warranted believing, their worth as means being determined by their pertinency and efficacy in "satisfying" condi-

16. *Op. cit.*, pp. 405, 404.
17. *Op. cit.*, p. 405.

tions that are rigorously set by the problem they are employed to resolve.

At this stage of the present discussion, I am, however, more interested in the passage quoted as an indication of the difference between us than as a manifestation of the nature of Mr. Russell's wrong understanding of my view.[18] I believe most decidedly that the distinction between "true" and "false" is to be found in the relation which *propositions*, as means of inquiry, "have to relevant occurrences." The difference between us concerns, as I see the matter in the light of Mr. Russell's explanation, the question of *what* occurrences *are* the relevant ones. And I hope it is unnecessary to repeat by this time that the relevant occurrences on my theory are those existential consequences which, in virtue of operations existentially performed, satisfy (meet, fulfill) conditions set by occurrences that constitute a problem. These considerations bring me to my final point.

V

In an earlier writing, a passage of which is cited by Mr. Russell, I stated my conclusion that Mr. Russell's interpretation of my view in terms of satisfaction of personal desire, of success in activities performed in order to satisfy desires, etc., was due to failure to note the importance in my theory of the existence of indeterminate or problematic situations as not only the source of, but as the control of, inquiry. A part of what I there wrote reads as follows:

Mr. Russell proceeds first by converting a doubtful *situation* into a personal doubt. . . . Then by changing doubt into private discomfort, truth is identified [upon my view] with removal of this discomfort . . . [but] "Satisfaction" is satisfaction of the conditions prescribed by the problem.

18. I venture to remark that the words "wrong" and "right" as they appear in the text are used intentionally instead of the words "false" and "true"; for, according to my view, understanding and misunderstanding, conception and misconception, taking and mis-taking, are matters of propositions, which are not final or complete in themselves but are used as means to an end—the resolution of a problem; while it is to this resolution, as *conclusion* of inquiry, that the adjectives "true" and "false" apply.

In the same connection reference is made to a sentence in the Preface in which I stated, in view of previous misunderstandings of my position, that consequences are only to be accepted as tests of validity "*provided* these consequences are operationally instituted."[19]

Mr. Russell has made two comments with reference to these two explicitly stated conditions which govern the meaning and function of consequences. One of them concerns the reference to the consequences being "operationally instituted." Unfortunately for the cause of mutual understanding, it consists of but one sentence to the effect that its "meaning remains to me somewhat obscure." Comment upon the other qualification, namely, upon the necessity of "doubtful," problematic, etc., being taken to be characteristic of the "objective" situation and not of a person or "subject," is, fortunately, more extended:

> Dr. Dewey *seems* to write as if a doubtful situation could exist without a personal doubter. I cannot think that he means this; he cannot intend to say, for example, that there were doubtful situations in astronomical and geological epochs before there was life. The only way in which I can interpret what he says is to suppose that, for him, a "doubtful situation" is one which arouses doubt, not only in some one individual, but in any normal man, or in any man anxious to achieve a certain result, or in any scientifically trained observer engaged in investigating the situation. *Some* purpose, i.e., *some* desire, is involved in the idea of a doubtful situation.[20]

When the term "doubtful situation" is taken in the meaning it possesses in the context of my general theory of experience, I *do* mean to say that it can exist without a personal doubter; and, moreover, that "personal states of doubt that are not evoked by, and are not relative to, some existential situation are pathological; when they are extreme they constitute the mania of

19. The original passage of mine is found in Vol. I of the *Library of Living Philosophers*, p. 571 [this volume, p. 55]. It is also stated as one of the conditions, that it is necessary that consequences be "such as to resolve the specific problem evoking the operations." Quoted on p. 571 of the *Library* from p. iv, of the Preface of my *Logic* [*Later Works* 12:4].

20. *Op. cit.*, p. 407.

doubting. . . . The habit of disposing of the doubtful as if it belonged only to *us* rather than to the existential situation in which we are caught and implicated is an inheritance from subjectivistic psychology."[21] This position is so intimately and fundamentally bound up with my whole theory of "experience" as behavioral (though not "behavioristic" in the technical sense that the word has assumed), as interactivity of organism and environment, that I should have to go into a restatement of what I have said at great length elsewhere if I tried to justify what is affirmed in the passage quoted. I confine myself here to one point. The *problematic* nature of situations is definitely stated to have its source and prototype in the condition of imbalance or disequilibration that recurs rhythmically in the interactivity of organism and environment;—a condition exemplified in hunger, not as a "feeling" but as a form of organic behavior such as is manifested, for example, in bodily restlessness and bodily acts of search for food. Since I can not take the space to restate the view of experience of which the position regarding the existential nature of the indeterminate or problematic situation is one aspect (one, however, which is logically involved in and demanded by it), I confine myself to brief comments intended to make clearer, if possible, differences between my position and that of Mr. Russell. (i) All experiences are interactivities of an organism and an environment; a doubtful or problematic situation is, of course, no exception. But the energies of an organism involved in the particular interactivity that constitutes, or *is*, the problematic situation, are those involved in an ordinary course of living. They are *not* those of doubting. Doubt can, as I have said, be legitimately imputed to the organism only in a *secondary* or derived manner. (ii) "Every such interaction is a temporal process, not a momentary, cross-sectional occurrence. The situation in which it occurs is indeterminate, therefore, with respect to its *issue*. . . . Even were existential conditions unqualifiedly determinate in and of themselves, they are indeterminate [are such in certain instances] in *significance:* that is, in what they import and portend in their interaction with the organism."[22] The passage should throw light upon the sense in which an existential

21. *Logic*, p. 106 [*Later Works* 12:109, 110].
22. *Logic*, pp. 106–107 [*Later Works* 12:110].

organism is existentially implicated or involved in a situation as interacting with environing conditions. According to my view, the sole way in which a "normal person" figures is that such a person investigates only in the actual presence of a problem. (iii) All that is necessary upon my view is that an astronomical or geological epoch be an actual constituent of some experienced problematic situation. I am not, logically speaking, obliged to indulge in any cosmological speculation about those epochs, because, on my theory, any proposition about them is of the nature of what A. F. Bentley, in well-chosen terms, calls "*extrapolation*," under certain conditions, be it understood, perfectly legitimate, but nevertheless an extrapolation.[23]

As far as cosmological speculation on the indeterminate situations in astronomical and geological epochs is relevant to my theory (or my theory to it), *any* view which holds that man is a part of nature, not outside it, will hold that this fact of being part of nature qualifies his "experience" throughout. Hence the view will certainly hold that indeterminacy in human experience, once experience is taken in the objective sense of interacting behavior and not as a private conceit added on to something totally alien to it, is evidence of some corresponding indeterminateness in the processes of nature within which man exists (acts) and out of which he arose. Of course, one who holds, as Mr. Russell seems to do, to the doctrine of the existence of an independent subject as the cause of the "doubtfulness" or "problematic quality" of situations will take the view he has expressed, thus confirming my opinion that the difference between us has its basic source in different views of the nature of experience, which in turn is correlated with our different conceptions of the connection existing between man and the rest of the world. Mr. Russell has not envisaged the possibility of there being another generic theory of experience, as an alternative to the pre-Darwinian conceptions of Hegel, on the one hand, and of Mill, on the other.

The qualification in my theory relating to the necessity of con-

---

23. *Behavior, Knowledge, Fact* (1935), Section XIX, "Experience and Fact," especially, pp. 172–179. The passage should be read in connection with section XXVII, "Behavioral Space-Time." I am glad to refer anyone interested in that part of my view that has to do with prehuman and pre-organic events to Mr. Bentley's statement, without, however, intending to make him responsible for what I have said on any other point.

sequences being "operationally instituted" is, of course, an intimate constituent of my whole theory of inquiry. I do not wonder that Mr. Russell finds the particular passage he cites "somewhat obscure," if he takes it in isolation from its central position in my whole theory of experience, inquiry, and knowledge. I cite one passage that indicates the intrinsic connection existing between this part of my theory and the point just mentioned—that concerning the place of indeterminate situations in inquiry. "Situations that are disturbed and troubled, confused or obscure, cannot be straightened out, cleared up and put in order, by manipulations of our personal states of mind."[24] This is the negative aspect of the position that operations of an existential sort, operations which are actions, doing something and accomplishing something (a changed state of interactivity in short), are the only means of producing consequences that have any bearing upon warranted assertibility.

In concluding this part of my discussion, I indulge in the statement of some things that puzzle me, things connected, moreover, not just with Mr. Russell's view, but with views that are widely held. (i) I am puzzled by the fact that persons who are systematically engaged with inquiry into questions, into problems (as philosophers certainly are), are so incurious about the existence and nature of problems. (ii) If a "subject" is one end-term in a relation of which objects (events) are the other end-terms, and if doubt is simply a state of a subject, why isn't knowledge also simply and only a state of mind of a subject? And (iii) the puzzling thing already mentioned: How can anybody look at *both* an object (event) and a proposition about it so as to determine whether the two "correspond"? And if one can look directly at the event *in propria persona*, why have a duplicate proposition (idea or percept, according to some theories) about it unless, perhaps, as a convenience in communication with others?

I do not wish to conclude without saying that I have tried to conduct my discussion in the spirit indicated by Mr. Russell, avoiding all misunderstanding as far as I can, and viewing the issues involved as uncontroversially as is consistent with trying to make my own views clear. In this process I am aware of the acute bearing of his remark that "it is because the difference goes deep

24. *Logic*, p. 106 [*Later Works* 12:109–10].

that it is difficult to find words which both sides can accept as a fair statement of the issue." In view of the depth of the difference, I can hardly hope to have succeeded completely in overcoming this difficulty. But at least I have been more concerned to make my own position intelligible than to refute Mr. Russell's view, so that the controversial remarks I have made have their source in the belief that definite contrasts are an important, perhaps indispensable, means of making any view sharp in outline and definite in content.

I add that I am grateful to Mr. Russell for devoting so much space to my views and for thus giving me an opportunity to re-state them. If the space I have taken in this reply seems out of proportion to the space given to questioning my view in Mr. Russell's book, it is because of my belief of the importance of that book. For I believe that he has reduced, with his great skill in analysis, a position that is widely held to its ultimate constituents, and that this accomplishment eliminates much that has been vague and confused in the current view. In particular, I believe that the position he has taken regarding the causal relation between an event and a proposition is the first successful effort to set forth a clear interpretation of what "correspondence" *must* mean in current realistic epistemologies. Statement in terms of a causal relation between an event and a proposition gets rid, in my opinion, of much useless material that encumbers the ordinary statement made about the "epistemological" relation. That I also believe his accomplishment of this work discloses the fundamental defect in the epistemological—as contrasted with the experiential-behavioral—account of correspondence will be clear to the reader. But at least the issue is that much clarified, and it is taken into a wider field than that of a difference between Mr. Russell's views and mine.

The Objectivism-Subjectivism of Modern Philosophy

I

In his *Adventures of Ideas,* Whitehead writes as follows: "It is customary to contrast the objective approach of the ancient Greeks with the subjective approach of the moderns. . . . But whether we be ancients or moderns we can deal only with things, in some sense, experienced."[1] Since I agree fully with this statement, my only comment is that it involves repudiation of the view that approach through experience is *ipso facto* subjective. There is a further statement of Whitehead's which I wish to use as a peg from which to hang some remarks of my own, as preachers use a text. "The difference between ancients and moderns is that the ancients asked what have we experienced and the moderns asked what can we experience."[2] I propose to develop the distinction between "what *has* been" and "what *can* be" experienced, in explanation of the difference between ancient and modern philosophy, in a way that has no authorization in Whitehead's treatment. In fact, my development is in a direction contrary to what Whitehead goes on to say. For that reason I feel the more bound to say that the particular interpretation he gives the distinction commands, within the limits set by the point he is making, my full assent. For he is concerned to show how the notion of experience was narrowed by the criteria set up by some moderns for judging what *can* be experienced. There can be no doubt as to the existence of this criterion nor as to its restrictive consequence.

1. P. 287.
2. *Op. cit.*, p. 288.

[First published in *Journal of Philosophy* 38 (25 September 1941): 533–42.]

The limitation is due, as Whitehead justly says, to two errors. "The first error is the assumption of a few definite avenues of communication with the external world, the five sense-organs. This leads to the pre-supposition that the search for data is to be narrowed to the question, what data are directly provided by the activity of the sense-organs. . . . The second error is the presupposition that the sole way of examining experience is by acts of conscious introspective analysis." [3] When applied to such writers as Locke and Hume on one side and Kant on the other side nothing could be truer than these statements. The outcome was a definite and to my mind disastrous narrowing of the field of experience. Upon the face of the matter, then, the view I am going to advance seems to be contradicted by facts. For what I wish to say is that ancient philosophy is the one which is restricted, since it could not venture beyond what had already been accomplished in the way of experienced things—using "things" to designate activities and institutions as well as "objects," while modern experience is expansive since it is marked off by its constant concern for potentialities of experience as yet unrealized, as is shown, for example, in its interest in discovery and invention. In consequence what *can* be experienced stands for something wider and freer than what *has* been experienced.

II

There is an undeniable discrepancy involved in admitting the justice of what Whitehead says about the way in which the idea of what "can be experienced" was used to narrow the experiential field and the position I am here taking. As to the views about experience literally expressed by modern philosophers of both the experiential and the *a priori* schools, I have no desire to explain away the discrepancy. What I intend to point out is that the spirit and direction of modern philosophy is of quite another sort, since it has been occupied with breaking down fixed barriers, with novelty, expansion, growth, potentialities previously unforeseen; in short, with an open and "in-

---

3. *Op. cit.*, p. 289 and p. 290. Cf. the following from p. 269, "Warping has taken the form of constant reliance upon sensationalist activity as the basis of all experiential activity."

finite" world instead of the closed and finite world of the Greeks. If this statement does not apply to the general movement and implicit intent of modern philosophy, we are faced with a much greater discrepancy than the one just mentioned: that between the actual tendencies of modern experience and the philosophy that has been produced on the ground of this experience.

Accordingly, I do not think it is a necessary part of my task to account for the view nominally taken by modern philosophers about what *can* be experienced. At the same time, I do not believe the paradox is as great as it seems to be on the surface. The very fact that modern philosophy has been concerned with conditions of experience which lie beyond the range of what *has been* experienced in the past made it peculiarly sensitive to the existence of certain barriers to their acceptance and realization; namely, the barriers that are products of past culture and are sanctioned by the philosophy which reflected that culture. In behalf of their own interest in the prospective, in possible expansion, philosophers were obliged to assail the beliefs and habits which stood in the way. They needed a criterion and method for carrying on their battle. In short, the positive side of modern philosophy, what I have called its spirit and direction of movement, was such as to give great importance to the negative work that had to be done. The readiest instrumentality of destructive criticism was identification of valid beliefs with those authorized by experience when experience is reduced to material of direct observation; namely, to simple ideas, impressions, sense data. The incompatibility of this reduction to the positive faith which animated the modern philosophers was concealed from view by their intense belief that if only obstructions inherited from the past were once done away with, the forces inhering in experience would carry men forward. Even more instructive than what was explicitly said about experience is the revolution that took place as to the respective outlooks of "experience" and "reason." In ancient philosophy, experience stood for the habits and skills acquired by repetition of particular activities by means of selection of those which proved successful. It was a limiting principle, while reason, insight into reasons, was emancipatory of the bonds that were set by acquired habits. Francis Bacon and his experiential followers took exactly the opposite view. The "rational," when disassociated from personal experience, was to them the lifeless, the secondhand. Personal "experience," irrespective of any technical definition, was the means of initiation into living realities and provided the sole assurance of entering pastures that were fertile as well as fresh. Empiricism and liberalism were allies; the possibility of growth, of development, idealization of change as progress, were all, whether rightly or wrongly, connected with faith in experience. Technically, or in strict formal logic, the *tabula rasa,* the blank sheet of paper, view of mind to be written upon by "external" impressions, should have led to the conclusion that human beings are passive puppets. Actually, the feeling that if hampering and restrictive traditions and institutions could be got rid of, firsthand experience would ensure that men could and would go ahead, was the dominant factor.

III

If we consider Greek thought in an analytical way, we shall be persuaded, in any event, that from its own standpoint it can not be called *objective.* If the term is used, it is from our own present standpoint; that is, on the ground of the contrast of Greek thought with subjectivistic tendencies of modern philosophy, tendencies which, however, could not be identified as such, were it not that the distinction between the cosmological and the psychological, the "objective" and the "subjective," had been consciously made and become current. And it is precisely this distinction which does not appear in Greek thought. "Being" was set over against becoming, the latter containing an element of non-being or imperfection; the everlasting, immutable, and immortal were marked off from the transitory, and mortal imitations or images were set over against their originals. But the nearest approach to anything like the modern distinction of subjective-objective was between that which is by *nature* and that which is by *institution* or *convention.*

What may be truly said of ancient philosophy in contrast with modern is that it is naïve, using that word to designate a condition in which the distinction between the subjective and the objective is not made. Since naïveté suggests freshness and directness of approach, due to absence of artificial sophistication, one may apply the word "naïve" eulogistically to Greek philosophy. Of the Greek attitude, we could say that it fused qualities we now distinguish, were it not that fusion suggests prior differentiation, and it is just this antecedent differentiation that is lacking. In every characteristic expression of the Greek genius, the qualities we call emotional and volitional, and hence attribute to persons, are used to clothe things that we call physical and lacking in such qualities. The atomists, literally interpreted, are an exception to this statement. But one has only to read Lucretius (or Santayana today), and to reflect upon what is known regarding Democritus, to see that their interest in cosmology was a moral interest rather than a scientific one in the modern sense. In all influential and widely held ancient cosmologies, the physical world was marked by qualitative and teleological traits which modern physics has stripped away. Until this stripping had taken place there was no ground for anything like sharp opposition of the animate and inanimate; the human and the non-human; the "subjective" and "objective." In the matter of accounting for human traits in terms of generic cosmological qualities, there is no difference between Plato and Aristotle on one side and Democritus on the other.

There is a positive point involved in the foregoing negations. Greek philosophy moved and had its being in and among the things, the subjects, of *direct* experience, the world in which we human beings act, suffer, and enjoy. There is no particular point in saying their attitude was *animistic*, as if they had *first* discriminated certain qualities as psychic and personal and had *then* projected them into an "external" and purely physical (in our sense) world. As a contemporary writer has said in a criticism of the idea about animism entertained by such writers as Tylor, Spencer, and Lang:

> Our present day dichotomy of *behavior* has isolated two types: the type directed toward things, which follows strictly a cause and effect sequence; and the type directed toward persons, which runs the gamut from love to manipulation. . . . Animism considered as *behavior* is nothing more than this; properly speaking, it is only the expression of a state of mind that has not made our distinction between *behavior* toward persons and behavior toward things, but which brings the whole field under one rubric, treating the entire external

world according to the pattern learned in dealings with fellow beings.[4]

The fact that philosophers refined and systematized what is involved in this habitual attitude does not militate against the other fact that they retained it intact as far as its fundamental moral and qualitative implications are concerned. Until the type of physical science which we call modern had become established, what alternative did philosophy have save to describe the world in terms of basic properties of the material of direct experience? If we did not have an alternative in the *pou sto* provided for us by present-day physical science, we too should "naturally" describe the world in teleological and qualitative terms. Any other procedure would strike us as artificial and arbitrary. I was strongly reminded of this fact in reading recently a book by a writer deeply imbued with the spirit of classic Greek philosophy. He uniformly refers to "philosophies of experience" in a disparaging tone. But, as uniformly, his own account of Nature is couched in moral and poetic terms appropriate only to Nature as it is directly presented in experience and inappropriate to nature as disclosed to us in physics.

IV

For the purpose of the present article, the point of the foregoing is the necessity of distinguishing between the things of *direct* experience (which may also be called everyday experience if the latter word is extended to include the relatively extraordinary experiences of poets and moral seers), and something else. What name shall be given to this something else? It may be called *physical* subject-matter in the sense of material of the physical sciences. But this name only makes the *problem* more precise; it offers no solution. And here I recur to the special postulate of this particular discussion: The postulate, namely, that "whether we be ancients or moderns, we can deal only with things, *in some sense,* experienced." From the standpoint of this postulate, the

4. Article, by Ruth Benedict, on "Animism" in the *Encyclopaedia of the Social Sciences,* Vol. II, p. 66. I have italicized "behavior" in order to emphasize the point made.

problem is to discover *in terms of an experienced state of affairs* the connection that exists between physical subject-matter and the common-sense objects of everyday experience. Concern for the *conditions* upon which depend the activities, enjoyments, and sufferings, constituting direct experience, is an integral part of that very experience when it is marked by faith in the possibility of its own indefinite expansion. The hypothesis here offered is that physical subject-matter represents in its own distinctive nature the *conditions* upon which rest the having, and the averting, of things in direct experience. What other method of getting outside and beyond the things of direct experience is conceivable save that of penetration to the conditions upon which they depend?

It is a commonplace that the sole method of controlling the occurrence of specific events—whether as to production or prevention—is by means of knowledge of their connections. It is also a commonplace that modern science, as distinct from ancient, is occupied with determination of such conditions, and also that their discovery has been attended with creation of all sorts of technologies by means of which the area of things experienced and experienceable has been indefinitely widened. Every student of philosophy knows that Greek philosophy subordinated its account of things in terms of "efficient" causation to the account of them in terms of "formal" and "final" causation: that is, it was concerned with stating, by means of definition and classification, *what* things are and *why* they are so (in terms of the ends they serve), rather than with the quite subordinate question of *how* they come into being. The habit of viewing the history of philosophy in isolation from the state of culture in which philosophical theories are produced explains why this undeniable fact has not been linked to the fact that technologies for production and prevention of specifiable objects did not then exist; at least not outside of certain arts and crafts which, in any case, were products of past experiences, or of what *had* been experienced, not of scientific insight. Under these circumstances, the part of intelligent persons was to make as much as possible of characters, of natures, or essences, that "make things to be *what* they *are*" in their own alleged non-relational or "inherent" being. The connections of space, time, motion, that are so important in modern science could not possibly have appeared to be of more than secondary significance until the use of these connections in making possible a control of experience had been demonstrated in experience.

It is not a new discovery that the word "object" is highly ambiguous, being used for the sticks and stones, the cats and dogs, the chairs and tables of ordinary experiences, for the atoms and electrons of physics, and for any kind of "entity" that has logical subsistence—as in mathematics. In spite of the recognized ambiguity, one whole branch of modern epistemology is derived from the assumption that in the case of at least the first two cases, the word "object" has the same general meaning. For otherwise the subject-matter of physics and the things of everyday experience would not have presented themselves as rivals, and philosophy would not have felt an obligation to decide which is "real" and which is "appearance," or at least an obligation to set up a scheme in which they are "reconciled." The place occupied in modern philosophy by the problem of the relation of so-called "scientific objects" and "common-sense objects" is proof, in any case, of the dominating presence of a distinction between the "objective" and the "subjective" which was unknown in ancient philosophy. It indicates that at least in the sense of awareness of an ever-present problem, modern philosophy is "objective-subjective," not just subjective. I suggest that if we gave up calling the distinctive material of the physical sciences by the name "objects" and employed instead the neutral term "scientific subject-matter," the genuine nature of the problem would be greatly clarified. It would not of itself be solved. But at least we should be rid of the implication which now prevents reaching a solution. We should be prepared to consider on its merits the hypothesis here advanced: namely, that scientific subject-matter represents the *conditions* for having and not-having things of direct experience.

Genuinely complete empirical philosophy requires that there be a determination *in terms of experience* of the relation that exists between physical subject-matter and the things of direct perception, use, and enjoyment. It would seem clear that historic empiricism, because of its commitment to sensationalism, failed to meet this need. The obvious way of meeting the requirement is through explicit acknowledgment that direct experience contains, as a highly important direct ingredient of itself, a wealth of *possible* objects. There is no inconsistency between the idea of direct experience and the idea of objects of that experience which are as yet unrealized. For these latter objects are directly experienced *as* possibilities. Every plan, every prediction, yes, every forecast and anticipation, is an experience in which some non-directly experienced object is directly experienced *as a possibility*. And, as previously suggested, modern experience is marked by the extent to which directly perceived, enjoyed, and suffered objects are treated as signs, indications, of what has *not* been experienced in and of itself, or/and are treated as means for the realization of these things of possible experience. Because historic empirical philosophy failed to take cognizance of this fact, it was not able to account for one of the most striking features of scientific method and scientific conclusions—preoccupation with generality as such.

For scientific methods and scientific subject-matter combine highly abstract or "theoretical" considerations with directly present concrete sensible material, and the generality of conclusions reached is directly dependent upon the presence of the first-named type of considerations. Now in modern philosophy, just as scientific "objects" have been set over against objects in direct experience, thereby occasioning the *ontological* problem of modern philosophy (the problem of where "reality" is to be found), so identification of the experiential with but one of the two factors of the method of knowing has created the *epistemological* problem of modern philosophy: the relation of the "conceptual" and "perceptual"; of sense and understanding. In terms of our hypothesis, the distinction and the connection of the distinguished aspects rests upon the fact that what *is* (has been) experienced is of cognitive importance in connection with what *can* be experienced: that is, as evidence, sign, test, of forecast, anticipation, etc., while, on the other hand, there is no way of valid determination of objects of possible experiences save by employing what *has* been experienced, and hence is sensible. Anticipation, foresight, prediction, depend upon taking what is "given" (what has indubitably been experienced) as ominous, or of prospective reference. This is a speculative operation, a wager about the future. But the wager is subject to certain techniques of control. Although every projection of a possible object of experience goes beyond what has been experienced and is in so far risky, this fact does not signify that every idea or projected possibility has an equal claim. Techniques of observation on one side and of calculation (in its broad sense) on the other side have been developed with a view to effective cooperation. Interactivity *of the two factors* constitutes the method of science. Were it not for the influence of the inertia of habit it would be fairly incredible that empiricists did not long ago perceive that material provided by direct sense-perception is limited and remains substantially the same from person to person and from generation to generation. Even when we take into account the additional sense data furnished by artificial instruments, the addition bears no proportionate ratio to the expansion of the subject-matter of the sciences that is constantly taking place. Were it not that "rationalist" theories of knowledge are in no better case with respect to accounting for increase in scientific knowledge (which is its most striking trait in modern times), the marked impotency of sensationalist empiricism would long ago have effected its disappearance.

V

I have presented the more difficult aspect of my position and argument first. Few persons, I take it, would be rash enough to deny that an *actual* experience of a definite thing depends upon the operation of factors which have to be distinguished from those of *physical* subject-matter. It is better at first to refer to these latter factors denotatively, rather than to apply the word "subjective." From the denotative point of view, no one will deny that an experience of light involves an optical apparatus and not simply the existence of certain physical vibrations and quanta, and similarly with experiences of sound, temperature, solidity, etc. In the logical sense of "objectivity," these organic conditions are as objective as those described in physics. The organism is one "object" among others. However, the function of organic factors is so distinctive that it has to be discriminated. When it is discriminated, it is seen to be so different in kind from that of physical subject-matter as to require a special name. As a candidate for the name, "subjective" has one great disadvantage, namely, its traditional use as a name for some sort of existential stuff called psychical or mental. It has, on the other hand, the advantage of calling attention to the particular agency through which the function is exercised: a singular organism, an organism that has been subjected to acculturation, and is aware of itself as a social subject and agent.

The difference in function is, in any case, the important matter. Physical subject-matter consists of the conditions of *possible* experiences in their status *as* possible. It does not itself account for any actual experience. It is general and remote. Objects of direct experience are singular and are here and now. The "subjective" factor (using the word to designate the operations of an acultured organism) is, like "objective" (physical subject-matter) a *condition* of experience. But it is *that* condition which is required to convert the conditions of *kinds* of objects, which as kinds represent generic possibilities, into *this* object. Since every actual or direct experience is of some *this,* here and now, it is imperative to distinguish this type of condition from the type supplied by generic "objective" subject-matter. Greek thought failed to recognize the existence of this "subjective" factor as a condition of positive control. It took account of it only as a ground for indiscriminate scepticism. Or, when convention and institution were regarded as more important than "nature" (as it was by one Greek school) it was because nature was regarded as so crude, raw, wild, that the most arbitrary escape from it was better than subjection to nature. What is not sufficiently noted is that definite differentiation of personal-social factors in their functions in production of things of experience is now part of the technique of controlling the experienced presence of objects; with further advance of behavioral psychology it will become of constantly increased importance. The old stock-in-trade of wholesale scepticism, namely, dreams, illusions, hallucinations, the effect of organic defects, of beliefs locally current, is now in practical fact a positive resource in the management of experience.

I hope what has been said will at least serve to explain the title I have given this article. It is true that modern philosophy is "subjective" as ancient philosophy was not.

In its concern with what *can* be experienced whether or not it *has* been experienced, it has systematically taken account of the operation of *specific* personal-social factors. But it is equally true that modern philosophy has been "objective" in a way in which ancient philosophy was not. It is impossible to make sense of the problems with which modern philosophy has been pre-occupied unless this fact is recognized in its full force. The outstanding defect of modern philosophy is that these problems have taken form by means of setting the two sets of conditions in opposition to one another. This fact is explicable only in terms of the projection into the modern situation of certain heritages from the earlier philosophy which originated in and reflects a different state of culture. Philosophy will become *modern* in a pregnant sense only when the "objectivism-subjectivism" involved is seen to be one of cooperative interaction of two distinguishable sets of conditions, so that knowledge of them *in their distinction* is required in order that their interaction may be brought under intentional guidance. Without such knowledge, intelligence is inevitably held down to techniques for making mechanical permutations and combinations of things that *have* been experienced, and mankind is dependent upon accident for introduction of novelty. The fact that mankind is still far from realization of the power contained in its ability to distinguish certain conditions of experience as physical and others as socio-psychological is true enough. This fact indicates the special responsibility of philosophy today.

Presenting Thomas Jefferson

Thomas Jefferson was fortunate in his birth and early surroundings, being a product both of the aristocracy of the time and of the pioneer frontier. He was fortunate in his contacts and his experiences. The United States is fortunate that he had them. The fact that he occupied certain offices is of little account in itself; comparative nonentities have been foreign envoys and presidents. The use he made of these positions is what counts, and the use includes not only the political policies he urged and carried through, but even more the observations he made and the reflections they produced. His duties, for example, in Paris were few and not very important, "the receipt of our whale-oils, salted fish and salted meats on favorable terms." But the French Revolution began while he was there and he was its keen and intelligent observer. It is typical of him that the political offices he held are not mentioned in the epitaph he wrote for his tombstone. He wished to be remembered as "the author of the Declaration of Independence, the statute of Virginia for religious liberty, and father of the University of Virginia."

His activities in public life provided for him the opportunity for the experiences which inspired and matured his ideas. His republican convictions were formed early in his life; they were absorbed into his life upon what was then the western frontier; they seem to have been crystallized when he was only twenty-two years old by hearing a speech of Patrick Henry in opposition to the British Stamp Act. From that time on he was a leader in every movement for freedom and independence, usually somewhat in advance of other "rebels," finding what he said or wrote disapproved of at the time, only to win later assent. He developed with

[First published in *The Living Thoughts of Thomas Jefferson*, Presented by John Dewey, Living Thoughts Library, ed. Alfred O. Mendel (New York: Longmans, Green and Co., 1940), pp. 1–30.]

the experiences enlarged responsibilities gave him, but it was un-
interruptedly in one direction. Political expediency may have
caused him to deviate on special points, but there are few men in
public life whose course has been so straight. Natural sympathies,
actual experiences, intellectual principles united to produce a
character of singular consistency and charm.

Two days before he retired from the presidency, he wrote to his
French friend, de Nemours, as follows: "Nature intended me for
the tranquil pursuits of science by rendering them my supreme
delight. But the enormities of the times in which I have lived have
forced me to take part in resisting them." Later "the hermit of
Monticello," as he sometimes called himself, remarked in a passage that comes nearer to tapping a poetical vein than almost
anything he ever wrote "The motion of my blood no longer
keeps time with the tumult of the world. It leads me to seek for
happiness in the lap and love of my family, in the society of my
neighbors and my books, in the wholesome occupation of my
farm and my affairs, in an interest or affection in every bud that
opens, in every breath that blows around me, in an entire freedom of rest, of motion, of thought, owing account to myself
alone of my hours and actions."

I do not quote these passages in order to make them the text
for a defense of Jefferson's sincerity, which has been questioned
on the ground that while he purported to live in the retirement of
a country gentleman, he was in fact the focal point of all policies
and movements that maintained the integrity of republican institutions against what seemed to him to invade them in any way.
I quote them to illustrate what I believe to be the key to the work
and character of our first great democrat: the vital union of attitudes and convictions so spontaneous that they are of the kind
called instinctive with fruits of a rich and varied experience:—a
union that was cemented by the ceaseless intellectual activity
which was his "supreme delight." But in a more conventional
way, he was that rare person in politics, an idealist whose native
faith was developed, checked, and confirmed by extremely extensive and varied practical experience. It is seldom, I imagine, that
an unusually sincere and unified natural temperament has been
so happily combined with rich opportunities for observation and
reflection. If he left the stamp of his idealism upon the course of
events, it is because this experience added realistic substance to

the inherent bent of his natural disposition. If it is true, as he wrote to Adams, that "whig and tory are terms of natural as well as of civil history," the pages of the latter may be searched to find another man whose native constitution so properly destined him to espouse the liberal cause and whose career so happily furnished the conditions that gave that constitution opportunity for articulate expression in deed and word.

As long as there are different parties in the United States, there will be dispute as to the soundness of the respective political philosophies associated with the names of Hamilton and Jefferson. If Jefferson was right, the source of the difference lies deep in the varying attitudes of human nature. But it would be a great pity if partisan differences are allowed to identify the teachings of these two men with party strife so as to disable us from appreciating the greatness of our common American heritage. We should do well to declare a truce in party controversy till we have congratulated ourselves upon our great good fortune in having two extraordinarily able men formulate the fundamental principles upon which men divide.

Considering the small size of the American population a hundred and fifty, a hundred and twenty years ago, we may well be amazed, as well as grateful, at the spectacle of the intellectual and moral calibre of the men who took a hand in shaping the American political tradition. The military and moral, although not especially the intellectual, repute of Washington has made him a part of a common heritage. There are also Jefferson, Hamilton, Madison, followed at some distance by Franklin and John Adams, and at a greater distance by Monroe. There were giants in those days. It is more than a pity if either partisan differences or a vague indiscriminate adulation of the Founding Fathers is allowed to produce and create indifference to what they contributed to American institutions and to what we still may learn from them. There still exists among us a kind of intellectual parochialism which induces us to turn to political philosophers of the old world who do not measure up to the stature of our own political thinkers—to say nothing of their remoteness from our own conditions.

Before speaking specifically of Jefferson's social and moral philosophy, something will be said about the range and depth of Jefferson's interests. Irrespective of any question of whose political ideas are sound, there is no doubt that Jefferson was the most universal as a human being of all of his American and perhaps European contemporaries also. We cannot pride ourselves that he was a typical or representative American. He is too far above the average for that. But we can say that he embodied in himself typical American characteristics that are usually dispersed. His curiosity was insatiable. The passage of Terence, accounting nothing human foreign, made trite by frequent usage, applies with peculiar force to him. His interest in every new and useful invention was at least equal to that of Franklin; his sayings are without that tinge of smugness that sometimes colors Franklin's reflections on life. He occupied practically every possible position of American public life, serving in each not only with distinction but marked power of adaptability to the new and unexpected.

The more one reads his letters and other records, the more surprised is one that a single person could find time and energy for such a range of diverse interests. As a farmer, he kept abreast with every advance in botanical and agricultural theory and practice. His notes of travel in France and Italy include the most detailed observations of soils, crops, domestic animals, farm implements and methods of culture. He is moved by what he sees to design a new mouldboard for a plough, having minimum mechanical resistance. Just before retiring from the presidency he notes with pleasure the invention in France of a plough, which was proved by test with a dynamometer to have increased efficiency. He was busy in correspondence with European societies and individuals in exchange of seeds. Of his introduction of the olive tree into South Carolina and Georgia and of upland rice into the same states, he says, "The greatest service which can be rendered any country is to add a useful plant to its culture; especially, a bread grain; next in value to bread is oil."

As far as I have discovered, his inclusion of a professorship of Agriculture in the faculty of the University of Virginia marks the first recognition of the subject for study in higher education. He himself ranked it as of equal importance with the professorship in Government that was provided. The plan he drew up for the institution of a system of Agricultural Societies includes most of the topics now forming the studies of our agricultural colleges, save the problem of marketing. His constant attention to the checking of theory by practical experience is seen in his desire for a report upon "the different practices of husbandry, including the bad as well as the good," with the statement that a selection of all the good ones for imitation and the bad ones for avoidance "would compose a course probably near perfection."

There is no discovery in natural science to the credit of Jefferson similar to that of Franklin in electricity. But his faith in scientific advance as a means of popular enlightenment and of social progress was backed by continual interest in discoveries made by others. When helping his grandson with his scholastic mathematical studies, he writes to a friend that he had resumed that study with great avidity, since it was ever his favorite one, there being no theories, no uncertainties, but all "demonstration and satisfaction." He notes in a letter the superiority of French mathematicians of the time due to their development of analytic methods and expresses his pleasure that English mathematicians are adopting them and are also abandoning the method of fluxions in calculus. His most active interest was in the natural sciences. The foundations of modern chemistry were laid during his life time. Priestley is one of the correspondents with whom Jefferson has closest intellectual sympathy. His "utilitarian" interest is manifested in an expression of regret that chemists had not followed Franklin in directing science to something "useful in private life"; with a hope that their science would be applied to "brewing, making cider, fermentation and distillation generally, making bread, butter, cheese, soap, incubating eggs, etc." He was also skeptical about theories not backed by evidence gained through observation, and thought the French *philosophes,* whose acquaintance he made, indulged in altogether too much unverifiable speculation. He says in one letter: "I am myself an empiric in natural philosophy, suffering my faith to go no further than my facts. I am pleased, however, to see the efforts of hypothetical speculation, because by the collisions of different hypotheses, truth may be elicited and science advanced in the end."

Because of the evidence it provides regarding Jefferson's belief in the union of theory and experience—or practice—it is worth while to quote a passage in which he expresses his opinion about medicine, the passage being taken from a letter to a physician in which he explains that he is sending a grandson to Philadelphia to study botany, natural history, anatomy, possibly surgery, but not medicine. "I have myself lived to see the disciples of Hoff-mann, Boerhaave, Stahl, Cullen, Brown, succeed one another like the shifting figures of a magic lantern, and their fancies, like the annual doll-babies from Paris, becoming, from their novelty, the vogue of the day, and yielding to the next novelty their ephemeral favor. . . . It is in this part of medicine that I wish to see a reform, an abandonment of hypothesis for sober facts, the first degree of value set on clinical observation, and the lowest on visionary theories. . . . The only sure foundations of medicine are an intimate knowledge of the human body, and observation of the effect of medicinal substances on that." It is characteristic of him to end his letter with the following statement: "At any rate the subject has permitted me for a moment to abstract myself from the dry and dreary waste of politics, into which I have been impressed by the times on which I happened, and to indulge in the rich fields of nature where alone I should have served as a volunteer, if left to my natural inclinations and partialities."

It would be a mistake, however, to suppose that Jefferson's interest in science was confined to the field in which useful applications were favorable. He somehow found time to keep up with progress made in astronomy; he made personal observations in the case of a total eclipse of the sun, obtaining a specially accurate chronometer in order that his observations of times might be accurate; he recommended the use of platinum in mirrors of telescopes; he interested himself in the problem of a new method for determining longitude, which he wished to apply also to correction of maps made by ordinary methods of surveying. His letters on weights and measures are quite extensive; he favored a decimal metric system but was opposed to the French selection of its basis. He expended a good deal of ingenuity in devising a standard pendulum swing as a more natural basis, and seems even to have entertained the hope that his project might—after Bonaparte was defeated in war—take the place of the French system. His geological interest was aroused by the existence of fossils, from bones of mammoths to sea shells found thousands of feet above the sea—a subject on which he rejected all theories advanced at the time, holding that more evidence was required before an adequate theory could be framed. His interest in mineralogy was great but mainly practical, since he thought the controversies between "Vulcanists" and "Neptunians" futile. He regretted the backwardness of meteorology and in addition to keeping weather records himself, urged others to do so.

"Science" is used by Jefferson, in agreement with the habit of his day, as an equivalent of *knowledge*. It included what we now call scholarship as well as what we call science. Jefferson was interested in language theoretically as well as practically. He discussed the contemporary pronunciation of Greek—with which he became acquainted while in Paris—in relation to that of classic Greece. He made a collection of vocabularies of fifty different Indian tribes. He began the collection as part of a project for writing a history of the Indians—in whose fate he took a civilized interest not characteristic of the usual attitude. For thirty years he took every opportunity to obtain from correspondents a list of about two hundred and fifty words, covering such objects and acts as every tribe would have names for. He compared names common to these lists with vocabularies of races in Eastern Europe as they were published in Russia, for he was convinced that "filiation of languages was the best means of studying filiation of peoples." His great and abiding interest in Anglo-Saxon undoubtedly had a political bias. For he was convinced that the liberal element in the British constitution was derived from Anglo-Saxon sources while the Norman sources introduced the "Tory" element. As a reason for introducing Anglo-Saxon into the subjects taught in the University of Virginia, he said "the learners will imbibe with the language their free principles of government."

Finally, it is instructive, if not especially important, to note his attitude on the growth of the English language, his idea on this special point being completely consistent with his general philosophy. After saying he is a foe of purisms and a friend of neologisms, since language grows by their introduction and testing, he says: "Dictionaries are but the depositories of words already legitimated by usage. Society is the workshop in which new ones are elaborated. When an individual uses a new word, if ill formed it is rejected in society; if well formed, adopted, and after due time laid up in the depository of dictionaries. And if, in this process of sound neologisation, our trans-Atlantic brethren shall not choose to accompany us, we may furnish, after the Ionians, a second example of a colonial dialect improving on its primitive." The principles here expressed are now generally accepted, but I doubt if a half-dozen men in the country were bold enough to assert them when Jefferson gave expression to them.

Jefferson's ideas about the fine arts suffer from his habit of subjecting things in which the old world was more advanced than the new to the test of utility as a measure of the value of their introduction here. Only in the case of architecture, gardens, and music does he allow his own personal taste free manifestation—and in the former case, motives of utility also enter. It was, however, a lifelong concern of his, both in theory and practice. Of music, he says it is the one thing in France about which he is tempted to disobey the Biblical injunction against coveting. In literature (in the sense of belles lettres), only the classics command his complete admiration. He regarded them as luxuries, but as "sublime" ones. "Homer in his own language" was his chief delight and he goes so far as to say that he thanked God on his knees for directing his early education so as to put him in "possession of this rich source of delight." Of modern poetry, the following is, as far as I am aware, all he has to say: "Pope, Dryden, Thomson, Shakspeare, and of the French, Molière, Racine, the Corneilles, may be read with pleasure and improvement." The factor of "improvement" bulked rather large in his mind, since he seemed to have limited the scope of "luxury" to Greek and Latin authors. Novels he regarded as mostly a "mass of trash, fostering bloated imagination, sickly judgment and disgust toward all the real businesses of life." The exceptions he admitted were those which were "interesting and useful vehicles of a sound morality." However, while he ranked the writing of Miss Edgeworth among the latter, he gave the palm to Sterne. Nevertheless, external evidence bears out the truth of his statement (made in a letter to John Adams)—that he "could not live without books." While he was in France, he collected a library by spending "every afternoon in which I was disengaged in examining all the principal bookstores, turning over every book with my own hand, and putting by everything that related to America and indeed whatever was rare and valuable in every science." He attempted to have the duty on foreign books removed. He introduced bills for establishment of libraries at public expense, and hoped to see a circulating library in every county. It is doubtful if any public man today could quote as freely from the classics as he and John Adams did in their correspondence with each other.

While Jefferson's views on the arts, as on science, reflected the preferences of Franklin—and of Americans generally—for the useful and the practical, his standard of utility and of practical value was that of the benefit of the people as a whole, not that of individuals or of a class. I have quoted in the text a passage from a letter written to John Adams, in which he says that America has given the world "physical liberty"; contribution to "moral emancipation" is a thing of the future. Just before leaving France, he wrote as follows in acknowledging the receipt of the degree of Doctorate of Laws from Harvard University: "We have spent the prime of our lives in procuring them (the youth of the country) the precious blessing of liberty. Let them spend theirs in showing that it is the great parent of *science* and of virtue." Jefferson, when at liberty to give his personal interests free range, was much less limited than some of the quotations given above might suggest. The quotations, taken in their full context, are not so much evidence of his personal taste as of what he thought was the immediate need of a new nation occupying a new and still physically unconquered country. If his *acting* principle had been expressed, it would have been: "Necessities first; luxuries in their due season."

Just as it was the "people" in whom he trusted as the foundation and ultimate security of self-governing institutions, so it was the enlightenment of the people as a whole which was his aim in promoting the advance of science. In a letter to a French friend, in which he says that his prayers are offered for the wellbeing of France, he adds that her future government depends not on "the state of science, no matter how exalted it may be in a select band of enlightened men, but on the condition of the general mind." What is hinted at in these remarks is openly stated in other letters. As the French Revolution went on from its beginnings, which aroused his deepest sympathies, until there followed the despotism and wars of Napoleon, he became increasingly sceptical of the social influence of a small band of enlightened men— like the French *philosophes*. His most extreme reaction is found in a letter to John Adams: "As for France and England, with all their preëminence in science, the one is a den of robbers, and the other of pirates. And if science produces no better fruits than tyranny, murder, rapine, and destitution of national morality, I should wish our country to be ignorant, honest and estimable, as our neighboring savages are." A more temperate statement of the response evoked in him is found in a letter written in 1811 in which he acknowledged the receipt of a history of the French Revolution. "Is reason to be forever amused with the *hochets* of physical science, in which she is indulged merely to divert her from solid speculations on the rights of man and wrongs of his oppressors? it is impossible." At the same time, in speaking of freedom, he throws in the phrase "the first-born daughter of science." Jefferson's emphasis upon the relation of science and learning to practical serviceability had two sources. One of them was the newness of his own country, and his conviction that needs should be satisfied in the degree of their urgency. Political liberty—or as he calls it in one place, physical liberty—came first. A certain measure of material security was needed to buttress this liberty. As these were achieved, he was confident that the spread of education and general enlightenment would add what was lacking in the refinements of culture, things very precious to him personally. Jefferson was a child of both the pioneer frontier and of the enlightenment of the 18th century—that century which he and John Adams regarded as the inauguration of a new era in human affairs.

The other cause of Jefferson's subordination of science and arts to social utility was his European experience. Science, no matter how "exalted," did not prevent wholesale misery and oppression if it was confined to a few. In spite of his very enjoyable personal relations with the leading intellectuals of Paris, his deepest sympathies went to the downtrodden masses whose huts he visited and whose food he ate. His affection for the "people" whose welfare was the real and final object of all social institutions and his faith in the "will of the people" as the basis of all legitimate political arrangements made him increasingly sceptical of advances in knowledge and the arts that left the mass of the people in a state of misery and degradation.

The balanced relation in Jefferson's ideas between the well-being of the masses and the higher cultivation of the arts and sciences is best expressed in his educational project. Elementary popular schooling educated the many. But it also served a selective purpose. It enabled the abler students to be picked out and to continue instruction in the middle grade. Through the agency of the latter the "natural aristocracy" of intellect and character would be selected who would go on to university education. State Universities have carried forward Jefferson's idea of a continuous educational ladder, that of Michigan being directly influenced by him. But in some respects, the plan is still in advance of what has been accomplished.

Jefferson's stay in France gave rise to the notion that his political philosophy was framed under French intellectual influence. It is easy to understand why, after the reaction produced by the excesses of the Revolution, Jefferson's political enemies put forward the idea as an accusation, extremists calling him a participant in Gallic atheism, licentiousness and anarchy. Just why scholars have entertained the same idea, not as a charge against him, but as evidence of close intellectual relations between American social theory and the French Enlightenment is not so clear. Every one of Jefferson's characteristic political ideas (with one possible exception) was definitely formulated by him before he went to France. It is probable that his inclination toward the moral ideas of Epicurus, among the classic writers, dates from acquaintance made in Paris, but that did not affect his political ideas nor even his working ethical views. Rousseau is not even mentioned by him. The moderate French Charter of Rights—a practical not a theoretical document—receives fairly extensive notice; the Rights of Man the barest casual mention.

The fact is—as selections in the text show clearly—in Jefferson's opinion the movement, intellectual and practical, was from the United States to France and Europe, not from the latter to America. The possible exception, alluded to above, is found in Jefferson's emphasis upon the moral inability of one generation to bind a succeeding generation by imposing either a debt or an unalterable constitution upon it. His assertion that the "earth belongs in usufruct to the living; that the dead have neither powers nor rights over it" was general in scope. But his argument (in a letter written from Paris) closes with a statement of the importance of the matter "in every country and most especially in France." For, as he saw, if the new government could not abolish the laws regulating descent of land, recover lands previously given to the Church, abolish feudal and ecclesiastical special privileges, and all perpetual monopolies, reformation of government would be hamstrung before it got started.

The genuine and undeniable influence of France upon Jefferson is shown in a letter he wrote expressing his amazement upon finding the prevalence of monarchical ideas upon his return to New York, when, as he says, "fresh from the French revolution, while in its first and pure stage," he was "somewhat *whetted up* in my own republican principles." The real significance of the question of French influence upon him is found in a larger matter. The text which follows quotes at some length what Jefferson had to say about the sources of the ideas he expressed in the Declaration of Independence. I do not believe his remarks are intended, in their denial of indebtedness to this and to that writer, to set up a claim for originality. On the contrary, I believe his statement is to be taken literally that his purpose was simply to be "an expression of the American mind in words so firm and plain as to command assent." There was nothing that was novel in the idea that "governments derive their just powers from the consent of the governed," nor did it find its origin in Locke's writings—"nearly perfect" as were the latter in Jefferson's opinion. Even the right of the people "to alter or abolish" a government when it became destructive of the inherent moral rights of the governed had behind it a tradition that long antedated the writings of even Locke.

There was, nevertheless, something distinctive, something original, in the Declaration. It was not, however, in ideas at least as old as Aristotle and Cicero, the civil law as expounded by Pufendorf and others, and the political philosophy of the Fathers of the Church. What was new and significant was that these ideas were now set forth as an expression of the "American mind" that the American will was prepared to *act* upon. Jefferson was as profoundly convinced of the novelty of the *action* as a practical "experiment"—favorite word of his in connection with the institution of self-government—as he was of the orthodox character of the ideas as mere theory. The novelty of the practical attempt was, indeed, only set out in higher relief by the lack of novelty in underlying principles.

Jefferson used the language of the time in his assertion of "natural rights" upon which governments are based and which they must observe if they are to have legitimate authority. What is not now so plain is that the word *moral* can be substituted for the word *natural* whenever Jefferson used the latter in connection with law and rights, not only without changing his meaning but making it clearer to a modern reader. Not only does he say: "I am convinced man has no natural right in opposition to his social duties," and that "man was destined for society," but also that "questions of natural right are triable by their conformity with the moral sense and reason of man." In his letter to his French friend de Nemours, Jefferson develops his moral and political philosophy at some length by making a distinction "between the structure of the government and the moral principles" on which its administration is based. It is here that he says, "We of the United States are constitutionally and conscientiously demo-crats," and then goes on to give the statement a moral interpreta-tion. Man is created with a want for society and with the powers to satisfy that want in concurrence with others. When he has procured that satisfaction by institution of a society, the latter is a product which man has a right to regulate "jointly with all those who have concurred in its procurement." "There exists a right independent of force" and "Justice is the fundamental law of society."

So much for the moral foundation and aim of government. Its structure concerns the special way in which men jointly exercise their right of control. He knew too much history and had had a share in making too much history not to know that governments have to be accommodated to the manners and habits of the people who compose a given state. When a population is large and spread over considerable space, it is not possible for a society to govern itself directly. It does so indirectly by representatives of its own choosing; by those to whom it delegates its powers. "Governments are *more or less* republican as they have more or less of the element of popular election and control in their com-position." Writing in 1816, he said that the United States, mea-sured by this criterion, were less republican than they should be, a lack he attributed to the fact that the lawmakers who came from large cities had learned to be afraid of the populace, and then unjustly extended their fears to the "independent, the happy and therefore orderly citizens of the United States." Any one who starts from the just mentioned moral principle of Jefferson as a premise and adds to it as another premise the principle that the only legitimate "object of the institution of government is to se-cure the greatest degree of happiness possible to the general mass of those associated under it" can, with little trouble, derive the further tenets of Jefferson's political creed.

The will of the people as the moral basis of government and the happiness of the people as its controlling aim were so firmly established with Jefferson that it was axiomatic that the only alternative to the republican position was fear, in lieu of trust, of the people. Given fear of them, it followed, as by mathematical necessity, not only that they must *not* be given a large share in the conduct of government, but that they must themselves be controlled by force, moral or physical or both, and by appeal to some special interest served by government—an appeal which, according to Jefferson, inevitably meant the use of means to corrupt the people. Jefferson's trust in the people was a faith in what he sometimes called their common sense and sometimes their reason. They might be fooled and misled for a time, but give them light and in the long run their oscillations this way and that will describe what in effect is a straight course ahead.

I am not underestimating Jefferson's abilities as a practical politician when I say that this deep-seated faith in the people and their responsiveness to enlightenment properly presented was a most important factor in enabling him to effect, against great odds, "the revolution of 1800." It is the cardinal element bequeathed by Jefferson to the American tradition.

Jefferson's belief in the necessity for strict limitation of the powers of officials had both a general and a special or historic source. As for the latter, had not the Revolution itself been fought because of the usurpation of power by the officers of a government? And were not the political opponents of Republicanism, in Jefferson's opinion, men so moved by admiration of the British constitution that they wished to establish a "strong" government in this country, one not above the use of methods of corruption— not indeed as an end in itself but as a means of procuring the allegiance of the populace more effectively and in a less costly way than by use of direct coercion? On general principles, Jefferson knew that possession of unusual and irresponsible power corrupts those who wield it; that officials are, after all, human beings affected by ordinary weaknesses of human nature, "wares from the same work-shop; made of the same materials." Hence they were to be continually watched, tested and checked, as well as constitutionally limited in their original grant of powers.

There are, however, two important points in which popular representations of Jeffersonian democracy are often at fault. One of them concerns the basic importance of the will of the people in relation to the law-making power, constitutional and ordinary. There is no doubt that Jefferson was strongly in favor of specifying in the constitution the powers that could be exercised by officials, executive, legislative and judicial, and then holding them, by strict construction, to the powers specified. But he also believed that "every people have their own particular habits, ways of thinking, manners, etc., which have grown up with them from their infancy, are become a part of their nature, and to which the regulations which are to make them happy must be accommodated." As he states the principle elsewhere "The excellence of every government is its adaptation to the state of those to be governed by it." In this matter, especially, Jefferson's theories were tempered by practical experience.

His idealism was a moral idealism, not a dreamy utopianism. He was aware that conclusions drawn from the past history of mankind were against the success of the experiment that was being tried on American soil. He was quite sure that Latin American countries would succeed in throwing off the yoke of Spain and Portugal, but he was decidedly sceptical about their capacity for self-government, and feared their future was one of a succession of military despotisms for a long time to come. He was conscious that chances for greater success of the experiment in the United States were dependent upon events which might be regarded either as fortunate accidents or as providential dispensations:—the wide ocean protecting the country from oppressive governments in Europe; the "Anglo-Saxon" tradition of liberties; even the jealousies of religious denominations that prevented the State Establishment of any one church, and hence worked for religious liberty; the immense amount of free land and available natural resources with consequent continual freedom of movement; the independence and vigor that were bred on the frontier, etc. Even so, he had fears for the future when the country should be urbanized and industrialized, though upon the whole, he says, he tended by temperament to take counsel of his hopes rather than his fears.

In direct line with his conviction on this point was his belief in the necessity of periodic revisions of the constitution, one to take place every twenty years, and his belief that the process of ordinary amendment had been made too difficult. His faith in the right of the people to govern themselves in their own way and in their ability to exercise the right wisely—provided they were enlightened by education and by free discussion—was stronger than his faith in any article of his own political creed—except this one. His own convictions as to the proper forms of government were strong, and he contended ably for their realization. But he was conciliatory by temperament and by practical policy. Students and historians have criticized him for not trying harder to put into effect after the "revolution of 1800" the reforms he had been urging before that time, especially as he based his opposition to Adams upon their absence. Doubtless he was moved by considerations of political expediency. But there is also no reason to doubt the sincerity of those expressions of his which set forth his willingness to subordinate his own political policies to the judgment of the people. Trust in the popular will was temperamental, constitutional with him.

In any case, he was no friend of what he called "sanctimonious reverence" for the constitution. He adhered to the view, expressed in the Declaration of Independence, that people are more disposed to suffer evils than to right them by abolishing forms to which they are accustomed. It was the more important, accordingly, to recognize that "laws and institutions must go hand in hand with the progress of the human mind" and that institutions must change with change of circumstances brought about by "discoveries, new truths, change of opinions and manners." Were he alive, he would note and scourge that lack of democratic faith which, in the professed name of democracy, asserts that the "ark of the covenant is too sacred to be touched." Jefferson saw that periodical overhauling of the fundamental law was the alternative to change effected only by violence and repetition of the old historic round "of oppressions, rebellions, reformations, oppressions. . . ." There was but one thing which was unchangeable, and that was the "inherent and inalienable rights of man."

The other point in which Jefferson's ideas have not been adequately represented has to do with his belief that state governments are "the true barriers of our liberty"; and his fear of centralized government at Washington:—not that he did not have the belief and the fear, and hold them with strong conviction, but that the ideas with which he supplemented them have not received due attention. In the main text which follows there are selections, of considerable extent, which show the importance he attached to self-governing communities of much smaller size than the state or even the county. He was impressed, practically as well as theoretically, with the effectiveness of the New England town meeting, and wished to see something of the sort made an organic part of the governing process of the whole country. Division of every county into wards was first suggested by him in connection with organization of an elementary school system. But even from his early service in the legislature of Virginia to the latest years of his life he urged his plan and expressed the hope that while it had not been adopted, it would be at some time. In a letter written after he had reached the age of three score years and ten, he says, "As Cato concluded every speech with the words '*Carthago delenda est*' so do I every opinion, with the injunction, 'Divide the counties into wards,'" referring in 1816 to a bill he had introduced forty years at least before, at the time when his other bills for abolition of entails in land and of primogeniture were adopted.

While the first aim of the division into small local units was the establishment and care of popular elementary schools, their purpose extended, in the mind of Jefferson, far beyond that function. The aim was to make the wards "little republics, with a warden at the head of each, for all those concerns, which being under their eye, they would better manage than the larger republics of the county or State." They were to have the "care of the poor, roads, police, elections, nomination of jurors, administration of justice in small cases, elementary exercises of militia." In short, they were to exercise directly with respect to their own affairs all the functions of government, civil and military. In addition, when any important wider matter came up for decision, all wards would be called into meetings on the same day, so that the collective sense of the whole people would be produced. The plan was not adopted. But it was an essential part of Jefferson's political philosophy. The significance of the doctrine of "states' rights" as he held it, is incomplete both theoretically and practically until this plan is taken into the reckoning. "The elementary republics of the wards, the county republics, the State republics and the republic of the Union would form a gradation of authorities." Every man would then share in the government of affairs not merely on election day but every day. In a letter to

John Adams, written in 1813, he says he still has great hope that the plan will be adopted, as it then will form "the key-stone of the arch of our government." It is for this reason that I say this view of self-government is very inadequately represented in the usual form in which it is set forth—as a glorification of state against federal governments, and still more as a theoretical opposition to all government save as a necessary evil. The heart of his philosophy of politics is found in his effort to institute these small administrative and legislative units as the keystone of the arch.

As was suggested earlier, the essentially moral nature of Jefferson's political philosophy is concealed from us at the present time because of the change that has taken place in the language in which moral ideas are expressed. The "self-evident truths" about the equality of all men by creation and the existence of "inherent and inalienable rights," [1] appear today to have a legal rather than a moral meaning; and in addition, the intellectual basis of the legal theory of natural law and natural rights has been undermined by historical and philosophical criticism. In Jefferson's own mind, the words had a definitely ethical import, intimately and vitally connected with his view of God and Nature. The latter connection comes out more clearly if possible in the Preamble, in which he refers to the necessity of the American people taking the "separate and equal station to which the laws of nature and of nature's God entitle them."

These phrases were not rhetorical flourishes nor were they accommodated for reasons of expediency to what Jefferson thought would be popular with the people of the country. Jefferson was a sincere theist. Although his rejection of supernaturalism and of the authority of churches and their creeds caused him to be denounced as an atheist, he was convinced, beyond any peradventure, on *natural* and rational grounds of the existence of a divine righteous Creator who manifested his purposes in the structure of the world, especially in that of society and the human conscience. The natural equality of all human beings was not psychological nor legal. It was intrinsically moral, as a consequence of the equal *moral* relation all human beings sustain to their Cre-

---

1. "Certain" was substituted for "inherent" by the Congress. The first manuscript draft, later changed by Jefferson himself, read that "all Men are created equal and independent; that from that equal Creation they derive Rights."

ator;—equality of moral claims and of moral responsibilities. Positive law—or municipal law, as Jefferson termed it—and political institutions thus have both a moral foundation and a moral criterion or measure.

The word "faith" is thus applied advisedly to the attitude of Jefferson toward the people's will, and its right to control political institutions and policies. The faith had a genuinely religious quality. The forms of government and law, even of the Constitution, might and should change. But the inherent and inalienable rights of man were unchangeable, because they express the will of the righteous creator of man embodied in the very structure of society and conscience. Jefferson was not an "individualist" in the sense of the British laissez-faire liberal school. Individual human beings receive the right of self-government "with their being from the hand of nature." As an eighteenth century deist and believer in natural religion, Jefferson connected nature and Nature's God inseparably in his thought. He writes that he has "no fear but that the result of our experiment will be that men may be trusted to govern themselves without a master. Could the contrary of this be proved, I should conclude either that there is no God, or that he is a malevolent being." These words are to be taken literally not rhetorically, if one wishes to understand Jefferson's democratic faith. He even engages in construction of the following syllogism. "Man was created for social intercourse; but social intercourse cannot be maintained without a sense of justice; then man must have been created with a sense of justice." The connection of justice—or equity—with equality of rights and duties was a commonplace of the moral tradition of Christendom. Jefferson took the tradition seriously. The statements of Jefferson about the origin of the Declaration of Independence, statements already quoted, are confirmed in what he wrote shortly before his death. "We had no occasion to search into musty records, to hunt up royal parchments, or to investigate the laws and institutions of a semi-barbarous ancestry. We appealed to those of nature, and found them engraved on our hearts."

Other days bring other words and other opinions behind words that are used. The terms in which Jefferson expressed his belief in the moral criterion for judging all political arrangements and his belief that republican institutions are the only ones that are morally legitimate are not now current. It is doubtful, however, whether defense of democracy against the attacks to which it is subjected does not depend upon taking once more the position Jefferson took about its moral basis and purpose, even though we have to find another set of words in which to formulate the moral ideal served by democracy. A renewal of faith in common human nature, in its potentialities in general and in its power in particular to respond to reason and truth, is a surer bulwark against totalitarianism than is demonstration of material success or devout worship of special legal and political forms.

Jefferson wrote no set treatises. In reply to a suggestion that he write a history of his own times, he replied that "while in public life I had not the time, and now that I am retired I am past the time." He probably would have made a similar reply, couched in even more emphatic terms, to a suggestion that he write a book on the principles of government. He would have been content to point to the record of his activities. But he was an indefatigable letter writer. In a letter written after he was seventy years of age, he says he engages in correspondence till noon every day, some days from sunrise to one or two o'clock. In his eightieth year he reports that having counted the letters in his file of the previous year, he found they amounted to 1267, "many requiring answers of elaborate research." The published letters of the first month of 1816 add up to over 12,000 words. It is from these letters and his public documents that the material of the following pages is drawn. I believe they make up in actuality and in sincerity what is lacking in system. The problem of selection was easier to solve than that of arrangement, since it is clear that there is no preordained logical arrangement for the materials of a correspondence that extends over a period of sixty active and full years. Many schemes of arrangement suggest themselves. I have been guided chiefly by a desire to combine the more theoretical statements with passages recording his own observations, and illustrate thereby that union of principle and practice which seems to me to constitute the greatness of Jefferson.

Jefferson's life was peculiarly divided, almost split, between his public career and his private and domestic activities. It is probably owing to something pretty fundamental in his own character that for the most part he preferred to permit the former to speak for itself, and that, when questioned about the latter, he said they were substantially similar to those of any other American citizen of the time. Consequently, in spite of the autobiographical notes which he wrote, there is curiously little material available of a strictly personal kind. We know he was a cultivated gentleman, of personal charm. That he was of handsome physique is proved by the portraits painted of him by Stuart, Peale, Desnoyers, Sully, and by the statues of Powers and d'Angers. Strongly opposed to extravagance and debt in public affairs, he was never out of debt himself. He must have spent several small fortunes in building, tearing down, and rebuilding his home at Monticello and experimenting with the buildings for the University of Virginia, whose architect and supervisor he was, down to personally deciding by chemical experiment the composition of the cement used in laying the brick walls.

His father was a pioneer frontiersman, one of the first three or four to venture to what was at that time the western limit of settlement in the Virginia territory, a man with slight opportunity for schooling and yet so "eager after information" and so bent on improvement that he made of himself a skilled surveyor who, in company with a professor of mathematics, fixed the boundary line between Virginia and North Carolina, and who insisted upon giving his son the best classical education attainable at that time in America. Doubtless it was from him and from the pioneer environment in which men were compelled to be jacks-of-all-trades that Thomas Jefferson derived his lifelong interest in all mechanical inventions and gadgets, and his abiding respect for personal industry and handicraft. His respect for labor is expressed in a letter he wrote to a friend in France when, upon his return from that country, he found that the deranged state of his farms required him to find a new source of revenue: "My new trade of nail-making is to me in this country what an additional title of nobility or the ensigns of a new order are in Europe." It is not unduly speculative to suppose that it was from his frontier experience that he also derived that sense of the inevitable continental expansion of the United States which seems to have marked him alone among the statesmen of the time, and which later expressed itself in the Louisiana purchase and in his attitude toward Florida and even Cuba.

We know that Jefferson married, when approaching the age of

thirty, a widow twenty-three years old, the daughter of a successful local lawyer; that for ten years before her death they lived in great happiness, and that Jefferson never remarried. But again it seems characteristic of the sharp line drawn by Jefferson between his public career and his private life that he left little record of her and his life with her, save a statement in a letter to a French friend that having "rested all prospects of future happiness on domestic and literary objects, a single event wiped away my plans and left me a blank." This blank, caused by his wife's death, he intimates to be the main reason why he was willing to accept his appointment as Ambassador to France, to succeed, but *not,* as he always said, to "replace" Benjamin Franklin, "The greatest man and ornament of the age and country in which he lived." During the ten years of married life, five daughters and one son were born to them. The son lived less than a month; the husbands of two of his daughters were among the closest of Jefferson's correspondents, but even with them ideas and public affairs are discussed rather than intimate personal and family matters.

The combination in Jefferson of a kind of objective pride in his public career and a frequently expressed preference for a life of retirement devoted to management of his estate, to reading and writing, to making scientific observations and studies, and to domestic happiness, finds expression in his replies to correspondents who asked him for material for a biography. The uniform tenor of his response is that "The only exact testimony of a man is his actions" and of these others must be left to be the judge. Aside from his public activities, there was nothing in his life worthy of special record. After his fame was firmly established he even refused to state the date of his birth on the ground that the only birthday he wished to have recognized was "that of my country's liberties."

The combination of reserve and dislike for public office with extraordinary skill and success as a practical politician laid Jefferson open to the charge of inconsistency and even insincerity. Such charges are impossible either to support or to refute long after the events which occurred, and are unprofitable. That Jefferson disliked controversy and was disposed to be conciliatory and compromising there is, however, no reason to doubt. The exceptions made in the case of Hamilton and to a lesser degree in that of Chief Justice Marshall are of the kind that prove a rule. The latter is exemplified in the pain he felt at the break with John Adams and the great joy he experienced in the restoration of friendly relations. What he said about the conduct of Franklin at the French Court might almost be taken as defense of charges sometimes brought against himself: "His temper was so amiable and conciliatory, his conduct so rational, never urging impossibilities, so moderate and attentive to the difficulties of others, that what his enemies called subserviency, I saw was only a reasonable disposition,"—not that he was charged with subserviency, but with inconsistency between professed principles and actual behavior. In any case, if Jefferson is better known for his political ideas and his public acts than as a human being, it is just what he would have wished for himself. Considering his times and the difficult and important part he played in them, there remains the image of a magnanimous, high-spirited public gentleman who subordinated himself with complete devotion to what he conceived to be the welfare of the country he loved. I do not see how any one can doubt that he was careless of his own future fame when that was put in comparison with the future of the democratic ideas he served, nor that, on the other hand, he felt sure of his own reputation as long as those ideas were safe.

Creative Democracy—
The Task Before Us

Under present circumstances I cannot hope to conceal the fact that I have managed to exist eighty years. Mention of the fact may suggest to you a more important fact—namely, that events of the utmost significance for the destiny of this country have taken place during the past four-fifths of a century, a period that covers more than half of its national life in its present form. For obvious reasons I shall not attempt a summary of even the more important of these events. I refer here to them because of their bearing upon the issue to which this country committed itself when the nation took shape—the creation of democracy, an issue which is now as urgent as it was a hundred and fifty years ago when the most experienced and wisest men of the country gathered to take stock of conditions and to create the political structure of a self-governing society.

For the net import of the changes that have taken place in these later years is that ways of life and institutions which were once the natural, almost the inevitable, product of fortunate conditions have now to be won by conscious and resolute effort. Not all the country was in a pioneer state eighty years ago. But it was still, save perhaps in a few large cities, so close to the pioneer stage of American life that the traditions of the pioneer, indeed of the frontier, were active agencies in forming the thoughts and shaping the beliefs of those who were born into its life. In imagination at least the country was still having an open frontier, one of unused and unappropriated resources. It was a country of physical opportunity and invitation. Even so, there was more than a marvelous conjunction of physical circumstances

[First published in *John Dewey and the Promise of America,* Progressive Education Booklet No. 14 (Columbus, Ohio: American Education Press, 1939), pp. 12–17, from an address read by Horace M. Kallen at the dinner in honor of Dewey in New York City on 20 October 1939.]

involved in bringing to birth this new nation. There was in existence a group of men who were capable of readapting older institutions and ideas to meet the situations provided by new physical conditions—a group of men extraordinarily gifted in political inventiveness.

At the present time, the frontier is moral, not physical. The period of free lands that seemed boundless in extent has vanished. Unused resources are now human rather than material. They are found in the waste of grown men and women who are without the chance to work, and in the young men and young women who find doors closed where there was once opportunity. The crisis that one hundred and fifty years ago called out social and political inventiveness is with us in a form which puts a heavier demand on human creativeness.

At all events this is what I mean when I say that we now have to re-create by deliberate and determined endeavor the kind of democracy which in its origin one hundred and fifty years ago was largely the product of a fortunate combination of men and circumstances. We have lived for a long time upon the heritage that came to us from the happy conjunction of men and events in an earlier day. The present state of the world is more than a reminder that we have now to put forth every energy of our own to prove worthy of our heritage. It is a challenge to do for the critical and complex conditions of today what the men of an earlier day did for simpler conditions.

If I emphasize that the task can be accomplished only by inventive effort and creative activity, it is in part because the depth of the present crisis is due in considerable part to the fact that for a long period we acted as if our democracy were something that perpetuated itself automatically; as if our ancestors had succeeded in setting up a machine that solved the problem of perpetual motion in politics. We acted as if democracy were something that took place mainly at Washington and Albany—or some other state capital—under the impetus of what happened when men and women went to the polls once a year or so— which is a somewhat extreme way of saying that we have had the habit of thinking of democracy as a kind of political mechanism that will work as long as citizens were reasonably faithful in performing political duties.

Of late years we have heard more and more frequently that this is not enough; that democracy is a way of life. This saying gets down to hard pan. But I am not sure that something of the externality of the old idea does not cling to the new and better statement. In any case we can escape from this external way of thinking only as we realize in thought and act that democracy is a *personal* way of individual life; that it signifies the possession and continual use of certain attitudes, forming personal character and determining desire and purpose in all the relations of life. Instead of thinking of our own dispositions and habits as accommodated to certain institutions we have to learn to think of the latter as expressions, projections and extensions of habitually dominant personal attitudes.

Democracy as a personal, an individual, way of life involves nothing fundamentally new. But when applied it puts a new practical meaning in old ideas. Put into effect it signifies that powerful present enemies of democracy can be successfully met only by the creation of personal attitudes in individual human beings; that we must get over our tendency to think that its defense can be found in any external means whatever, whether military or civil, if they are separated from individual attitudes so deepseated as to constitute personal character.

Democracy is a way of life controlled by a working faith in the possibilities of human nature. Belief in the Common Man is a familiar article in the democratic creed. That belief is without basis and significance save as it means faith in the potentialities of human nature as that nature is exhibited in every human being irrespective of race, color, sex, birth and family, of material or cultural wealth. This faith may be enacted in statutes, but it is only on paper unless it is put in force in the attitudes which human beings display to one another in all the incidents and relations of daily life. To denounce Naziism for intolerance, cruelty and stimulation of hatred amounts to fostering insincerity if, in our personal relations to other persons, if, in our daily walk and conversation, we are moved by racial, color or other class prejudice; indeed, by anything save a generous belief in their possibilities as human beings, a belief which brings with it the need for providing conditions which will enable these capacities to reach fulfilment. The democratic faith in human equality is belief that every human being, independent of the quantity or range of his personal endowment, has the right to equal opportunity with every other person for development of whatever gifts he has. The democratic belief in the principle of leadership is a generous one. It is universal. It is belief in the capacity of every person to lead his own life free from coercion and imposition by others provided right conditions are supplied.

Democracy is a way of personal life controlled not merely by faith in human nature in general but by faith in the capacity of human beings for intelligent judgment and action if proper conditions are furnished. I have been accused more than once and from opposed quarters of an undue, a utopian, faith in the possibilities of intelligence and in education as a correlate of intelligence. At all events, I did not invent this faith. I acquired it from my surroundings as far as those surroundings were animated by the democratic spirit. For what is the faith of democracy in the role of consultation, of conference, of persuasion, of discussion, in formation of public opinion, which in the long run is self-corrective, except faith in the capacity of the intelligence of the common man to respond with commonsense to the free play of facts and ideas which are secured by effective guarantees of free inquiry, free assembly and free communication? I am willing to leave to upholders of totalitarian states of the right and the left the view that faith in the capacities of intelligence is utopian. For the faith is so deeply embedded in the methods which are intrinsic to democracy that when a professed democrat denies the faith he convicts himself of treachery to his profession.

When I think of the conditions under which men and women are living in many foreign countries today, fear of espionage, with danger hanging over the meeting of friends for friendly conversation in private gatherings, I am inclined to believe that the heart and final guarantee of democracy is in free gatherings of neighbors on the street corner to discuss back and forth what is read in uncensored news of the day, and in gatherings of friends in the living rooms of houses and apartments to converse freely with one another. Intolerance, abuse, calling of names because of differences of opinion about religion or politics or business, as well as because of differences of race, color, wealth or degree of culture are treason to the democratic way of life. For everything which bars freedom and fullness of communication sets up barriers that divide human beings into sets and cliques, into antagonistic sects and factions, and thereby undermines the democratic way of life. Merely legal guarantees of the civil liberties of free belief, free expression, free assembly are of little avail if in daily life freedom of communication, the give and take of ideas, facts, experiences, is choked by mutual suspicion, by abuse, by fear and hatred. These things destroy the essential condition of the democratic way of living even more effectually than open coercion which—as the example of totalitarian states proves—is effective only when it succeeds in breeding hate, suspicion, intolerance in the minds of individual human beings.

Finally, given the two conditions just mentioned, democracy as a way of life is controlled by personal faith in personal day-by-day working together with others. Democracy is the belief that even when needs and ends or consequences are different for each individual, the habit of amicable cooperation—which may include, as in sport, rivalry and competition—is itself a priceless addition to life. To take as far as possible every conflict which arises—and they are bound to arise—out of the atmosphere and medium of force, of violence as a means of settlement into that of discussion and of intelligence is to treat those who disagree—even profoundly—with us as those from whom we may learn, and in so far, as friends. A genuinely democratic faith in peace is faith in the possibility of conducting disputes, controversies and conflicts as cooperative undertakings in which both parties learn by giving the other a chance to express itself, instead of having one party conquer by forceful suppression of the other—a suppression which is none the less one of violence when it takes place by psychological means of ridicule, abuse, intimidation, instead of by overt imprisonment or in concentration camps. To cooperate by giving differences a chance to show themselves because of the belief that the expression of difference is not only a right of the other persons but is a means of enriching one's own life-experience, is inherent in the democratic personal way of life.

If what has been said is charged with being a set of moral commonplaces, my only reply is that that is just the point in saying them. For to get rid of the habit of thinking of democracy as something institutional and external and to acquire the habit of treating it as a way of personal life is to realize that democracy is a moral ideal and so far as it becomes a fact is a moral fact. It is to realize that democracy is a reality only as it is indeed a commonplace of living.

Since my adult years have been given to the pursuit of philosophy, I shall ask your indulgence if in concluding I state briefly the democratic faith in the formal terms of a philosophic position. So stated, democracy is belief in the ability of human experience to generate the aims and methods by which further experience will grow in ordered richness. Every other form of moral and social faith rests upon the idea that experience must be subjected at some point or other to some form of external control; to some "authority" alleged to exist outside the processes of experience. Democracy is the faith that the process of experience is more important than any special result attained, so that special results achieved are of ultimate value only as they are used to enrich and order the ongoing process. Since the process of experience is capable of being educative, faith in democracy is all one with faith in experience and education. All ends and values that are cut off from the ongoing process become arrests, fixations. They strive to fixate what has been gained instead of using it to open the road and point the way to new and better experiences.

If one asks what is meant by experience in this connection my reply is that it is that free interaction of individual human beings with surrounding conditions, especially the human surroundings, which develops and satisfies need and desire by increasing knowledge of things as they are. Knowledge of conditions as they are is the only solid ground for communication and sharing; all other communication means the subjection of some persons to the personal opinion of other persons. Need and desire—out of which grow purpose and direction of energy—go beyond what exists, and hence beyond knowledge, beyond science. They continually open the way into the unexplored and unattained future.

Democracy as compared with other ways of life is the sole way of living which believes wholeheartedly in the process of experience as end and as means; as that which is capable of generating the science which is the sole dependable authority for the direction of further experience and which releases emotions, needs and desires so as to call into being the things that have not existed in the past. For every way of life that fails in its democracy limits the contacts, the exchanges, the communications, the interactions by which experience is steadied while it is also enlarged and enriched. The task of this release and enrichment is one that has to be carried on day by day. Since it is one that can have no end till experience itself comes to an end, the task of democracy is forever that of creation of a freer and more humane experience in which all share and to which all contribute.

The Case for Bertrand Russell

The defense of Bertrand Russell in connection with his appointment to the chair of philosophy in the City College of New York has quite properly centered about two points. One of them is the legal authority of a court to overrule and nullify the action of an administrative board created according to the statutes of New York State. The other is whether writings upon matters of great social importance addressed to adults shall be used to deprive the author of the power to teach his own special and very different subject in classrooms of higher institutions of learning. If courts have the power claimed for them, appointments in tax-supported institutions—and possibly in private institutions—will be thrown into a state of uncertainty till they have dragged through the courts, while educational administrative bodies are deprived of responsibility as well as of power. If Justice McGeehan's action is upheld with respect to the second point, the effect will be to muzzle university teachers on subjects not directly connected with their specialties of instruction.

There is another issue which should not be lost sight of. The profuse outgivings of the attorney for the complainant and of the justice who passed on the case have surrounded what Mr. Russell actually wrote with such a disgusting and loathsome aura that many otherwise fair-minded people have been misled as to what he said. The public interest in discussion of such matters of sexual morals as the use of contraceptives, the stability of family life, the sex education, direct and indirect, of children, the population problem, eugenics, and the like, even more than fair play to Mr. Russell—which has been conspicuously lacking in the treatment given him—raises the questions: What has Mr. Russell actually said and in what spirit has he said it? Neither of these

[First published in *Nation* 150 (15 June 1940): 732–33.]

questions can be even approached, much less settled, on the basis of passages torn out of their context.

In the first place, it is necessary to mention a few facts about moral theory which are elementary to all modern students not committed in advance to some scheme of supernatural and theological ethics. One fact recognized by such students is that the bases and sanctions of morals are found in human relations and their bearing upon human welfare. Another is that cultural lag is nowhere more evident than in the discrepancy existing between the conclusions of specialists in anthropology, medicine, psychology, and so on upon general matters of ethical theory—not just special matters of sexual ethics—and popular beliefs, which, when they have not been received from some dogmatic institutional source, have usually been picked up from the flotsam and jetsam of old traditions. Because of this discrepancy any public discussion based upon results reached by scientific investigators but couched in words that can be understood by those without specialized technical training is bound to be disturbing, and even shocking. This fact, especially weighty in connection with all matters of sexual morality, where in any case the discrepancy between actual social practices and traditional opinions is greatest, is easily taken advantage of by those who believe in the theological bases for the morality that is taught and sanctioned by ecclesiastical "authorities." Unless this fact is borne in mind, it is impossible to understand either the animus of the attack upon Mr. Russell or the effect produced by quotations from his writings upon the minds of those who do not share that animus.

Mr. Russell's discussion, in his writings, of the need for a new sexual ethic has been too successfully represented as if it were a repudiation of any sexual ethic whatever. His argument, based upon facts derived from a variety of sources, that the current sexual ethics, more honored in words than in fact, contain many elements of superstitious origin, while the social practices based upon them have lost their efficacy because of political and economic changes, is completely passed over. Emotional panic is aroused in the breasts of many good people by the mere suggestion that the old sexual ethics have broken down. The treatment that has been accorded Mr. Russell is then more significant as evidence of the gap that lies between the attitude of scientific students and the tenor of prevalent opinions than it is of anything else. And the basic issue is not whether Mr. Russell's own views are correct but whether efforts to bridge the existing gap shall be prevented or at least discouraged by abuse of anyone who engages in public discussion not couched in highly technical language.

The spirit in which Mr. Russell approached the topics discussed is important. To a student of social psychology there is nothing surprising in the fact that an audience which feeds willingly on flippant and easygoing discussion of sex in the novels it reads should be shocked by a serious discussion of sex. For Mr. Russell's discussion is serious in spite of an occasional regrettable asperity of tone. The following passages could be multiplied many times over: "I do not think that the new system any more than the old should involve an unbridled yielding to impulse, but I think the occasions for restraining impulse and the motives for doing so will have to be different from what they have been in the past"; and again, "The doctrine I wish to preach is not one of licence; it involves exactly as much self-control as is involved in the conventional doctrine." For, as he says, "Sex cannot dispense with an ethic, any more than business or sport or scientific research or any other branch of human activity." He accepts the idea now generally held by competent students that impulses are to be trained rather than suppressed. He holds that very many of the evils which he in common with other moralists deplores are due to the existence of conditions which give misdirection to impulse and desire. Consequently there is something ironical in the attacks upon him which proceed from persons who hold that all natural tendencies are so inherently bad and all sexual impulses so intrinsically indecent that not only they but any reference to them should be suppressed.

Regarding the principles which are used in providing the criteria for a sound sexual ethic, Russell writes:

> Sex morality has to be derived from certain general principles, as to which there is perhaps a fairly wide measure of agreement, in spite of the wide disagreement as to the consequences to be drawn from them. The first thing to be secured is that there should be as much as possible of that deep, serious love between man and woman which embraces the whole personality of both and leads to a fusion by which

each is enriched and enhanced. The second thing of importance is that there should be adequate care of children, physical and psychological.

As Mr. Russell indicates, not all who accept these principles and who attempt to draw consequences from them in the light of the best knowledge available will agree with all the conclusions upon special points which he reaches. It happens that personally I agree with some of his conclusions and disagree with others; and to me it appears that in the cases in which I disagree Mr. Russell adopts a logic more appropriate to mathematical than to social and moral subjects—a logic, that is, of one-way reasoning from a single set of premises. But any such difference in conclusions is not only no reason for penalizing one who discusses in a serious spirit the issues involved but is a possible reason for having the issues publicly discussed, so that light may be gained from a variety of sources. The only thing ruled out is the dogmatism and intolerance that would forbid discussion.

In any case the persons, if there be such, who go to Mr. Russell's writings in search of filth and obscenity will be disappointed. These things are so lacking that the intemperate and morally irresponsible way in which they are charged against Mr. Russell is good reason for believing that those who put them forth hold such an "authoritarian" view of morals that they would, if they had power, suppress all critical discussion of beliefs and practices they want to impose on others.

Social Realities *versus* Police Court Fictions

In 1929 there was published in New York City a book dealing with the social and personal ethics of the family from the conjugal and familial points of view, the latter having to do especially with the interests of children but also including economic aspects of the family as a household unit. The public reception of the book at the time is fairly represented by the following extracts from reviews in New York City papers. By one critic the author is said to "deal most competently and completely with practically every ramification of sex and sex life that occurs in modern sociology and psychology"; the critic referred specifically to the book's "dignified pages." Another reviewer flatly said of the book that it was "the most humane and persuasive volume in the recent books on marriage," while a third one said that the book "is valuable for being at once fundamental and clear, unbiased and persuasive," that the author is writing "as a humanist, defending the happiness of man against many moral prejudices."

Several years before the appearance of the book in question, a writer of the Roman Catholic persuasion had written in the *Catholic World* concerning the author, whose reputation was already well established, as "a religious atheist." Although, of course, the Catholic writer rejected the "religious atheist's" views, he said of him: "He is a man of high intellectual achievement, and of undoubted honesty of purpose"; "one of our clearest and most penetrating thinkers, and, whatever our judgment of his ideals, undoubtedly an idealist." In another place this Catholic writer said, in a passage directly relevant to the theme of the later work of the author: "In the chapter on 'Marriage' in

[First published in *The Bertrand Russell Case,* ed. John Dewey and Horace M. Kallen (New York: Viking Press, 1941), pp. 55–74.]

Principles of Social Reconstruction we read: 'As religion dominated the old form of marriage, so religion must dominate the new.' It is good that Mr. Russell should see so clearly that no legal rules or permissions can, by themselves, solve the problems of sex relationship, that these are soluble by religion alone." Regarding the general position taken by the author whom the Catholic writer was discussing, the latter quotes the following passage as typical: " 'If life is to be fully human, it must serve some end which seems, in some sense, outside human life; some end which is impersonal and above mankind, such as God or truth or beauty,' " and after citing other passages says: "Such is the religious witness of Mr. Russell, valuable surely as the witness borne by one of the keenest intellects to which naturalism can appeal for support."

Eleven years after the appearance of the book of which reviewers spoke so highly in 1929, its author was characterized by a lawyer, representing a client in an alleged court of justice, as "lecherous, salacious, libidinous, lustful, venerous, erotomaniac, aphrodisiac, atheistic, irreverent, narrow-minded, untruthful, and bereft of moral fiber . . . he is a sophist; practices sophism; by cunning contrivances, tricks, and devices, and by mere quibbling he puts forth fallacious arguments . . . all his alleged doctrines which he calls philosophy are just cheap, tawdry, worn out, patched up fetishes and propositions, devises [*sic*] for misleading the people."

The judge who passed upon the case in court said that the contention that "immoral and salacious doctrines" were taught in the books written by the author in question was amply sustained; that they are full of "filth"; that the principle of "academic freedom was being used as a cloak to promote the popularization in the minds of adolescents of acts forbidden by the Penal Law"; that the writer was a man whose life and teachings run counter to the doctrines "which have been held sacred by all Americans, preserved by the Constitution of the United States and of the several states, defended by the blood of its citizens"; that the man in question "teaches and practices immorality and . . . encourages and avows violation of the Penal Law of the State of New York."

It is no secret to the reader that the book thus denounced is *Marriage and Morals* and that the author thus excoriated is Bertrand Russell.

The full story is told elsewhere in the present volume, and the bearing of the decision upon the well-being of schools, public and private, is competently discussed. These matters are outside the scope of my particular contribution to this book. I shall say nothing of the extensive acquaintance of the lawyer with the vocabulary of obscenity or of the fact that the "justice" who heard the case indulged in language which if uttered where it did not have the protection of judicial position would have been outright libelous, although he also took advantage of the same judicial position to deny Mr. Russell a chance to appear and to exercise the ordinary right of self-defense. I gladly leave these men, lawyer and judge, to the kind of immortality in the annals of history they have won for themselves.

I shall not even raise a question that is of great social importance: How and why is it that in eleven short years there has been such a growth of intolerance and bigotry? My part in this volume of record and protest is to point out the immense difference between the realities of the case in what Mr. Russell actually said about the past, present, and possible ethics of marriage and sex, and the opinion, involving unbridled misrepresentations, expressed by attorney and Court. The opinion of the Court was allowed to pass, with no opportunity for Mr. Russell to obtain a hearing, and his right of appeal to a higher court was denied on a technicality which is irrelevant to the merits of the case. As Americans we can only blush with shame for this scar on our repute for fair play.

But, it may be asked, whatever be said about the Court's interpretation, are not the passages cited by it actually found in the book? They are, and yet, by adopting the method employed by the Court, I could show that Mr. Russell's opinions are in substantial harmony with the best traditional views on the topics discussed. For the method was the cheap device of quoting passages without reference to their context and without reference to the purpose of the arguments in which they appear.

For example, the following passages are infinitely more representative of the purpose of the discussion and of the question of decency *versus* filth than are the extracts arbitrarily selected by the Court—or by whoever wrote its decision: "Marriage is something more serious than the pleasure of two people in each other's company; it is an institution which, through the fact that it gives rise to children, forms part of the intimate texture of society and has an importance extending far beyond the personal feelings of the husband and wife." "I believe marriage to be the best and most important relation that can exist between two human beings." "Custom should be against divorce except in somewhat extreme cases."

So much for marriage. As for sex and the sexual act, I quote the following passages: "A comprehensive sexual ethic cannot regard sex merely as a natural hunger. Sex is connected with some of the greatest goods in human life, lyric love, happiness in marriage, and art." "Love increases in value in proportion as more of the personalities of the people concerned enters into the relation." "I wish to repeat, as emphatically as I can, that an undue preoccupation with this topic [sex] is an evil." "One of the most dangerous of fallacies is the reduction of sex to the sexual act." "We regard it as wrong to steal food. . . . Restraints of a similar kind are essential where sex is concerned, but in this case they are more complex and involve much more self-control." Mr. Russell criticizes novelists who "view sex intercourse merely as a physiological outlet"; "love," he holds, "has its own ideals and its own intrinsic moral standards."

I could quote many other passages of the same tenor. If, however, they were permitted to stand alone they would fail to do justice to the purpose and spirit of Mr. Russell's book. While the passages are, as I have said, representative, and Justice McGeehan's extracts are misrepresentative, they occur in the course of a criticism of the traditional and conventional ethic of sex and of marriage. It is this ethic, according to Mr. Russell, which fails to conform to the ideal character of love, and which tends to degrade the sex-act to something inherently unworthy and, even according to the views of St. Paul and many of the Church fathers, intrinsically indecent; the prevalence of this ethic being the main cause of taboos on proper instruction of the young. Indeed, the sole charitable opinion that can be formed, by stretching charity to the utmost, of Justice McGeehan is that he himself, because of his education and environment, shares those views so fully that he regards *any* discussion of sexual matters as intrinsically indecent.

Mr. Russell's book is, then, an outright criticism of the traditional views of sex and marriage, views which have profoundly influenced law and public opinion. The book is a plea for views, for legal institutions, for social customs, and for public opinion, which will, in Mr. Russell's considered judgment, represent a more humane ethic and better serve the general welfare of society. Mr. Russell does not regard any position he takes as beyond criticism. But he would wish the criticism to be made on the same grounds of rational examination, free from superstitious traditions, and in the light of the moral standard of general well-being and happiness, upon which he rests his own views. He was not unaware of the interpretation that would be put upon his views by men of the mental and moral habits of the justice, several clerics, and such outstanding authorities as Mr. George Harvey of Queens and various lodges of the Ancient Order of Hibernians; for in his book he said: "The writer who deals with a sexual theme is always in danger of being accused, by those who think that such themes should not be mentioned, of an undue obsession with his subject. It is thought he would not risk the censure of prudish and prurient persons unless his interest in the subject were out of all proportion to its importance. . . . I am quite in agreement with the Church in thinking that obsession with sexual topics is an evil, but I am not in agreement with the Church as to the best methods of avoiding this evil."

I am aware that people who are sincere and in general high-minded, have been so deeply influenced by the taboos which surrounded the subject of sex in their early education that many of them, although they had not read Mr. Russell's book, were willing to take the outcry against the book and its author for what it pretended to be. But those who *are* genuinely sincere and high-minded will be willing, even if they retain their own traditional views, to admit that a man who is a scholar and who is deeply concerned for social values may hold other views than their own, and may hold them on definite moral grounds. If they believe in the value of free intelligence and inquiry, they will concede to others the right of public examination and discussion, provided those are conducted in a way that is intellectually competent and morally serious.

This brings me to the important point in insistence on social realities against court-room fictions, namely, the ethic actually held by Mr. Russell. What is this ethic? His own statement is explicit. "Sex morality has to be derived from certain general principles, as to which there is perhaps a fairly wide measure of agreement, in spite of the wide disagreement as to the consequence to be drawn from them. The first thing to be secured is that there should be as much as possible of that deep, serious love between man and woman which embraces the whole personality of both and leads to a fusion by which each is enriched and enhanced. The second thing of importance is that there should be adequate care of children, physical and psychological." It may be doubted whether the original complainant, Mrs. Kay, her attorney, Mr. Goldstein, or the justice, Mr. McGeehan, can find (upon the unlikely supposition that they ever read the book) anything "lecherous, salacious, libidinous, etc., etc." in this passage, expert as they assume to be in such matters. The following passage represents the contrast Mr. Russell finds existing between the conclusions he draws from these principles and those drawn from views more widely held: "The doctrine that there is something sinful about sex is one which has done untold harm to individual character—a harm beginning in early childhood and continuing through life. By keeping sex love in a prison, conventional morality has done much to imprison all other forms of friendly feeling, and to make men less generous, less kindly, more self-assertive, and more cruel. Whatever sexual ethic may come to be ultimately accepted must be free from superstition and must have recognizable and demonstrable grounds in its favour." "Sex," says Russell, "cannot dispense with an ethic, any more than business or sport or scientific research or any other branch of human activity. But it can dispense with an ethic based solely upon ancient prohibitions propounded by uneducated people in a society wholly unlike our own. In sex, as in economics and in politics, our ethic is still dominated by fears which modern discoveries have made irrational. . . . It is true that the transition from the old system to the new has its own difficulties, as all transitions have. . . . The morality which I should advocate does not consist simply of saying to grown-up people or adolescents: 'Follow your impulses and do as you like.' There has to be consistency in life; there has to be continuous effort directed to ends that are not immediately beneficial and not at every moment attractive; there has to be consideration for others; and there should be certain standards of rectitude. . . . It is impossible to judge a new morality fairly until it has been applied in early education."[1]

There is another point to be taken into consideration when passing judgment upon the book. It certainly is essential that the tone and temper of the discussion should be in keeping with the underlying moral principles which are advocated, that it should be serious and dignified. In a book that in important matters goes contrary to current beliefs it is especially indispensable that the discussion be carried on with high seriousness as well as candor. No quotations of mine, short of citing the whole book, can be conclusive on this point. But anyone who with honest spirit has read the book as a whole, knows, and if he be honest will be ready to testify—regardless of whether he agrees with its argument or does not agree—that the book is addressed to adults who are supposed (perhaps overgenerously) to have, themselves, a serious moral interest in the subject and to be capable of drawing their conclusions on the basis of facts and reasonable arguments. The chapters of the book consist of anthropological, historical, sociological, and psychological data, assembled from recognized authorities in these fields. That the book is addressed to adolescents—such as would be taught in a college class—is a falsehood; it is equally false that if it were read by adolescents (as it might well be) it would be found to advocate looseness of conduct, judged even by conventional standards, on their part. What it advocates, consistently and without exception, is a change in public opinion which will make possible a sexual ethic and moral habits, personal and social, which, in the opinion of Mr. Russell, are of a higher order than those which now exist. It is impossible to characterize any other opinion of the book, even though it be put forth in an alleged court of justice, as anything except a deliberate misrepresentation.

I come now to the specific points upon which the Court based its condemnation of Mr. Russell and gave as reasons for nullifying his appointment by the Board of Higher Education. Mr. Russell made some remarks on the evils of methods that are in vogue of dealing with the practice of masturbation. The remarks are

1. I have quoted liberally because it is an incidental irony that this book, so bitterly denounced, is no longer in print and cannot be bought through the regular channels of trade.

commonplaces of competent medical discussion. The really important matter in this connection is not the remarks of Mr. Russell, which are supported by experience and, as I have said, by practically universal medical opinion. The really important matter is the fact that the method used by the Court gives convincing evidence of the latter's intent to make out a case without reference to the state of fact. For the Court's intent is to place Mr. Russell in the light of advising the practice of masturbation. Consequently, he omits a passage in which Mr. Russell explicitly recommends the use, in the endeavor to check it, of procedures other than direct prohibition which is accompanied by threats of dire consequences (insanity, etc.). These other procedures, if adopted, would tend to reduce the likelihood that children will indulge in the practice. Of course, had this passage been quoted, it would of itself have been enough to disprove the contention that Mr. Russell was promoting and sponsoring the practice of masturbation.

Extracts from what Mr. Russell has written on the topic of nudity in children and adults are also brought forward as a ground for condemning him as a man of such immoral character that he ought not to be permitted to teach youth. Mr. Russell advanced the view that "It is good for children to see each other and their parents naked, *whenever it so happens naturally*." No fuss should be made either way. This view appears monstrous to Justice McGeehan, and he quoted the passage as a proof that Mr. Russell's appointment is in effect an establishment of a "chair of indecency." It is typical of McGeehan's judicial processes that he makes no reference to the reasons given by Russell for coming to this conclusion: that the opposite practice evokes "the sense that there is mystery, and having that sense they [the children] will become prurient and indecent." This belief is one item of Mr. Russell's indictment of conventional ideas and practices. For the conventions have enveloped sex in an atmosphere of mystery and secrecy, and by so doing have done very much to create and to foster the very indecencies which are nominally deplored. Quite independently of anything Mr. Russell ever said on the subject, hundreds and hundreds of intelligent and honorable parents in our country have reached a similar conclusion as a result of their own experience. In what concerns nudity and children, the attitude commended by Mr. Russell has long been standard.

As to adults, Mr. Russell writes: "There are many important grounds of health in favour of nudity in *suitable circumstances* such as out-of-doors in sunny weather." Utterance of this hygienic commonplace is perhaps the ground for the statement of the attorney purporting to speak for Mrs. Kay that Mr. Russell once personally conducted a nudist colony; apparently, no interpretation of what Mr. Russell has said and done was too absurd or too arbitrary to keep Mr. Goldstein from perpetrating it. The bathing costumes now in vogue on most beaches in the country would certainly once have caused the arrest of people wearing them; if such bathing-suit cases had ever come before Justice McGeehan one can infer from his handling of the point in the matter of Mr. Russell's appointment with what relish and gusto he would have dealt with them. It is also true that the change in the public attitude is evidence for Mr. Russell's contention that much of the sense of indecency which has been attached to certain customs disappears when the customs in question change.

The matters just mentioned fall within the scope of the things which Justice McGeehan said gave him no ground for interference. For it is one of the extraordinary features of the extraordinary opinion of the Court that more than half of it is an attack upon Mr. Russell's views and conduct in matters which, by the justice's own admission, were quite out of his jurisdiction. In his own words, "As to such conduct, this court is powerless to act because of the power conferred by law on the Board of Higher Education." The space given to abuse of Mr. Russell in matters which according to the Court's own statement were none of its judicial business is enough by itself alone to prove the existence of a concealed animus back of the whole affair.

The opinion of the Court is so confused and so mixes up the things regarding which it said it had no power to act with the matters in which it assumed it had power to nullify the action of the Board of Higher Education, that it is not easy to tell, on the ground of what Justice McGeehan states, just what views of Mr. Russell tended in the Court's opinion to "aid, abet, encourage" violations of the penal code, so that the Board had acted "to sponsor or encourage violations of the Penal Law." For the justice quotes, with his usual relish, provisions of the penal code against abduction and rape, which even he did not and could not accuse Mr. Russell of advising and recommending. The probability,

however, is that the things he makes the basis of his claim to jurisdiction are Mr. Russell's views on extra-marital relations of
husband and wife; on sexual relations between young men and
young women, especially university students, before marriage;
and on homosexuality. Aside from details of the Court's treatment of these points, there is one feature which marks everything
that the Court said: nowhere does His Honor allude to the reasons that Mr. Russell advanced for putting forth his particular
views, and everywhere he treats Mr. Russell's argument in favor
of a change in public opinion which will finally result in a change
of custom and law as if it were a recommendation to people to
engage in practices that are contrary both to traditional opinions
and to the law as it now stands.

I begin with the question of homosexuality. In *Marriage and
Morals* Mr. Russell discusses the inadvisability of laws regulating
obscenity. He argues that no such law can be so drawn that it may
not be used to suppress the public discussion and the literary
productions that should have the right to appear. In the course of
this argument Mr. Russell calls attention to the fact that, according to English law, not only is "any treatment of homosexuality
in fiction illegal" but also that "it would be very difficult to
present any argument for a change in the law which would not
itself be illegal on the ground of obscenity." According to English
law, "homosexuality between men but not between women is illegal," so that, Mr. Russell remarks, the effect of the law on
obscenity has been to promote retention on the statute books of
a law which "every person who has taken the trouble to study
the matter knows is an effect of a barbarous and ignorant superstition." Justice McGeehan does not cite this passage, possibly
because the passage itself, even if his practice of consistent ignoring of context had been dropped, made it clear that change in
existing law was the aim of the discussion. His Honor does quote
the following passage from an earlier book of Mr. Russell's, *Education and the Modern World:* "It is possible that homosexual
relations with other boys would not be very harmful if they were
tolerated, but even then there is danger lest they should interfere
with the growth of a normal sexual life later on." This hypothetical statement of a *possibility*, accompanied as it is with an
argument *against* rather than *for* the practice, becomes in the

Court's opinion advocacy of a "damnable felony." Just what the honorable judge would say about physicians who have written much more unguardedly than has Mr. Russell in case their writings came before him may be left to the imagination. I hope that quotation of the following sentence from *A Survey of Child Psychiatry* written by Dr. J. R. Rees (1939) will not get its author into trouble or be interpreted as an endorsement by me of homosexuality among boys. "Homosexuality may be regarded as a normal phase of development in both sexes. . . . Provided the general emotional situation of the child is as it should be, there will be a natural development through this phase on to heterosexuality." [2]

Mr. Russell's views upon the subjects of sexual relations between unmarried youth of opposite sexes and in certain cases upon extra-marital relations on the part of husband and wife are undoubtedly shocking to upholders of the conventional moral code. They are also the views most likely to arouse dissent of a certain amount and kind among persons whose ideas on the standpoint from which sexual matters and marriage should be considered are similar to those of Mr. Russell. What is at issue, with respect to Justice McGeehan's method of treatment and his characterizations of Mr. Russell (which, I repeat, would be libelous if their author could not shelter himself behind the privilege of a court), is not the correctness or the wisdom of Mr. Russell's particular views. What is at issue is the wisdom or unwisdom of public discussion of sex and marriage when these topics are approached in a scientific manner and with serious, ethical interest. Anyone who reads Mr. Russell's complete text in a frame of mind at all reasonable will find that he states his views, be they wise or unwise, in a way that well satisfies both of these conditions. Such a reader will note that Mr. Russell is definitely concerned with moral evils in customs which do undeniably exist already alike among unmarried youth and married adults. Such a reader will note that it is in the interest of a change in public

2. In fairness to the author, it should be noted that "homosexuality" is used in a very wide sense by members of the Freudian school. It covers "emotional interest in persons of the same sex" as against such interest in persons of the other sex, and includes more than commission of overt acts of the type to which the word "sexual" is usually limited outside of psychiatric circles.

opinion, custom, and in legal rules that Mr. Russell advocates an alternative ethic.[3]

According to an account of an interview with Mr. Russell published recently in a newspaper, he himself has found reason, in one important matter, for modifying views earlier expressed. He now thinks divorce more often preferable to trying to patch up an unsatisfactory marriage. Changes such as this are an indication of his general scientific method and moral seriousness. They tie up with the fact that nowhere in his writings is there any claim that the views expressed are final or intended for any purpose other than the ultimate promotion, by means of scientific discussion, of a higher type of ethic than now exists.

Other persons have written in this volume about the legal aspects of the case and about its connection with educational policies. I have said what I have to say in the conviction that, quite apart from the baleful consequence of the Court's decision in respect to school and education, this decision is to be condemned on two other grounds. One of them is the flagrant injustice done a gentleman and a scholar. Probably not one-tenth of one per cent of members of the various organizations that rushed to attack Mr. Russell's supposed views and to support Justice Mc-Geehan ever read anything of Mr. Russell's save perhaps the passages extracted (or extorted) by the justice in his opinion and repeated in a gloating press. Hundreds, and perhaps thousands, of other persons who knew nothing of what Mr. Russell actually teaches were thus led to look upon him with moral suspicion and aversion. In these circumstances, I regard it as a personal privilege to express publicly my deep conviction of the wrong done Mr. Russell.

The other reason for my particular contribution to this volume is more serious, and would be regarded as such, I am sure, by Mr. Russell himself. Wicked as is the personal injustice which has been done him under cover of what purported to be judicial

3. The disingenuousness of the Court is on the surface in the case of what is said about "companionate marriage." For in this matter it is obvious on its face that the discussion concerns change in existing law, and that the change is argued for on the precise ground that the effect of legalized "companionate" marriage would be to reduce casual, surreptitious sexual relations among youth, and to promote relations prompted by serious and perhaps enduring affection in contrast with the strength of mere sexual desire now so common in actual practice among youth of all sects.

action, it is, as he himself declared, relatively insignificant beside the question whether the issues and problems of social morals, in fields where conventional taboos are very strong, are or are not to be publicly discussed by scientifically competent persons. Many people believe that present practices and customs are morally much lower than they need be and that one cause of this lowness is the taboos upon discussion of sexual matters, taboos which preclude proper instruction of the young with respect to sex. Such people may be deterred from saying and doing what they might (and should) do toward the creation of a higher condition of moral practice, because they are not willing to undergo the unrestrained abuse heaped upon Mr. Russell. Especially are they held back when they learn that even the common, ordinary right to appear in their own defense is likely to be denied them. The net effect of the McGeehan decision, thus, can only be to maintain the low standards which prevail in practice; to keep up the convention that if existing habits are not publicly discussed they do not exist. The decision serves, then, only to perpetuate the belief that no matter how undesirable are existing habits, they should not be mentioned publicly, since human nature is so constituted that nothing can be done—a belief I hold to be more current among "respectable" people than we like to admit. The action of Justice McGeehan was bad enough in its consequences. The evil was increased by the attitude of the Corporation Counsel in refusing to appeal the case, and by the complaisance of a "reform" Mayor who, after straining at Bertrand Russell, swallowed a Jimmy Walker.

It would seem as if all intelligent persons interested in a social ethic which is based upon social realities scientifically made known and which is directed to just and humane social ends could at least agree that darkness always attends suppression of the possibility of public discussion, and that the darkness, here as elsewhere, makes it easier for evil customs to endure and to flourish. I would not have legal measures censure even the mass of cheap sexuality presented on the stage and in public prints. But what is to be said of the state of a public opinion which delights in the former, yet is easily rallied to oppose serious intellectual discussion of sex and to revile those who act upon a belief that such discussion is a precondition of a better social ethic? The load of hypocrisy, conscious and unconscious, that is borne along on the shoulders of public opinion is one of the things most discouraging to those who would like to keep their faith in the possibility of a more enlightened and more honest public morality.

The evocation, the promotion, and the solidification of hypocrisy because of the way in which the Russell appointment was treated is an event which by comparison makes the wisdom and unwisdom of particular changes advocated by Mr. Russell of no great moment. If they are unwise, surely public discussion, upon the basis of free inquiry and scientific knowledge employed by Mr. Russell, would lead to statement of and agreement upon wiser views. On the other hand, the action of the Court and of the institutional forces which promoted and supported its action tend to cut off discussion even on the grounds of reason and knowledge, although such discussion alone would be sure to uncover whatever mistakes there may be in Mr. Russell's proposals. The prospect of a better, a more sincere, and a more intelligent social morality, as well as of sound education in the school, has been blacked out.

The hopeful feature of the situation is the number and quality of scholars, scientific men, public-spirited citizens, and educators who have risen in defense of the scientific freedom for which Mr. Russell stands. I am privileged to have some part, however small, in this defense.

The Basis for Hope

I hesitate to predict anything whatever about the outcome of the present war. I am moved in my hesitation by something other than the fear of indulging in Pollyanna anticipations
just by way of offset to the dire forebodings in which it has become customary to engage. For I believe that both pessimistic
and optimistic expectations are likely to be based upon old data,
while it is highly possible that the world is undergoing a crisis
which makes precedents and old data irrelevant to forming an
estimate of the future. Were past events an adequate ground for
prognostication, I could easily fluctuate between anticipation of
a Europe, and possibly a world, torn by another Thirty Years
War, but leaving civilization in a state of greater ruin, and pictur-
ing a Europe which has at least started on the road of a Con-
federation which will end in a United States of Europe.

The most definite hope for the future which I am able to entertain, with any confidence, concerns not external political and
economic results of the war, but a change which is already beginning in human attitudes, the factors which in the end influence
external results. It may be that by the time these lines are published, the all but universal earlier predictions about destructive
war waged against civilians will have begun to be realized. Even
so, I think there are dependable signs that both abroad and in
this country, belief in war and sheer force as the source of production for needed social changes has suffered greatly. There is
even a possibility that belief in war as an agency for this end will
have received a mortal wound by the time the war is over. In that
case, if destructive wars continue to be resorted to—as they may
be—it will be because of outright relapse into barbarism and not
as an agency for advancing civilization and culture. In other

[First published in *Common Sense* 8 (December 1939): 9–10.]

words, I think there are grounds for belief that the world is passing from a pacifism which is mainly subjective to a realistic attitude based upon technological and scientific grounds—which
diplomats and political leaders must henceforth take into account in making their plans.

Industrial and business interests, aside from stock-market
speculators, have also changed their attitude about war. Upon
the whole, although not absolutely, the old socialist charge of an
intrinsic alliance between capitalism and militaristic adventure
has lost its element of truth. It would seem as if, in time, this
change would react upon imperialistic tendencies. As an offset,
however, I cannot rid myself of the belief that the existing war
situation strengthens a nationalistic spirit, which is already too
strong. Representatives of the reactionary wing of the Catholic
Church are, for example, just now vying with the Communists in
wrapping themselves in the American flag.

The other hopeful sign of a change in attitude and morale is
associated with the alliance of Soviet Russia with Nazi Germany.
One must be aware of the dangers for the world that are involved
in this alliance. But as far as human attitudes (which ultimately
determine policies) are concerned, I think the effect of having the
underlying principles of method common to the two brought out
into the open is going to prove an encouraging healthful event.

For the last ten to fifteen years genuine liberalism—upon
which we in this country have to depend—has been either arrested or deflected by ideology that won its prestige because of
the Bolshevist Revolution. The seeming success of the latter had
a hypnotic effect upon many in this country who had become
impatient with the slow progress made in dealing by democratic
methods with our serious economic ills. Discounting all the special criticisms that are passed upon Bolshevist Communism, it
remains true that it operated in this country to divert attention
and energy away from methods that are in harmony with American habits.

The hypnotic spell is now broken. I am willing to make one
prediction, namely, that trust in panaceas and wholesale devices
has received a shock from which it will not easily recover. We are
now more prepared to realize that our reliance must be put upon
intelligent human beings who bring their knowledge and their
skill to bear in organized cooperation upon special problems that

confront us. As the realization develops, democracy will take on a new significance and a new lease of life. As far at least as our own country is concerned, I do not think it utopian to believe that something of this kind is possible, and I am confident that the *ground* for the change has been provided by the chief event, so far, of the present War, the alliance of the two great totalitarian countries. As we appreciate the inherent connection existing between attempts at wholesale social change and the methods of dictatorship, we shall be made ready to employ genuinely democratic methods more systematically and more intelligently than we have in the past.

The Meaning of the Term: Liberalism

Words that apply to moral attitudes and aspirations have broad meanings and attempts to define words that have broad meanings are exposed to two opposite dangers. One may try to pin them down. Then the meaning becomes not only narrow and technical but also in all probability conventional or partisan. In avoiding this error one may fall into such complete vagueness that the word ceases to have any particular application; or one may simply tell the kind of emotion a word arouses in himself and that he would like to have it evoke in others.

The noun "Liberalism" is peculiarly caught in this predicament. On one side, it has been used as the rallying cry of a particular political party and of a particular school of economic theory and action. If one thinks the word should be given a precise, sharply marked-off signification on the basis of its most specific historical usage, one may come to believe that this meaning is the only legitimate one. He will then laud or condemn liberalism on the basis of his attitude to special political and economic movements. On the other hand, if one neglects all historical usage one will only be able to tell what he personally thinks liberalism ought to mean, and thus find himself in the position of defining the word on the ground of some personal and perhaps private preference.

History itself affords some guidance, however. The word has never been associated in this country with *laissez-faire* economics and hands-off governmental action, as it has been in England and especially on the continent of Europe. It has been used in connection with what is vaguely called a forward-looking and progressive attitude, and in opposition to the kind of conservatism that looks back in time to the extent of being reactionary.

[First published in *Frontiers of Democracy* 6 (15 February 1940): 135.]

The original use of liberal in anything like a technical sense was in connection with schools and studies, when the word meant that which was adapted to the character and needs of free men in distinction from training that was imposed from without, that was routine and that fitted men for mechanical and subservient pursuits. The association of liberalism with liberty remains a permanent deposit. The historic signification of the word is associated also with liberality and generosity, especially of mind and character. It points to an open mind, to emancipation from bigotry and from domination by prejudice.

I have mentioned these familiar facts of historic usage because, while I am persuaded the word must be defined so as to mean a moral attitude and ideal, I do not wish in what follows to express merely a personal choice. Choice is involved as it must be in connection with every moral matter. But the choice in this case is only a selective emphasis out of the meanings sanctioned by past usage; it is not arbitrary and private.

What then is the moral attitude towards which liberalism points? Upon the side of even the narrower political movement, we find a clue in the emphasis of liberalism upon the Bill of Rights and civil liberties. The latter are concerned with freedom of belief and thought combined with the right of free expression and communication, limited only by responsibility for antisocial criminal consequences. These liberties, so fundamental in the liberal faith, obtained meaning in the concrete because of the existence of powerful institutions in church and state which, in the former case, denied freedom of religious creed and worship and, in the latter case, forced all political and social convictions into a mould of rigid uniformity.

This particular meaning gains wide and even universal force because of the persistent existence of enemies to free inquiry, free communication and choice of objects of supreme loyalty. These enemies come from within and without. In a country like our own, having a measure of democratic institutions, internal foes are more dangerous than external ones, since it is only when an illiberal mind exists that external enemies are permanently dangerous.

It is quite possible to be active in an illiberal spirit in behalf of ends which are historically associated with liberalism. This betrayal of liberalism is especially rife and especially harmful at the present time. Certain goals, economic and political, are set up and are then striven for in the most dogmatic and illiberal spirit. Genuine liberalism thus finds itself attacked by both reactionary conservatives and by the bitter foes of the latter.

The meaning of liberalism then consists in quiet and patient pursuit of truth, marked by the will to learn from every quarter. Liberalism is humble and persistent, and yet is strong and positive in its faith that the intercourse of free minds will always bring to light an increasing measure of truth.

Art as Our Heritage

During the early years of the depression, when I was crossing the Atlantic, I fell into conversation with a fellow passenger. She was a gracious white-haired woman, and in telling her plans she said that since she had lost a great deal of her money because of bank failures and bad stock investments, she was now going to buy herself something nobody could take away from her. She was going to Athens to see the Acropolis and the Parthenon.

She knew what too few persons know, the difference between an investment in physical things that are perishable, at the mercy of external accidents, and an investment in something that is imperishable, because it enriches personal life and becomes a part of one's very self. But the incident has another face, a face which has a real bearing upon the cause that has brought us here together this evening. It was the art of Greece which was taking this woman on her pilgrimage just as the cathedrals and public buildings, the paintings, statues, and literature of Europe have taken countless thousands of Americans there. The art, the vision of which was an enrichment of her personal life, is that which has given Greece her enduring glory among nations. Material acquisitions and possessions have by themselves never given any people a sure place in the memory of mankind or an assured place in history.

It is by creation of the intangibles of science and philosophy, and especially by those of the arts, that countries and communities have won immortality for themselves after material wealth has crumbled into dust. What has been true of other peoples will be true of our own. Creation, not acquisition, is the measure of a

[First published in *Congressional Record,* 76th Cong., 3d sess., 29 April 1940, 86, pt. 15:2477–78, from a 25 April radio address over WMAL, Washington, D.C.]

nation's rank; it is the only road to an enduring place in the admiring memory of mankind.

There is a good reason why achievement in science and art is the criterion by which a nation's place in civilization is finally judged. In the case of material things, possession by one excludes possession, use, and enjoyment by others. In the case of the intangibles of art the exact opposite is the case. The more the arts flourish, the more they belong to all persons alike, without regard to wealth, birth, race, or creed. The more they flourish the less they are privately owned, and the more they are possessed and enjoyed by all. This is what is meant when we say that art is universal—more universal than is that other intangible, science, since the arts speak a language which is closer to the emotions and imaginations of every man. Accordingly, whether we like it or not, even whether we believe it or not, the question whether this country of ours is to be narrow and provincial, or whether it is to attain to that which is universal, will be finally decided by what we do and what we are capable of appreciating, and enjoying, in those intangible things of which the fine arts are the outstanding examples. It is on this account that I esteem deeply and gratefully the opportunity to be here this evening and to express, as best I can, not only gratitude as a citizen, to Edward Bruce for initiating and conducting the Section of Fine Arts in the Public Buildings Administration, Federal Works Agency, but also my sense of the great significance of this work in the development of a worthy American civilization.

The work is significant both as a symbol and as an actual force in inspiring and directing activities, which will extend as time goes on far beyond what is done in post offices and other public buildings. As a symbol it is an acknowledgement from official sources, with the active encouragement of persons high in the government, of the importance to our Nation of the development of art and of ability to enjoy art products. Ned Bruce has shown me a letter from the postmaster of one of the smaller towns whose public building now has a mural upon its walls. In his letter of enthusiastic thanks for what has been done for his town, he included a sentence which might almost be a motto of the whole project: "How can a finished citizen be made in an artless town?" How indeed can an all-around and complete citizenry be developed without that development of creation and enjoyment of works of art to which the government, itself, must contribute?

Our public buildings may become the outward and visible sign of the inward grace which is the democratic spirit, while too often, especially in municipal halls and county courthouses, they have not even been kept clean.

As a symbol, the work carried on by the Section of Fine Arts is a service to democracy, so important, even in its present comparatively limited scale, that to starve it or allow it to lapse would be a defeat for democracy as genuine as one taking place on a physical battlefield. For the same reason, this governmental activity is more than a symbol. Hundreds of thousands of persons all over this broad land now have opportunities to see and enjoy works of art which they had not before. They are developing, within themselves, germs that were part of their being but which never had a chance, because of lack of nourishment, to grow.

If the arts come forth from museums to which they have retired, if they become a living part of the walk and conversation of the average man, and thereby parts of the legitimate heritage of a democratic people, a great debt will be owed to the stimulus provided by this governmental section in the buildings which belong to the common people and where they daily assemble.

Old World countries have been able to develop the fine arts by means of the patronage of the nobility and the wealthy. Their healthy development in our country will depend upon the active response of the civic consciousness of the common people. For this reason, I do not want to close without mentioning a fact which I could bring home to you only if television were at my command. For if you could see for yourselves reproductions of the murals which are now found in public buildings from Maine to the Gulf, from the Atlantic to the Pacific, you would see that the paintings combine the values of the arts which nourish the human spirit with the accomplishment of our past history which strengthens that legitimate pride, which enables one to say, "I am an American citizen!" Secretary Morgenthau, Mr. Carmody, and Mr. Bruce, may your work go forward to even greater triumphs.

"Contrary to Human Nature"

Opponents of projects for bringing about social change have a number of defense devices they resort to almost automatically. One of the commonest, and laziest, of these devices is the assertion that the proposal goes contrary to human nature. More sweepingly still, it is often said that human nature is so unalterable by its very constitution that the proposal is bound to fail and therefore shouldn't even be tried. It is always dangerous from an intellectual point of view to try to oppose a practical movement with an argument drawn from a purely abstract idea. At the very best, such a procedure tends to divert the eye from the business that needs attention, namely, critical examination of the actual merits of the proposal in question. It fastens attention upon a matter so remote from actual conditions that it cannot be subjected to any practical test. At the worst, this device is only an expression of a strong prejudice clothed in the garb of an idea in order to appear respectable.

The use of the idea of the unchangeability of human nature as a means of opposition to special projects for political and economic change belongs in the latter class. That the new project is contrary to some traits of human nature *as they exist at the time* is certain. For the proposed policy is openly one for a change; therefore of course it goes against those particular habits which have been formed by the very conditions it is proposed to alter.

Considering that the course of human history is a record of changes in human habits, considering that every proposal from the time of primitive savagery to the present for any important change has been fought by the beneficiaries of things as they have

[First published in *Frontiers of Democracy* 6 (15 May 1940): 234–35.]

been, considering that every step in advance has been taken by overcoming opposition of habits entrenched in positions of advantage, it would seem as if argument based on the immutability of human nature would have lost its force by this time.

The fact that it has not done so is instructive. For while it does not prove the constancy of human nature, it does prove the inertia of established customs. It is an old story that habit is "second nature." Any one who is observant of what goes on around him knows that one of the things which happens most frequently is the confusion of second or *acquired* nature with *original* nature. What people have become used to supplies their ordinary standard for what is natural and for what is contrary to nature. Looked at from this point of view, the tendency to fall back upon the idea of the fixity of human nature in opposition to policies for change in social arrangements is highly instructive. It testifies to the extent in which men's *minds,* as well as their actions, have fallen into the grip of habit. And while the tendency is most marked in the case of those who obtain onesided advantage from customs as they exist, it is strong enough to hold in subjection many of those who are put at a disadvantage by those customs.

There is some encouragement to be gathered from the fact that today the argument that something is "contrary" to nature tends to take the form of contrary to *human* nature. In the past, changes in institutions, that is in fundamental customs, have been opposed on the ground that they were contrary to Nature in its most universal sense, and hence to the will and reason of God as the Founder of Nature. One has only to go back to the arguments advanced against the abolition of human slavery to see that such was the case. More recently still, many opponents of the idea of enfranchising women used the argument that it was contrary to the very laws of Nature and of Nature's God. Such facts prove how strong is the tendency to use well-established habits as the proper standard and measure of what is natural and unnatural. Even among a people as intelligent as the Greeks, institutions that now we accept as a matter of course were regarded as contrary to the inherent structure of Nature; a philosopher like Aristotle could use as his most convincing argument against a proposed policy that it was impossible by nature since it had never existed in the past.

Although the argument from fixity of human nature is but a "rationalization" of existing habits, including prejudices and onesided interests which have become institutionalized, proponents of social changes have something to learn from it. The first thing to learn is the importance in human behavior of habit, once it is established. Because of the inertia—and momentum—of habits it is a great practical as well as theoretical error for those who would introduce fundamental reforms to ignore or make light of the positive force exercised by custom. "Revolutions" never go as far or as deep as they are supposed to go; it takes time, usually a long time and a succession of partial changes, to carry one through, since carrying it through signifies the establishment of habits which will be as deep-seated and as "natural" as those which have been displaced. There will be fewer disillusioned liberals and radicals when they learn that, because of the place of habit in human nature, no single measure of social change can of itself accomplish what its enthusiastic devotees expect from it. There is nothing discouraging in this lesson. For it is more than a protection against future disappointment. If the lesson is learned, it enables those interested in change to direct their efforts more effectively so as to avoid waste motion.

There is another and perhaps more positive or constructive thing to be learned about the strategy and tactics of promotion of policies of social change. There exist certain underlying things in human nature which are relatively constant, and whose constancy is of a much less artificial quality than that of customs, whose existence at a given time in human history up to the present has been more or less a matter of accident. These most constant things in human nature are *Needs*. It is quite obvious for example that all human beings have a recurring need for food, and that unless this need is satisfied a human being dies.

I have used an extreme example. The case of need for food as a constant element in human nature is too obvious to be capable of being denied. When other needs are viewed, they are found to shade off from its general class to needs that are fluctuating and superficial. But in any case promulgators of policies of social change have much to learn by considering first, the needs of human beings which, being central, are most constant in human nature; and secondly, the means, available at a given time, for the most extensive and fullest satisfaction of these needs. Viewed in this way consideration of the constitution of human nature may become an aid in promotion of desirable social change instead of, as in the past, an obstruction.

If the idea is applied to proposals for change in existing economic habits, its meaning will become clearer. Economic systems must, if they are to be in accord with *constant* requirements of human nature, be such as to meet the need for support of healthy vigorous life. To suppose that the present "capitalistic" system (which is demonstrably the product of special historic conditions), is the only one which can effect this result is to fall, on a large scale, into the same kind of error which tribes or families fall into, on a small scale, when they think that only the particular foods to which they have become accustomed are fit for human consumption.

But the need for food does not stand alone. "Man does not live by bread alone." The value of a proposed change in economic habits and relations must be considered in its bearing upon other needs, many of which are less tangible than the need for food. It must be analyzed, for example, in its bearing upon the need for companionship, for freedom of choice, for rivalry or emulation, for security, etc. Doubtless the conditions of the problem are rendered more complex by this approach than when some single idea is used as an adequate standard for accepting and urging a particular policy. But all history and all experience show that the simplifications which end in leaving out of account some of the conditions which are active anyway defeat themselves.

I do not think it is too much to say that for the first time in human history we are beginning to have within our grasp the means for the discovery in two areas: on one hand, of what needs are the most central and active in human nature; and upon the other hand, of what are the means for systematic effort in satisfying these needs in a way which recognizes the claims of each, instead of sacrificing some in a onesided way to others. An intelligent attitude toward the problems of the relation of human nature to social policies is capable of giving efforts at social reforms a new start.

Address of Welcome to the League for Industrial Democracy

It is an honor for me to have the privilege of welcoming an audience like this upon an occasion like this. Thirty-five years is about the length of time conventionally assigned to a generation, so we are here to celebrate the completion of the first generation's life of the League for Industrial Democracy. I shall not attempt to report its notable achievements nor tell the story of its past. There are, however, two aspects of its history that I cannot refrain from mentioning. This is the first of a long series of years in which Robert Morss Lovett is not the President of this organization. I know you will all join me in paying a tribute of respect and admiration to the man who has always given so generously of himself to every cause that promises advance in human freedom and brotherhood. And I know that your thoughts have already anticipated anything I can say in expression of our gratitude to Harry Laidler for his untiring devotion through all these years to the L.I.D. and all the excellent things for which the L.I.D. stands. I am afraid the phrase "the scholar in politics" hasn't much meaning. If it had more significance, I should unhesitatingly nominate my friend, the friend of all of us, the Executive Director of the L.I.D., for the position of "gentleman and scholar" in political public education.

For while the L.I.D. is an educational rather than a political organization, yet in a democracy the two things, education and politics, cannot be separated from each other. Indeed, even totalitarian states differ from previous despotic states in history because they have learned that, under the conditions which exist today, even dictatorships must have a popular support which

[First published in League for Industrial Democracy, *Thirty-Five Years of Educational Pioneering—and a Look Ahead* (New York: League for Industrial Democracy, 1941), pp. 3–6, from the presidential address delivered at the thirty-fifth anniversary dinner of the L.I.D. in New York City, 28 November 1940.]

only some kind of education can furnish. The noble distinction of a democratic society lies in the kind of unity it establishes between education and politics. It is for the people to instruct their officials, not for a few officials to regulate the sentiments and ideas of the rest of the people; the final criterion and test of what is done by our legislative bodies from the United States Senate to the humblest village Common Council is what effect their actions have upon the ideas and emotions of the citizens of the country.

So much is said now on the subject of democracy that one almost feels like apologizing for adding anything to the stream. But in speaking for the L.I.D., it is not out of place to remind you that democracy above all else is an educational enterprise; that it rests upon faith in public opinion and upon faith that the democratic process will result in the growth of a public opinion which is capable, enlightened and honest. Voluntary organizations have to play a role and have a duty to perform in carrying on this educational work. The conditions that originally brought the L.I.D. into existence, not merely my own lifelong occupation with college education, make it appropriate to say something first about the work the L.I.D. attempts to do with and among college students. Probably everybody is aware that in Germany the universities were hotbeds of the reaction that prepared the way for Hitler's arrival at supreme power. We do not have anything of that particular kind to fear in this country. But insecurity and uncertainty as to jobs and future careers on the part of youth are things which prepare the way for lack of confidence in the democratic way of life and for willingness to worship strange gods. Protection against these dangers is education in the fact that democracy is a moving thing; that its possibilities are far from exhausted, and that its great need is expansion into the industrial field. It is the special task of a League for *Industrial* Democracy to bring this lesson home to college youth. What young men and women need above all else is a sense of unrealized possibilities opening new horizons, which will inspire them to creative effort. It is this phase of the democratic way of life, not as yet realized, which it is the special office of the L.I.D. to bring to the attention of youth in our colleges, thereby giving them the sense of something fine and great for which to live.

But much the same task faces us in connection with the general public with which we have contact. We hear now on all sides about defense. Defense is the most conspicuous thing before the public; no advertisement is complete without some reference to it. The other day I noticed ads on the public highways urging persons to attend the movies as a means of national defense. Now defense pure and simple is a negative aim; it sounds too much like keeping things away, holding them at a distance. The military maxim that offense is the best defense has a social counterpart if we translate *aggressive* to mean positive and constructive. The only sure way to defend democracy in the long run is to fight to extend it here and now, here at home, to fields of action hitherto not touched by it.

I recently read a book by a German now living in exile because of his profound revolt against Nazi oppressions and cruelties. In spite of his personal experience of these things and his horror of them, he says that the great danger of western democracies is that they will regard what has happened in totalitarian countries of Europe as symptoms of a passing unrest, while, in reality, they are the signs of profound change in the very structure of society. The danger is especially strong with us because of our distance from the immediate scene of upheaval. It falls in with the notion that defense is a negative matter, a kind of armed quarantine against infection from abroad. But one sure thing about the present state of the world is that it is not going to be the same world we have known in the past, no matter what happens on the battle field.

There are periods when forces that have been slowly gathering in the past come to a head, and produce a great change more or less abruptly. Unless all signs fail, we are now living in one of the three or four most fateful periods of all history. If it sounds pessimistic to say this, it is because of assumption that the change must be for the worse. It is also possible that, after suffering and agony, the change may be for a better society, making possible a freer and more secure life for all. This better prospect can become an actuality only as our defense takes the form of creative activity to make the democratic way of life a deeper and wider reality than it has been. One hundred and fifty years ago we were the undenied and undisputed leader in pointing the nations of the world to a more just, because freer, form of government. We are still a young nation measured in years of existence. We are old in spirit if we cannot once more by the example of our own form of life point out the way in which the nations of the earth can walk in freedom and cooperative peace.

The task ahead is a hard one and will be accomplished but slowly by the combined efforts of great numbers. The L.I.D. is but one of the many forces that may carry us forward—and very fortunately so. But it has a special field to cultivate, a special audience to reach, and even if that audience is comparatively limited and the work the L.I.D. can do but a humble scene in the vast historic drama that is unrolling, it behooves us to play well that part. In welcoming you as guests to this dinner to celebrate the thirty-fifth anniversary of the existence of this organization, I am in a deeper sense also welcoming you to opportunity to take part in the creative activity of constructing a social order which shall be democratic all the way through, and this activity is as inspiring in its possibilities as the present world situation is dark and depressing in its actuality. We cannot help asking: Where do we go from here? The only possible answer, in spite of all difficulties and in spite of the reactionary forces that always gather strength in time of war, is Forward, not Back. And while we have an enormous amount to learn, we can learn what we need to know in the very process of acting together to create a democracy that shall be a living reality in every aspect and reach of our common life.

Education: 1800–1939

It is fitting on this day to recall that in addition to one who deserved the name of *the* Founder, this University has had a succession of Founders. The roll includes all who have contributed to its growth—material benefactors who have given of their monetary means, and the teachers and administrators who have given of their ideas, plans and dreams to provide the soul of which these buildings and their equipment are the body. The roll includes even educators, statesmen, thinkers who never had any personal connection with the University but whose work gave inspiration and direction to those who labored here. Ira Allen had a spiritual ancestry from whom he derived the desires and the impetus that led him to work to establish this University; we are indebted to him because he in turn was indebted to others.

For every living institution is a cooperative creation, in which the work of joint creation goes on as long as an institution has life. Universities like families and like nations live only as they are continually reborn, and rebirth means constant new endeavor of thought and action, and these mean an ever renewed process of change. If then I mention that it is now sixty years since the class of which I was a member graduated from this institution, it is not to indulge in reminiscence about the good old days, and certainly not to suggest to you that youngsters today miss something that we oldsters enjoyed when we were young. It is because what has happened educationally in these sixty years gives a measure by which we can judge of the changes which have gone on everywhere in education. For although sixty years are considerably less than one-half the life time of this institution, yet the changes that have occurred in this time are not only much greater than in

[First published in *Vermont Cynic*, 1 May 1939, p. 7, from address at the forty-sixth annual Founder's Day ceremony at the University of Vermont, Burlington, Vt.]

the earlier period but are much greater than those which had taken place in the two hundred and fifty years of the history of the oldest college in the land.

I do not mean, of course, that no expansion occurred in the earlier period. The number of students and of the faculty grew and new courses were added. But for the most part the expansion occurred within limits which had been set by the main purpose of higher education all during that period. The changes which have taken place in the last fifty or sixty years have been steadily in the direction of service to purposes to which the older education paid no attention. The earlier aim and ideal may be called the classical, not simply because of the role of ancient languages in the curriculum but because the chief aim was transmission of what was called the cultural heritage. In other words, the studies looked to the past not to the future. The only callings for which they prepared were the three recognized learned professions; and even then they were prepared for indirectly rather than directly. Even though the greater number of graduates went into teaching at least temporarily, there was no preparation for that vocation beyond knowledge of subject matter. Even when the natural sciences found their way into the course of study they were largely taught in an academic way; that is, by communicating through text and lecture that which was already known with little participation by students in the processes by which knowledge had been attained.

If then I mention changes taking place in this institution during the last half century it is because they are symptoms of the kind of change that has gone on everywhere in higher education in this country, the change being in the aim which has controlled the introduction of new courses, new studies and new methods. Union of the University with the State Agricultural College had taken place before we entered college. Nominally the University had already taken on a new responsibility and a new aim. But there was in those days no farm, no experimental station, no organized extension work, no agronomy building. There was also a medical school and a good one of the kind that commonly existed at that time. But its sessions were not for a full academic year and, like almost every other school for training physicians at that date, it was conducted by a group of physicians as a semiprivate undertaking. Only thirty years ago did the trustees take over its complete control and management, and only a decade later were two years of regular collegiate work required for admission. The point is that in neither of these matters did the University lag materially behind the course of events in other institutions of the country. Once more, although the University had been a pioneer among the colleges of the country in introducing at an early date a course in civil engineering, yet its scope was limited: there was no distinct college of engineering and no separate building; in fact, one teacher did practically all the technical teaching in that field. There were courses in the natural sciences required for a degree, even for the Bachelor of Arts. But there was no well-equipped science building, and the number of students who had any experimental laboratory work was limited. Instead of the present fine museum facilities, there were such collections as the personal interests of teachers led them to gather.

So far I have been speaking of the expansion that took place along lines for which there had been a certain amount of previous preparation. You will note that they all point in one direction—a special education for those engaging in the vocations and more attention to the foundations of these callings in science. But there are also the developments that strike out entirely in novel lines. As I have said, there were no special courses for the training of even high school teachers while the idea of college training for elementary school teachers was an unheard of thing. Not only was there no business school curriculum but there was only one course in the whole field of economic theory, a course for one term in the senior year. There were no courses in music, and while a course of lectures in general esthetic theory was one of the distinctive things in the teaching of philosophy, practical training in any of the fine arts would have been regarded as out of the proper province of an institution of higher learning. Finally, there was no such thing as graduate work in this University; indeed, a graduate had only to live three years and pay a small fee to obtain, if he wished, a master's degree "in course"—which meant as a matter of course. Only in the seventies was graduate work systematically available anywhere in this country. Students who desired it had always gone to Europe, especially to Germany.

I repeat that I am citing these facts not as historical information in things already well known and certainly not to indicate the poverty of the training we got in those days, but as evidence of the change in the purposes that has occurred that in the end regulate subjects and methods—and in the latter connection it is worth noting that we had no electives of any kind. We went through a list of courses one after the other, without its even occurring to us that they were prescribed, so much were they a matter of course. Yet were my purpose that of reminiscence of old days, which it is not, it would be a pleasure to call the roll of stimulating contacts with teachers who were devoted scholars in their fields. But the object of the recital of the changes is simply to present evidence drawn from the history of the institution, with which we who are here today are most familiar, of the kind of change in educational ideals and purposes that has been going on in the last half century, a change which is revolutionary when compared with the prior history of institutions of higher learning. What does this great shift signify? Why did it come about? What is its future?

These questions are much too large to receive proper attention at this time. But certain things as to the cause of the change stand out. The changes haven't come about by the wilful choice of those conducting educational institutions. They have come about because of social changes which created new needs and new opportunities. Colleges had to recognize them if they were to keep in contact with living forces about them. The first of the changes created the demand for specially trained persons in a variety of callings and vocations which the older education did not touch: Teaching, Business, the Fine Arts, Farming, Engineering and technological work. The pressure of social conditions that was caused by the transition from a simple mostly agrarian life to conditions predominantly urban and industrial called for a special equipment and special knowledge which had not been necessary in earlier conditions. The effect was not merely to increase the number of professional subjects and schools. There was a definite reaction back into the subjects of so-called general and cultural education. They became more or less pre-professional courses, and there was a tendency to arrange groups of studies so that they would lay a fairly definite basis for the later specialized preparation for medicine, teaching, engineering or whatever.

In the second place, the sciences reached a stage of development in which they play and are bound to continue to play an ever larger part in preparation for intelligent ability to practice successfully any calling. There was a time, and not so very long ago, when life on the farm was upon the whole the best preparation for being a farmer, especially if supplemented by a knowledge of the chemistry of fertilizers and the principles of seed selection which could easily be obtained without spending years in a school of agriculture. Neither the calling nor the state of science was such that there was any especially vital bond of union between the farm and specialized training. As long as the farmer had a nearby market and was fairly free from competition with farmers at a distance, there was no special point in agricultural economics. I am not a farmer and even if I were this is no place for a dissertation upon the need by agriculture of the kind of assistance which only specialized scientific knowledge can give. The change in conditions is so evident that the calling of a farmer stands as an example of what has taken place in almost every vocation. Modern industry rests definitely upon the applications of science. If a person is to engage in any one of the multitude of forms of modern production or distribution in other than a blind or routine way, he has to have an equipment of knowledge and skill in the sciences that have created the technological operations of present production and transportation. An age of steam, of electricity, of miracles wrought by chemistry, demands that those who enter into its complexities have an education that cannot be acquired by the old-fashioned type of apprenticeship.

What of the future in higher education? At a time of very rapid social change, a time when experimentation is occurring in almost every educational institution in the country, a time in which the situation is in flux, it would not become anyone to speak dogmatically about what will take place in the future in the colleges and universities of the country. But the fact that the changes of which I have spoken have come about in response to the actual conditions and needs of society affords sure ground for the conclusion that there is not going to be any general movement backward. The social changes which education has had to meet have taken place with extraordinary rapidity; more extensive changes have happened in the last fifty or seventy-five years than in as many preceding centuries all put together. There is confusion and conflict in education because there is confusion and conflict in social life. This much is inevitable. But that we are going back to that complete separation between knowledge and practice, between the intellectual life and the natural sciences, which existed in earlier days is but a fantasy of those who do not understand why and how the present educational system has grown out of its earlier condition. There is room at present for all kinds of collegiate institutions so that up to a certain point all kinds of experimentation and variation are welcome. If a leisure class is going to exist in this country for a long time to come, and if there is a demand for the kind of education which suits the needs of those whose economic condition liberates them from taking part in the useful work of the world, there is no reason why there should not be an institution or two whose curriculum is based upon reading and discussion of literary masterpieces, where the medieval trivium of grammar, rhetoric and logic is taken to be sufficient for the requirements of the life they propose to lead. But to urge this kind of education as *the* way out of all educational confusion and conflict is possible only for those who fail to recognize the realities of social change and their connection with the kind of change which education must undergo. The way out will be found as we effect a more intimate and vital union between theory and practice, science and action, culture and vocation, not by trying to keep them in separate compact work.

I began by saying that our University, like every other living institution, is a cooperative creation. The creation is still in process. It will continue as long as the University endures. Tradition looks forward as well as backward. To transmit the powers and achievements of our own day to the future is as important as to transmit the past to the present. Indeed, the more aware we are of the fact that we are builders of a future world, the more likely are we to be intelligent in our attitude to the past and in our estimate of the values we inherit from it. The time which we select to do honor to the Founders of the things we now enjoy is the very time we should be most solicitous about what we here and now are engaged in doing upon which those who come after us may build. For we are creators of the future as well as heirs of the past.

In national life as well as in our scholastic undertakings we best honor those whom we call Founding Fathers by trying to do for our own conditions what they accomplished in their time. Political and economic activities, as well as educational activities, have to adapt themselves to changed conditions. Democracy has to be continually fought for and won over again by every generation. It cannot stand still; unless it moves forward to meet the demands of new conditions of life it degenerates and will finally die. We cannot live upon the past in our national life any more than we can in our bodily life. In one as in the other, life is a process of renewal and the process demands effort and struggle. Especially is this true of the students in educational institutions who have received abundantly from those who have labored in the past. It is you young people who are here today and those like you all over this land who have the opportunity and responsibility to help build in a troubled and distracted world the democratic society of the coming years in which freedom, peace and security will be the common heritage.

Higher Learning and War

Recollections of the events of the last war forcibly remind us that our institutions of higher learning are not immune to war hysteria. They tell us that the atmosphere created by war enables interested parties to use this hysteria for their own ends, by means of suppression of free inquiry and free expression. We have every reason to hope and many reasons to believe that we shall not become directly involved in the present war. But some amount of emotional and intellectual involvement is inevitable and this involvement has its dangers for the intellectual interests which colleges and universities are supposed to serve and to represent.

Our best protection is to be prepared in advance. The alpha and omega of this preparation is realization that no matter what our sentiments and our preferences, or our loyalties, to the causes which we believe are at stake in the European war, our primary obligation and all-controlling responsibility and loyalty are to the freedom and objectivity of inquiry and communication for which universities are supposed to stand; and to which we, as constituents of the universities, are morally committed.

Past experience shows that the existence of this loyalty can not be taken for granted even among the scholars who are found in our universities. Already there are signs that some of them feel more strongly about the rights or the wrongs of this or that nation engaged in the present war than they do about the cause of intellectual freedom and scientific objectivity. I would not hold for a moment that sympathies and antipathies can be or should be avoided by college teachers. Since they are human beings, their occurrence can not be avoided. But there is a deeper respon-

[First published as an editorial in *Bulletin of the American Association of University Professors* 25 (December 1939): 613–14.]

sibility incumbent upon those who claim to be representatives of the spirit of scholarship and of the scientific attitude. It is a sign of weakness and indeed of disloyalty when this interest is subordinated to any other interest.

There are plenty of persons and groups who will present and who will urge with vigor nationalistic, political, economic, and ideological interests of different kinds. It is our business to stand up with at least equal vigor and aggressiveness for the cause of freedom and objectivity of mind to which our profession commits us. These remarks may seem to some aloof from the actual and practical needs of the present world-scene. But it is this feeling against which these remarks are directed, since they are actuated by the belief that as teachers and scholars we too are soldiers in a cause which is as definitely ours as that of any nation at war in Europe is that of the soldiers who are fighting in its special behalf.

It is more or less of a commonplace today to refer many of the present troubles of the world to the defects of the Versailles treaty. These defects had, however, *their* cause. Failure of educated men and women, including those in universities, was a part of this cause. Let us make sure that we do not share again in this guilt, especially as in our case it is more of an act of treachery to our supreme end than it is in the case of others.

I believe that our Association can and should be a power in maintaining and fostering the professional *esprit de corps* which will keep educators and scholars faithful to their own cause. The time to begin is now, not when emotions are still more stirred.

The Basic Values and Loyalties of Democracy

Values and loyalties go together, for if you want to know what a man's values are do not ask him. One is rarely aware, with any high degree of perception, what are the values that govern one's conduct. Observe a person's conduct over a period long enough to note the direction in which his activities tend and you will be able to tell where his loyalties lie, and knowing them, you will know the ends which stir and guide his actions: that is to say, the things that are values in actuality, not just in name. And if I begin with emphasizing the importance of observing the direction taken by behavior over a period of time rather than judging by words, it is because at no time in history have words meant as little as they do today.

One of the worst corruptions that totalitarianism has engendered is its complete violation of integrity of language. There is some truth in the saying, "at the border line, it is not easy to tell where education stops and propaganda begins." But the propaganda of the Soviet Union, Italy, Germany and Japan is easily identified by the fact that in every important matter the words used have to be read in reverse. They are selected and weighed with no reference to anything but their effect upon others. Criteria for judging slight deviations from fact are in the possession of every reasonably mature person, for his experience enables him to judge of probabilities. But complete inversions of truth are astonishingly confusing. They produce a state of daze that endures long enough to enable its creators to accomplish their will while darkness still prevails.

In short, a primary, perhaps *the* primary, loyalty of democracy at the present time is to communication. It cannot be denied that our American democracy has often made more in words of the

[First published in *American Teacher* 25 (May 1941): 8–9.]

liberties of free speech, free publication and free assembly than in action. But that the spirit of democracy is, nevertheless, alive and active is proved by the fact that publicity is a well established habit. It gives the opportunity for many silly and many false things to be uttered. But experience has confirmed the faith that silly things are of so many different kinds that they cancel each other over a period of time, and that falsities come out in the wash of experience as dirt comes out in soap and water.

The freedom which is the essence of democracy is above all the freedom to develop intelligence; intelligence consisting of judgment as to what facts are relevant to action and how they are relevant to things to be done, and a corresponding alertness in the quest for such facts. To what extent we are actually democratic will in the end be decided by the degree to which the existing totalitarian menace awakens us to deeper loyalty to intelligence, pure and undefiled, and to the intrinsic connection between it and free communication: the method of conference, consultation, discussion, in which there takes place purification and pooling of the net results of the experiences of multitudes of people. It is said that "talk" is cheap. But the hundreds and hundreds of thousands of persons who have been tortured, who have died, who are rotting in concentration camps, prove that talk may also be tragically costly, and that democracy to endure must hold it immensely precious.

It has been discouraging to American democrats to see how shallow has been loyalty to this value in those fellow Americans who, while professing democracy, have still defended suppression of liberty of speech, press and creed in the Soviet Union. One would have supposed that any American would by this time have enough of the democratic spirit in his very blood so that he would need nothing more than suppression to enable him to judge the policy of a country, no matter what one supposes it can say for itself on other matters. We are warned that we must feed and nourish this particular loyalty with much more energy and deliberate persistence than we have done in the past—beginning in the family and the school.

Since I cannot discuss all the loyalties that define the values of the democratic way of life, I confine myself to those which are emphasized by contrast with contemporary totalitarianism. In theory, democracy has always professed belief in the potentialities of every human being, and all the need for providing conditions that will enable these potentialities to come to realization. We shall miss the second most important lesson the present state of the world has to teach us if we fail to see and to feel intensely that this belief must now be greatly extended and deepened. It is a faith which becomes sentimental when it is not put systematically into practice every day in all the relationships of living. There are phrases, sanctioned by religion, regarding the sacredness of personality. But glib reciting of the verbal creed is no protection against snobbishness, intolerance and taking advantage of others when opportunity offers. Our anti-democratic heritage of Negro slavery has left us with habits of intolerance toward the colored race—habits which belie profession of democratic loyalty. The very tenets of religion have been employed to foster anti-semitism. There are still many, too many, persons who feel free to cultivate and express racial prejudices as if they were within their personal rights, not recognizing how the attitude of intolerance infects, perhaps fatally as the example of Germany so surely proves, the basic humanities without which democracy is but a name.

For it is humanity and the human spirit that are at stake, and not just what is sometimes called the "individual," since the latter is a value in potential humanity and not as something separate and atomic. The attempt to identify democracy with economic individualism as the essence of free action has done harm to the reality of democracy and is capable of doing even greater injury than it has already done.

So I close by saying that the third loyalty which measures democracy is the will to transform passive toleration into active cooperation. The "fraternity" which was the third member of the democratic trinity of the France of the Revolution has never been practiced on a wide scale. Nationalism, expressed in our country in such phrases as "America First," is one of the strongest factors in producing existing totalitarianism, just as a promise of doing away with it has caused some misguided persons to be sympathetic with Naziism. Fraternity is the will to work together; it is the essence of cooperation. As I have said, it has never been widely practiced, and this failure is a large factor in producing the present state of the world. We may hope that it, not the equality produced by totalitarian suppression, will constitute the "wave of the future."

For a New Education

There was never a time when the words *New Education* and *Fellowship* were as significant in what they stand for as they are to-day. This statement is true whether the words are taken separately or together. It would be unjust to the schools and to millions of faithful teachers who are doing the best they can under adverse circumstances to hold the old education accountable for the present state of the world. But it can be said with justice that upon the whole the older type of education was a part of the old social order, whose bankruptcy constitutes the present epoch of history. A new social order must be built and a new type of education must be worked out as an integral part of the construction of this inclusive human order. Probably the most inept statement uttered in the present crisis is one put forth by a professed publicist, who claimed that abandonment of the old education is the cause of the present confused and conflicting state of the world. The fact that the first act of totalitarian dictatorship is to close every school of the newer type, every school affiliated with the New Education Fellowship, is the sufficient answer.

The present state of the world bears witness also to the fact that any desirable new education must express and must create fellowship. Fellowship is more than the opposite of war, discord, hatred, and intolerance. It provides the only sure and enduring guarantee that these evils will not continue to plague mankind. Education in and for and by fellowship, through cooperation and with a cooperative society as its aim, is an imperatively required factor in an education that will arise in contrast to the world now engaged in destroying itself.

The freedom to which schools of the New Education are com-

[First published in *New Era in Home and School* 22 (June 1941): 134–35.]

mitted has taken on a new and deeper meaning. In the past it was emphasized as a right. The urgent demand for cooperation to replace enmity, for fellowship to replace suppressive force, emphasizes the fact that freedom is a responsibility which imposes duties; it cannot exist save in a social order whose members respect one another and show their respect in acts of friendly contact and intercourse. Some phases of existing totalitarianism are reactions which were inevitable, humanely speaking, against the individualism of isolation. Evil in this case as in others can be overcome only by good. Social unity which is the product of force can be displaced only by the social unity that expresses Fellowship, and by it alone.

Reviews

America in Midpassage, Vol. 3,
by Charles A. Beard and Mary R. Beard.
New York: Macmillan Co., 1939.

Nobody but the Beards could have even commenced to write the contemporary history of the United States, 1924–1938, in a volume of less than a thousand pages so as to produce an account having the scope, fullness, accuracy of detail, unity of plan, and dramatic literary presentation found in *America in Midpassage.* To say that it forms a worthy companion to their monumental *Rise of American Civilization* is inadequate praise. For the present book attempts a more difficult task. It is an account of a movement still going on and a movement in which we are all, for better or worse, caught up. To achieve the objectivity that marks the Beards' account of the unfinished turmoil of the last fourteen years demands a closer realistic grip upon events than was needed in writing of the past.

Were I asked for the cause of this achievement, I should say that in addition to thorough scholarship—obviously a necessary condition—the clue is suggested by the word "Midpassage" in the title. The sense of an unfinished process of transition, the sense that no one can be sure of the issue of the events in which we are involved, is manifest in every chapter. The writers have their preferences as to what the issue should be. But their abiding feeling of an ongoing historic process prevents their adopting it as a method of interpretation and criterion of judgment. In the account of the development of foreign policies in the United States the preference of the writers seems to me to appear more emphatically than in their dealing with other topics. But, after an account of four competing policies, it is added, "As in all such cases, history to come would pass judgment on the competing conceptions." A phrase used in another connection, "outcomes of history and forerunners of destiny to come," expresses, I be-

[First published in "Atlantic Bookshelf," *Atlantic Monthly* 164 (July 1939).]

lieve, the spirit in which the book is written, and the authors, in spite of warm convictions, show no desire to usurp the place of destiny.

The scope of the book is extraordinarily inclusive. That it covers the range of political events from the "summer solstice of Normalcy, the high plateau of permanent peace and prosperity," of the Coolidge administration, through the "dissolutions" of the Hoover administration and the subsequent "detonations" in finance and industry, and then through the promulgation of the New Deal, the election of '36, and the policies of the next two years, and that the treatment keeps politics and economics in constant alliance, is what would be expected from the past record of the writers. Nor is it a cause for surprise that one chapter should be given to discussion of the "Interplay of Court, Congress, and President," since Charles Beard's interest in the history of the Supreme Court is familiar from his previous writings. If the treatment of labor in the chapter entitled "Urban and Rural Labor in Evolving Economy" does not seem to have as unified a pattern as the subjects of most of the other chapters, the fault, if it be one, probably lies in the confused and uncertain position of labor itself rather than with the authors.

As in the earlier volumes on American Civilization, the political-economic record is supplemented by well-documented chapters dealing with the arts of entertainment, including the rise of radio and movie, with literature, painting, and music, with science, and with "the frames of social thought," about two fifths of the whole book being given to an account of developments in these subjects since 1924. There will doubtless be differences of opinion about the importance of men and women selected for especial notice, but there can be none about the range of the documentation.

The volume ends with a chapter called "Toward a Reconstruction of Democracy" which points out how events have compelled a revival and closer scrutiny of the idea of humanistic democracy. In this chapter occurs a summary of the role of President Roosevelt in carrying forward the tradition of humanistic democracy which has been a dynamic in American life since colonial days. The Preface is dated "Winter, 1938." There is in consequence no complete account of the reaction which has grown so rapidly during the last year. But I should have greater confidence in the healthy development of the American ideal of humanistic democracy in the coming years if every editorial writer, every radio commentator, every legislator, and every administrator in the United States had beside him and used for constant reference the Beards' account of our unfinished midpassage course. A subtitle might well be "Lest We Forget."

Social Religion, by Douglas Clyde Macintosh.
New York: Charles Scribner's Sons, 1939.

In view of the all but exclusive emphasis of the present
book upon the social aspects of Christianity, fairness to the author requires that attention be called to a point mentioned in the
Preface, namely, that the present book is the first part of a work
on *Religion Today and Tomorrow,* the other parts dealing with
personal religion and with theology. In view, however, of the importance attached to the social phases of religion, the nature of
the author's transition to the last named topic, theology, will be
awaited with interest by those who are concerned especially with
the philosophy of religion. Doubtless there is a metaphysical
view appropriate to the present interest in the "social," but the
view is still inadequately represented in philosophical writings,
and it would seem as if the position taken in the present volume
committed its author to a further development of this metaphysics when he undertakes a theological treatise.

Although the title of the volume is general, it is probably no
ground for surprise that the book itself discusses but one religion, namely Christianity. Professor Macintosh would not, I am
confident, deny that the social aspects and implications of other
great historic religions are worth examining, even though they
fall outside the scope of this book. In any case, the reader must
be grateful to him for the candor and thoroughness with which
he has dealt with the problem facing every Christian believer who
insists upon the intrinsic social message of the Christian faith—
the relation existing between this insistence and the teachings of
Jesus as they are recorded in the New Testament.

Mr. Macintosh's book is divided into two parts, the second
part being given to certain specific practical social problems of
contemporary western life, with reference to which the author

[First published in *Review of Religion* 4 (March 1940): 359–61.]

believes that the Christian gospel has something significant to say. These problems are the prevention of war, the abolition of poverty, the safeguarding of civil liberties, and the reformation of government and political methods. Doubtless for many persons what Mr. Macintosh has to say about the bearing of Christian faith upon these concrete matters will prove the most vitally interesting part of the book, and this reviewer would not minimize their significance. But the author is, after all, a professor of theology in a school of divinity, and his purpose would be misrepresented were it not explicitly noted that his views on practical points are applications of a conclusion reached in the first and theoretical part of his work.

This first part, "Principles of Social Religion," is an examination of the meaning of the idea of the Kingdom of God as that is presented in the New Testament when it is taken to be *the* central and controlling principle of the Christian faith. Whatever be thought of the conclusions arrived at—and Christian theologians as well as non-Christians will differ in their judgments on this point—there should be complete agreement as to the fairness and completeness of the author's discussion of the topic. For, while there is no parade of scholarship, the author's range of reading is very wide; it includes, not only the literature, English and foreign, expounding the social quality of the Christian gospel, but also writings that are adversely critical of this view. Of the first, he mentions some twenty authors who have presented the social interpretation of the teaching of Jesus. But he then proceeds to consider with complete candor all the main dissenting and opposed interpretations, at least as far as they have been put forward by Protestant and non-Christian scholars.

Special attention is given to writers who hold that the moral teachings of Jesus were so deeply influenced by his acceptance of the current idea of the speedy ending of the existing world that his moral principles were intended to refer (according to one group of commentators) either to a Kingdom still to come, after the catastrophic destruction of the existing order, or (according to another group) to the short interim remaining between the time in which he taught and the coming of the supernaturally introduced order.

As far as the present writer can judge, Mr. Macintosh does full justice to what has been urged regarding the influence of eschatological beliefs upon Jesus. He also accepts many of the conclusions of what used to be called "higher criticism" regarding interpolations in the record and attributions to Jesus of interpretations made in the light of later events. But he holds that, even when the mode of expression of Jesus is influenced by the idea of a sudden eschatological change, what he asserted were ethical principles intended to be universally applicable. This position is supported by examination of the social contents of the Old Testament literature with which Jesus was presumably familiar, and by a detailed examination of the records of his teachings, especially the parables. Mr. Macintosh is a constant critic of the view that the undeniably ideal character of the moral principles set forth is consistent only with faith in some supernatural intervention by which they will be applied in practice, upholding the view that they are consistent—and *moral* principles consistent *only*—with the view that they are directions and inspirations to a life to be lived now. His treatment of recorded passages about wealth and pacifism are peculiarly pertinent in connection with this point.

There can be no doubt that many Christian theologians will feel that Mr. Macintosh is taking too literally the teachings of Jesus. They will continue to prefer a more esoteric interpretation which places a lighter burden of responsibility upon the professing Christian. Non-Christians may feel that the author's emphasis upon the strictly moral character of the principles set forth in the New Testament is more consistent with a naturalistic-cultural moral position than with one which gives a unique position to the Christian religion; or, otherwise stated, that Mr. Macintosh has gone so far in his "liberalism" that he should go further. But no reader who vies with the author in simple candor can fail to be impressed with the sincere and courageous spirit which shines through all the pages of this book. It should not be necessary to urge every reader to begin with the Preface, where personal acquaintance may be made with the humane attitude which animates Mr. Macintosh throughout.

The Human Enterprise: An Attempt to Relate Philosophy to Daily Life, by Max C. Otto. New York: F. S. Crofts and Co., 1940.

The adventure of mankind as it is discussed in this book has reference on one side to the present plight of humanity and on the other side to the function and responsibility of philosophy in this juncture. One era of history, Dr. Otto says, is running out and another is coming in; but what the new era is to be is still to be determined, and the special role of philosophy is to ally itself with the forces which can work to forward realization of the better potentialities of human nature. The obligation imposed upon philosophy is the more serious because, with the running out of the old era, "the most precious thing that has emerged—human uniqueness—is everywhere in peril." The author is quite aware that his view of the nature and task of philosophy conflicts with that of its classic and genteel tradition, and a portion of the book, not disproportionate under the circumstances, is devoted to criticism of the latter.

The definitely philosophic core of the book is found, unless I am mistaken, in its treatment of "experience," "reality," and "man," the latter on the basis of conclusions reached in analysis of the first two topics. The account given of experience and reality brings the book into conflict with that aspect of the classic tradition which holds that the concern of philosophy is with discovery and grasp of an ultimate reality behind experience, the latter being limited to mere appearances or "phenomena." On the basis of a radically different idea about reality and experience, Mr. Otto makes an eloquent, often poetic, plea for development of the kind of philosophy which, upon a reasoned basis, will do in this period of change and uncertainty something of the work which religion once did but is now failing to do because it no longer commands loyal intellectual support. The distinctive

[First published in *Journal of Philosophy* 37 (23 May 1940): 303–5.]

feature of this book as I read it is that it interprets through the legitimate terms—but not the conventional language—of philosophy a view of the potentialities of man and his experience which instates on a human foundation the *values* that historic philosophies have usually placed upon a cosmic foundation—which has now crumbled. The sense of the crisis occasioned by the unsettlement of the old foundations and of the necessity for henceforth finding direction for the human enterprise within the conditions of human experience pervades and determines the whole book.

There is, in consequence, some danger that, as far as some readers are concerned, the book will fall between the two proverbial stools. Professional philosophers will miss the language through which epistemological and metaphysical problems have become endeared to them, while they will be conscious of the criticisms levelled against traditional philosophy on the ground of its impotency to assist men in the present crisis. They may accordingly miss the point of the book and even relegate it to the class of would-be edifying popularizations. The so-called general reader, on the other hand, may find so much of the genuine substance of philosophy in the book that he will be unprepared to assimilate what the subtitle truly calls the book, "An attempt to relate philosophy to daily life." Furthermore those who have looked for salvation to science as a purely abstract pursuit independent of human desire and emotion may be disturbed by the fact that Mr. Otto insists upon the limitations of this science, although he completely accepts its critical impact upon the religions and philosophies of the past.

In any case I shall utilize this possibility so as to say a few words about the philosophy of "reality" and "experience" which underlies and animates the book's conclusions. This philosophy is "realistic idealism." There is nothing new about this collocation of words. But as the author uses them they have a moral, not an epistemological, reference. The all-pervading characteristic of the book is, then, its union of a thoroughgoing naturalism with faith in the actuality and the potency of ideals. This union is expressed in the philosophy of "experience" and of "reality" that is set forth. Experience is not just interaction with raw physical forces. For a world which is the product of human ingenuity enters also into the structure and contents of experience. Even more important in the consequences for present humanity than change in the science of physical nature is the fact that "traders, inventors, entrepreneurs, and scientists, working together, produced capitalistic, industrial, machine civilization. They contrived to set up a world between mankind and the natural environment" (p. 79). Even empirical philosophers have managed to deal with experience as a theoretical abstraction and have neglected its actual contents and the problems the latter have created. It is, I think, in harmony with the spirit of the book to say that the challenge to "human uniqueness" which is now so vigorous and widespread is a product not of the wicked intent of any man or nation, but is an expression of the fact that industrial life as it now exists has entered into human experience in such a way as to deprive many men of the conditions through which distinctively human values can be realized. A similar conclusion is reached in the chapter on "Reality." I can not summarize the argument on which it rests but its gist is set forth in this sentence: "Some people choose to restrict the term reality to that abstract something which exists independently of man and forever. . . . We have included what reality is experienced to be, and this has given us, among other realities, those which are an interweaving of human and nonhuman elements" (p. 190), from which is drawn the practical conclusion that some "realities are in the keeping of mankind and can be thrown away or used with imaginative intelligence" (p. 191).

One of the specific bearings of this practical conclusion is seen in the treatment of the belief in God. For the author distinguishes between cosmic atheism, which he rejects since he has reached, he says, "an affirmative faith in the nonexistence of God," and the moral atheism which denies the reality of ideals, purposes, and values as genuine elements of human experience and hence of "reality." In consequence of acceptance of the latter, the cosmic "nontheist is pledged to an uncommon moral independence in the face of the two commanding voices of our time—the strident voice of business and the proud voice of science. He prizes attitudes of mind and heart that transcend practical demands and elude intellectual formulas" (pp. 340–341). The philosophy of experience as an interaction of factors of desire and purpose with the world that physical science intellectually reports, an interaction in which the human factors contribute something precious and unique to nature and to reality (something which is as important for philosophy as for the human enterprise) is then to me the distinctive contribution of this book. The author would be the first to admit that the basic idea is not new. But I know of no book in which humanistic naturalism is set forth with the consistence and the wealth of application which attend its exposition in this book.

The Techniques of Reconstruction

Man and Society in an Age of Reconstruction,
by Karl Mannheim.
New York: Harcourt, Brace and Co., 1940.

Dr. Mannheim has had the great advantage of living in both Germany and England in the years of crisis. He has a thorough German training, but he also has a mind flexible enough to learn what new conditions have to teach. The present book represents a combination of experiences in the two countries by a man who is expert in all branches of social theory, who has an open mind, and who is capable of seeing conditions in two very different countries as parts of one and the same social world.

From what happened to the Weimar Republic and the coming of Naziism to power he learned that existing civilization "is faced not with brief unrest, but with a radical change of structure." He reached the conclusion that unless the causes of the social disintegration are understood countries which have not experienced the full impact of the crisis will not be able to "control the trend of events by democratic planning so as to avoid dictatorship, conformity, and barbarism." Living in a country in which "liberal democracy functions almost undisturbed" he was led to consider the means by which societies of the traditional liberal order can re-adapt themselves to the crisis in which the whole modern world finds itself. In Germany he reached the opinion that political democracy had run its course, in England he changed to the belief that if the dissolution of the old social order is admitted, its causes grasped, and the democratic techniques are created, reconstruction can be achieved by other than totalitarian means.

Dr. Mannheim is quite aware that persons in a country like the United States are those who are likely to believe that local causes account for the rise of dictatorships in Europe, and to suppose the idea that the whole social order is undergoing transformation is just a case of shaken nerves. That, as he sees the matter, is just

[First published in *Saturday Review of Literature* 22 (31 August 1940): 10.]

their danger. It will keep persons in democratic countries repeating worn out social creeds so as to justify and support a social order that is bound, in any case, to pass.

When he says that scientific analysis, experiment, and planning are required to develop new techniques if justice and freedom are to be maintained, he may seem to be saying only what is urged from almost every quarter. But one who goes to the book itself will find in it, I think, the best account that exists anywhere of the causes which, in his words, have changed liberal democracy into mass democracy, and how and why it is that these causes tend to create a totalitarian order in the name of mass democracy. By planning exercised in behalf of freedom, he doesn't mean what is called a planned society nor even "planned economic order." He means rather the strategy, consisting of carefully developed techniques, by which a democratic community can maintain itself as a free community—and not just as an aggregate of self-seeking persons who are constantly subject to mass and massive forces.

Mannheim is first of all a social psychologist who sees institutions, historic movements, and emotional and moral attitudes engaged in constant interplay with one another. From the standpoint of the influence the book should have, its weakness is that it tries to combine in the same work an exposition of the methods appropriate to the study of society and a brilliant and—to the present writer—convincing application of this method to the study of what has brought European civilization to its present pass. As a consequence, I fear that the persons who occupy strategic positions in politics, industry, and in what is called intellectual life will be repelled by the scholarship of the book and fail to learn the lessons which Mannheim clearly sets forth when he applies the method to interpretation of actual events. Mannheim's book is free from dogmatism, from stock phrases, and from clichés. In a word, it exemplifies its own teaching, the need of study directed by a fresh outlook.

The Philosophy of George Santayana, Library of Living Philosophers, vol. 2, edited by Paul Arthur Schilpp. Evanston and Chicago: Northwestern University, 1940.

In accord with the general plan of the series of volumes of which the present one is the second, the book opens and closes with statements by the philosopher who is the subject of discussion. The first part bears the general title of "A General Confession" and consists of two sections which admirably complement each other. First there comes a kind of intellectual autobiography, previously published under the title of "Brief History of My Opinions," and then follows a retrospective summary reprinted from the Preface to the Collected Edition of the author's works. The last hundred pages, under the caption "Apologia Pro Mente Sua," restate the main doctrines of Santayana with a view to meeting adverse criticisms that have been passed by the other contributors to the volume, clearing away misunderstandings, and elaborating the philosopher's own tenets. There are eighteen commentators and critics and their essays cover almost every aspect of Santayana's writings, his poetry and novel not being left out.

A reviewer is embarrassed in dealing with a book of such varied contents. The task is almost like that which would devolve upon a person who undertook to write in a single article about philosophic views expressed by nineteen different philosophers about the state of the world in general, the nominal subject, whether philosopher or the world, continuing to go the same way in which he or it was going before, when all is said and done. Nevertheless, in the case of the present volume there is a unity that is other than nominal.

The quality of this unity may be expressed by saying that the book affords no great promise of fulfilling the expectation quoted by the Editor from F. C. S. Schiller in the general Introduction; namely, that interminable controversies would be avoided if a

[First published in *Mind* 50 (October 1941): 374–85.]

living philosopher were asked by other living philosophers a few searching questions. But just as somehow the differing comments of philosophers on the nature of the world finally add to its depth of meaning for the rest of us, so the appraisals and comments offered us in this volume serve a worthier purpose than putting an end to controversy. We have an enriched exposition of the doctrines of Santayana and we have, through the medium of comments and criticisms, the gift of many statements that are intrinsically significant, whether or not they are relevant to Santayana as their alleged theme. The present book, moreover, is strikingly free, as a whole, from arguments based merely upon previously fixed systems. The writers discuss *problems* with which Santayana has concerned himself rather than reiterate their own 'isms.

The variety of interpretations put forth may almost be taken as an ironical confirmation of one aspect of Santayana's own philosophy—his belief in thoroughgoing relativity, and the fact that he does not altogether, in this special instance, welcome its exhibition suggests a difficulty inhering in his own position. The variety and relativity is a reminder that a reviewer who expresses any responses of his own is assuming, uninvited, the position of a further contributor. Hence to make clear at the outset my own position I shall say that I have found the first essay in the volume, that of Mr. Brownell, the one which most fully and sensitively arouses my intellectual sympathy with respect to both the positive and the negative aspects of the philosophy about which he writes. Brownell says of Santayana that he "reveals things to you by his insight; this is his inspiration; he does not stimulate you by his purpose." He is a former student in Santayana's classes at Harvard; he has evidently continued to be a student of the writings of his old teacher, and he has imbued himself with the method he ascribes to the latter. Of the great versatility of Santayana, he says, "This is less the objectivity that usually is attributed to him than a kind of cosmic sympathy for all the forms and variations of being." This sympathy finds expression in the manifest textural qualities of Santayana's thinking, his interest in contextual quality and the union in his work of poetry and dialectic.

What is called "interest in contextual quality" is expressed, according to Brownell, in the distinctive color assumed by universals in the philosophy of Santayana. For the universals of the latter emerge from "contextual matrices warm and glowing," they are "literary universals, not mathematical"; they are not imposed, as the latter are, "from without." Since "contextual colors and suggestions change with every breath, shimmering and moving like the surface of the sea, the universals arising in them are temporary." This statement does not contradict the uniform assertion of Santayana that universals are eternal. For it is of universals beheld by "spirit" that Brownell is speaking, and Santayana's dominant interest is in universals in precisely this relation. The insouciance with which spirit—and also Santayana—dismisses one essence and accepts another one is part of the "deliverance" that is the good and the joy of the spiritual life. To the spirit, some essences are *ideals,* and the latter, Santayana says, are ends not in the sense of an accomplished work, but as "the *good* of that finished work in the vision and emotion it can awaken in the mind that, *at some supreme moment,* understands it best." And "this moral ideality, he expressly says, being relative to appreciation, may accrue or may lapse."

I believe that Brownell is right in thinking the fact that "the color and poetry of thought" is the chief concern of Santayana is the main source of the difficulty experienced in grasping his meaning; if, indeed, it is properly subject to the rude act of grasping. It is rather to be felt by a kind of empathy. There is something of this direct quality in every philosopher who has something new and different to say. But it is at its height in Santayana. It is at this point that, according to Brownell, Santayana himself has difficulty in making his poetic strain fuse with the dialectic; or, since fusion is too much to expect, difficulty in getting them to live in the same house. For poetry is akin to the *natural,* which in Santayana's view is the material, the existential, while dialectic is concerned with the non-existential, with essences that are non-material. Both poetry and the natural, according to this commentator, "arise in the dense and uncontrollable experience of life. They press up irresistibly. They are concrete or many sided, stubborn, integral in themselves. . . . They are lyrical, both of them, in the sense that they are gratuitous, spontaneous songs, as it were, in our experience. Essence and dialectic belong elsewhere." And in his "General Confession," Santayana says, "The intention of my philosophy has certainly been to attain, if possible, such wide intuition and to celebrate the emotions with which they fill the mind"—a sentence in which "such" refers to moments when "routine gives place to intuition, and experience is synthesized and brought before the spirit in its sweep and truth"—truth being not so much literal as an embodiment of essence in existence.

Santayana objects to having the epithet "aesthetic" applied to his philosophy, the word being to him, I believe, redolent of objectionable "aestheticism." But I cannot see that he would or could object to having his point of view called poetic, especially if "religious" is understood in connection with poetic. I believe this phase of his philosophy is that which has given to so many readers that which I myself have derived from it: instruction, wealth of suggestion, added insight, and the kind of "inspiration" that enables one to face the conditions of life more happily. It is in this direct field rather than in the technical realm of his later works that his own genius has, I believe, found congenial expression. To quote from Brownell once more: "Santayana's philosophy is mainly moral in interest and is concerned with the conditions of life, the emergence of values and the possibilities of happiness. . . . Santayana is not interested in nature from its own point of view, as the scientist is or thinks he is, but in the bearing of nature on man, on his possibility of knowledge and his chances for happiness." I cannot take this statement as an adverse criticism. For to me it expresses the difference between the aim and quality of the love of wisdom, which is philosophy, and love of knowledge, which is science.

It is not at this place, then, that arise the difficulties which inhere in Santayana's thought. These difficulties are, I think, indicated by Brownell when he says that Santayana's philosophy may be regarded as a "Naturalism honestly docile to obvious facts but so tortured by memories of scholasticism that the face of it is hardly recognizable." I find this sentence contains the gist of all serious criticisms that may be brought against Santayana. In order that it be applicable we must, however, broaden the scope of the word "scholasticism." We have to take into account what is—(what, that is, seems to me to be)—the subordination of his own insight and quality to a number of historic systems. There is the memory of Plato (with judicious eliminations) in his theory of essence; of Aristotle in the theory of substance (at least, in name, for I doubt if Aristotle would recognize his immutable and eternal beings in the plastic, potential and completely contingent "matter" of Santayana); of Democritus and Lucretius in his "materialism." Memory of Spinoza is manifested in his psychophysical parallelism—though here again the historic correctness of this interpretation may be doubted—and his moral relativism. The memory of Locke and of Locke's psychological successors saturates his view of immediate experience, resulting in what he calls transcendentalism. This memory is the source of his "solipsism of the moment," and thereby of the necessity for treating "matter" as a mere, although necessary, "presupposition." The intensity of this memory is the source of what he supposes is thoroughgoing scepticism, although if he had ever entertained any doubt whatever about the validity of an interlude in modern epistemological psychology, his *wholesale* scepticism would have itself been sceptically viewed.

It is the complex of these memories that determines the formulation of Santayana's own otherwise delicate, free, sensitive insights. In consequence, he is diverted from developing them in their own direction. I do not mean that scholarly knowledge is not a necessary part of philosophical equipment, but that in his case it is used to hinder rather than help the growth that seems to be intrinsic to his humanistic naturalism. In view of the contrast and conflict between the parts of Santayana's writings which express his own direct experience with its poetic color and depth, reflecting his personal observations of life, and those parts which provide the formal skeleton of his system (whose bones protrude in his later works), Brownell's use of the word "tortured" hardly seems too strong. However, there is so much in present-day philosophy that is all but entirely composed by piecing together remnants of older systems that we are grateful to Santayana that he has given us so much from his own proper sources. But at the same time, this very gift is what makes one regretfully aware of the obtrusive presence of the other constituent.

I have done injustice, outwardly at least, to other contributors in allotting so much space to Brownell's article. But I have an excuse in the fact that what I have quoted from him strikes a note sounded in most of the other essays; in sympathetic and adverse ones alike. There is practically no writer who does not have occasion to speak of the diverse strains composing the system of Santayana. It was practically inevitable, in view of his topic, "Santayana's Philosophical Inheritance," that Mr. Sullivan, the author of the second essay, should notice it. He closes by saying, "I have completed this brief survey of three traditional themes in Santayana's philosophy, his Platonism, materialism and scepticism." In a later contribution, Boas, in his acute and instructive essay on "Santayana and the Arts," writes, "One of the secrets of Santayana's power as critic and philosopher of art lies in the threefold nature of his philosophy. A lesser man would have felt the necessity of 'reconciling' the realms of matter, essence and spirit. He would have reduced two of them to the third and left us a universe so neat and orderly that the world we live in would have become inexplicable." This is well said, and so is his earlier sentence which remarks that "each realm turns out to be incomplete and to give no satisfactory picture in itself of the entire universe." There is, however, an alternative to reducing two of these elements to the third one. In a less confined treatment of the underlying naturalism, life and mind would both present themselves as direct and vital manifestations in which inherent potentialities of nature are expressed. Exploration of this possibility might have found a common source for all three, while a diversity of manifestations, incompatible with artificial neatness and trimness, would also have appeared.

It would be wearisome to pursue this particular theme literally throughout the whole series of essays. It is, however, pertinent to one central topic, morality as pre-rational, rational, and post-rational, to note that Rice's article on "The Philosopher as Poet and Critic" holds that Santayana's prose is more successfully poetic than his verse, while it connects each one of the three poets discussed in Santayana's *Three Philosophical Poets* with one of the three historic strains mentioned. He quotes from Santayana a pertinent passage to the effect that a complete poet would unite elements that are divided in the three men who are discussed. Namely, the immediate experience of Goethe; the naturalism of Lucretius; and the spirituality of Dante. For he "'should live in the continual presence of all experience and respect it; he should at the same time understand nature, the ground of that experience; and he should also have a delicate sense for the ideal echoes of his own passions, and for all the colors of his possible happiness.'" It would seem as if in the work of this complete poet the three strains would not exist side by side in different "realms," which turn out to be Santayana's philosophy of water-tight compartments, but would have the vital connection with one another which springs from community of origin and nurture.

Mr. Cory seems more the disciple, not just the student, than other contributors. And in connection with the crucial place of the problem of the relation of the pre-rational, rational and the spiritual, or post-rational, it is noteworthy that he finds that the earlier books, constituting the biography of *The Life of Reason*, are infected with a moral taint so that the series beginning with *Scepticism and Animal Faith* is philosophically superior, since free from this taint. It is suggested that the infection was a product of the American environment, where the domination of morals by Calvinistic Puritanism combined superstitious elements with predestination to worldly success and wealth. Santayana was thereby led to wish to present happier and more human morals. It is at least significant that in his reply to criticisms, Santayana attributes the hostility of his Harvard colleagues, James and Royce, to their respective "moralisms" and thinks that it continues to be the "latent and permanent source of almost all the hostility I encounter," including the "more severe strictures passed upon me in this book."

It would seem inevitable that *any* philosophy which is naturalistic would concern itself with the problem of the connection between the pre-human and pre-moral base and the moral interests that play so large a part in human life. It would seem that a naturalistic philosophy would have to face this question quite apart from moralistic concern. It is the central issue of all modern thought, being statable, in non-moral terms, as the problem of the relation of the subject-matter of the physical and biological sciences to all phases of human experience, knowing included. There can be no doubt that "the severe strictures" of the present volume are those of Munitz, Edman and Vivas, and that they are directly concerned, in one way or another, with the split which

they find existing between the alleged naturalistic base of Santayana and his treatment of morally and scientifically human
experience.[1]

While these three essayists arrive at the conclusion that the
split which Santayana finally makes between naturalism and human experience in its scientific, artistic and moral aspects is not
inherent in naturalism, being the product of an arbitrary factor
in Santayana's thought, they reach the conclusion by different
paths. Edman points out that even in the *Life of Reason* there are
two important tenets which foreshadow the doctrines of the later
works. But his main purpose is to show that the later Santayana
has deserted the road which he opened at first and which he
walked in for the most part.

The premonitory symptoms were the fact that the practicality
assigned to thought is Pickwickian, and that *ideal society* is defined not in terms of relationships of human beings with one another, but in terms of association of a human being, conceivably
solitary, with ideal images, the latter being the essences of later
doctrine. But in the early volumes "art was an activity of remaking the natural conditions of life so that they were more appropriate to, and more expressive of, ideal interests. Science was a
technique of efficacious control, religion was an art of moral expression and significant metaphor or myth. Spirituality was a
name for a life lived in terms of a comprehensive ideal called harmony." The substance of Edman's essay is an exposition of the
deliquescence of these three ideas in the later series.

The position of Munitz is not very different, but he traces in
some detail the conflict between the interpretation of the aim and
function of *science* which is given in the *Life of Reason* and the
radical challenge to science that seems to him to mark the series
beginning with *Scepticism and Animal Faith*. The discussion contains what, given the point of view of the writer, is a significant
essay on the proper function of scepticism, and the conversion

1. It is to be regretted that in his reply to the two first named critics, Santayana
for once abandons the urbanity which otherwise marks even his most ironical
comments. It was unnecessary to the point of gratuitousness to attribute their
attitude to "political and racial zeal," and in a less irritated mood Santayana
might perceive that the collection of passages which Munitz finds to be inconsistent with one another is not the product of "personal animus," but of preoccupation with a *problem* which Munitz, whether rightly or wrongly, finds to
be of central importance.

by Santayana of this office into something wholesale, a transformation that is metaphysically rather than logically necessitated. Vivas is more critical than these other writers of the views set forth by Santayana in the *Life of Reason,* finding in substance that they prophesy later developments. His belief in Santayana's inherent continuity is perhaps one reason why Santayana feels that Vivas misrepresents him less than do the other two writers.

Santayana's reply to Vivas does not touch upon the latter's suggestion that the moral theory of the *Life of Reason* was unduly influenced "by the biological approach current in his day," thereby missing or misconceiving the role of the cultural or social. Something said by Vivas has led Santayana, however, to make an explicit statement of just what he affirms and what he denies in his theory of epiphenomenalism; denial of the efficacy of thought as consciousness and spirit, although in some passages efficacy is ascribed to reflection and reason. In passages of the latter tenor, reflection, Santayana says, is an integral part of the "dynamic material world." Sensation, emotion, and thought are materially efficacious just because or as far as they are material. There is no intention to deny that a thoughtful person will behave differently from a thoughtless one. But it is the person, with a body, or rather as a body, which thus behaves; and not a hypostatic consciousness or spirit. Whether persons in general, as distinct from some philosophers, have ever really held any other view than this of the efficacy of intelligence might be worth consideration. In any case, it bears out in this particular point Santayana's contention that his philosophy makes articulate the intent of common sense. However, from the standpoint of Santayana's *system,* his epiphenomenalism is but a reassertion that existence and only existence acts, essence never.

The discussion has trenched upon two of the most important phases of Santayana's philosophy: his materialism as to natural existence and his idealism—in its epistemological sense—as to consciousness and ideas;—the latter being the result of, in his own words, the belief that "we must oscillate between a radical transcendentalism, frankly reduced to a solipsism of the living moment and a materialism posited as a presupposition of conventional sanity." Dennes' article upon "Santayana's Materialism" is a carefully documented study of the nature of matter as it is presented in the writings of Santayana. He has no difficulty

in showing that "matter" is used as a name for *existence* in so far
as *existence* is both enduring and, in its very endurance, powerful and therefore continually manifesting itself in change. Matter
is plastic because it is potential. The union of change and permanence constituting existence is the reason, apparently, that Santayana applies to existence the name "substance," following in
this respect Kant, I should say, rather than Aristotle or Spinoza,
with whom he nominally connects the category of substance.
Existence is called *matter,* I take it, for two reasons. It is what is
studied in physical science, and it is independent of and the cause
of everything mental or psychological. Putting aside, as it is occasionally a pleasure to do, the question of names, Santayana's
position here seems to be that of common sense rendered can-
didly explicit. In one of his comments upon Dennes' paper, Santayana makes a clarifying remark about the mental as *existence.*
It exists, he says, as "the ultimate phase of explicitness, in which
potentiality becomes actuality." He asks "how should this moral
actualisation of existence be less existent than the physical potentiality of it?" It is interesting to speculate what the result
would have been if Santayana had worked out his whole philosophy in harmony with this remark, instead of making the denial of
the existentiality of the given a main tenet.

Dennes' difficulty is not with the view of the nature of substantial existence put forward by Santayana. On this point, he in-
clines to finding in Santayana an expression of the naturalism
towards which contemporary philosophers, "usually called natu-
ralists, empiricists, or positivists, the most critical and careful have, in the last decades, and rather laboriously, won their
way. . . . They have shifted from basic categories like matter, motion, sensations, mechanism, to such relatively neutral categories
as event, quality and relation." This statement is one of the many
significant remarks scattered throughout the book which render
it important, independently of its theme. Dennes finds, however,
one outstanding exception in this matter of the underlying similarity between Santayana's views and those toward which empirical naturalism has been moving since he began writing. This
exception is Santayana's "dogma that nothing given exists," and
the accompanying denial that what exists can be *known,* an assertion that, in ultimate analysis, it can be merely *presupposed.*

This fundamental difference does not seem to me to be an accident in Santayana's system. I should take it rather as proof that Santayana had not made, much less anticipated, the kind of shift which Dennes finds (quite justly) to mark much contemporary philosophy.

In the following single passage, Santayana shows that he has retained intact the earlier categories of "intrinsic character" and "causation"; and he also shows the effect of this retention upon his ideas of the spiritual life and of the ideality of data. How, he asks, "should the feelings (namely, those produced by 'matter') thereby aroused in the organism present the *intrinsic* character of the surrounding things? Evidently they will transcribe only the *effects* of those things *on* the organism." ("Intrinsic" is italicised in the original; "effects" and "on" are not.) The non-relational nature of *character* and the survival of the prehistoric, pre-continuous, notion of *cause* in its relation with *effect*, explain his belief in the non-existential character of data and the necessity for postulating matter by an act of faith. The latter theory reminds one, as it stands, of the phenomenal character of all experienced things on account of which Kant reached up to things-in-themselves by an act of *moral* faith. Santayana seems to be bent on rivalling Kant by doing for ordinary objects by means of animal faith what Kant accomplished for his higher noumenal objects by moral faith.

The failure of Santayana's views to conform in this respect to Dennes' assimilation of them to recent naturalism seems to me to confirm the feeling of Brownell that Santayana suffers from an attempt to unite old beliefs and new ideas which in fact are incompatible. The same point is made by Vivas; indeed the latter quotes from Santayana a passage in which the latter says that he has sought to "build a system of philosophy out of disparate and complex allegiances, 'combining them as well as logic allowed, without at heart disowning anything.'" There is, accordingly, the more cause for regret that none of the contributors examines critically either Santayana's uncritical implicit acceptance of what he (somewhat strangely) calls "transcendentalism" or his view of animal faith. Quite frequently, Santayana deserts, as far as words are concerned, the idea of *faith*, and has recourse to *action*. In the latter passages, which certainly are the ones agreeing with unprejudiced observation, there is no more need to bring in an act of faith to account for experience of the natural events which condition all "mental" existences, than there is to account for the fact that, say, a vegetable is able to interact with non-vegetable things like air, light and soil. Since human beings live only by interacting with things of the environment, it is strange that faith in the existence of the latter is said to be a *precondition* of their ability to act and experience.

I am aware of the great danger in quoting passages in isolation from their context, so when I quote the two following passages it is not by way of proof of what I have just said, but by way of invitation of students to reflect upon them in their total context. From the reply in the present volume I take the following: "We believe because we act, we do not act because we believe." [2] From an earlier essay, on "Tragic Philosophy," I quote the following: "There is inspiration wherever there is mind. The sensuous images and categories of thought on which common knowledge relies are themselves poetic and wholly original in form, being the product of a kind of inspiration in the animal organism. But they are controlled in their significance and application by experiment in the field of action"—of *action*, not a *faith* lying back of action, be it noted.

The problem of morals, as has been intimated in the course of the foregoing remarks, is central in the interpretation of Santayana. It receives attention in the essay of Pepper, "Santayana's Theory of Value," of Lamprecht, "Animal Faith and the Art of Intuition," and somewhat more remotely in the contributions of Schilpp, Schaub and Russell. It appears whenever the question of value comes up. When, however, I say "problem of morals" I do *not* mean the problem as to what is the genuine nature of morals, but the question of what is the attitude of Santayana's philosophy toward morals. Put as briefly as possible: Is Santayana's system as a whole fundamentally a theory of morals? Is what many writers would call his metaphysics, using the word in a different sense

2. Compare with this remark, the following from the introductory "Confession": "The object of this faith is the substantial energetic thing *encountered* in action"; and also pp. 512, 518, 531, "My whole reliance on action, intent and environment in generating knowledge." I am quite aware how dialectically easy it might be to translate such passages into the official doctrine of Santayana. I quote them to suggest to a sensitive reader what might have happened if what these passages seem to say had been freely developed in their own terms instead of in those of prior acceptance of a psychological doctrine whose necessary implication is the "solipsism of the moment."

from his use when he denies he has any metaphysics, fundamentally a part of his doctrine about morals, or is it independent of the latter; independent, moreover, in a way which makes it so fundamental that the theory of morals, important as it is in its place, is relatively superficial in the whole system? I do not intend to try to answer the question thus raised. In addition to pointing out the frequent recurrence, throughout essays on nominally different subjects, of this question, I want to say a few words about why and how, as far as I can see, the question is a basic problem for the understanding of Santayana's views.

Santayana quotes with approval two sentences from the essay of Friess and Rosenthal, "Reason in Religion and the Emancipated Spirit," saying in effect that it gives the clew to a sympathetic interpretation, as distinct from a misunderstanding, of what is most important in his doctrine. The passage reads as follows: "Does not the same foundation, materialism, serve his intellectual and his spiritual emancipation? This view-point, I mean, is the ground not only of his critique of belief, but also of his freedom to confront the world, as he puts it, 'martially . . . with courage and good humor, rather than supplications and fears'?" Santayana comments: "Exactly: this hits the nail on the head, but I think the nail might be driven in still further." And he goes on to restate his "transcendentalism" as to immediate experience and his description of the spiritual life, adding that his "materialism is therefore simply ordinary perception, sustained in its impulsive trust but criticized in its deliverance." It seems to me that as long as this strain is uppermost what I have called the place of the problem of morals in the philosophy of Santayana is resolved by giving it a secondary and derived place. And this view seems to be the only one consistent with the large place occupied by "deliverance" in "spiritual life." Religion appears to be "taking a moral holiday" in a deeper sense than that meant by those who first used the phrase. On the other hand, in reply to questions asked and criticisms made by some of the contributors—and also if I mistake not questions he has at times asked himself—Santayana seems to hold that the supreme place given to spiritual life is due to its being the supreme *good*. Although it is an instance of post-rational morality, yet it is said that rational morality must provide a place for it in its own scheme. There is even an intimation that it presents the consummate flowering of the highest impulse in *pre*-rational morality. While it would be proper, on a more fitting occasion, to consider these apparently different conceptions from the dialectical point of view, the reason for bringing up the matter here is non-dialectical. It is that this aspect of Santayana's doctrine, when it is viewed as stating a problem, exemplifies what upon the whole is the controlling issue of all modern philosophy: The relation (or lack of relation) to each other of the elements with which the sciences (physical, biological and anthropological) are concerned and the moral qualities of human life, in the widest sense of "moral."

Whether one regard the present volume from the standpoint of Santayana's philosophy or as a document illustrating varied phases of contemporary philosophic reflection, it is abundantly rewarding. I regret in corresponding measure that the particular line of exposition I have adopted has prevented mention of the essays of Hartshorne, Strong, and Banfi, and has permitted only mere mention of three or four others. The contribution of Bertrand Russell is, for example, a very interesting running commentary upon a whole series of points in Santayana's philosophy, throwing light also upon points in which each have influenced the other's views. Fortunately, the book, like the world, is open and accessible, and each person can take from it according to his ability. I do not wish to close without speaking of the unusually high literary quality of the different contributions. This quality is assuredly a tribute to the power of poetic and persuasive expression characteristic of the subject of the essays. It is not merely that every writer refers to Santayana's power in this respect. It is as if having to write about him had acted as a spur and even to some degree as an inspiration.

Addresses

Message to Friends of the John Dewey Labor Research Fund

It is a source of much regret to me that I am not able to be with you who have gathered here this evening in order to welcome you, and to express my deep appreciation of the spirit which has animated you in coming here. I feel honored in being entrusted with this project under whose auspices the present occasion has been arranged. It combines in happy practical fashion three ideas in whose union I have long believed—labor, education and science. Looking back over many years and looking ahead to the future which in many respects is so uncertain, I am convinced that the possibility of a free, prosperous and creative culture is bound up with the fruitful interrelation and cooperation of these three ideals—labor, as representing the solidarity of all progressive forces, education, as the enlightenment necessary for action, and science, as the method of extending the boundaries of knowledge and providing the means of making action intelligent and effective.

I should also, if I were able to be present, express my warmest thanks to Mr. S. Feinstone of Philadelphia, Pennsylvania, for the generosity which made the initiation of this project possible, as well as to all the members of the cast who give such pleasure to the audience. Having seen the play, in thanking them for the enjoyment they provide, I will also congratulate the audience upon having the opportunity to see one of the most entertaining plays that has appeared on the New York stage. I should be ungrateful indeed if I did not extend my heartiest thanks to all the members of the Committee who have given so unstintingly of their time and energy to make this occasion a success.

[From an unpublished typescript in the Sidney Hook/John Dewey Collection, Box 1, folder 6, Special Collections, Morris Library, Southern Illinois University at Carbondale, for the message read at a benefit performance of *What a Life!* at the Mansfield Theater in New York City on 6 February 1939.]

Lessons from the War—in Philosophy

1. Typescript

If the present state of the civilized world with its clash of arms, social policies, forms of institutions, ideas and ideals is capable of teaching anything to future philosophy, then the past of philosophy must have had something to do with forming the conditions that culminate in the present catastrophe. If so, adequate discussion of the present would require a critical survey of the main trends of thought for at least the last two or three centuries. Since that is out of the question, I shall touch upon a few points that strike me as important.

In the first place, I would say that it is easy, especially for those of a professional intellectual class, to exaggerate the influence exerted by intellectual formulations, philosophies included. The chief influence is the other way around. Events, social movements, come first. Reflective analysis and systematic report come later. Often they come so much later that by the time they arrive the state of affairs has changed. Nevertheless, taking it by and large, philosophical formulations have exercised two functions. Ideas may run ahead of action, and persons who are acutely sensitive may feel movements that have a great future while they are still inchoate. Systematic formulation of practical social movements serves also to provide men with reasons for what they are doing and undoing, making them more aware of the significance of what they are practically engaged in. Every important social movement of modern times has had its own ideology, and the ideology has served as means of defense, on rational grounds, of

[Part 1 from an unpublished typescript and Part 2 from a tape recording of an address at Cooper Union in New York City on 7 December 1941, both from the John Dewey Collection, Special Collections and Archives, Rutgers University Libraries, New Brunswick, N.J.]

what men were trying to accomplish; and as a weapon of offense against hostile movements. By indirect means, through habits which are formed, through institutions in which something is incorporated from the arena of ideas, through education, that which once was an intellectual proposition becomes a sustaining part of a later state of culture.

Roughly speaking, the course of modern philosophies is marked by two main tendencies. There have been men who have devoted themselves mostly to trying to justify, on intellectual grounds and in a reasoned way, the newer tendencies which had an adverse effect upon beliefs and institutions coming from an earlier period; to be more specific, from the middle ages. They stood, indirectly at least, for new departures in religion, morals, politics, economics, and the physical sciences. Aside from traditionalist defenders of tradition, there have been also philosophical schools that thought they could best defend what they regarded as sound in the newer or modern movements by interpreting them, with changes of language and of detail, in terms derived from old and classic philosophies.

Still speaking roughly, the first named type has been empirical and liberal. When I said that an adequate survey would have to note what past systems of opinion have done in producing the conditions which have manifested themselves in the present upheaval, I had in mind the fact that there must have been defects and distortions in historic liberal empiricism and that they played a part in forming conditions which now exist. There must have been something about them which at least provided the opportunity for large scale development of absolutistic and totalitarian philosophies. When and if, for example, we emphasize the influence of Hegel and other German philosophers alike upon Bolshevik and Nazi totalitarianisms, we must not forget there were things in British and French empirical and liberal philosophies which called out the German movement by way of reaction. When for example in the nineteenth century English thinkers wished to combat the disintegrating influences of earlier British empiricism and laissez-faire liberalism, they found no other intellectual weapons at hand than those they borrowed from the German philosophical arsenal, even though they wanted to employ them to build a firmer foundation under an essentially democratic society.

I now come to a more direct discussion of the topic of the day. Readers of the periodical press will be aware that one particular diagnosis of the cause of present troubles and evils is now filling its pages. We are told that their source is our undue concern with the "materialistic" phases of life, and the remedy is to return to the "spiritual." Here is a ready-made answer to the question of what the war can teach philosophy. It would doubtless simplify my task today if I could fall in with the stream of speech coming to us from theologians and also from literary critics and from some sociologists. I find, however, that the exact import of the terms "material" and "spiritual" is either left so vague as to arouse questions or if definite is of a kind so definitely reactionary as to evoke protest.

When we get out of the vagueness that virtually uses "material" to stand for whatever is regarded as low and "spiritual" for what is esteemed to be high, fair and noble, the following questions suggest themselves: Just what in *concrete* terms *are* the material things to which we have been unduly devoted? We need a bill of particulars on this point in order to be able to judge in what ways our too exclusive concern with them has produced the evils from which we suffer. Having information on this point, we ask our second question: Why is it that human beings generally have become as engrossed as they are said to be in pursuit of things that are base? Finally, just what is meant in the concrete by the "spiritual," and how are men to be brought to that state of devotion to the spiritual which is said to provide the only sure way out of present troubles?

There are those whose attitudes, beliefs, and practices do not suffer from vagueness. They are quite specific as to the cause of the present world condition and as to the remedy. We have deserted the philosophy of the supernatural, and we have deserted the institution, the Church, authorized to represent divine wisdom, goodness and power. An injunction to return, to go back, is, upon this view, the lesson the war may teach us. There are however others who agree in the necessity of return to first and ultimate truths about ultimate Reality (as they were formulated in Greek philosophy and worked over in medieval scholasticism) who have not, as yet, identified these truths with supernatural authority nor taken refuge in a particular institution. They content themselves with claiming that much of our present confusion and conflict is due to philosophies which have leaned upon the weak reed of experience for intellectual and moral guidance. They do not, as yet, assert that the desertion of necessary truths is heresy in the sense of wilful sin. They even seem to suggest at times that improvement in education and other secular matters would do much to bring us back to right paths—a view which, I fear, will be regarded as itself heretical by those who belong to the institutional ecclesiastical wing of the philosophy of beliefs. The latter persons at least are not out on a limb. They have behind them the pragmatic advantage of beliefs worked out systematically and with great dialectic ingenuity in the past, and also of embodiment of these beliefs in a special social institution. On the other hand, from the standpoint of those who do not believe that distinctively modern movements in natural science, naturalism and secularism are due to deliberate or wilful disobedience, it suffers from the disadvantage of trying to turn backward the clock of time.

In lieu, then, of the historic survey which is here impossible, I suggest that past philosophies have contributed something, both by acts of commission and omission, to the intellectual and moral insecurity, confusion and conflict expressed in the present world situation. They have done so because they have been caught between the new and the old. They have been to a considerable extent a mixture of incompatible, clashing ideas and values. The net result in one respect is to give an immediate strategical advantage to the philosophy that is consistently framed out of the older beliefs which have also achieved institutional incorporation.

But for others the lesson the war is capable of teaching philosophy is that we should go on, go forward, not backward; and that the way to go forward is to get rid of those elements of our heritage from the past which hamper, load down and distort clear and coherent intellectual articulation of the attitudes, interests and movements which are distinctively modern. The issues at stake will then at least be squarely joined intead of being confused. If the Americas are a *New World* in any other than a topographic sense, it would seem to be peculiarly true that in this country philosophy should devote itself in a radical and complete way to all effort to grasp and state the potentialities which inhere in modern movements, and to make much clearer than it now is the direction in which they must move if these potentialities are to be actualized.

The proposition that there is such a radical incompatibility between some fundamental elements in the philosophies inherited from Greek and medieval times and dominant traits of what is modern that confusion and conflict is bound to result from any attempt at moral and intellectual combination is a sweeping one. From the side of those who consistently represent the older philosophy, the proposition is confirmed by the fact that they regard the tendencies which are most characteristically modern as lapses from truth and from the divine. At its best, Greek philosophy and science were framed in a pre-scientific age. In intent, however, Greek thought was inquiring, free from control by external authority, political or ecclesiastical, and was based upon trust in the ability of human reason to attain truth. In the medieval period, the method used in such science as the Greeks achieved was neglected, while its conclusions were arrested and petrified. What was vital and moving in Greek culture dropped away. The natural world for which Greek genius had affinity was treated as corrupt and unworthy because it was corrupted by the fall of man. Human reason at its best required both confirmation and extension in every important matter by supernatural revelation.

If the beliefs and principles which form the heart of ancient pre-scientific times, had been the possession of a small group of persons who called themselves philosophers, they would probably have had little general influence. But in connection with the formulation of religious faith, they became a part of the common intellectual and moral fibre of the western world. They entered into the social memory and imagination of Christendom; they became a part of the tradition that is taken for granted and they determined the horizons of man's vision. Under these circumstances, it is not surprising that modern movements had great difficulty in finding appropriate expression of their own meanings, and that modern philosophy is weakened and confused by its attempt to combine things inherently incompatible.

What is true of the modern science of nature in its sharp contrast with ancient science is true also of the other most conspicuous feature of modern life: political and industrial revolution and its consequences upon human relations, activities and values. Something that bears the name democracy existed in Athens but it had little in common with the democratic movement of modern times. Economic conditions were openly radically different from those now existing. As for our heritage from the medieval period, it is well to remember occasionally that its political and economic philosophy was framed in the age of feudalism, and is hardly well adapted to give guidance in dealing with the serious political and industrial problems of the present age.

So far then as modern philosophy is a mixture of principles, standards, methods derived from inconsistent elements in past and modern cultures it is unfitted to be of avail in coping with the problems of modern life. Society abhors a vacuum in a deeper sense than was once said to be the case with respect to nature. The philosophy underlying the revolutionary upheaval precipitated by totalitarian powers is an amalgam of the absolutistic standards and methods inherited from past philosophies with the positive organized use of those results of modern science and modern industrial technologies that meet the requirements of aggressive modern political nationalism. It is for this reason that I say what philosophy has to learn is the necessity for a thoroughgoing positive intellectual analysis and registration of the significance of the scientific, industrial, and political movements which are distinctively modern: the need for a philosophy which shall formulate its conclusions in terms of forces and tendencies that are modern, liberated from the confusion and conflict due to injection of alien elements. I do not for a moment suggest that such a philosophical development will resolve the crisis which is upon us. I do say however that whatever positive directive function comprehensive intellectual outlooks and attitudes are capable of exerting depends in the present juncture upon a purgation and a constructive development of the kind just indicated.

I shall now present three problems of a philosophical nature which have practical counterparts in issues with which we are confronted in the present state of the world. One of them is anticipated in words at least by what was said earlier about the conflict set up between "material" and "spiritual." The second has to do with the conflict of the absolutistic and the experimental and experiential. The third concerns the division and conflict between emotions and desires on one side and knowledge and ideas on the other.

The ancient idea that matter is something inherently low, indifferent to, if not opposed to, all "higher" ideal interests and efforts has persisted and has operated to prevent and deflect the service that modern science and modern technologies might otherwise have rendered us. The philosophical theory of the complete separation of matter and mind, of the physical and the ideal, is a fusion of pre-scientific Greek physics, of the medieval belief in the radical corruption of the natural world, and the necessity under which modern physical science found itself of finding a subjectmatter of its own with which it could operate free from control by injection of irrelevant moral and religious considerations. Because of the persistence of earlier philosophical notions about the respective natures of the material and the spiritual, this division has operated nonetheless to prevent and to divide and confuse the service the methods and results the physical sciences might have rendered negatively, in getting rid of obstructions to freer and more equitably arranged social life, and positively, in providing the means for looking ahead, foreseeing consequences, and guiding ourselves accordingly.

What is true of the causes for our failure to make actual the potentialities contained in the scientific revolution is true also of the industrial revolution which is a product of the control of the energies of nature made possible by the revolution in science. In consequence, troubles and evils that are the result of the injection of beliefs and attitudes from the pre-scientific and pre-industrial ages are often attributed to the trust, only half-hearted at best, we have put in science and in industry. They are employed as arguments in favor of systematic return to the type of authority modern forces and resources have discredited. Give a bad name to anything and we cannot expect good to come out of the things to which the bad name is given. The heritage of ancient philosophy which was adopted in and confirmed by the religious heritage of the middle ages has systematically given a bad name to the operations and methods of modern science and modern technology, on the ground they are concerned with the things and events to which ancient philosophy and medieval theology cursed with the name "material."

I do not mean that in and of themselves the methods and conclusions of natural science or the processes of industrial technology are found to be of positive social benefit. They take practical and social effect of any kind, good, bad or indifferent, only as they interact with human habits and efforts. The contribution from the human side is at least an equal partner, if not more than equal, in deciding the sort of consequences scientific knowledge and an industrial regime actually produce. What I am saying is that perpetuation of old beliefs and attitudes about matter have made their way into the existing constitution of human agents with an outcome of failure and deflection in possible social consequences.

It is a common practice to find the physical sciences praised because of their results in the industrial field. They owe a good deal of their current prestige to the obvious utility of many of their industrial applications as well as to the consequences of application in public health and banishing of plagues and epidemics. But commendation on this ground has generally fallen in with the belief that their practical application is confined to the material and the bodily. The view currently taken of economics as a science is that it is concerned with social phenomena that centre about provision for the "material needs" of human beings, a statement that is meaningless unless material needs are set in opposition to some other kind of needs to which economic activities are wholly irrelevant.

I am not suggesting as an alternative that moral judgments about right and wrong be introduced into the inquiries and conclusions of economic theory. That is not necessary. No one can doubt that as matter of fact industrial and economic conditions and agencies are the most potent of all forces at work today in affecting the concrete relations human beings sustain to one another, deciding their effective opportunity to share in the esthetic, intellectual, and other social values which constitute a civilized life. If inquirers were not still weighed down, largely unconsciously at that, by attitudes which accept division between "material" and other human needs as necessary, they would be able to trace scientifically the relations of cause and effect existing between concrete conditions of the industrial and economic setup and their human and social results. They would also be able to propose, on purely scientific grounds, hypotheses about different economic arrangements and the probable consequences they would produce.

The vacuum left by systematic neglect of the connection of science and industrial technologies with the structure of society, in their bearing upon human welfare and misery, is one factor that has given totalitarian philosophies their present power. Criticism of Marx and the Marxists for holding the theory of exclusive materialistic determination of social phenomena should in fairness be conjoined with recognition that Marx did not originate the idea that economic phenomena are materialistic in nature. That idea he found ready made in prior philosophies that claimed to represent ideal and spiritual interests and ends. All he had to do so as to develop his own theory was to unite this idea with observation of the effect the forces released by the industrial revolution were actually having upon the relations human beings sustain to one another. That a totalitarian political entity like Bolshevist Russia should try to put the doctrine into effect and that an excess of destruction over construction should result is not especially astonishing. Nor is it surprising that German totalitarianism, backed by German capacity for organization and subordination, should take literally the purely material character of physical science and then systematically utilize all the resources of physical force put at its disposal by technologies also regarded as purely material to try to put over its aggressive nationalistic social philosophy. The social aim of nationalism is so limited that it demands destruction of other national social groups. But at least there was some kind of a social aim set up to fill the vacuum caused by all but complete neglect of the social results of science and industrial technologies.

I would express my agreement with what was said here last week from the standpoint of anthropology. The failure of democratic countries that esteem freedom, equality and fraternity to pay attention to the methods which the social sciences indicate would serve to accomplish these ends has been an invitation to anti-democratic countries to use the techniques for *their* ends. I would add that the statement need not be confined to the social sciences. It applies also to the failure of democratic countries to take active interest in the question of how the results of physical science can be used to further the values they profess to prize. Failure to use new resources for liberal ends which are distinctly modern has helped create the social vacuum in which these resources are used to support a new kind of despotism. The heritage from philosophies which thought to advance the cause of the ideal and spiritual by cutting it off from the material has played some part in creating the conditions that have done something to give Nazi ideas and practices their opportunity.

What has been said is so intimately connected with the second illustration of my main proposition that I can deal with the latter rather briefly. Respect for what may be learned from experience and especially for the great part played by the experimental method in experience has operated to develop natural science and to produce inventions that have revolutionized production and distribution of commodities and services. The heritage of attitudes and habits formed in earlier states of civilization has operated to limit the application of the experimental attitude to regions called physical in distinction from, in opposition to, interests and fields regarded as moral and ideal. The latter have in consequence been static while the former changed.

I had occasion some years ago to quote from a representative of the medieval form of absolutistic philosophy the statement that if morals abandons the dogma of absolute standards, "we shall have merely the same certainty that now exists in physics and chemistry." There are those who would prefer the certainty of a method which makes for continuous detection of existing errors, for substitution of enlightenment for ignorance, and for ever-renewed discovery of facts and truths not previously known, to the kind of certainty afforded by dogmas purporting to have absolute and final truths. The issue involved in the conflict of philosophies resting upon experience with philosophies of the world, nature, man and human destiny professing another foundation centres at this point. The claim to possession of absolute truths, and of final, unalterable standards might be practically harmless, it might conceivably be even a boon, if everybody had the same set of absolute truths and standards, or if there were in existence some method by which differences could be amicably ironed out and men brought to agreement. What upholders of absolute principles always forget is the vulnerability of their implicit assumption that the principles which *they* advance are *the* absolute principles which any can accept.

The claim to possession of first and final truths is, in short, an appeal to final arbitrament by force. For when the claim to possession of the truths by which life should be directed is asserted to have its origin outside of anything in actual experience, and when the claim is asserted to be incapable of being tested by anything in experience, and nevertheless different systems are asserted to possess ultimate truth, there is no reasonable, no practicable way of negotiating their differences. Stark and absolute opposition and conflict covers the whole situation. The only way out is trial by force, the result of which will give the side having superior force the ability to impose acceptance of its dogmas, at least for as long a time as it has superior forces.

Before leaving this phase of the topic, I will be specific upon one point. Throughout the nineteenth century Germany was the special home of systems of philosophy and metaphysics bearing the label "Idealism." How does it come about that a people brought up in idealism, and taught by its traditional national philosophy to draw a sharp line between physical science and the imperatives of the ideal, arrived at a general acceptance of Nazi philosophy? Of course there are many diverse concrete events which brought Hitler to power, and I have no intention of offering the influence of a philosophical doctrine as a substitute for these concrete events. What I have in mind is the question why and how the transition occurred from idealism to what seems from the outside to be a philosophy of glorification of brute force.

The reply is that the transition is not so sharp as it seems. It will be shocking and probably seem absurd to many persons to say that the idealistic system in vogue in Germany lent itself to the transformation which occurred when the specific concrete events just referred to took place. But the ideals in question were asserted to be above experience in origin and test. There is no intrinsic reason then why experiences connected with one kind of institutions should not be brought under the ideals in question just as readily as some other kind. And the interpreter of Naziism makes a great mistake who supposes that thousands, probably millions, of the most devoted adherents of Naziism do not find in that system idealistic values which justify the use of force. The transformation from one kind of idealism to another social system which regarded itself as idealistic was, moreover, furthered by two factors. The practical one was that the German people regarded themselves as the source and chief upholder of absolute and final idealistic principles in a world progressively given over to naturalism and empiricism and liberal democracy. This belief could readily be used to justify use of force, on the ground that the use would in the end be a means of bringing the lesser breeds to acceptance of the higher idealism. Even in this country a representative of the medieval brand of absolutism is on record to the effect that Hitler was a lesser menace to this country than are those who teach naturalism and empiricism. The other reason is more theoretical. German philosophical idealists had been forced by the weight of facts to realize that the presence of ultimate ideals does not of itself guarantee the exact contents or filling that these ideals will have in the course of history. This admission certainly left it open for the Nazi system to offer itself as the concrete filling appropriate to the present historical juncture.

My third illustration concerns the dividing-up of human nature into a number of separate water-tight non-communicating compartments. One of these compartments is said to contain reason and all the intellectual factors and capacities by which knowledge and valid ideas are attained. The other one consists of appetites, impulses, desires, wants, everything that is brought under the head of emotional life in its widest sense. Acceptance of the philosophies of the past (spilling over into psychologies that purport to be scientific) which erected this division has resulted in formation of what from a technical point of view is probably the main problem of philosophy at present: the relation between fact and value.

This technical problem is however, the remote and pallid reflection of the most urgent problem of education in its broadest and deepest sense: The formation of the attitudes and dispositions in human beings which take effect in the sort of behavior which is prized and is engaged in. For the habits formed decide in the long run, through the cumulative combination of consequences the kind of customs and institutions which come to prevail socially. Separation of ideas and knowledge from emotions creates an intolerable vacuum. When one hears from authentic sources the ardor, the abounding zeal, with which the young have devoted themselves in totalitarian countries to the policies of those countries, one is on safe ground in inferring that there was a vacuum of this sort, and that totalitarian philosophies alike in Germany and Russia, somehow succeeded in uniting intellectual beliefs and the well-springs of emotion in a way that filled, as is said in advertisements of novelties, a deep-felt want.

With respect to more immediate consequences, one is perhaps justified in saying that the chief lesson the war has to teach philosophy is the importance of the problem of the relation of those factors in the human make-up that are emotional and those that are intellectual. It is now commonplace that desires and emotions are the source of our activities as far as these are not of a merely automatic nature and that ideas move to action only when they carry an emotional charge. If the division between the factors that admittedly determine action and those which are embodied in our knowledge and verified ideas is as ultimate and fixed as the philosophies which have emphasized reason, knowledge and science have claimed, then the particular connection made between them at any particular time is external and for all practical purposes accidental. If there is any reasonable ground in human nature for believing that sound ideas, what in general we call intelligence, can become effective on any considerable scale in management of human affairs, it must be found in the evidence of biological, anthropological and psychological facts which prove the falsity of the doctrine of separation, and which indicate the terms on which emotion and tested knowledge can cooperate with one another in setting the pattern and providing the contents of human behavior.

I said that the lesson taught by the war is the *problem* of the relation of emotion and knowledge, of vital desires and ideas, not that the particular solution of the problem is the lesson. Historic systems have never faced the issue. There are historic factors which have made philosophy dodge it, a main one being probably the fact that new ideas create disturbance enough in any case and philosophers and scientific men have found the best way in which to acquire a safe and peaceful place in which to work effectively at their own special jobs is to disclaim that what they find out has any bearing upon important social issues. Just at the present time, for example, there is an immense emphasis upon purely formal aspects of philosophy. A special point is made of insisting that the main connection of valid philosophy is with mathematics and that mathematics is the science that has nothing to do with anything which actually exists either in man or nature. This self-denying ordinance of philosophers is in part by way of doing penance for exaggerated claims previous philosophers have put forth. But it is also in effect if not in intention a way of evading contact with social issues. It is no matter of surprise then that this school of philosophy has made an alliance with linguistic students who hold that if we only eliminated all emotive quality and bearing from the words we use, thereby depriving them of any connection whatever with what we do and have to do, the great step needed for advance in the social sciences would be taken. The problem, the difficult but urgent problem, of whether emotional charges that are not warranted can possibly be replaced by desires that are linked up with our best knowledge is evaded. Yet this is the problem which we are compelled to face if we ask whether human behavior is capable of being directed by other means than either superior force, external authority, uncriticized customs, or sheer emotional outbursts not controlled by authenticated ideas.

Nothing I have said indicates disrespect for the importance that is now taken by the study of language in contemporary philosophy. On the contrary, communication, which is, I take it, the definitive trait of language, is the central social fact. The dual relation of language, its connection on one side with ideas and emotions, and on the other side with the social process, only affords another reason why one basic problem of philosophy at present concerns the relation of emotion and intelligence in the make-up of human beings.

What I have said, is said, obviously, from the standpoint of empirical and experimental philosophy, and with the emphasis the latter puts upon relationships and connections instead of upon absolutes and isolates. But nothing said implies that historic empirical philosophies are free from harmful entanglement with alien ideas inherited from the past, nor that the mixture found in historical empiricisms has not made its special contribution to existing confusion and conflict. What underlies what I have said is the belief that we now have the knowledge and the social experience that contain within themselves the means of creating a philosophy which shall be faithful to the movements, interests and values that are distinctively modern, and that the embroiled state of the world is a challenge to create this kind of philosophy.

2. Address

Mr. Chairman, ladies and gentlemen. I hardly need say that when the arrangements were made for my speaking this evening, and when I prepared my remarks, I need not say that at neither of those dates did I have any idea of what would happen on the day of the evening that I was going to speak. I have nothing, had nothing, and have nothing now, to say directly about the war. My remarks are rather philosophical in nature, on the philosophy side, and philosophy is a somewhat remote, and, sometimes, I fear, a rather arid subject. And I would begin by saying that it is very easy to exaggerate the closeness of the relation between philosophy and social league movements, social activities, even those of an important kind. It's easy, I think, for the intellectual class particularly, to exaggerate the influence which their ideas, reflections, have upon the course of social events. Philosophy, intellectual operations in general, are likely to come after events, as a sort of *ex post facto* enterprise, and very often by the time the philosophy is formed events have changed so much that there isn't much for the ideas to lay hold of. Speaking, however, moderately, I think history shows that philosophy has done something in connection with more important social interest movements. Philosophy, to some extent—even those that seem to be very remote and abstract—does something to make human beings more aware of what they are doing, and what they're trying to do, what they're trying to undo. Of course, all language does that: to give a name to a thing gives us a sort of hold on it that we didn't have before. When we can verbalize anything, put it in propositions, we get it outside of ourselves where we can look at it better.

[tape interrupted] in two ways. Certain persons in the world are somewhat peculiarly sensitive to the direction in which things are moving. If they don't, can't, prophesy or predict with accuracy, but they have a sort of feeling for things before they happen because they're responsive to the direction in which things are moving, and so they help others see better the possibilities in what is going on, they anti[cipate] what's going to happen to some extent and thereby they promote, they foster, its happening. And another thing which philosophies, historic philosophies, have done is to make people aware of what they're doing by trying to justify what is going on—what the theologians, perhaps, call "apologetics," or what the psychoanalysts call "rationalization." They give reasons that people hadn't thought of, especially after they've done a lot of things and they've looked back and find very good reasons for what has been going on.

Now, the first type of philosophy is, you might say, on the liberal order. I mean by that, it's interested in the future, in things that are going to happen, and is more likely to take an unfavorable view of the past, a critical view, that is to say intellectually. The other type of philosophy finds meaning in things and makes people aware of those meanings and they serve the significance of things, and that serves as a kind of justification. Now there's no philosophy that's wholly on one side or the other, but philosophies generally fall—their emphasis falls—on one side or the other, either looking ahead and trying to promote changes, to lead people to think of ends, values they hadn't been aware of, or the emphasis falls more on the justification of institutions.

Now, modern philosophy, so far as it is modern, has come about in a modern world, which means a world in which changes were going on very rapidly. Mr. Whitehead has said that the last fifty years has probably seen more changes in knowledge and in activities depending on that, than thousands of years before, and in general, since the Middle Ages, the world has been changing rapidly.

Now, what my main proposition about what philosophy has to learn, not from the war, of course, in any military sense, but what we have to learn from the conditions which have brought about the war, the confusion in the modern world, the uncertainties, the insecurities, the conflicts, that are going on, is that our philosophy, even that which we call the modern philosophy, has been modern in only a half-hearted way. Just as ancient conditions and institutions have, after all, projected themselves, and perpetuated themselves, in the times we call modern, so, naturally, ancient types of thought, ancient ideas and ideals and standards and ways of looking at things have projected themselves and injected themselves into even the philosophies that had thought that they were fairly modern, taking cognizance simply of modern events and movements. [tape interrupted] the world has been a combination, an amalgamation, or an attempt at a union of things that are incompatible with each other. And as far as the present war is a great deal more than a war in the military sense, so far as it is a very fundamental clash and in all human probability one of the markings, one of the turning points, in the course of events in the history of civilization, it is because things that are modern have been loaded down, have been deflected, distorted, by the projection into them of principles, ways of acting, habits, customs, and institutions that are very definitely pre-modern. Or put it in another way, you might say the lesson of the present war is that we've either got to go backward, in a more systematic and unified way, to old principles and standards, or we have got to face the things in modern life that are genuinely modern, and do what we can to liberate them from the burden of old and incompatible institutions that are weighing them down, that are holding them back, that are creating uncertainty, confusion, and conflict.

Now, of course, there are those who take advantage of a situation like the present to regard it as the evils and troubles, as the result of deserting, abandoning, the philosophies, theories, creeds, faiths, religious creeds of the past, and take this evil then as a sign that we should look backwards, that our ideas and principles should turn back. Now, that is an intelligible, clear-cut position. And over against that we have, as I see it, the only other clear-cut position, the contrary one, that we can get rid of the underlying sources of conflict only if we more frankly, more completely, more courageously—if anyone wants to put it that way— deal with the forces that are distinctly modern.

Now, if you read periodicals and books, and read your poets, some sermons, or lectures, you are aware that there is one ready-made answer given to this question of what we now have to learn—or what philosophy has to learn—from the conditions that are manifested, that express themselves in the war, something that is said by theologians, preachers, said by sociologists (Sorokin of Harvard recently got out a book with [indiscernible word]), literary critics like Van Wyck Brooks. The trouble is, they say, that we have given ourselves up to things that are materialistic, and the only way out is to put our minds, thoughts, hearts, once more on things that are spiritual. Well, as a general saying that sounds well in all events. The question that might be raised is whether it's a little vague, whether it means much more than saying we've devoted ourselves too much to low things and now we ought to devote ourselves to higher things. [tape interrupted] in the concrete, just what are they? And just why is it that human beings on a wide scale have become so engrossed, so absorbed, and taken up with it? Why should they desert higher things and systematically cultivate lower ones, and what in the concrete, are the spiritual and ideal things? And just how are people going to be, if they know what they are, how are they going to be induced to give the necessary attention to them?

Now, what I want to say first, the chief reason I bring this point up, is this idea that anything that is material is somehow low and base is a part of that heritage of past principles, beliefs, and standards which injected into the present has prevented our getting the values, the uses, out of modern things that we might otherwise have got. Just as a matter of fact I suppose no one would deny that two of the most distinctive traits of the modern world have been the rise of the physical sciences—in other words, the scientific revolution which, while it had germs and seeds earlier, dates on any large scale from the seventeenth century, or late sixteenth and seventeenth, the time of Galileo and the astronomers, Sir Isaac Newton—and the Industrial Revolution which followed, really as a consequence of the scientific revolution, because ancient science did not enable people—they called it science, but it was not the kind of knowledge that gave people any control over the energies of nature. When people found out about heat and light and electricity, chemical changes, then there followed—they invented the techniques—the technology by which modern industry has been revolutionized.

Now, the general point that I just made has its concrete effect or bearing in the fact that both the natural sciences and all of our industrial methods, the whole field, the rate of the economic, has to do with what ancient philosophy put a curse on, by calling it "matter," "material," and regarding matter and the material as something inherently low and base in value as compared with the higher ideal and spiritual thing. Now, what I am saying, then, comes to this—that the modern world has been prevented from getting the full advantage that it might have got for the advancement of a juster, more equitable, a more kindly, more friendly, more rapidly developing life and society because it has not taken advantage of the possibilities, the resources, of the natural sciences and of all of our new industrial technologies, methods, because the inherited philosophy, the philosophy that came down to us from the past, has done what I call putting this curse—at least of the disparagement of treatment [tape interrupted] these things must be thought inferior if they are material and because the material is set over against everything that is called spiritual and ideal. [tape interrupted] past and the prestige which attaches to it is very great. There is a very strong feeling in the background of people's minds (which is more than we realize a deposit from philosophies of the past) that, after all, the physical sciences are important in purely material, purely physical, matters, that they have nothing particular to do with the more serious values of life, even if they are not really actively opposed to them.

I noticed that the speaker here two weeks ago, speaking from the standpoint of what anthropology has to learn from the war, said that one thing, that very fundamental thing in her view of the situation, was that the totalitarian countries had recognized the power that was available in the techniques which the social sciences had made possible, that the totalitarian states—of course Germany is the great example with its great power of organization—had utilized all of the resources of the social sciences to put over and advance their particular ideas, that the other nations, those we call democratic, have never given their minds, their attention, to the question of what the techniques of the social sciences might do to advance the ideals, the objects, and values for which the democratic countries stand. I think not only is that correct but that we can go further. The totalitarian countries have realized not merely that the social sciences but that the physical sciences and the techniques of the physical sciences can be utilized to advance a particular social objective; namely, the nationalistic and racial one of those countries.

Now, our other philosophies, our liberal philosophies, have taken a very *laissez-faire* attitude, not merely in the field of economics but in that of science. Now, I don't mean by that that moral judgments of right and wrong should be introduced either into the physical or the social sciences. What I do mean is that through inventions and new technologies, control of natural energies, industry dealing with these things which have been called material and matter has, on that account, failed to reckon with the forces that as matter of fact are having more social influence, more effect, more consequences upon the relations of human beings to each other than anything else in the world. Now, whatever we think of totalitarian countries, and what we think of their policies, at least there is a recognition that it is possible to lay hold of the conclusions of the physical and the social sciences, to organize them and use them for some social end. And then what I think we have to learn is that if we do not like—as we do not like, presumably—the ends for which those nations are organizing and utilizing the results of science, that philosophy—I'm saying now "this philosophy"—I mean all intelligent and thoughtful people, however, have got to consider [tape interrupted] something that is of the nature of a revolution. My understanding of that is that, having produced all of this scientific knowledge, having produced it by using methods of which the ancient world, even the Greek, medieval world, knew nothing at all, we have now got to face the question of how those things are going to be systematically organized and used for human ends. And to do that we have got to do, as I have suggested, considerable elimination, purging, critical purging, of the ideas of the past which have made us look askance upon the conclusions of the natural sciences and the processes of industry simply because they were dealing with things to which the names "matter" and "material" had once been given.

Now, another closely connected aspect of this same thing: the holding over of ideas from the past into the present because habits, and customs, and institutions, and traditions have held over also. I would like to say that the whole power of the things we call ideal in man has been weakened just because so-called ideals, spiritual things, have been put over in a world by themselves and in the minds of an indefinite number of people, have been regarded as supernatural and having supernatural authority, and put over against the natural things and the things that we can learn from experience. I think that great many people, including many of our intellectual refugees who have come to this country from Germany, totalitarian countries, would be profoundly shocked at any suggestion that idealism—professional, philosophical idealism—had had considerable to do with bringing the Nazis to power. On the face of it, it looks absurd to say that idealism, philosophical idealism, highly spiritualized philosophy, would have anything to do with bringing to power a group who, when looked at from the outside, rely exclusively upon force and superiority of force to dominate their neighbors or the world. But we must remember that Germany, at least, was the country that all through the nineteenth century was the stronghold of philosophical, idealistic theories from the time of Kant onward through the whole period. How did it happen that the very country which had been the birthplace and the stronghold of modern metaphysical idealism, spiritualistic theories, was the country which most completely turned over to the use of present methods? And in asking that question we have to remember that a great deal of idealistic emotion, a great ardor, a burning fervor in the cause, has been awakened for the Nazi policies, especially in the youth of Germany. Whatever it seems to be from the outside, from their standpoint they have ideals to which they are devoted and, having them, they feel that they not only have a right, they have a responsibility [tape interrupted] of the world, and if they can't [tape interrupted] them by force, why then in the long run it's for the good of these other people that they be enforced upon them. Now that may seem somewhat extreme, but there's a teacher of philosophy in the University of Chicago who, in this city a little over a year ago, said that Hitler, Naziism, wasn't as much of a menace to this country as the professors of philosophy in the universities who are teaching naturalism and empiricism. They've deserted all of these standards of the past. Well, now, if an American can feel that way, I don't know why Germans shouldn't feel that as the great representatives of idealism that they should be entitled to bring it, rather forcibly if need be, to the attention of people who had gone off for lower things. There used to be a saying which didn't turn out very true in natural science, "Nature abhors a vacuum." Well, human beings abhor a vacuum, society abhors a vacuum, and if ideals aren't made concrete in terms of concrete life and actual institutions that we know are here and events that are going on around us, well, that vacuum will be filled in some very untoward way.

The third illustration—because these after all, of course, are only illustrations that I can give—is that modern philosophy and psychology (and in doing this, of course, they've simply reflected—they didn't invent these things, they reflected them, they mirrored them and formulated them in words) has made a split in human nature. An official definition, for instance, to go back to a matter I've already touched upon, of economic science— political economy or economic science—is that it considers those social phenomena that have to do with the satisfaction of man's material wants. Well, there's no sense in that statement "to satisfy a man's material wants" unless his material wants are put in opposition to some other wants that are supposed to be not only different but of a higher, more ideal and spiritual nature. Well, we've not only cultivated that kind of division, separation in the make-up of human beings and human nature, but a very profound split has been made between science, between knowledge, between ideas that are of an intellectual character, everything that has to do with our getting knowledge and correct ideas, profound split has been made between that and everything that's included in our emotional life, in our impulses and desires, what the ancients used to call our "passions" (but not meaning anything as vile as the word means now). Now, it's practically a commonplace that our actions, we are moved to action—in all action that isn't purely mechanical and routine—by desires, by impulses, by emotions. The psychiatrists have popularized the importance of what they call "the unconscious," which I think is a very poor name, but it does stand for something vital in the things that move us to action and something that is not of a strictly rational, intellectual nature. Without desire, without the whole plane, area, and arena of the emotional life, people do not act. Now, if there is a split [tape interrupted] thinkers today that all our ideas about ends and values, the things that we regard as good and bad, just represent either a kind of emotional ejaculations, a kind of wail, "Oh, I like that! Isn't that lovely?" or "I don't like it!" but purely arbitrary emotional reaction with no intellectual ground, or else they are simply disguised commands given to other people, especially from superiors to inferiors. In other words, I say "That's good" (especially parents say it to children), that means you better do it or you'll get into trouble; and if "It's bad," that I don't want you to do that, and you shouldn't do it, and all of our moral judgments from that point of view, because they are expressions of something in our emotional life and life of desires, lack any kind of intellectual backing and authority.

Now, in some ways, I think that the relation between the things that move us to action and our store of knowledge and ideas and methods by which we reach it, whether these things can cooperate or whether they are separate and divided, I think that in some ways it's the most important question of modern life and therefore the most important thing that philosophy, as a problem, has to face. It's a problem because it has been so little considered that there are no ready-made solutions. Unfortunately, a good deal of recent philosophy is an escape from facing that problem. Sometimes it would seem as if it were almost a deliberate escape. One very popular view, now, in philosophical circles in our colleges and universities, is that mathematics is the branch of knowledge with which philosophy is most directly and intimately concerned, and mathematics is the science that has nothing whatsoever to do with anything that exists, either in nature or in the human mind directly. And by devoting itself to purely formal statements and formal analyses, philosophy, or philosophers, have found a way of escape and evasion from these more serious problems.

I want to read something from an intellectual autobiography by Mr. [Robin G.] Collingwood who is a teacher of philosophy at Oxford. The statements are extreme and they're bitter, but sometimes some exaggerated statement of exaggerated emphasis brings a point home better. Speaking of some of his Oxford colleagues in philosophy—whom he evidently didn't like very well, or didn't like their teachings—he says, "They were proud to have excogitated a philosophy so pure from the sordid taint of utility that they could lay their hands on their hearts and say it was of no use at all, a philosophy so scientific that no one whose life was not a life of pure research could appreciate it, and so abstruse that only a whole-time student, and a very clever one at that, could understand it. They were quite resigned to the contempt of fools and amateurs. If they differed from them on these points, it could only be because their intellect was weak or the motives of the others bad." Then he said again of a certain group of his whole school, of his colleagues, "If these men had wanted to train up a generation of Englishmen and Englishwomen expressly as the potential dupes of every adventurer in morals and politics, commerce or religion, who should appeal to their emotions and promise them things which he neither could procure them nor even meant to procure them, no better way of doing it could have been discovered." As I said, those remarks are colored by probably some personal strong emotion.

[tape interrupted] is the young people, is that they have held up to them certain ends, objects, which did excite their emotions and which they could use, as I've said before, their knowledge and their techniques to bring into actuality. So beyond all other things I should say what philosophy has to learn from the war is at least the importance of facing the problem of getting some kind of unified view of human beings in which ideas and emotions, knowledge and desire, would cooperate with each other instead of either going entirely separate ways or being brought into harmony with each other only through some outside power.

Miscellany

Introduction to James's *Talks to Teachers on Psychology*

It is now almost half a century since James first gave the lectures out of which grew the volume modestly entitled *Talks to Teachers,* and almost forty years since they appeared in print. During the intervening years, the study of psychology has greatly expanded; new methods of investigation have appeared; topics formerly beyond the range of scientific investigation have been brought within its scope; branches of psychology that were in their infancy have grown to maturity. Educational psychology has developed into a special subject taught in all schools for teachers, and workers in its field now make independent researches into practically every phase of education.

For these reasons there are probably some who suppose that what James said more than a generation ago is now only of historic interest rather than of present significance. Our conviction that the opposite is the case accounts for the republication of this book. A survey of school practices throughout the country would probably show that teachers are still far from having made their own what is sound in the teachings of James, while a survey of the advances made in psychological science since his day might show that apart from technicalities, they enable teachers of the present day to profit by the book more readily and fully than did those who first read it.

The artistic power of James is a commonplace. His ability to set forth scientific generalizations in vivid and popular (because human) language is one reason why his writings are fresh today. As he says in his Preface, teachers are least interested in analytical technicalities and care most for the concrete and for practical applications. The outstanding merit of the writings of James

[First published in William James, *Talks to Teacher on Psychology,* new ed. (New York: Henry Holt and Co., 1939), pp. iii–viii; written with William Heard Kilpatrick.]

is that he states general principles stripped of everything irrelevant to actual teaching: of everything, that is, that is not an aid to the teacher in observing and understanding what is going on in the processes of individual human beings. As James said, psychology is of avail to the teacher only as the teacher is possessed of sensitivity, tact, and power of sympathetic divination as to the life-processes of other human beings. His own possession of these traits is one great source of his enduring timeliness. It is probably as true as when he wrote that many teachers are disappointed at not deriving from the study of psychology the direct practical help they had been led to hope for. The method of presentation which he practised is a protection against this disappointment.

In one important respect, James underestimated in the text of these *Talks* the significance of what he had to say for even the teachers of his own day. He felt called upon to say that in his humble opinion there was no such thing as a new psychology. It is not difficult to see why he spoke thus. He had a wide knowledge of the past and deep appreciation of the contributions made by its great thinkers. He was, we may imagine, hurt by the flagrant disregard of their work exhibited in blatant claims of complete novelty occasionally put forth for contemporaneous work. But in spite of the fact that there is nothing in any science for which complete novelty can be claimed, there was a new spirit animating psychology at the time he wrote and this new spirit is peculiarly alive and active in his own work.

This new spirit is directly connected with the value of his book for teachers today. It is the source of his emphasis upon the active and the motor; upon the principle of the vital connection of expression and impression and his accompanying refusal to separate the body of the pupil through which activity is carried on from the pupil's mental processes. It provides the basis for his demand that teachers think of their pupils as "behaving organisms," a principle which, as it is stated in the early chapters, contains what is sound in later "Behaviorism" without its exaggerations. It accounts for the perennial timeliness of his chapter on habit; for the vitality of what he has to say about attention and interest, and for the emphasis put in his discussion of moral education upon the supremacy of the positive and constructive over the inhibitory and negative—a discussion which even if it stood alone would justify the claim of this book for serious attention by the teachers of the present day.

And everything said about the usefulness of the *Talks* for the teachers of today holds if anything even more pointedly for those preparing to teach. The penetrating insight which James had and stated so engagingly is what the prospective teachers need most of all as they build the conceptions which are to guide them in dealing with the young. Happy are these beginning teachers when they can catch thus early not only the insight, but the fine enthusiasm, "the inflamed ardor of zest," from so competent a guide as William James.

There is however a word of warning that we should give. When James wrote, a new type of education was just beginning to make its appearance. James lauds this new trend, perhaps extravagantly, when he speaks of the "most colossal improvement" that lay in the introduction of "the manual training schools" (a now outmoded term) not for the specific skills they taught but "because they give us citizens with an entirely different intellectual fibre." It was the work of James and others to lay a foundation on which later educators have carried forward in marked degree the new type of education thus foreshadowed.

But while James praised the promising new, he was as regards school-keeping still the child of his age and time. He thought that a school must be the kind of place where much if not most of the work will of necessity be dull and at first repulsive. In fact, he said explicitly that just these things are "inevitable, let the teacher do what he will." To get this repellant work done he considered that the teacher must use "external methods." It was in keeping with this that he could speak of the "extreme value of verbal recitation" (though his discussion shows that it was words as the carriers of ideas that he sought). And similarly in keeping are his remarks on the use of marks and prizes. In all of these things James was, we think, looking backward not forward. He was right to speak against "making things interesting" as "soft pedagogy," for so it was and is; but he was wrong in thinking the school has to be essentially the kind that he had known, that study and learning have to be repellant. In these things the discerning reader must sift the wheat from the chaff, the old that ought to die from the new that was coming into being. The wheat is there to be found, and great riches which even yet have not been fully realized.

So we close as we began. James has given us in this little book so much truth, expressed in such clear and vigorous language, that we who knew it when it first came out are not willing that it should stand unused on library shelves. For the message it still has to give we wish it read and studied afresh by the teachers of our country. It is their gain that we seek and the good that they may thereby do to the young in our land.

Introduction to *Problems of Ageing*

It is a common experience that solution of one type of problem brings with it new and unforeseen problems that require for solution a very different approach from that which was earlier employed. This is especially true with problems capable of isolation and dealt with by specialized techniques. The first steps in what is now known as the industrial revolution were, for example, taken simply to produce more cheaply a larger amount of woolen goods. The problem seemed to be a purely technical one and capable of solution by technical improvements in the machinery of spinning and weaving. The final social consequences of the adoption of similar methods in all fields of production were unforeseen and unforeseeable. Yet they were such as to bring about a state of affairs in which more than anything else are rooted all of our present social and political problems, domestic and international.

Upon its face, the problem of saving a greater number of lives was a similar special problem. It was a definitely medical question. It was met by improvements in medical care and by improved dietaries and measures of public sanitation. Just as more efficient methods of manufacturing were the result of new physical scientific knowledge, so the improvements in production of personal and public health were the results of new physiological and chemical knowledge. But it is now becoming evident that the changes which have brought about great reduction of infant mortality and the lengthening of the span of life for those who survive the hazards of infancy have had important social effects so that social conditions have been created which confront civilization with issues of the most serious nature.

[First published in *Problems of Ageing: Biological and Medical Aspects,* ed. Edmund Vincent Cowdry (Baltimore: Williams and Wilkins Co., 1939), pp. xxvi–xxxiii.]

For a considerable period, say roughly till the beginning of the present century, the effects of the new methods of industry on one side and of new methods of care of the sick and protection of public health on the other side practically coincided. The result was an immense increase of population in all industrially advanced countries. The birth-rate was stimulated by new economic opportunities; more children were kept alive; philanthropic zeal cooperated with new medical knowledge and skill to keep alive the enfeebled who formerly would have perished, and new biological knowledge of the sort represented by Pasteur's epoch-making discoveries checked the ravages of the plagues and infectious diseases that had previously made such inroads upon whole populations. The net effect of all these changes was what the biometricians call the population pyramid: for the distribution of the population by ages could be graphically represented by a pyramid, children forming a broad base gradually tapering off to a narrow apex of a comparatively few aged persons.

Recent years have made a marked change. The present distribution of the population by ages, throughout the western world at least, would be represented by something shaped more like an egg cut off at the base, than by a pyramid. The reduction of infant mortality has proceeded apace. But the birth-rate has steadily declined so that the increased survival of infants and children has not checked the decrease in the ratio borne by the youthful element in the population to the older elements. Concurrently with decrease in the relative number of the young has been a dramatic increase in the span of life. Better medical care and more adequate nutrition have effected the survival of ever larger numbers of older people. As compared with the earlier pyramidic form, we now have a narrowed base, a wider middle aged group and a much enlarged group of the aged at the top.

As the chapters in this volume clearly show, present society in Europe and the United States is now approaching a stabilized, even possibly a declining, total population with a larger older population, both absolutely and relatively, than any country in the world has ever known before. In the United States, with decrease of birth-rate and the limitation of immigration (which had been mainly of the young and vigorous) we now have an unprecedented situation. Over one-third of the total population will soon be over fifty years of age. In 1980 the number of persons over sixty-five will be more than double that today.

The most obvious aspect of the social problem thus created is the economic. It is a matter of common knowledge that persons above fifty are experiencing ever greater difficulty in finding employment and that even those above forty are not immune from the effect of the industrial developments which have put a premium on youthful vigor and a discount upon the experience of those who are older. While the change is a matter of common knowledge rather than of statistics scientifically obtained, yet one record of the latter sort may be noted as typical. Reports of almost half a million of persons who have been subjects of public relief show that individuals between the years of twenty-five and thirty-five have found re-employment and been taken off relief-rolls at the rate of two to one as compared with those of the ages from even as low as thirty-five to forty-five.

That this economic shift has political repercussions is manifest in the general movement for old-age pensions on one side, and on the other side in the efforts, such as legal restrictions on child labor, to hold a larger number of jobs open for persons in the middle years. Even the legal rights and powers of individuals are coming to be defined, both as regards the older and the younger groups of the total population, on an age basis. So far this re-definition is occurring in response to special conditions, but it is not too much to predict that finally it will mean the conscious emergence of new social standards and ideals. Indeed, the recent economic crisis which prevented the normal entrance of the young into industrial and professional employment has already rendered the problem of youth a conscious social problem both economically and educationally. In its political bearings as to the older group, it should be noted that under existing cultural conditions, and probably to some unknown degree biologically, conservatism increases with age, so that in the degree in which the older group expresses itself politically we have the curious and indeed ironic condition that at just the time when measures of social readjustment are most needed, there is an increasing number of those whose habits of mind and action incline them to resist policies of social readjustment.

This latter remark provides a natural transition to consideration of aspects of the new social problem that are less tangible than the economic one; for after all, the population group which is economically handicapped by age is not a statistical affair. It consists of individuals, each one having his or her own individual

past career, his or her own temperament, personal needs, and desires, and his or her own special relations to other persons, especially of his or her family group, and, though less directly, to his
or her community. The psychological, educational and moral
ramifications of this phase of the new social problem are as end-
less as they are subtle—and as little understood. Many years
ago, Mrs. Florence Kelly asked me if I could give any references
in literature to the psychology and sociology of growing old.
When I was compelled to admit my ignorance, she remarked, "It
is strange that the one thing that every person looks forward to is
the one thing for which no preparation is made." The situation
is not measurably better today save that the importance of the
problem is now recognized as it was not a generation ago.

The present volume of studies is itself evidence of the new recognition of the importance of the problem of ageing. No reflective and informed person will question that the foundation of
any serious consideration of the problem of ageing and of methods of dealing with the problem is provided by biological and
related chemical knowledge. Whatever else human beings are or
are not, they are biological creatures whose physiological process, normal and abnormal, can be understood only by means of
adequate physical and chemical knowledge. The studies of this
nature which are presented in this book are the necessary foundation for attack upon the more intangible psychological and social aspects of the problem. They provide the needed base line,
for they disclose basic conditions which in any case must be
taken into account. As they continue to develop they will reveal
means and methods by which such anomalies and disorders as
now exist can be dealt with in their causes and not simply as
symptoms.

For the purpose of the present discussion, these studies may be
interpreted as presenting a problem that forces upon us an investigation of every form of human relation: the problem, namely, of
the relation of the biological and the cultural. Take the matter of
the increased conservatism that emerges with increased age.
While specific studies of a scientific quality are not numerous,
this increased conservatism may be taken as a matter of public
knowledge. In a general way, it is a reasonable inference that biological factors play some part. For a declining store of physical
energy may be expected, on theoretical grounds, to result in less-

ened initiative and readiness to undertake new lines of activity. But when it is asserted that large past experience and maturity in general tend to render human beings more and more sceptical of the value of innovation and "reforms," we have left the biological ground for the cultural.

For there is no well grounded way of connecting conservatism of this type with any inherent biological processes. We do not know the extent to which growing aversion to the new and to change is a product of the *quality* of past experiences, rather than to the bare fact of experience, nor the exact extent to which that quality is due to conditions provided by the social environment rather than to anything intrinsic, the social conditions being moreover, socially modifiable. There certainly exist exceptions to the rule of fixation of ideas and belief with increased age. Admitting that there are in these cases, special individual genetic conditions favorable to retention of the plasticity and the interest in growth that are characteristic of youth, the important question is what role education and other cultural influences play.

I have referred to this matter of increased conservatism simply as an illustration of the general problem. There are aged persons who are repining and querulous and who make life difficult for their families and immediate associates; who live in the past and who get their chief happiness in recalling the good old times that are no more. But there are other aged persons having exactly the opposite traits. Nobody knows how the two groups compare in numbers. But the very existence of these two kinds of old persons is strong reason for believing that the source of the difference may not be wholly biological and fixed, but may be social and cultural and therefore amenable to change, provided changed social and educational conditions are brought to bear.

The preference of employers for the younger group which has been referred to is not wholly a matter of the greater physical vigor, power of endurance and of greater speed on the part of the young. It is also due to conditions of industry which render past experience of little value in machine operations. The latter may be mastered in a short time. In the older hand industry, on the contrary, length of experience was a positive asset, since it meant increase of judgment, skill and taste. Social conditions, in other words, come into play. Now extend the point to include the common belief that individuals tend with age to get into a rut and lose power to adapt themselves to new conditions. If we admit that this tendency is biologically grounded, we reach a highly pessimistic conclusion, for it means that maturing is quite as much a curse as it is a blessing.

The fact that the conclusion is pessimistic is not of itself a sufficient reason for rejecting it. But it is a reason for examining closely into the reasons why increasing age now tends to render individuals less flexible and less adaptable, with all the personal and social loss that is a consequence of this failure. The age-long quest for the fountain of eternal youth, taken merely in its physical form in the past, has failed. Perhaps a happy ending to the search would be better approximated if we turned the quest in another direction. That conditions and methods of education have *something* to do with retention and with loss of power of re-adaptation to changed conditions will not be denied. Just how much it has to do with it we do not now know, and we shall not know until we employ every available experimental resource to find out. And when I say "education" I mean more than schooling, although I think it is demonstrable that much of current schooling tends automatically to artificial production of habits which arrest growth and create inability to readjust and reconstruct.

The emphasis that is placed in contemporary educational schemes upon production of mechanical forms of skill and mechanical reproduction of information is itself a reflex, moreover, of social conditions. In present culture, the dominant interest is upon the whole the economic, and successful pursuit of this interest is conditioned upon the existence of a large body of persons who are operators of machines. In this work, emphasis falls upon accuracy and speed in the performance of repetitious processes. There is not only little call and little chance for personal initiative and judgment, but the mental and physical strains involved are such as to create demand for artificial diversion and "stimulation" in non-working hours: just as children in a mechanically operated school tend to react to the other extreme when they get outside the school walls. For the condition under which activity is carried on involves strain because it is *contrary* to normal biological demands, so that compensatory activities are evoked.

When this point is applied to the relatively old, it indicates two things. One of them is the failure, which now exists, of the usual conditions of experience to create the interests and the capacities which will occupy later years fruitfully and happily. The other is the positive side of the same problem: the need of study to ascertain and develop the kind of activities in which the older part of the population can engage with satisfaction to themselves and value to the community. I do not think it is too much to say that this whole field is a practical blank at the present time. There are here and there individuals who have managed to work out a solution, but, as far as I can see, such cases are a matter of combination of a fortunate personal temperament and lucky surroundings. They do not exist because of any general social policy which provides conditions for achieving this happy outcome. It may be that when the number of the old was relatively small, the problem was not an urgent one. With the prospect of over a third of the total population above fifty years in age, it is a pressing problem.

To be laid upon the shelf, to find one's self socially useless and hence socially unwanted, even when other members of the family are personally kind and considerate, is a fate which goes contrary to even normal biological conditions. Upon the social side, it means that accumulation of experience is not regarded as a social asset. I take it that the moral of Shaw's *Back to Methuselah* was that the process of gaining and using experience is now so constantly interrupted by death that human beings do not gain the wisdom which is necessary if human affairs are to be successfully managed. The idea that wisdom would accumulate and would be applied if only the span of life were sufficiently extended stands, however, in ironic contrast with the present situation. For as that is constituted, we have gone far beyond the ancient adage "If youth only knew, and age only could." For there is now no socially organized means by which the aged have (or at least are supposed to have) even the *knowledge* which is relevant to the conditions of social life, much less have the opportunity of applying it.

The underlying problem, both scientifically and philosophically, it seems to me, is that of the relation of ageing and maturing. We are at present more or less in the unpleasant and illogical condition of extolling maturity and deprecating age. It seems obvious without argument that there is some connection between the two; that we cannot separate the processes of maturing from those of ageing even though the two processes are not identical. The split that now exists between the two, in terms of both individual activity and happiness and of social usefulness, would appear to be socially or culturally produced, rather than to be biologically intrinsic. That there should be a gradual wearing down of energies, physical and mental, in the old age period it is reasonable to expect upon biological grounds. That maturing changes, at some particular age, into incapacity for continued growth in every direction is a very different proposition. We may not be able to affirm with the poet

> Grow old along with me
> The best is yet to be,

but there is something abnormal in the situation if we are obliged to admit that after a certain period nothing *better* in any direction, individual and social, can occur because of the process of growing old.

In the previous discussion, I have made a certain separation between the problem of the measures that can be socially organized and administered in ameliorating the estate of the aged and the psychological and moral problems presented by the older part of the population. I do not mean, however, that the two things are independent of each other. I think we can safely foresee the extension of old age allowances, together with provision for the young, which will relieve the aged from a burden they now carry. I do not think that it is a sign of undue extension of imagination to anticipate a time when organized administrative care for the aged will extend not only to greater facilities in the way of hospitalization and old-age homes, special nurses and special forms of medical care, including psychiatric; but to special housing, including perhaps provisions for living in especially congenial climates and special recreational facilities.

But such measures, while important and necessary, are mitigative rather than constructive, unless they are accompanied by changes in the cultural social structure which will give the group of older persons a status of moral security and social value as well as material security. The attitude taken toward the aged has at all historic periods been a function of the general social pattern. Today it is largely a function of the economic and educational pattern of present society. External material improvements can be instituted without going far outside the existing social pattern. But I am unable to see how the basic *human* problem can be solved without social changes which ensure first to every individual the continual chance to have intrinsically worthwhile experience, and secondly provide significant socially useful outlets for the maturity and wisdom gained in this experience.

What has been said has probably made it clear to the reader that it is my conviction that the many perplexing problems now attendant upon human old age have a psychological-social origin. Yet the main purpose of these introductory remarks is to call attention to the fact that there is a *problem* and one of a scope having no precedent in human history. Biological processes are at the roots of the problems and of the methods of solving them, but the biological processes take place in economic, political and cultural contexts. They are inextricably interwoven with these contexts so that one reacts upon the other in all sorts of intricate ways. We need to know the ways in which social contexts react back into biological processes as well as to know the ways in which the biological processes condition social life. This is the problem to which attention is invited.

Recognition of the seriousness of the problem as well as application of the knowledge that is already in our possession is impeded by traditional ideas, intellectual habits and institutional customs. There is urgent need for a philosophy of personal and institutional life that is consequent with present knowledge. Biological science has a great contribution to make to formation of the theory and practice of a new pattern of living, aside from what it can do in provision of special techniques. For biology as a science brings to the foreground of attention the significance of Growth in a way which underlying physical sciences do not. The special technical problems of ageing are all connected with processes of growth, but in addition our philosophy of all life and of all social relations demands reconstruction of traditional beliefs upon the basis of Growth as the fundamental category. When we shall envisage social relations and institutions in the light of the contribution they are capable of making to continued growth, when we are capable of criticizing those which exist on the ground of the ways in which they arrest and deflect processes of growth, we shall be on our way to a solution of the moral and psychological problems of human ageing. Science and philosophy meet on common ground in their joint interest in discovering the processes of normal growth and in the institution of conditions which will favor and support ever continued growth.

Foreword to Clapp's *Community Schools in Action*

From the viewpoint of this book and of the work it represents introductory words by me are superfluous. The trite saying about "speaking for itself" applies in full measure. Nevertheless, I have welcomed as a pleasure the opportunity to write a few words. It is a pleasure because reading the book has vividly recalled to me many stimulating conversations with its author in which the two schools were mentioned, and because of a most enjoyable visit to one of them, that at Arthurdale. But my greatest pleasure would come if anything I may say would advance the cause of education by calling the attention of others to the extraordinary significance for education of the work reported in this book. Education is itself a continuing process. Administrators and teachers will add to their own education by becoming acquainted with the work of these schools, and thereby the larger educative process be promoted. I am happy to have the chance to act as an intermediary, however incidental, in the continuing process.

If I said the book is a record of a highly significant undertaking in the field of community education, it would sound as if schools had in addition some other field of operations. In fact they do not have. Miss Clapp remarks that "A great deal is said in calling a school a 'community school.'" If the school lives up to that name, everything is said. The present book portrays what is involved in terms of schools that do fulfill their function. The portrayal is so adequate that I can but underline some points. A great deal is now said about the social function of schools; more is said than is done. In this book we have an account of something actually done and of how it was done. Perhaps the first lesson it

[First published in Elsie Ripley Clapp, *Community Schools in Action* (New York: Viking Press, 1939), pp. vii–x.]

teaches us is that schools function socially only when they function in a community for community purposes, and communities are local, present, and close by, while "society" at large is something vaguely in the distance. The reason, I believe, why more is said and written than done about the social function of schools is that "society" is taken as a kind of sociological and academic entity, instead of as the lives of men, women, boys, and girls going on right around us. Under such circumstances, writing becomes pale and shadowy—abstractions dealing in remote language with an abstraction. The neighborhood is the prime community; it certainly is so for the children and youth who are educated in the school, and it must be so for administrators and teachers if the idea of socially functioning schools is to take on flesh and blood. There is no occasion for fear that the local community will not provide roads leading out into wider human relations if the opportunities it furnishes are taken advantage of.

This, then, is one point I would underscore. Here is one report of one of the small number of schools in our country which have made a reality out of theories about the social function of schools, and which has done it by creating a school to which Lincoln's words about democratic government apply: a school not only for, but of and by the community; the teachers being leaders in the movement, since they are themselves so identified with the community.

An important aspect of this point is that those who were teachers in the schools prepared themselves for their work by becoming citizen members of the community in the most intimate way. They became acquainted with their neighbors by being part of the neighborhood. They knew the other members in a face-to-face way. They kept up all the time they were there this process of educating themselves as to the community's needs and resources, its weaknesses and strong points; they learned that only in this way could they engage in further education of the community. They did not "survey" the community; they belonged to it. Results proved the immeasurable value of this phase of community education. It was not just a question of staying "after school"— which is a part of the duties of many teachers. There were literally hardly any hours of night or day that would be said to be *after* school work—that is, educative work—was finished. In spite of the tax on time and energy that was involved, no one can read about the school without getting the feeling that teaching in it was free from the drudgery and monotony that often attend teaching. It was a continuous experience, enlivening as well as enriching, a process in which the joy of discovery and growing was never absent.

The way in which subject-matter to be taught was selected and the way in which methods for teaching it grew directly out of knowledge of community conditions are so concretely reported in the pages of the book that I hardly need to underline the point. I do wish to add from personal knowledge, however, that the vital responsiveness of the members of the community, young and old, to the school as a centre of its own life is understated rather than exaggerated in the pages which follow. Closely connected with the warmth and extent of the response is the fact, I believe, that the community was a rural community. For I am convinced it is a mistake to believe that the most needed advances in school organization and activities are going to take place chiefly in cities—especially in large cities. From the viewpoint of genuine community education, country districts provide the greatest opportunity as well as exhibit the most crying need—the most vocal even if not in fact the deepest.

The connection of school activities with out-of-school activities is indirect in the city. It is immediate, close at hand, in villages where there are gardens, shops, and a variety of household activities to meet family needs. First-hand acquaintance with nature, which is the background of scientific study, is obtained with great difficulty in the city. It exists as a matter of course in country districts, and yet is rarely taken advantage of for educational purposes. The completeness with which the study of science in the Arthurdale School was a study of the community has value sufficient to make its record worth study, even were it, as it decidedly is not, the only significant achievement of the school. And while in speaking of rural districts we think first of their needs, the report given of both schools indicates the resources, the positive values, that are there in tradition, in history, in folklore and music, indeed in all the conditions out of which the arts grow when their development is healthy.

Even at the risk of stating the obvious, I conclude by pointing out how central are the problems of health, recreation, and of occupations carried on for a livelihood in any community; how conspicuously these problems stand out in a rural community where they offer themselves as direct personal issues. But I want to point to the book as evidence of how the school as well as the community gains when these basic interests of life are made fundamental in education. I might also say that it is surprising how many alleged pedagogical problems relating to such matters as "discipline and freedom, motivation," etc., either vanish or are greatly reduced when a school is a living part of a community. I do not know that there is much danger that the social function of education will be thought of exclusively as the question of what schools could and should do for the community. But if there is any danger at all, the schools here reported upon show that the relation is a two-way process. They prove what the community can do for schools when the latter are actually centres of community life. Here are cases in which communities develop themselves by means of schools which are the centres of their own life. In consequence, there is no detail of the following report which will not repay study. The report is a demonstration in practice of the place of education in building a democratic life.

Foreword to Johnson's *Mars in Civilian Disguise!*

The vast majority of American citizens are opposed to involving this country in a foreign war. The opposition is as sincere as it is deepseated. In spite of this opposition, militarists are taking advantage of the feelings of fear and insecurity which develop in wartime to increase the size of our army and navy to unheard of proportions. Public moneys are needed for the peaceful maintenance of an industrious and prosperous citizenship. But they are being diverted to the cause of war.

The facts adduced by Mr. Johnson raise the question as to whether the Federal government's student pilot training program is not a camouflage for a definitely militaristic project. Why has it been thought necessary to sell a military campaign to the American people under the guise of a civilian project? Does not the fact that this line of tactics has been adopted in this case throw suspicion upon the whole military program now put forward? The methods used in this case strengthen the belief that the American opposition to war is being used by interested parties to sell the American people down the war-river. Under the name of defense, measures are proposed that have no sense unless the American people are being prepared to engage in war. Since the American people are opposed almost to a man to this idea, it is necessary to put blinders upon them in order to lead them toward war.

The project discussed in this pamphlet comes home with especial force to the authorities of our institutions of higher learning. Do they want educational institutions harnessed to a scheme of preparation for war? Do they want the harnessing

[First published in Edwin C. Johnson, *Mars in Civilian Disguise!* (New York: Committee on Militarism in Education, 1939), p. 2.]

to be done under the claim that the measure is civilian? If persons in charge of colleges and universities favor this plan, what shall the American people with their strong opposition to being involved in war think about what the colleges and universities are doing?

Introduction to *The Bertrand Russell Case*

It is fitting to say a few words about the origin of this book. When it became apparent that the forces of reaction, bigotry, and political cowardice were powerful enough to obstruct the cause of fair play and of intellectual freedom in the case of Bertrand Russell's appointment to a chair of philosophy in the College of the City of New York, Dr. Albert C. Barnes engaged him for a period of years at the Barnes Foundation, Merion, Pennsylvania. Russell's lectureship is now progressing successfully and to the satisfaction of all concerned. No one, Justice McGeehan to the contrary notwithstanding, has been instigated to commit any "damnable felony." It may, indeed, be doubted whether the Justice really believed anything of the kind would happen if Mr. Russell were appointed to a chair in City College.

But Dr. Barnes was not satisfied with this action in behalf of religious toleration and intellectual freedom. He felt that the social importance of the case demanded there be a public record of the issues involved. This book is a result of his suggestion. Fairness to him and to the writers of the essays makes it advisable to say that the authors of the essays were selected not by him but by a group representing the Committee for Cultural Freedom, one of the first organizations to take an active part in condemnation of the attack on education and culture involved in the Russell case. Nor did Dr. Barnes make any suggestions, much less give any advice or instruction, as to what contributors could or should say.

The various contributors represent different philosophical and social standpoints. They are agreed upon one point: the unqualified necessity of honest discussion by competent persons, using the method of intelligence, the scientific method. For they

[First published in *The Bertrand Russell Case*, ed. John Dewey and Horace M. Kallen (New York: Viking Press, 1941), pp. 7–10.]

know the alternative is some aspect and degree of totalitarianism. It is probably true that because the war waged by totalitarian powers came at a time when it distracted attention from the Russell case it became easier for the cohorts of darkness to "get away" with their campaign against the democratic method of discussion. But it would be a bitter irony if protest against totalitarianism abroad should be a factor in fostering recourse to totalitarian methods in this country.

The writers are also agreed that the social importance of the present case far transcends the injustice done to Mr. Russell personally, great as that is; and that it also transcends the question of the merits or demerits of the particular views he set forth. The reasons for this belief are given in the essays that follow. The Mayor, who has to accept a share in the responsibility for allowing an attack upon moral and intellectual freedom to go by default, had occasion later to protest when the Justice, who appropriated for himself the duty of appointment belonging to a duly constituted public agency, did the same sort of thing in the case of a public commission having authority in the matter of public transit. In the latter case, the act of the Justice was found to approach usurpation. There are those who believe that public access to the sources of knowledge and light are as important as means of access to rapid transit. But this aspect of the action of the Justice, who stood steadily in the way of permitting an appeal to a higher court and in the way of allowing Mr. Russell to exercise the supposedly elementary right of self-defense, is but the technical manifestation of an underlying attempt to apply the lynch law of popular outcry to settle an issue where the enlightened judgment of competent educators who have no political or theological ax to grind was on the other side.

Legally speaking, the particular case with which this volume deals is now a closed issue. But the issue underlying it is no more settled than the Dred Scott case settled the slavery issue. There are events which do more than tell in what direction the wind is blowing at a given time. They have a pivotal, a crucial, importance. They may become precedents for later activities in the same direction. Then a change of angle that subtends a small arc at the outset comes in time to include a vast space. Or the same event may arouse protest; it may stir forces that had been lulled into apathy. So far as public institutions of higher education are concerned, and so far as the whole cause of unfettered public discussion of social and moral issues is at stake, it may well turn out that the Russell case is an event of this pivotal kind. The turgid rhetoric and the dishonest abuse engaged in during the process of winning a temporary legal victory for reaction and intolerance may possibly contribute to creation of a long black period in our intellectual life. But the extreme this reaction went to in flouting of fair play and of freedom may, on the other hand, help clear the atmosphere of foul vapors and so assist the light of intelligence to shine more brightly.

Belief in the social importance of public discussion of moral problems, when it is conducted upon the plane of scientific method and with a sense of public responsibility, is, as I have said, the bond which unites those who have written this book. The belief is accompanied by the hope that this book may contribute in the same degree to the happier conclusion of the two possible ultimate results for the freedom of the human spirit and the democratic way of life.

Foreword to *Educational Trends*

Interpreters and critics of events are practically unanimous in the conviction that the world is arriving at one of those critical points of history in which a change of direction takes place. The signs are manifest in our own nation, in European and in Oriental affairs. No one can state with an assurance which is based upon reason what the nature of the change is going to be. The forces at work are too vast and are too precariously poised to enable us to speak dogmatically about the future. We only know that it is as if the affairs of the world were turning on a hinge but cannot tell which way they are going to swing.

This condition is a challenge to serious thought and to those who have the responsibility for giving effect in action to thought. This bromidic remark may acquire concrete significance if it is translated into the idea that the challenge comes with special intensity to philosophers and educators. Structures do not crack and threaten to collapse unless there is structural weakness. The bare fact that the structures were erected to serve a good purpose does not protect them if such weakness exists. The world would hardly find itself in its present state if our religion, our education, our nationalism, our politics, our democracy, were all that we have liked to believe they were.

Insecurity and fear lead men to strive to seek some safe place of refuge. For some reason or other, the fortress of safety is most often looked for in some past state of existence. Tendencies toward reaction grow strong in times like the present ones. Instead of an intelligent search for the causes of weakness and failure, emotional disturbance leads to an intellectually heedless retreat. Philosophers as professed lovers of wisdom are not immune from

[First published in *Educational Trends* 7 (November–December 1939): 5.]

this tendency. Those who do not give way to this temptation may react to an almost equally thoughtless defense of what they take to be new and progressive.

There are peoples like those of the warring European countries, who have to act because they are caught in an immediate emergency. They do not have the time and the room—the space—in which to think. But we in this country are not in that position. We are summoned to think, to inquire, examine, weigh, rather than to decide, or at least before we decide. There have doubtless been times in the past when the summons was as imperative and the consequences of failure to respond as momentous. But I do not believe they have occurred in the lifetime of any persons who are now on the earth. There is need for a searching re-examination of our habits and our professed principles, a need which applies alike to those of all philosophical schools, and which should unite them, in spite of differences among them, against all who fail to perceive in the present crisis the urgent need for critical reflection.

Educators, using the word in the large sense in which it includes more than schoolmasters, are those who work systematically to give effect to the results of thought by so incarnating them in the characters and attitudes of men that they influence conduct. They too are summoned by the present state of the world to take stock of their practices and even more of their beliefs, of the ideas which, perhaps unconsciously more than consciously, control what they do. I would not under-rate what educators have accomplished in this country nor depreciate the value of the instrumentality they have at command. But I do not think there has been a time in the history of the country when it was so fundamentally necessary to ask what it is all about, and what the instrument should be used for. In response to the kind request of the editor that I say a few words for publication in this present issue, I have thought that it might be more important to emphasize the point of need for thinking rather than to try in any way to anticipate what the conclusions of the thinking might or should be. Emergencies, crises, are bound to come about, but their final issue depends upon whether or not they evoke thorough and sincere reflection.

Introduction to *American Journal of Economics and Sociology*

There is nothing new in the enunciation of the idea that political economy cannot be separated from sociology. Long ago, Auguste Comte criticized classic English economics on the ground that it attempted a divorce in theory that is impossible in practice, a divorce which, applied in practice, resulted only in confusion and disintegration. The connection of political economy with politics is embodied in the very name. Although many recent workers in the field have tried to introduce the neutral name "economics," they have also insisted that economics is one of the social sciences. The fact that only a comparatively small number of workers and writers have ventured to hold that there is an intrinsic connection of politics and economics with ethics, as a social science, is proof of how empty and verbal is the current notion of "social science." As it is now commonly used, it is only a word. For what is the sense in calling ethics, politics, economics and sociology "social sciences" when it is also held, in practice if not in so many words, that there is no necessary, no intrinsic connection among these various subjects? It is as if some one, proclaiming the importance of the physical sciences, then went on to assume that there is no inherent connection between the facts and principles of astronomy, physics, chemistry, etc. The present state of the world cannot be laid at the door of the separation held and proclaimed by many scholars. Its causes are deeper. But it can be truly affirmed that the chaotic, the divided, the hostile, state of the world and the intellectual division that has been built up in so-called "social science," are both of them reflections and expressions of the same fundamental causes. The attempt to break down the walls of separation, the un-

[First published in *American Journal of Economics and Sociology* 1 (October 1941): i–ii.]

natural barriers which have been erected, is therefore a necessary part of any movement toward greater social cooperation. The endeavor for synthesis should be welcomed by all persons of all creeds who are concerned with attainment of the harmonious relations which more and more are seen to be the sole alternative to collapse of civilization. Although the *American Journal of Economics and Sociology* is not committed to swearing loyalty to any one master, it is certainly fitting that an American endeavor at synthesis in the social field should honor the work of Henry George. For I know of no writer by whom the interdependence of all aspects and phases of human relations, economic, political, cultural, moral, has been so vigorously and so sympathetically set forth.

"No Matter What Happens—Stay Out"

I have rarely found myself in agreement with Herbert Hoover. But as I read his prediction that if the United States is drawn into the next war we shall have in effect if not in name a fascist government in this country, I believe he is completely in the right. The dire reaction that took place in the early twenties after the World War was mild in comparison with what would occur another time. It would begin earlier, be more rigid, and endure no one knows how long. We are forgetting that the years before the last war were a time of growth for a strong and genuine progressivism in this country, and that if its career had not been interrupted we should have made whatever gains have been accomplished by the New Deal much earlier and in a much less costly way.

It is quite conceivable that after the next war we should have in this country a semi-military, semi-financial autocracy, which would fasten class divisions on this country for untold years. In any case we should have the suppression of all the democratic values for the sake of which we professedly went to war.

The discouraging thing is that the very persons who a few years ago were sure that they would not allow themselves to favor our entering another great war, and that we had been deceived by propaganda in entering the last one, are now thinking and talking as if it were inevitable that we should again go in. This attitude is a precursor of an event that is in no way necessary. If we but make up our minds that it is not inevitable, and if we now set ourselves deliberately to seeing that no matter what happens we stay out, we shall save this country from the greatest social catastrophe that could overtake us, the destruction of all the foundations upon which to erect a socialized democracy. At the same time we shall destroy the means by which we can be of use to a stricken Europe after the end of its attempt at suicide.

[First published in *Common Sense* 8 (March 1939): 11.]

The Committee for Cultural Freedom

Sir: The editorial in the *New Republic* of May 31 contains the following: "The statement of the Committee for Cultural Freedom says in effect that we have entire liberty in America and that there is none at all in Germany, Italy or Russia." The sentence just quoted is wholly false. More space is given in the committee's manifesto to the dangers to cultural freedom found in this country than to anything else. The dangers existing here and now in America are the reason for the formation of the committee. The opening paragraphs about the rising tide of totalitarianism in other countries are introductory to a strong statement that it is spreading into other countries and explicit mention is made of the United States, together with specific instances of its presence here.

Is it perhaps significant "in effect" that the *New Republic* did not print the manifesto? If it had done so, even casual readers would have seen the disparity between what it says and the view attributed to it by the editorial writer.

There are other statements in the editorial, of minor importance in comparison with that just mentioned, which call for correction. The editorial says the committee "clearly implies that fascism and communism are both completely incompatible with freedom for the individual" and goes on to argue that the "charge is certainly not true of the theory of the socialist commonwealth." The document issued by the committee does not contain any such charge even by way of remotest implication. If the editor read the list of signers he must have noticed among them several well known Socialists, including the name of the last Socialist candidate for the presidency of the United States. The notion that Norman Thomas, to say nothing of a number of other signers, would put his name to a document that suggested, even

[First published in *New Republic* 99 (14 June 1939): 161–62.]

in a far-fetched fashion, that a socialist commonwealth and freedom for the individual are incompatible would be too fantastic for notice were it not that the editorial has put it forth.

In the final advice the writer gives the committee he refers in parenthesis to some of its members "widely supposed to be followers of the anti-libertarian Trotsky." By not indicating whether or not he shares the supposition he disassociates himself, in a way, from the writers in the Stalinist press who make the charge directly. Having no way of telling whether the writer also means to charge some of the signers with double dealing, or to suggest that "in effect" such is the case, I will explicitly state there is no "Trotskyite" among the signers.

Finally the writer admits that there is danger we shall embrace a large part of fascism, while probably calling it anti-fascism. Personally I agree with this statement. It is a strong argument for the belief of the Committee for Cultural Freedom that it is not enough just to denounce fascism, that it is not enough just to be anti-fascist, but that a positive and aggressive campaign is required against every sort of totalitarian influence in this country.

JOHN DEWEY, Chairman,
The Committee for Cultural Freedom

"Democratic Ends Need Democratic Methods for Their Realization"

Unforeseen commitments out of town have prevented me from attending the meeting at Town Hall to which I have looked forward with such great interest. I am proud of the work of the Committee for Cultural Freedom, and its efforts to defend and advance the integrity of cultural and intellectual life.

As we listen to accounts of the repression of cultural freedom in countries which have been swept by totalitarian terror, let us bear in mind that our chief problems are those within our own culture. In the modern world, every country under some circumstances becomes fertile soil for seeds out of which grow fanatical conflict, intolerance, racial oppression.

The attitude which prevails in some parts of our country towards Negroes, Catholics and Jews is spiritually akin to the excesses that have made a shambles of democracy in other countries of the world.

The conflict between the methods of freedom and those of totalitarianism, insofar as we accept the democratic ideals to which our history commits us, is within our own institutions and attitudes. It can be won only by extending the application of democratic methods, methods of consultation, persuasion, negotiation, cooperative intelligence in the task of making our own politics, industry, education—our culture generally—a servant and an evolving manifestation of democratic ideas.

Resort to military force is a first sure sign that we are giving up the struggle for the democratic way of life, and that the Old World has conquered morally as well as geographically.

If there is one conclusion to which human experience unmistakably points, it is that democratic ends demand democratic

[First published in *New Leader* 22 (21 October 1939): 3, from a message read at the first public meeting of the Committee for Cultural Freedom on 13 October 1939 at Town Hall in New York City.]

methods for their realization. Authoritarian methods now offer themselves to us in new guises. They come to us claiming to serve the ultimate ends of freedom by immediate, and allegedly temporal, techniques of suppression.

Or they recommend adoption of a totalitarian regime in order to fight totalitarianism. In whatever form they offer themselves, they owe their seductive power to their claim to serve ideal ends.

Our first defense is to realize that democracy can be served only by the slow day by day adoption and contagious diffusion in every phase of our common life of methods that are identical with the ends to be reached.

There is no substitute for intelligence and integrity in cultural life. Anything else is a betrayal of human freedom no matter in what guise it presents itself.

An American democracy can serve the world only as it demonstrates in the conduct of its own life the efficacy of plural, partial, and experimental methods in securing and maintaining an ever-increasing release of the powers of human nature, in service of a freedom which is cooperative and a cooperation which is voluntary.

We cannot sit back in complacent optimism. History will not do our work for us. Neither is there any call for panic or pessimism.

We, members and friends of the Committee for Cultural Freedom, must dedicate ourselves to the task of securing and widening cultural freedom with eyes open and minds alert to every danger which threatens it. We must always remember that the dependence of ends upon means is such that the only ultimate result is the result that is attained today, tomorrow, the next day, and day after day, in the succession of years and generations.

Only thus can we be on guard against those who paint a rosy future which has no date in order to cover up their theft of our existing liberties. Only thus can we be sure that we face our problems in details one by one as they arise, and with all the resources provided by collective intelligence operating in cooperative action.

Russell as a Moral Issue

To the *New York Herald Tribune:*

I wish to thank you for your calm and intelligent editorial discussion of "The Russell Decision" in today's issue. Its contrast with the wild hysteria of much of the attack upon Russell's appointment is very refreshing.

JOHN DEWEY

New York, April 1, 1940

[First published in *New York Herald Tribune,* 3 April 1940, p. 22.]

Investigating Education

The veiled assault on public education, which currently manifests itself in the form of "investigations" of one kind or another, must arouse progressive educators throughout the country to renewed vigilance, lest the careful work of the past four decades be undone in our day by elements in the community whose concern is not primarily with advancing free education.

In New York, Governor Lehman has approved a resolution carrying a $30,000 appropriation for a legislative investigation into the New York public school system. In Washington Mr. Martin Dies, chairman of the House Committee to Investigate Un-American Activities, has promised an investigation into the political and social affiliations of textbook writers.

Ostensibly in the public interest, both of these announcements have about them a vagueness that gives rise to legitimate apprehension on the part of all experienced observers. There can be no objection, certainly, to an investigation, either of the New York school system or of the authors of textbooks, provided that, in line with the best educational practice, the investigation has a clear-cut objective and that the investigators themselves are competent to pursue it without prejudice or favor.

In a democracy, any elected body of representatives has the right to look into the methods and practices which are in force in the schools supported by public taxation. Nor can a scrutiny of the writers of textbooks used in those schools be regarded as an unwarranted invasion of rights. The investigation of public-utilities corporations, which a handful of senators led by Thomas J. Walsh and George W. Norris forced the Federal Trade Commission to conduct in 1928, was extremely valuable in expos-

[First published on 6 May 1940 in *New York Times*, p. 16, and *New York Herald Tribune*, p. 18. For Merwin Kimball Hart's reply to this letter, see this volume, Appendix 3, and for Dewey's rejoinder, see p. 373.]

ing an intolerable abuse of privilege by a powerful group that did not scruple to buy the services of professors for its own anti-social ends.

A different purpose, however, would seem to animate those who are today bent on investigation. The quest today is for "subversive" activities and "subversive" textbooks; and the problem becomes one of determining what is "subversive" and what is not. Competence to recognize the distinction between the two is essential in anyone who conducts an investigation into educational methods and materials. The belief, entertained no doubt in many quarters, that any textbook which presents the theories of state and revolution advanced by Karl Marx, Nikolai Lenin or Leon Trotsky is ipso facto "subversive," would, if allowed to prevail, reduce the educational system of America to the condition of bondage which exists in the totalitarian states of Italy, Germany and Soviet Russia.

The term "subversive," employed indiscriminately, may easily become a weapon in the hands of those who would exercise an intellectual censorship that is in fact subversive of the best public interest.

Increasingly, attempts are being made to invoke such a censorship against some of our foremost textbook authors because, in common with most enlightened citizens, they see the need for change and improvement in our present social order, if it is to survive. Only last month the social science textbooks of one such writer, Professor Harold Rugg of Teachers College, Columbia University, were branded "subversive" and removed from the public schools of Binghamton, N.Y., at the instigation of Mr. Merwin K. Hart, president of the State Economic Council. This action climaxed agitation that has for years been inspired by groups in other communities to silence Mr. Rugg by forcing his books out of the schools. Nor is Mr. Rugg alone. In the recent past Professors Carl L. Becker, David Saville Muzzey, Roy Hatch and the late DeForest Stull were victims of similar persecution.

In the only true sense of the word, the works of these men are not subversive; they are, on the contrary, conducive of unfettered thinking, as opposed to unthinking stereotypes that leave no way out of our dilemmas but resort to violence and arms. The same freedom of inquiry characterizes, in another field, the works of Bertrand Russell.

We welcome any investigation of American education that has as its goal the development of thoughtful, intelligent, critical-minded students and citizens; we welcome evidence that agents of foreign governments are using the schools to undermine confidence in democracy as a way of life. But we stand unalterably opposed to those who would pervert a free educational system by opening it to the exploitation of prejudice, bigotry and unenlightenment; and we shall vigorously resist any attempt by pressure groups to gain control of the public schools by seeking to dictate what shall and what shall not be taught in them.

Censorship Not Wanted

To the Editor of the *New York Times:*

Merwin K. Hart, in the letter which appeared in the *Times* of May 9, would make it appear that to approve a book, whether textbook or not, one must accept the theories presented in it. This is an all too common fallacy which, if generally accepted, would result in shutting out all consideration of divergent views. Would Mr. Hart have us follow the example of Japan, and forbid the harboring of "dangerous thoughts" on pain of death?

The discussion of a wide variety of opinion, unorthodox and orthodox, with an intelligent teacher in the classroom, is the best protection the schools can afford against our students being later misled by unscrupulous propagandists of one doctrine or another. It is surely better for our young people to face controversial issues in the open atmosphere of the schoolroom, than to seek out what is forbidden in some dark, unwholesome corner. No thought is so dangerous as a forbidden thought.

And it is, I think, safe to say that a teacher who is going to preach the virtues of communism or nazism does not need a textbook for his purpose, and will not find the most orthodox of texts a handicap. There is, furthermore, no evidence that the leaders of conspiracies to overthrow the United States Government learned revolution in the public schools.

If the attacks on authors like Mr. Rugg came from educators, they might have more validity. Mr. Hart might approve such a censorship as prevails in Spain; but the enlightened citizens of this country have never regarded the educational system of any totalitarian State as a model to be emulated in America.

JOHN DEWEY

New York, May 11, 1940.

[First published in *New York Times,* 14 May 1940, p. 22. For Merwin Kimball Hart's letter to which this is a rejoinder, see this volume, Appendix 3, and for Dewey's first letter in this exchange, see pp. 370–72.]

Statement on Academic Freedom

No better statement of the function of the university could be made than that of President Butler. That the university should contribute to "analysis and understanding of the economic, social and political problems involved in the present war" and should do so without emotional excitement, "with calmness, good judgment and full knowledge," is a statement that cannot be improved upon.

Because of sympathy with this view I am unable to understand some other statements made in the same address. I should suppose, for example, that it is vitally important for students to have a share in this analysis and understanding. Hence I do not see what is meant by his denial of academic freedom to students.

Then President Butler seems to make a distinction between the freedom of the teachers in the faculty and the higher freedom of the university to pursue its own ideals. The demand that teachers subordinate their freedom to the higher freedom of the university does not seem to agree with the original statement. I do not know what a university is apart from students and its teaching staff.

I can hardly believe that President Butler intended to place the university in a realm so lofty that it is above the students and faculty and has the right to control their beliefs in the way in which churches set the creeds to which their members must conform. Such an idea seems to be identical, as far as it goes, with totalitarianism. Since President Butler is an opponent of the latter, I am forced to conclude that what he said does not convey his real meaning.

[First published in *New York Times*, 5 October 1940, p. 7.]

Dewey Greets Teachers Union

There is no single act that would have given me more pleasure, and few that would have given me as much, as to be present at this meeting of commemoration and celebration—all the happier because of the troubled times recently come through. If I were present in person I should want to pay my especial regards to old friends with whom I was associated in the past, and who never yielded the least ground in their battles for teachers, for the labor movement in association with teachers, and for the freedom of unionism from subjection to foreign political influences. Now that the first twenty-five years have been completed and the Teachers Union Federation of the American Federation of Labor has passed through its ordeal, the time has come to look to the future in remembering the struggles and achievements of the past. We must bring in all teachers who have social vision and personal realization of the part the public and other schools have to play in making the vision real. If we bring in those whose sympathies, social and educational, are in line with the ideals of our Federation, we shall not need to worry about the absence of the socially dull and the apathetic. An aggressive band of teachers united for our common cause can achieve great results, and we should not be modest in our hopes and ambitions; we should cause our energy to be on a par with them. Congratulations to the American Federation of Teachers and best wishes for its full prosperity in the next quarter century and all those which come after.

[First published in *American Teacher* 26 (October 1941): 31, from a message read at the twenty-fifth anniversary dinner of the American Federation of Teachers on 23 August 1941 in Detroit, Mich.]

Appendixes

Appendix 1
Some Difficulties in Dewey's Anthropocentric Naturalism [1]
By Morris R. Cohen

To those who are both conscientious and sensitive, philosophy, like other serious human pursuits, offers difficulties that are often baffling and dispiriting. There are times when not only does the truth which is our objective elude us but when we are tempted to abandon the arduous climb up the uncharted heights and to return instead to the complacent lowlands of Philistia. It is good, therefore, to have our faith strengthened by notable examples of steadfast devotion and heroic attainments. And today no man offers a record of such long, varied and distinguished devotion to philosophy as does John Dewey. For over 57 years he has been publishing the results of his philosophic studies in most diverse fields. With a tireless fidelity and a keen and sensitive eye for the workings of the human mind, his descriptions of what he sees are always penetrating and offer fruit for reflection even in those instances when they do not carry full conviction. It would be a grateful task for me to dwell on his beneficent influence in American life. I know of no one who has done more to keep alive the fundamental ideals of liberal civilization, and I am personally deeply grateful for the illumination and inspiration which I have drawn from his writings and from conversations with him since my boyhood days in 1899. His textbook on Psychology and his early volume on Leibniz were among the first readings that led me to philosophy. And in recent years I have found much nourishing food in his diverse writings on social and political questions, on education and especially on art. The book on Ethics which he wrote with Professor Tufts seems to me to have made that field a living study of actual problems instead of exercises in

1. Read, in part, at the meeting of the American Philosophical Association, December 28, 1939.

[First published in *Philosophical Review* 49 (March 1940): 196–228. For Dewey's reply, see this volume, pp. 141–54.]

traditional homiletics, which it used to be in our American colleges. In the field of jurisprudence and in the study of all social institutions he has mightily reinforced the old but ever-needed truth that the Sabbath was made for man, not man for the Sabbath. But my theme is his philosophy of nature, and here I regret, I cannot follow him.

Some of my difficulties are doubtless due to the limitations of my interests and temperament. To me the central problems of philosophy are the perennial or, if you like, traditional ones of ontology, of the nature of the world into which we are born and which we sooner or later leave. And I am bewildered when I find fundamental cosmic issues ignored or treated only in the interstices of the much more complicated, and to me always illusive, problems of the psychology of human thought or behavior. Many of my differences from Dewey may be differences of emphasis. But in philosophy as in music, emphasis is of the essence. In general I agree with Dewey's rejection of supernaturalism as well as with his humanistic theory of art and morals. But while philosophy to me is no longer theocentric, neither is it as anthropocentric as Dewey's seems to me.

Besides these subjective difficulties of mine there are, I am sure, objective ones which others besides myself find in trying to understand Dewey's thought. In the course of his long and active career, even since he left Chicago, his ideas have doubtless grown. But whether he is not aware of any changes or whether because of his indifference to systematization, he has not as a rule explicitly indicated which of his former expressions no longer adequately represent his views. Moreover, he often uses words such as *practical, experience, empirical, knowledge,* or *ideas,* in unusual meanings without there and then indicating the departure. For these and other reasons I am extremely skeptical as to my ability to make an accurate synthesis of the views expressed in his diverse writings. And so I at first declined the kind invitation of our Program Committee to take an active part in these festive proceedings. I have become more and more convinced that we generally do better to state what we ourselves see than to deny the vision of others that we cannot share. But the liberalism of which Dewey is such a notable protagonist regards the free expression of differences, even when based on misunderstanding, as itself a valuable aid to the progress of philosophy. The expression of my dissent may provide him and his distinguished disciples further opportunity to clarify his position. And even where my statements may (because of the exigencies of time) be dogmatic, their aim is to prevent some issues from being prematurely regarded as closed.

Dewey calls his philosophy humanistic naturalism. In view of the many uses to which the word humanism has recently been applied, to one of which Dewey's whole philosophy is anathema, it seems preferable to call it anthropocentric naturalism. It is undoubtedly a philosophy in which not physical cosmology but social anthropology or a doctrine of human experience plays the central rôle. It offers no vistas of nature beyond the human scene, and manifests no interest in such questions as the origin and future of our solar system or of life on our earth, or even in the natural conditions which are likely to bring about the disappearance of the human species. Now, it is perfectly legitimate for a philosopher to take a position anywhere and to try to survey the entire realm of being as it appears from that point of view. It is, however, difficult, if not impossible, for any human being to escape the bias which comes from emphasizing the things nearest to him, and not only belittling the things that are foreshortened by their remoteness but ignoring or even denying the existence of the things that are not in his field of interest. More especially is one tempted to deny, even if only by implication, that other points of view or perspectives besides one's own can also be legitimate. That is, I think, more or less the case with humans generally, and it would have been strange if John Dewey were an exception. His perspective is essentially that of a moralist, moving in the humanistic tradition. I have heard him define philosophy as reflective thought dominated by moral interests. And in his frequent criticism of other philosophies, he often emphasizes moral considerations such as the waste of so much human thought that could be used for the advancement of human welfare. This leads to a subordination of metaphysical to moral considerations which seems to me hurtful to both.

My remarks thus naturally fall into two groups, the first deals with general philosophical difficulties, and the second with their implications for moral or social theory.

I

After the great Hobbes stubbed his toes by hardy ventures into mathematics and physics on inadequate information, Locke prudently opened a new way for philosophy by turning it into a psychologic account of our ideas and of the conduct of our understanding. And Kant only followed when he made epistemology a necessary precondition for metaphysics, as if a theory of knowledge could possibly be built up without ontologic assumptions as to the knower and the universe in which knowledge takes place. Except for the important fact that Dewey substitutes a theory of active experience for the psychology of sensations and their association, he certainly belongs to the Lockian tradition that almost banishes the cosmologic interest from philosophy. It may at times be in revolt against the old theology, but it is at one with the latter in regarding man as the center of the world and viewing everything else solely in relation to him and to his salvation, in an earthly if not in a heavenly paradise.

Professor Hocking is to discuss Dewey's theory of experience. It is sufficient for my present purpose to indicate that in Dewey's actual usage, as in everyone else's, that sacred word of modern philosophy is restricted to what happens to human beings or to animals to the extent that they behave like humans. No one speaks of the experience of a dead or lifeless body; and we do not attribute it to the sea, to the rocks, or to the sun before human life appeared on our earth. An experience is therefore a certain kind of event in nature and not the whole of it. And Dewey cannot, as subjective idealists do, identify the existence of an object with our experience of it. He admits the existence of a world before human life came on the scene. But he condemns the contrast between the infinitesimal pettiness of man and the vastness of the stellar universe.[2] Passing over the moral question whether such a contrast is or is not "a cheap intellectual pastime," I should emphatically deny that it is logically illicit. In time as well as in space the existence of man *is* infinitesimal, and the forces at the basis of the stellar universe create and destroy man, while the converse is not true. And if the meaning of objects or events is not purely subjective but is to be found in their objective consequences, the

---

2. *Proceedings of the Sixth International Congress of Philosophy,* 538.

meaning of the stellar universe as distinguished from our apprehension of its meaning is not, except to professional psychologists, exhausted in the emotions or thoughts it arouses in human beings.

Dewey is so intent on proving that everything human is natural that at times he seems to drift into the converse view that all nature or existence can be described in the categories of human experience such as need, uncertainty, precariousness and the like.[3] Possibly the latter attitude is even more strongly influenced by the conviction that the categories of social life are so much richer than those of physical science[4] that they give us a better contact with "reality." But we cannot satisfactorily describe the whole cosmos in human terms unless we believe in thoroughgoing animism, which Dewey does not profess even in his theory of natural ends. I can, therefore, see no force at all in his attack on the realists[5] for holding what seems to me the obvious truth, *viz.* that search, inquiry, ignorance and the like are in the field of the personal and the psychologic but are not traits of *all* existence. While experience is personal not all objects are. Indeed, the categories in question are not even applicable to all organic beings. Dewey claims that "It is as much a part of the real being of atoms that they give rise in time, under increasing complication of relationships, to qualities of bitter and sweet, pain and beauty, as that they have at a cross section of time extension, mass or weight."[6] Now, it should be observed that the assumption that atoms have given rise to the human sense of beauty is not something that has ever been empirically shown. It is rather a deduction from the principle of physical determinism which realistic rationalists recognize but which Dewey cannot completely accept without raising certain difficulties (which I shall mention in the next paragraph). In any case, if physical objects cause pain or the thrill of beauty in human beings the reverse is not true. That certain foods are distasteful, for instance, is a fact that depends on certain chemical factors, while the chemical phenomena do not in the same way depend on our taste. In general, human pain and the sense of beauty occur in a passing episode of cosmic history

3. *Experience and Nature*, 64, 69, 253, 351, and esp. 413.
4. *Philosophy and Civilization*, 77–92.
5. *Experience and Nature*, 69.
6. *Op. cit.*, 109–110.

which might never repeat itself, while extent and mass are traits that atoms always have. Moreover, I think Dewey ignores the requisites of precise quantitative thought, which has done so much to advance physics, when he says "the domination of man by reverie and desire is as pertinent for the philosophic theory of nature as is mathematical physics."[7] No one doubts that human reverie is a natural event, but surely it is not one of the great controlling forces of nature that science uses to explain phenomena. For the understanding of the general processes of nature throughout time and space, the existence of human reverie and desire is surely not as illuminating as are considerations of mathematical physics. It illumines the human scene to understand the desire which made men refuse to accept the Copernican astronomy, but it gives us no light on the nature of planetary motion. The solution of human problems depends upon a knowledge of physiology, chemistry, and inorganic physics, but not vice versa.

Can Dewey whole-heartedly accept the principle of physical determinism? In the first place, it is difficult to see how a principle that claims a universal necessity can be fitted into a strictly empirical philosophy, since it cannot be conclusively verified in any single phenomenon or experiment or in any finite number of them. But a more important consideration is that in order to allow human judgments to make a change in the world the latter must be conceived as otherwise incomplete or undetermined. But physical determinism means a closed system of measurable magnitudes, such as ergs, and it is hard to conceive how judgments can be so expressed. Of course, we can abandon the absoluteness of physical determinism and even claim support in Heisenberg's much abused indeterminacy principle. But this not only leaves no basis for confidence in an unbroken chain between atoms and the human sense of beauty, but it weakens the basis for the absolute exclusion of all possible supernatural influence in human development.

Indeed, despite Dewey's insistently sharp dichotomy between his own views and those which he accuses of harboring traces of supernaturalism, he nowhere defines clearly the precise differences between the natural and the supernatural. He seems to think that the invocation of the principle of continuity settles the

7. *Op. cit.* (first ed.), 6.

matter. But what Dewey means by continuity in a pluralistic world containing admitted novelties is obscure to me. At one point he speaks of it as if it were a purely logical principle, so that its denial would involve self-contradiction. But this hardly fits into his own distinction between the logical and the existential. In the essay on the "Influence of Darwin," he argues as if the discovery that some (not all) species have changed in the course of time disproves the Aristotelian logic and the view that the world contains ultimately different kinds of things. But unless we also invoke the opposite principle of discontinuity, continuity would be indistinguishable from what Dewey condemns, namely that all existence is one, and comes under a single concept.

Dewey's predilection for the "thicker" categories of social psychology is closely related to his preference for the method of analysing experience in the gross as against the traditional way of explaining the actual as a synthesis of simpler elements. The abuse of the latter method is one of the enduring scandals of the intellectual life. But the analytic method is no less subject to limitations. For *what* and *how* we should analyse depend largely on the point of view that we assume to start with. Darwin long ago pointed out that a wrong observation is a much greater hindrance to the progress of science than a wrong theory. And Dewey himself has urged that what are the facts of a given case emerges at the end rather than at the beginning of our investigation. Now there can be no doubt that it is easier to determine the facts in the physical than in the mental or social realm. For not only are the former inherently simpler (since the social includes the physical), but physics also has so many more instruments and methods for eliminating false observations. This makes a consensus (or the elimination of differences of opinion) difficult in the social field. A philosophy therefore which begins with observations on human experience is bound to partake of the uncertainties and controversial differences which abound so much more in what we courteously call social science.

The opposition to all forms of dualism is one of the dominant notes of Dewey's philosophy. In this he relies on the popular philosophy of evolution, though he may also have in mind some of the indications of physiologic psychology. But, while the dualism between conscious and unconscious existence is rejected, he does not postulate any panpsychism to explain the rise of consciousness in an unconscious world. Indeed, in the course of his polemics he sets up dualisms of his own, *e.g.*, that between knowledge and perception, where an evolutionist might expect to find a continuous development of the former from the latter. In war, lines must be sharply drawn. You cannot preach a crusade to free the Zion of experience from the infidel rationalists if you admit that the sacred place is everywhere and that the infidels have some element of the truth in them. Thus, though he must reject the radicalism which attacks the historic past as trivial and harmful, the major part of *Reconstruction in Philosophy* is devoted to drawing a sharp antithesis between what he calls the modern and all previous views of the world, with a rather sweeping rejection of all the latter instead of integrating them in a wider outlook. I shall deal later with his exaggerated contrast between modern and ancient science.

One of the dualisms that Dewey both inherits and develops is that between the existence of particular things and the purely procedural character of logical and mathematical entities or relations.

The term *procedure* or *method* is one of the vaguest in modern philosophy and, next to *reality* and *experience,* most in need of critical challenge for its precise meaning. It is never used in the exact sciences except under precise specifications, so that it was not altogether unjust for Poincaré to remark that physicists discuss their results while their colleagues in the social field discuss their methods. In any case, Dewey himself recognizes that method cannot be completely divorced from subject-matter. Yet he adopts the absolute dualism of the formalists that the subject-matter of logic or pure mathematics "is not only non-existential in immediate reference," but is "free from existential reference of even the most indirect delayed and ulterior kind." [8]

The logical development of mathematics is "the story of [the] liberation of mathematical subject-matter from any kind of ontologic reference." [9] But if the marks or sounds, two plus two equals four, had no reference whatsoever to anything beyond themselves, they would have no meaning. The marks used by mathematicians would not be symbols if they did not symbolize something more than what they themselves are as immediate ob-

---

8. *Logic,* 396; *Experience and Nature,* 148–149.
9. *Logic,* 397.

jects. The objects of mathematics, to be sure, are wider than those of physics, since we can speak intelligibly of non-physical objects. But if there were no objects of any kind whatsoever, no discourse would be intelligible. There can be no possible world or universe of discourse except by reference to some variation from something actual.

If logical and mathematical relations were no part of the nature of things, only something extranatural or a pre-established harmony could explain their fruitfulness in leading to physical discoveries. On pragmatic grounds there is no reason why Dewey should not reject the detached particular as well as the abstract or detached universal. Do not the relations of an object enter into our experience of it as much as its unique particularity? Universality and particularity are in fact the two poles of existence. Each is necessary but insufficient without the other. And at times Dewey explicitly admits that nature has its relationships as well as its terms. Indeed, at heart he is at one with Aristotle in holding that the individual apart from universal traits cannot be the object of knowledge.[10] But the undue fear of rationalism often leads him to nominalism or conceptualism,[11] as Peirce complained.[12] To say that the universal is a habit gives us only its psychologic locus, not its denotation. Only our apprehension of the denotation or meaning of an idea is an event which may occur a finite number of times in a personal biography, and as such is the product of human association or interaction. The mathematical and logical relations that we apprehend, *e.g.*, the ratio between the circumference and the radius of a circle, are not human events or habits. They are invariant features of physical nature which we can and do ignore to our peril.

The question how a theorem arises in someone's mind is not the same as the analysis of its meaning or a study of its implications. We cannot by human association or interaction make any proposition the logical consequence of another. We can change the names we give things, but the logical consequences of any set of propositions such as Euclid's axioms do not depend on us. If,

---

10. *Experience and Nature*, 85, 86.
11. *Reconstruction*, 152.
12. See *Journal of Philosophy*, 1916. It is instructive to note that Peirce's pragmatism allows for purely mental experiments, "conceivable consequences," which Dewey cannot allow if he follows his opposition to the usual distinction between the mental and the physical.

from any set of propositions, we could derive any proposition we pleased, nothing could really be said to be proved.

If "meaning is objective as well as universal"[13] it should follow that at least some universals are objective. The fact that they are illuminating or instrumental does not prove that they are not also constitutive.

The traditions of empiricism, the distrust of universals or abstractions, often leads Dewey to an inadequate appreciation of the rôle of mathematics. The following passage is an instance. "When men insisted upon judging astronomical phenomena by bringing them directly under established truths, those of geometry, they had no astronomy, but only a private esthetic construction. Astronomy began when men trusted themselves to embarking upon the uncertain sea of events and were willing to be instructed by changes in the concrete."[14] But history shows that men sailed or guided their camels by the light of the stars before a science of astronomy was born. It was precisely when the phenomena were subsumed under the laws of geometry that the science began.

As a psychologist interested primarily in the way men think and acquire knowledge, Dewey views logic from the point of view of human inquiry. This is an important field of study, and it is not necessary for me to add to the many deserved encomia as to the value of Dewey's contribution to it. But there are two difficulties which I find in his view. The first has to do with the ignoring or denial of the ontologic basis of logical procedure, and the second difficulty is with his denial that scientific inquiry can be defined in terms of knowledge.

Like the positivists Dewey rejects as ridiculous the view that logic prescribes how we should think[15] (which, it seems to me, is precisely what logic does indicate, if we wish to avoid certain fallacies). Instead, he offers us the view that logic is a description of those methods of inquiry that are successful. But what is a method of inquiry? Science knows of methods of verification but there are no methods of discovery. If there were such, all we need would be discovered, and we would not have to wait for rare men of genius. Now the vagueness of the term *method* as a de-

13. *Experience and Nature*, 188.
14. *Human Nature*, 242–243.
15. *Reconstruction*, 136.

scription of actual human thinking is not at all clarified by the introduction of the word *successful*. What is the test as to when an inquiry is successful? Surely not anything practical in the ordinary sense of the word; for in practical affairs we often get sufficiently satisfactory (though not accurate) information by all sorts of accidents of good fortune in no way connected with the rules of logic. Even in scientific work men frequently arrive at the truth by logically false reasoning, as Galileo did in his argument that the velocity acquired by a falling body does not vary directly with the space through which it falls.

Shall we say that in the long run those methods which give us most truth are bound to be selected by a sort of survival of the fittest? That would give us no logical test before the run was sufficiently long, and how long that is no one knows. But, in any case, such a view would be an historical generalization for which I should like to see more evidence. There is certainly a good deal of evidence to the contrary in the decline of Greek science. Assuredly, prejudice, superstition, and logical fallacies persist; and Dewey himself has in one instance at least found a pejorative psychogenesis or bad ancestry for a certain view of philosophy to be a more effective argument against it than a logical refutation.[16] It is well for us if in practice we follow the rules of logic, but their validity does not depend upon how men actually behave.

Dewey himself rejects certain doctrines as self-contradictory. This rejection is surely not based on the assumption that it is impossible to think or express contradictions, for that is precisely what the holders of these doctrines are accused of actually doing. The real objection is that there cannot possibly exist anything objective denoted by these self-contradictory doctrines. The principle of contradiction therefore asserts something in regard to existence and not merely in regard to thought or that logical monstrosity, language that has no reference to anything other than itself that it can denote or mean. Logic may thus be viewed as the simplest chapter in ontology, as a study of the exhaustive possibilities of all being. Its laws are not derived from our intentions but express the fact that as regards determinate being or existence certain combinations are possible and others impossible. A world in which everything was possible, and nothing im-

16. *Op. cit.*, 24.

possible, would be a chaos; and science and common practice cannot proceed without assuming a world in which definite or determinate relations are discoverable. From the laws of logic we cannot deduce any specific matters of fact; but, without assuming that the laws of logic are relevant to existence, no inquiry can be launched, much less concluded. Logic indicates necessary but not sufficient determinants of empirical existence.

My second difficulty is with Dewey's assertion that knowledge is to be defined in terms of inquiry and not vice versa. Here as in other instances, Dewey's affirmation seems to me perfectly legitimate, but I see no justification for the denial; nor does Dewey carry it out consistently. Significant or scientific inquiry cannot take place except on the assumption of knowledge already had, together with knowledge of what kind of an answer would be relevant to our question. We must know what to look for if we are to discover anything. And previous knowledge of nature is necessary to understand what we observe. My difficulties increase when, to these observations which are duly recognized by Dewey himself on many occasions, I add his exclusively prospective view of knowledge, that "consequences, not antecedents supply meaning and verity."

That the logical consequences of a proposition are essential to its meaning seems to me an important insight which we owe to many thinkers from Socrates to Peirce. But that the antecedents of a proposition do not "supply meaning and verity" seems surprising when coming from one who places so much emphasis on the psychogenesis or origin of our ideas. In any case, judgments of probability, the abstemious empiricist's staple food, are meaningless apart from the antecedent evidence which forms their premises. Dewey maintains that previous knowledge is held subject to use and is at the service of the discovery which it makes possible, and has to be adjusted to the latter but not the latter to it. Here, as in so many other passages of Dewey's writings, he seems to me to add hasty negations to sound affirmations. Most emphatically is it true that a past generalization must be adjusted to new factual discoveries. But it is equally true that new scientific discoveries do and must involve adjustments to previous knowledge. And the empiricists at least should admit the historic fact that scientific discoveries are generally not made by ignorant people who decide to follow the Baconian method of getting rid of all anticipations of nature and starting with a free or empty mind, but only by those who do have knowledge and who have been able to give intense thought to the subject in hand. Scientific discoveries are interpretations of observations, and these interpretations involve assumptions as to the nature of our instruments and as to the constant relations of the observed to other phenomena of nature. When Lavoisier burned certain substances and found that their weight increased, that did not by itself overthrow the theory of phlogiston. That result came only because other antecedent truths of chemistry made the explanation in terms of the oxygen-theory a simpler one. When a new discovery upsets an old principle it is only because the old principle is thus proved to be inconsistent with other *known* truths. The bending of light-rays overthrows Newton's formula for the law of gravitation, but only when the bending of light-rays is viewed as a consequence of hitherto accepted principles of optics. Without accepting these old truths Newton's gravitational formula could not be impugned by new facts.

Dewey's philosophy may be viewed as one of the many efforts since Hume to introduce the experimental method of the physical sciences into philosophy and moral subjects. These attempts generally proceed on the naïve assumption that the only reason this has not been done before is that people didn't think of it or were prevented by sheer prejudice or by Aristotle. It is doubtless true that where human values are felt intensely most of us are unwilling to pursue the detached objectivity of science. But the human field is also inherently more complex and intractable. It is difficult, if not impossible, to vary one of its factors at a time as we can in the inorganic field. Even the biologic question of heredity becomes more difficult of solution when we consider the human species. The outstanding fact is that we cannot experiment on human beings as freely as we can on hydrogen-gas or guinea-pigs. I once heard T. H. Morgan take Raymond Pearl to task for leaving his fruit-flies to take up such a poor biologic specimen as man. Moreover, even when social experiments are tried, the pragmatic test of truth, or the appeal to experience, is indecisive as to fundamentals. For the question whether a doctrine works satisfactorily or not is itself determined by faith in it. Thus the doctrines of Christianity and Islam are in many points in direct opposition; and many peoples in Asia, Africa, and Eastern Europe have changed from the former to the latter. But in the main, each party finds that the experience of thirteen centuries proves it right. The case is similar in regard to Catholicism and Protestantism. And in our own day believers in democracy, fascism, and communism are equally convinced that the actual course of experience is proving their view to be the only true one. And this state of affairs may continue indefinitely as it has in the field of religion.

The hope of those who, following Bacon, aim at a reconstruction of philosophy on the model of experimental science, is generally supported by a conventional but apocryphal history which is plausible only because ancient and medieval science are for linguistic reasons not popularly accessible. On one occasion Dewey maintained that ancient science was demonstrative, while the life-blood of modern science is discovery. Now I submit that this is neither historically true nor can it ever be so. Mathematics, the most demonstrative of the sciences, grows by successive discoveries, and has proved the most fruitful source of even physical discoveries. For mathematical and logical relations are as objective matters to be investigated as are the velocities of the stars. Nor is it true, as is asserted by popular historians and by scientists when away from their laboratories on a philosophic picnic, that the Greeks did not resort to experiment. The work of Hippocrates, Archimedes, Hero, Hipparchus, and Eratosthenes amply indicates the contrary. Even Pythagoras had to experiment to discover the laws of musical harmony. It required experiment to determine the effects of diet, exercise, and climate on health and disease. It required refined measurement (which is still essential for exact experiment) to decide the choice between rival theories of astronomy such as those of epicycles and excentric motion, to determine the precession of the equinoxes, or the actual length of a degree of latitude on our earth. Moreover, an actual reading of the work of Copernicus, Kepler, Galileo, and Newton fails to justify the popular legend that the science of the sixteenth and seventeenth centuries was revolutionary in its attitude to previous science. It is a myth to suppose that modern science arose when it suddenly occurred to a few men to discard the authority of Aristotle and to examine nature for themselves. That was the bright idea of the lawyer, courtier, and literary artist, Francis Bacon, and it got him nowhere in actual science. Indeed, it made him ignore and even oppose the most significant scientific achievements of his day, such as the Copernican astronomy, the mechanical interpretation of physics, the physiologic discoveries of his own personal physician, Harvey, and the pioneer researches of Gilbert, whose writings were entrusted to him. If we read Copernicus' own work we see that he only revived the Pythagorean astronomy, that he accepted the method of Ptolemy, which is after all still the method of mathematical physics, and that his so-called revolution was after all only a simplification of Ptolemy by reducing the number of epicycles. Kepler was not only profoundly influenced by neo-Platonism, but one of his principle works is a commentary on the optics of a Medieval theologian, Vitello. To Galileo and Newton, Euclid and the other Greek mathematicians were the very basis of all physical science. It is amazing how relatively few mechanical experiments all these men made and how much they were influenced by the idea that the book of nature was written in mathematical terms so that the object of science was to find out this simple underlying mathematical pattern. Anyone who has ever tried to repeat Galileo's experiment of rolling balls on an inclined plane will need no assurance that without the prior faith in the simplicity of natural laws Galileo's actual results would have proved nothing at all. For under the conditions of his experiment the necessary degree of accuracy cannot possibly be attained. Even more is this the case with the supposed dropping of two weights from the Tower of Pisa. To prove what it is generally supposed to have proved, it would have been necessary to create a perfect vacuum by eliminating all the air between the tower and the earth. In any medium such as air or water, the resistance to and retardation of a falling body does depend on its mass, as Lucretius clearly pointed out in antiquity and as anyone can observe for himself if not prevented by reliance on the popular anti-Aristotelian mythology. Note that I am not denying the importance of experiment in modern or in ancient science, nor that, in America especially, many more men are now engaged in laboratories. But I think that a due regard for the essential rôle which mathematical or theoretical development plays in experimental work is not only necessary to explain the growth of science, modern or ancient, but also to remove the false dualism between experiment and rational determination.

Modern science has not abandoned the basic Hellenic idea of a constant order, law, or relation, in the flux of phenomena, nor has it adopted the cult of the limitless infinite, nor the even more recent illusion of function without substance, the grin without the cat. And it is simply not true that "Change rather than fixity is now a measure of 'reality' or energy of being."[17] According to the principle of relativity there is just as much rest and permanence in the world as there is motion and change, since neither set of categories has any physical meaning apart from the other. And even in the older physics, potential energy, the energy of position, is as real as kinetic energy. The subordination of one to the other is as foreign to physical science as the subordination of the north to the south pole.

When I read the *Politics* or the biologic treatises of Aristotle, or even works of medieval scholastics such as Adelard of Bath, Albertus Magnus, or Maimonides, I fail to find anything radically novel in the appeal to experience. And in view of Dewey's rejection of any dualism between reason and experience,[18] I cannot understand his own sharp contrast between empiricism and rationalism. The former, he says, consists in showing or pointing or coming upon the thing discussed, while the latter assumes the primacy and ultimacy of logical thought and findings. I see no basis for assuming these two attitudes to be incompatible, since Dewey himself admits that deduction or the logic that governs it is one of the things pointed out, found and shown.[19] In fact, the logical impossibility of deducing material propositions from purely formal ones was first brought out most clearly and cogently, not by the philosophers of the empirical school, but by the movement for logical rigor in mathematics. And the distrust of self-evident premises goes back to the great rationalist Leibniz. Even Kant, for whom Dewey seldom has a really kind word, has insisted that concepts without percepts are empty, just as percepts without concepts are blind. And to the extent that Dewey, though rejecting the old faculty-psychology, accepts the interdependence or polar character of the perceptual and the conceptual, that in every specific inquiry experimental and *a priori* considerations are both inextricably involved, I agree with him as he does with

17. *Op. cit.*, 61.
18. *Op. cit.*, 100.
19. *Experience and Nature*, first ed., 10.

Kant. But I think that the absolute dualism between the empirical and the rational with its rather unmeasured apotheosis of the former, should yield to a more precise analysis of the distinction between history on the one hand, and logic or pure mathematics on the other.

In challenging Dewey's account of the history of science as a support for his philosophy,[20] I by no means admit the legitimacy of the extent to which he often treats the birth-certificate of a doctrine as a guide to its truth. The fact that geometry arose out of surveying does not determine the truth or falsity of any theorem in it. But I do not want to discuss here the general validity of the passage from the chronologic to the logical order which an uncritical acceptance of Hegel and romantic evolutionism has made so popular. One specific point, however, is noteworthy. Dewey argues against the belief in a single ultimate and final good, that it is an intellectual product of the feudal organization, which is disappearing.[21] Now, I should not admit that any doctrine, say for instance, that of representative government, is bad because it originated in a system of society which no longer exists. The present worth of any doctrine should be examined on its own merits in the light of present conditions. But the assertion, that the doctrine of a single ultimate and final good does depend upon feudalism, is certainly not true. It is found among ancient and modern thinkers who have not lived under feudalism.

Brought up in the Protestant tradition, Dewey regards the Catholic philosophy of St. Thomas as overthrown. "It is already dim, faded, and remote." But to millions of men, as intellectual as ourselves, it is still the only true philosophy. I do not myself accept the Catholic philosophy and my people have no pleasant memories of the Inquisition. But philosophic issues have to be met in the intellectual arena, and I think St. Thomas and Duns Scotus worthy of more attention than some of our minor contemporaries. Neglect is not a philosophic refutation.

Here a word may be added on the close connection which Dewey sees between experience and democracy. One may share his ardent and lyric devotion to democracy in politics and social life without admitting its relevance to science and philosophy. After all, Archimedes, Copernicus, Galileo, Kepler, Harvey, New-

20. *The Quest for Certainty,* 92 ff.; *Reconstruction,* chap. iii.
21. *Reconstruction,* 162.

ton, Lavoisier, Gauss and a host of others did not live in democracies. Nor can I admit the validity of the current appeal to the common man as the ultimate judge of issues which he has never examined with sufficient care. Indeed, if the views of the common man were satisfactory, why should philosophy as critical reflection have arisen, on Dewey's own theory? When the common man has good sense, or the wisdom of humility, he recognizes his limitations and is willing to learn from those who have devoted more time and attention to philosophy than he has.

Dewey's preoccupation with the human or moral function of science, and his polemic against the spectator or contemplative theory of knowledge, leads to three characteristic instrumentalist doctrines, namely, that knowledge and reflection arise only to enable us to get out of trouble,[22] that science grows out of practical daily needs, and that philosophy is a reflex of the civilization of its period and should be directed to illumine contemporary social problems. These doctrines seem to me partial or half-truths that are misleading in their one-sidedness and in need of serious correction not only for the sake of more accurate truth but also for the sake of that humane liberalism which is at the heart of Dewey's whole intellectual effort.

As to the first point, philosophers and scholars are, doubtless, apt to magnify the rôle that knowledge plays in ordinary experience. But that is no reason for asserting that it is never its own purpose or justification. The desire to know for its own sake, to satisfy idle curiosity, is a fact of human nature. Children show it and adults, too, when not educated or shamed out of it. Common men and good women are interested in ascertaining baseball or football scores or in what was said or done by certain prominent statesmen, by movie stars or even by our less prominent neighbors. We do not always read our daily newspapers, biographies, histories, or works on philosophy for the sake of any application. And sustained reflection or study may occur more often in our leisure than when we are in practical trouble. Indeed, the latter is apt to prove an obstacle to persistent intellectual inquiry.

Invention or progress in science depends on a certain amount of leisure, and freedom from economic or vital pressure. Disin-

22. *Essays,* 20, 73; *Reconstruction,* 23, 30, 53; *Experience and Nature,* 51, 76.

terested curiosity is certainly one of the dominant, if not the dominant, force which leads men to science and makes progress in it possible. The history of many branches of science, such as electricity and magnetism from the days of Thales to those of Gilbert and of Faraday or paleontology from Xenophanes to our own day, shows how remote they were in origin from technologic interests. I am not denying that many problems of mathematics and theoretic physics have in fact been suggested by practical needs and have found useful applications. I am denying the universal proposition that all have been. Moreover, men do not make discoveries even in medical sciences such as pathology solely because they are anxious to relieve human suffering. We cannot solve problems of the pathology or chemistry of disease except by concentrating our attention entirely on the determining factors of the process. To be thinking of the human values of the results would be an irrelevance and therefore a hindrance to the investigation itself. Nor is it even true that men always do or should choose those problems which they think will contribute most to human welfare. Men get interested in certain mathematical, physical, chemical, or biologic problems, in the same way that those with less time and less intellectual equipment get interested in solving conundrums, crossword puzzles, charades, or detective mysteries, the great difference being that the subject-matter and procedure of science is so much richer and sustaining in its interest. To be sure, science today has become a professional occupation; but that does not deny that the great contributors to science, men like Newton, Lavoisier, Cavendish, or Willard Gibbs, have been drawn to it by an inner urge like that which leads men to compose music. And one of the greatest of recent contributors to medical science, Theobald Smith, once declared that, despite his very favorable official position, all the research he ever did was done by stealth. Devotion to science is often an infatuation or love which does not reckon with external consequences.

It cannot be too strongly emphasized that relatively few branches of science have had practical applications; and of many realms, such as the theory of prime numbers or the proof of theorems such as Fermat's, it is hard to imagine how they can possibly ever have any. It is told of a great mathematician that, when he announced the solution of a famous mathematical problem, someone asked him of what use it was, whereat he replied:

"Thank God it has none." A great American physicist is said to have dropped the study of radioactivity when he found it had practical application in medicine. Whether these specific instances are historical or not, I cannot vouch. But they are typical of many men engaged in pure science, who, with the most benevolent attitude to the social needs of their day, still feel ill at ease in the field of applied science where the immediate, the practical, and the approximate rather than the ideal of rigorous accuracy is dominant. In the minds of some men like Einstein the pursuit of science is motivated by what has been called cosmic emotion, which is akin to certain religious feelings that are highly individual and not at all social.

In the light of the foregoing considerations no account of the history of philosophy seems even plausible which neglects the rôle that curiosity about cosmic issues (or Aristotelian wonder) has played in its origin and maintenance. And Dewey seems to me to be straining the facts when he contends "that philosophy originated not out of intellectual but out of social and emotional material."[23] The origin of Greek philosophy is certainly connected with the interest in abstract mathematics and cosmology as distinguished from any technical or social applications. Thales and other Ionian thinkers doubtless had political and economic interests. But there is no evidence that these controlled the direction of their philosophy, or that their thought was dominated by the apologetic attempt to justify existing institutions by harmonizing them with practical knowledge, as Dewey's avowedly malicious account in the first chapter of his *Reconstruction in Philosophy* would have it. Melissus was a successful admiral; but his philosophy came from Parmenides and Zeno, who seem in their metaphysical speculations to have turned their backs on human affairs. Moreover, the exaltation of pure theory is explicitly professed by Aristotle as well as by Plato. It is only in the days of its decline, in later Greek and Roman times, that philosophy became almost entirely concerned with guiding human conduct.

I think it rather important in this connection to challenge the view, fashionable since Hegel, that the philosophy of any period is the reflex of the civilization under which the individual philosophers live. Reflection on the nature of number, time, space,

---

23. *Reconstruction*, 25.

mind, matter, and knowledge do not vary with political and economic views or changes. The outstanding fact is rather that in every age in which there is any philosophy at all relatively few are interested in it, and among them the most divergent views prevail, just as between idealists, realists, and instrumentalists in our own day, not to mention sceptics, mystics, authoritarians, and many others. The common institutions under which the men of a given period live cannot be the sufficient cause for what they do *not* have in common. On the other hand, the elements common to great thinkers of different countries and periods seem far more important for philosophy than those any one of them may share with his contemporaries who opposed or ignored him. Great philosophers speak to all time; only the minor ones are dated. Few generations have been interested in Plato's criticisms of the electoral machinery of the Greek democracies; but his doctrine of Ideas has, for good or ill, stirred men's minds throughout the ages. Kant has more in common with Plato than with Frederick the Great; Hobbes has more in common with Democritus than with Digby; and Bradley is more intimately related to Parmenides or Spinoza than to Herbert Spencer or William James. That which unites ancient and modern sceptics, materialists or idealists, or Hindu, Greek, Hebrew, Arabic, and Christian mystics, is more significant for philosophic truth than the external resemblances which a number of them may have because they lived at the same time. Not only do many philosophers frequently read their ancients more than their contemporaries, but there are certain differences of temper, say between the tough-minded and the tender-minded, which prevail in all ages. Thus many a man has turned to philosophy precisely because he was not like his neighbors or even his brothers absorbed in the passing problems of the day. And Dewey admits this when he condemns them for it, a condemnation which many of them would certainly accept as a tribute to their real wisdom.

It is interesting to note that in a concrete case, namely, as to the difference between Russell's philosophy and his own, he vehemently rejects the explanation in terms of English aristocracy and American democracy and appeals rather to the fact of different intellectual interests, Russell in mathematics, and his own in the experimental method of obtaining knowledge. Even Hegel's view of the state may be far more influenced by the reading of

Aristotle and Luther than by the actual Prussian state with which he came in contact rather late in life.

In this connection I must confess my inability to follow the strange doctrine that "philosophy is occupied with meaning rather than with truth." I find it difficult to reconcile this contention which makes the truth of the great philosophic systems relatively unimportant,[24] with his own persistent effort to refute them. Surely, his objection to them is not that what they have said is meaningless, since as philosophies they are admittedly significant; and in any case the meaningless cannot be refuted. His actual arguments are intended to prove that previous philosophies assert things which are not true, for example, that perception is a form of knowledge. If the method of sound philosophy is that of science, the distinction between the true and the false is the essential question. The difficulty is not removed by making truth play a negative rôle in philosophy. Of course, any philosophy that does not suffer from what Santayana calls near-sighted sincerity must extend its vision beyond the actually verified results of the special sciences. But hypotheses or even imaginative anticipations of the progress of science are true or false. I cannot see how meanings without any claim to possible truth can be the content of even the most speculative, much less empirical philosophy. When we speak of the meaning of the Hellenic çivilization we point to the wider historic antecedents and consequences of Greek institutions. But such historic connections did or did not take place, and assertions about them as well as about the history of philosophy are therefore true or false. And so are those assertions about the wider world which is the subject of philosophy.

II

We come now to the question about the moral value of theoretic science and speculative philosophy pursued for their own sake without regard to their application in human affairs. Orthodox pietists, puritan moralists, and efficiency-minded philosophers are agreed in condemning it as a waste; and to call phi-

24. *Proceedings of the Sixth International Congress of Philosophy, 537, 540.*

losophy an indoor sport commonly passes as a condemnation of it. This is entirely opposed to Dewey's humane ethics. He has impressively, and to my mind convincingly emphasized the importance of sport, play, and art as indispensable for moral sanity.[25] He has repeatedly and quite rightly insisted that by practical he does not mean narrow ends of the bread-and-butter type. And more recently he has disclaimed the intention to subordinate knowledge to action. But I think it is fair to distinguish between an author's conscious intention (of which he is the sole judge) and the bearing of what he has actually said, which is an objective social affair. For words, like arrows, have effects not always identical with the intention of the one who sets them loose. And I do not see how anyone can read Dewey's works without finding explicit as well as implicit subordination of theoretic knowledge to practical moral ends. The following passages seem quite typical. "For in an experience where values are demonstrably precarious, an intelligence that is not a principle of emphasis and valuation (an intelligence which defines, describes, and classifies merely for the sake of knowledge), is a principle of stupidity and catastrophe."[26] An interest in the theory of knowledge for its own sake is characterized as "a luxury and hence a social nuisance and disturber."[27] He rejects the view of the new realism that thinking "is instrumental simply to the knowledge of objects" and insists that it is "instrumental to a control of the environment."[28] Natural science "is something to be pursued not in a technical and specialized way for what is called truth for its own sake, but with the sense of its social bearing, its intellectual indispensableness. It is technical only in the sense that it provides the technique of social and moral engineering."[29] Indeed, his whole *Reconstruction in Philosophy* and the essay on the "Recovery of Philosophy" are devoted to the thesis that philosophy should be "a method of understanding and rectifying specific social ills."[30] He pours his scorn on contemplative surveys of existence, on monkish detachment, on the otiose observer who is

25. *Human Nature and Conduct,* 161.
26. *Influence of Darwin,* 44.
27. *Op. cit.,* 298–299.
28. *Essays in Exp. Logic,* 30.
29. *Reconstruction,* 173.
30. *Op. cit.,* 124.

content to be concerned with things past and done with. "Philosophy is of account only if, like everyday knowing, and like science it affords guidance to action." [31] To study history or to dwell upon the past for its own sake is condemned as a "substitution of the reminiscence of old age for effective intelligence." [32] The spectator view of knowledge is condemned as irresponsible estheticism, "a purely compensatory doctrine," a consolation for those "held back through lack of courage from making their knowledge a factor in the determination of the course of events." [33] If we were to adopt a clever argument of Russell, we might be tempted to say of Dewey that, having by definition ruled out the possibility of contemplative knowledge, its occurrence must be characterized as wicked. But that would not only be unfair but would miss what seems to me the underlying motive, and that is a strong sense of the social responsibility of the philosopher as a condition for making philosophy itself more alive and substantial. I should not wish to deny that social problems can be viewed as offering genuine philosophic issues; I have made some attempts in that direction myself. But I cannot agree that this is the only proper field for philosophic reflection. Taken literally Dewey's attitude on this point, or perhaps more accurately his expressions, would in principle condemn not only pure mathematics and all theoretic science that has not found and may never find any practical application, but also all music and fine art that has not been devoted to influencing the course of social events.

Such impoverishment of human life is obviously far from the intention of one so devoted to the tradition of liberalism. But opposition to the spectator-theory of knowledge, and zeal for social betterment, together with what may without offense be called an Anti-Aristotelian complex, lead Dewey to decidedly illiberal expressions like the foregoing. I do not suppose that he would condemn climbing mountains for the sake of the vistas which we can obtain from their peaks. Why then should he condemn its intellectual analogue or extension, Aristotelian contemplation or theoretic vision, which is the exercise of an intense human energy and adds by its very aloofness a much-needed serene sweetness and noble joy to human life? That the philoso-

31. *Creative Intelligence,* 60.
32. *Creative Intelligence,* 14.
33. *Reconstruction,* 117.

pher, scientist, or artist should subordinate all his thought to the welfare of the community in which he lives is, alas, the demand not only of the increasing number of partisans of the totalitarian state but of popular opinion in our and other democratic countries. In popular education for instance it would subordinate the claim of historic truth to those of patriotism. Hence those interested in the values of the intellectual life must resist the multitude which is ever ready to sacrifice philosophy, pure science and other forms of non-utilitarian learning for all sorts of immediate ends of a petty practical kind. At all times and places combatants in the social conflicts of the day despise the neutral. And the philosopher must often remain neutral in thought if he has a conscientious regard for intellectual integrity and recognizes that neither side has proved its case and that he himself has not sufficient information to decide all the questions at issue. What the various parties in our social conflicts generally demand of the philosopher is not enlightenment (which might possibly dampen the fierce ardor of the struggle) but partisan support; and when the philosopher does that he renders little aid to his party and grievous harm to his philosophy. This does not mean that we may not join any church or political party or other active group with a social program. Being a philosopher no more than being a mathematician, musician, or clergyman excuses one from ordinary domestic, civic, and political obligations. But the special duty of the philosopher is to put the pursuit of truth first whether his fellow citizens are interested or not; and this often requires ethical neutrality or indifference to the issues of the day. It may be well to be sensitive to the needs and problems of those with whom one is associated. But that does not mean that we must yield to the non-philosophic as to what problems are most important. We too are men, and we ought to know that the market-place does not exhaust the whole meaning of life.

As against Dewey's emphasis on the philosopher's participation in the problems of (other) men, I think it necessary to adopt a more critical attitude to the notion of the social responsibility of philosophy, and to the optimistic view of the power of human intelligence, in the face of nature's obstacles. Especially must we realize the limitations of atomic empiricism in social philosophy.

No sensitive spirit can fail to be stirred by Dewey's eloquent plea that we help our fellow men in the bitter struggle for a better world. But what should philosophy do about it? Must one who cannot swim jump into the whirlpool to save a drowning man? Surely it is not one's duty as a philosopher to plunge into the maelstrom of social efforts without adequate knowledge as to what would be a better world and what will actually bring it about. To accept blindly from our fellow men their current attitudes as to what is good or better is certainly not the way to bring them salvation. And surely, an empirical philosopher has no reason to feel that he can easily obtain adequate knowledge to solve all the problems of politics, economics, social hygiene, and other difficulties which have troubled mankind for thousands of years. Dewey is aware of this but boldly asserts: "Better it is for philosophy to err in active participation in the living struggles and issues of its own age and time than to maintain an immune, monastic impeccability." [34] I cannot share this preference. It seems to me foolish for philosophy deliberately to choose to fall into error when it can save itself by suspending judgment by recognizing that the practical necessity for making a choice does not remove our ignorance. Nor does wisdom require us to be frightened by epithets such as monastic, ivory tower, escapist, or compensatory. It is wisdom to leave a room that is filled with suffocating smoke, and in dark ages monasticism kept alive the remnants of civilization. And I should think monastic impeccability far more preferable both for philosophy and social sanity, than adding to the already large fund of error about issues that our fellow men think important.

Philosophy according to Dewey "must deny and eject that intelligence which is naught but a distant eye, registering in a remote and alien medium the spectacle of nature and life." [35] I venture to assert that relatively few sensitive and reflective minds have gone through this world without often feeling alien in its fetid air and needing to escape for a while into a rare and higher atmosphere. "My kingdom is not of this world" is an important element in a truly human life, a redemption from deadly worldliness. And most people do require quasi-monastic conditions in their study in order to engage in concentrated intellectual work which is not possible in the hubbub of crowds. The wisdom of

34. *Essays in Honor of William James*, 77.
35. *Creative Intelligence*, 66.

humility requires that the philosopher should not unduly exalt the importance of his special vocation. But neither should he envy the man of action, the one whose maxim is: "For God's sake, stop theorizing and do something practical!" Nor am I impressed with the argument that philosophers are economic parasites unless they direct their reflection towards practical objectives. We have as much a right to philosophize as to pray, to hear music, or to be spectators at dramatic performances. No one is really paid for philosophizing. Some, though not all, philosophers have been employed as teachers; but I should be surprised to learn that any got excessively rich thereby. The upkeep of philosophers is far from being such a staggering burden on society as to demand serious attention.

Though Dewey would hardly subscribe to Emerson's idealistic Platonism and the doctrine that the over-soul is everything, he shares Emerson's benign attitude in regard to the unconquerable natural ills which have dogged human existence throughout the ages. He rejects the view that our appetites and desires are the manifestations of unruly nature. For that would make democracy impossible.[36] "Man is capable, if he will but exercise the required courage, intelligence, and effort, of shaping his own fate. Physical conditions offer no insurmountable barriers."[37] But, if that were the case, why has not mankind exercised its intelligence to remove the stupid cruelties which darken the lives of men and women in our day as much as ever, in countries that are at peace, as well as those at war? If the cause is not in nature, human or non-human, what is there left but to invoke a supernatural source of evil? We are told to have faith in the active tendencies of the day.[38] But these tendencies may destroy all the values of civilization. As a temporalist Dewey puts the Golden Age in the future rather than in the past. Such hope strengthens men, and it cannot be refuted. But the philosopher who piously visits the cemetery of human hopes may well shake his head. And this attitude is not dismissed by calling it a counsel of despair. There is strength as well as solace in fearlessly looking at things as they are. But in the end no philosophy is really humane, or avoids needless cruelty, unless it recognizes the inevitability of human

36. *Influence of Darwin*, 59.
37. *Reconstruction*, 49.
38. *Op. cit.*, 212.

suffering, defeat, death, and destruction and provides some ano-
dyne through wisely cultivated resignation.

So long as human beings lack omniscience they will lack om-
nipotence and will therefore have to face insuperable difficulties
and evils. The acceptance of the inevitable, ceasing "to kick
against the pricks," seems to me the great wisdom of the old religious teachers who, despite their supernaturalisms, had keen ap-
preciations of the problems of actual living. This does not deny
that all human beings do and should pursue what may, in the
broader sense, be called economic ends, *i.e.,* the increase of the
means for the desirable kind of life. But human beings also have
a craving not only for worship, but for subordinating themselves
so as to avoid the intolerable distraction which often arises when
we have to decide on the basis of imperfect knowledge. Indeed
the history of such movements as Islam or Calvinism shows how
submission can liberate human energies. No man is as happy and
energetic as the one who is a glad slave to his beloved, whether it
be a person or a great impersonal cause. For this reason it would
be hazardous to deny that human beings have probably derived
as much happiness from accepting their lot as from efforts, so
often tragically vain, to improve it.

I am familiar with the argument that if we abandoned all
forms of resignation and strenuously devoted ourselves instead
to the improvement of actual conditions there would be no need
for resignation. But this seems to me wishful thinking requiring
much more evidence than has ever been offered for it. Doubtless
there is such a thing as unwise submission. But who will deny
that there is also an unwise obstinacy in refusing to accept our
limitations and thus wasting life in efforts that are fruitless if not
worse? We in America are especially in need of realizing that
perpetual motion is not the blessed life and that the hustlers may
not be the only ones, nor perhaps even the first, to enter the kingdom of heaven. I am not arguing against the necessity of effort
and work. But I do want to suggest a doubt about any moral
system that is too social and does not recognize the just claims of
rest, of vacations from the strenuous life, of retreats or escapes if
you like, from the depressing horrors of the human scene and its
brutal struggles. Like other intellectual workers the philosopher
must break away from the crowd, even as Jesus, filled with compassion for the multitude, retires alone to the mountain to pray.

Why should philosophy deny us any private nook in this wide universe which the soul may for a while call its own?

Dewey's optimism is based on a "positive respect for human nature when the latter is associated with scientific knowledge." [39] He greatly admires Bacon, who is frequently praised for his efforts to free philosophy from idle speculation and logic-chopping and to bring it down to man's business and bosoms, so that knowledge of nature may become a power for human welfare. But Bacon's Utopia of many men working to advance man's control of nature has been largely realized in the many researches which apply modern science to machinery. And the result has certainly not been free from new horrors (in peace as well as in war) added to human life thereby. Dewey, of course, is aware of some of the failures of the Baconian Utopia, but he discounts these as due to our relative inattention to the problem of control of human nature [by whom?] which he expects to be solved by our social sciences.[40] He seems to assume a relative neglect of the latter as the source of our evils. But it seems to me that since Bacon's day politics, economics, and ethics have received much more attention than physics. And the argument, that past social studies have not been sufficiently scientific, does not warrant the uncritical assumption that present social studies or any that we are likely to attain in the near future can be sufficiently advanced to solve our fundamental human difficulties. Such a degree of progress in science does not depend simply upon our willingness to follow one or other method. We are faced with insuperable difficulties. Moreover, when men do learn about the forces which control human nature the results are sometimes even more frightful. The psychology of persuasion as practiced by such eminently successful masters as Herr Hitler or Father Coughlin has shown that the constant and skillful repetition of demonstrable falsehoods is a far more effective way of influencing masses of men and women than any fair argument based on truth. These observations may be denounced as cynical, but any philosophy that ignores them smacks of the wisdom of the ostrich.

In his more sober moods Dewey is less optimistic, but still insists on active effort as the only way. And he claims that such

39. *Human Nature and Conduct,* 4.
40. *Characters and Events* (ed. Ratner), 719.

effort means something to the universe at large.[41] But that can hardly be established on an empirical basis. Nature seems quite indifferent to our human values. It gives us birth and sometimes joy, but also tragic disharmonies in our minds and bodies. In the end it kills all we love. It destroys in one moment all the work of the hard years. Poverty, disease, insanity, and abysmally stupid viciousness, prevail in all societies and mock man's pretension to be a god on earth. We cannot by thinking add a cubit unto our stature, not even stop the progress of cancerous growths, of arterial sclerosis, or of senescence, much less the rotation of the earth. Knowledge does not always help us to control the future. We often foresee the inevitable without being able to stop it. It is not lack of courage but real wisdom to recognize our limitations in the face of the larger world of nature that is not of our own making. The theory that we know only what we create or make[42] would, if consistently carried out, deny any knowledge of the world and of those who brought us into it. We cannot create the world into which we come. Indeed if we could not be mere spectators to events beyond our control, neither Dewey nor any one else could report evils without being responsible for what happened. In wiser moments Dewey, like James, recognizes that our vision extends beyond our manual reach or control, and that vision is itself an intense form of life.

Though Dewey himself is naturally interested in the analysis of general ideas such as the nature of the individual or the state, his distrust of universals makes him at times scorn all attempts to refine our "general concepts of institutions, individuality, state, freedom, law, order, progress, etc."[43] Especially does he turn his back on all discussions as to the nature of the *summum bonum* or ultimate good. He advocates instead concentration on the removal of specific evils. I think that this prevents him from formulating any adequate theoretic guide, any Ariadne thread out of the labyrinthian mazes of experience which philosophy should offer if it is to be of any help in the analysis of diverse social problems. Impressed with the difference of opinion among philosophers in regard to abstract questions, he seems to think that we can get more agreement on specific issues.[44] This seems to me to

41. *Experience and Nature*, 420.
42. *Op. cit.*, 428.
43. *Reconstruction*, 193; *cf.* 188, 190, 192.
44. *Op. cit.*, 165.

ignore the intensity with which people do divide on specific social issues. If theorists do not agree (because in fact they do not
want to), the disinclination comes from practical life rather than
from pure theory. Moreover, we can get little help from the maxim
that every situation must determine its own concrete good.[45] The
world does not break itself up into a number of distinct atomic
situations each with a determinate good. That which will remove
some economic evil may bring about worse political ones, and
vice versa. And we have no common unit to measure heterogene-
ous social values. This defeats the counsel to remove one evil at a
time. Nor do we get very far by saying that what is good in any
situation cannot be answered *a priori* but depends on actual conditions, if we have no guide as to the nature of the dependence.

In one phase of his thought, in his faith in progress, Dewey
does attempt a general formula as to the *summum bonum,* and
that is that growth is the only moral good. But, since all sorts of
viciousness also grow and spread, this formula offers us no discriminating test. And what on this view *is* the moral end for
those who are in homes for the incurable or are losing their
means of support, their health, or are dying too slowly under
helpless conditions? "Let us do the best we can," is meaningless,
if we have no idea as to what *is* best or how it can be found.

It would be absurd to charge Dewey with being altogether in-
sensitive to the values of enjoyment. But his writings do not seem
to appreciate the classic values of solitude. His psychology is too
behavioristic and social. He places too much emphasis on being
continually on the go, without regard to the places whereto it is
worth while to go in order to stay rather than merely to pass
through. This is analogous to the attitude which leads him to
suppose that physical science has banished the idea of substance
in developing the idea of function. In any case, against his view
that rest and enjoyment are to be viewed as merely re-creational
or instrumental for further activity, I think we should recognize
that they are ends in themselves and that life would not be worth
anything without them. Contrary to his explicit denial, I should
still maintain that many activities that are instrumental in enabling us to attain the things we enjoy, are still dreary and depressing. That indeed is the condition under which most men
work in order to procure the things that make life worth while

45. *Op. cit.,* 163.

for themselves and their families. It does not prove anything to say that enjoyments, or, in his own terminology, "consummatory values," that are not also instrumental will turn to dust and ashes in our mouths.[46] All life and activity will also do that in the course of our mortality. Rest is no more merely a means of activity, than peace is merely a means to war.

Throughout the ages, wise men have cultivated philosophical reflection regardless of its bearing upon the social struggle, not because they were cowardly or lazy members of a class of economic parasites, but because they recognize that in the pursuit of cosmic truth we are least subject to the uncertain turns of fortune and least likely to make others as well as ourselves suffer from the results of sowing vain hopes.

I must not conclude this ungracious task of devil's advocate without reiterating my profound conviction that in these days of morbid and deadly irrationalism John Dewey is rendering inestimable service in maintaining the liberal faith in enlightenment, based on free thought. But my criticism is not directed so much against his positive efforts as against incidental negations due to his unfortunate polemic against classical philosophy or to insufficient emphases on the things that are not in the center of his interests. The zeal which has actuated moralists and humanists aims at persuasion, at making others join our church or party rather than to suspend judgment where the evidence is inadequate. Ardor for social reform is admirable in any one, but detachment and a critical attitude are the special duties of those who as scientists or philosophers have to maintain the canons of intellectual integrity. Too often has devotion to temporal causes turned philosophical light into partisan heat. And Dewey surely agrees that we need to keep in mind the words of Emerson: He serves all who dares be true.

46. *Experience and Nature*, 365.

Appendix 2
Dewey's Concepts of Experience and Nature
By William Ernest Hocking

Ten years ago, when Mr. Dewey was only seventy years old, a session of the Association meeting in this place was devoted to a phase of his philosophy. I seem to remember reading a paper at that session in which I recounted the tragedy of thirty-two years occupied in refuting Dewey while Dewey remained unconscious of what had happened!

I have now a different and happier report to make. Not, I hasten to say, that Dewey has changed, but that I have largely ceased to read him with polemical intent: I read him to enjoy him. In this I succeed far better, in fact I am almost completely successful! Only, the question continues to trouble me whether Dewey, if he knew about this, would regard it as an improvement on my part or as a retrogression.

Let me enlarge briefly on this parable.

Experience, as Dewey says, consists in the first instance not of highly theorized contents, but of things *had and enjoyed*. And even highly theorized contents, sciences, and philosophies, in so far as they are among the facts of the world, we must also as empiricists count among the objects to be, first of all, had and enjoyed. Dewey suggests that he can take even a transcendental philosophy that way, as well as all the (other?) dreams, illusions, enthusiasms, superstitions of the race. For every mode of thought and feeling has its history; it has been begotten somewhere and somehow; there is a motivation which attends its genesis and its continued seat in the minds of active men. In brief, there is a factual *psychological englobement* of the theory, which is bound to be instructive because it is human; and by way of this englobement, empiricism becomes or should become the most hospita-

[First published in *Philosophical Review* 49 (March 1940): 228–44. For Dewey's reply, see this volume, pp. 141–54.]

ble of all attitudes of the mind. All modes of thinking, feeling, speculating, fancying, believing, come to an ultimate democracy on this level of experience.

I am reminded that Kant introduced a similar democracy, but from a different angle. When he said that the "I-think" can always be prefixed to any notion we may entertain, he defined the *logical englobement* of ideas, or what has since been called the "logo-centric predicament." Dewey's empiricism makes in substance the same remark; but the "I-think" (or "they-think") which Dewey can always prefix is not a mere logical point of reference; it is a bit of history having its date, and arising in the quandary of an actual thinker and doer; it defines the psychological[1] englobement of that notion or thought.

On the face of it, this addition of the psychological "I-think" gives us a completer view of the whole situation. But—and here is the puzzle—with the addition *something seems to have escaped.* To assert "John is a rascal" is less complete than to say "I think John is a rascal," but it is more forceful: the prefix "I think" may relieve me from an action for libel, because in telling the truth more circumspectly it withdraws the force of assertion from the outer world. Just because we can all take Zen Buddhism as one of the empirical shapes of human self-discipline it falls short of the way Zen Buddhism would like to be taken. And if I halt at the point of taking Dewey's philosophy that way, as a mode of thought to be had and enjoyed in its psychological englobement, I am paying it less than its due respect. Just because the psychological "I-think" (or "he-thinks" or "they say") is a sun which shines equally on the just and on the unjust, it is an absolute which evades the battle. If we examine the psychology of the teacher in the moment of his teaching, his motive contains the paradoxical demand that the personal and historical origins of his propositions shall be forgotten, and that his teaching be taken in its naked propositional force.

Thus when we celebrate today the eightieth birthday of John Dewey, we do so because Dewey's philosophy is not merely a philosophy thought out today and yesterday by John Dewey, but also a majestic body of thought to which the years and their

---

1. The biological englobement, fundamental in Dewey's thought, may be taken as implied in this term; "historical englobement" might be used to cover both.

story are irrelevant. If I may venture the paradox, what makes history important is that it englobes something superhistorical; the *meaning of the particular is in the universal*.[2] This is the substance of what I shall here try to illustrate, by way of comment on Dewey's concepts.

I shall begin with the concept of Experience.

I. Experience

In the second edition of his Carus Lectures, Dewey abandons the remark that experience is a weasel word, and says instead that experience is a double-barrelled idea. This change implies, I think, an improvement in the moral status of the weasel; a residue of his duplicity has seemed on reflection to be worth keeping. In the undivided totality which experience is, there can be distinguished (1) a stuff of experience and (2) a way of dealing with it. We never know what experience is by simply knowing the grist fed into the mill of perception. Somebody has "gone through the experience" of having smallpox or has "had the experience" of trying to climb Mount Everest; in such expressions we habitually denote the experience by its subject-matter; but the question of interest is, *How did he take it?* Did he whine through it? did he "get a kick out of it"? did he make something of it? is there a *story* in it?

Why should any experience give rise to a story? Because a given stuff may be *taken* in an incalculable variety of ways. The physician's case-record of the smallpox patient, or the log of the expedition, makes no story; but in the way this stuff is taken there is emotion, imagination, moral and esthetic meaning; and the true empiricist will include all this, because it is all *there*. Experience is a grist interfused with the way of taking it.

The grist itself has to be understood as that which we mean to be dealing with; and since we mean to be dealing with *things* and not with *sensa,* with chairs rather than with odd perceptions, shapes, colors, experience is of *things*. In calling attention to the "doing and suffering" which make experience, Dewey has no in-

---

2. This is but a half-truth. It is also true that the universal means the particular. I want here to emphasize the fact that "meaning" is a two-way conception.

tention of dissolving its objects into perceptions. Men "do and suffer" farming (for example): but they experience not only farming but the farm, the fields, the wood-lots, the stock, the implements, the weather, the crops. Experience is the inseparable engagement of the objects of our concern with the concern, the beings loved and hated with the loving and hating.

(So far, I think I am on the ground of Dewey's conception; and I believe I shall be still within his meaning if I make a simple inference. The objects of experience blend into their own backgrounds; as we experience things, we experience the setting of things. Some of these backgrounds—like space and time—are common backgrounds; and the common setting of all things having such common backgrounds is briefly describable as "nature." If this is the case, we establish one point in the relation between the conceptions of "experience" and "nature," namely that nature is a persistent object, a constant in all experience. Experience is *of nature*, as incorporated into our doings and carings; or, Experience is our doing and caring "penetrating into nature and expanding through it.")

It is this undivided totality which for Dewey is the beginning and ending of all thinking: it is near to what some of our Continental brethren have been calling the "Concrete," and some others "*Existenz*"; and if I am not mistaken it is akin to what Muensterberg once called "*die reine Erfahrung.*"

II. Thought as a Function within Experience

Now, for Dewey, thought is a function within experience, understood in this concrete fashion.

As I understand the contrast which he wishes to make between his way of thinking and other ways, it lies here: he points out that thought always has a working relation to its beginning and ending in gross experience; it has something to resolve and to clarify through its task of enquiry; and *what thought is* must be judged by that temporal function.

It is for this reason that Dewey regards scientific method as exemplary for philosophy also.

For the theoretical journey of science is everywhere understood to be a part of experience: it debouches in experience; its terminal wire is well grounded. If the conceptions devised in this journey hold good, they provide control of the course of events and also an enlargement of the meaning of the plainest of plain facts. Philosophical thought ought to have the same kind of rôle: it should be applicable to experience and testable by experience; it should enlarge the meaning of experience. And *its* conceptions have "reality"—if we wish to use this dangerous term—(or "validity" if we do not) (and I do, because the substitutes are worse)— only because and in so far as they fulfil these conditions.

Lumping together scientific and philosophic thought, we might, I believe, resume the position as follows. Thought is a function within experience, engaged in *remaking experience* by enlarging our resources for the understanding and control of nature (*i.e.*, for our ways of *taking* the grist); and there is no "reality" outside this process with which either experience or thought have anything to do.

And this conception of the work of thought adds an important trait to the conception of experience. Experience is a history in which the world (including nature itself, so far as it is "incorporated into our doings and carings") is being progressively remade by thought. The sardonic comment of Karl Marx to the effect that "philosophers have been engaged in interpreting the world, whereas the task is to change it," is here met by the doctrine that to interpret the world in a truly empirical sense *is to change it*.

III. Emerging Questions

The only apology I can offer to Mr. Dewey and to you for so truncated an exposition, or for any exposition at all, is an instrumental apology; I had to avow the jumping-off place for the comments I now have to offer.

With the conceptions of experience and nature so far sketched out I am in general agreement. These conceptions have a good cutting edge, and most of what is cut away and rejected by them seems to me worthy of rejection. They exclude any scheme which sets up a result of analysis as candidate for the honorific position of "the real," in the sense of the unit of all being. The sense-datum, the physical object, the mental state considered as "idea," the neutral entity, the eternal entity or essence, are all alike disqualified for *this* ambitious rôle. Analysis surely has something to do in philosophy as well as in science; but it is not to discover the metaphysical atom.

I agree also that the philosopher's balloon must confess the circumstances of its flight, and that once ascended it must not anchor itself in the sphere of the fixed stars. Unless it returns to do work in the world it left, and in the same situation as launched its voyage of enquiry, it affords no answer to *that* question.

Dewey's work has been so well done, that some of his propositions which were contentious in his youth have become almost the axioms of the world of his mature age. But our fraternity, for whom the play of thought is the most germane expression of our seriousness, needs continually to be reminded of the profound human stake in the issues with which we deal, and owes perennial gratitude to the man who has so unswervingly done that reminding.

The point at which I tend to diverge from the conceptions as stated has to do, first, with the relation between experience and reality, and second with the relation between the products of thought and that same reality. I begin to feel this divergence in Dewey's account of the meaning of scientific method; let me then first say a few words about that.

Scientific questioning and answering have the virtues which Dewey attributes to them; they arise (ultimately) from gross experience and report back to the same sort of situation in which they arose. But, *en route,* the process is intellectualized to the last limit. The question is altered so as to refer to a body of existing theory; it reads, How must this theory be amended or developed to provide for phenomenon X? And experience is interfered with, so that a single sense-datum will provide a straw looking to an answer. Experiment may be defined as an arrangement of controllable events such that a terminal sense-fact shall *mean a verdict of life or death to a theory.* That terminal sense-fact, pointer-reading or what not, stands at the extremest distance which any grist of experience can reach *from immediacy,* or from that minimal cognitive burden which "gross experience" carries.

And this disparity between starting point and the consummatory moment of answer-getting is the *peculiarly scientific thing.* Refined, and ever more refined, speculation is there embedded in the course of facts, and there is no way to un-embed it! The weight of bodies near the earth continues to mean, for our experience, terrestrial gravitation, until we get a better theory. There are to be sure three ways of escaping awareness of this meaning: forgetfulness, the artificial naïveté of the artist, the acquired integrity of the mystic. But these anodynes are passing, and the mischief done by the scientist remains; for by the nature of his calling, he is transforming experience for all mankind; we all suffer the fate of having to see things through his eyes. That is why science is front-page news for our time and henceforth.

My point is that this highly theorized moment of cognitive contemplation in which the fact means the theory is, to my mind, the characteristically scientific moment, rather than that flood of subsequent moments in which gross experience is lifted by the improved theory to a new level for all mankind. And it is so, I believe, because science in crowding the maximum of theory into the narrowed flux of event supposes itself to be coming nearer to the goal we call "reality," rather than removing us from it.

This brings me to my main enquiry, that of the relation between experience and reality.

(Idealistic metaphysics is supposed to have a vested interest in denying reality to the conceptual terms in which physical equations are couched, physical substances of whatever sort, atoms, electrons, positrons, or what not, and in indicating that these entities mean simply calculable relations between moments of overt experience. The fine-spun theoretical mesh of physics means no more and no less than precise reliability in succession; its particular terms are in a literal sense "constructions," not reals. And contemporary physics is inclined to accept the idealist analysis to the extent of saying that it has no interest in non-phenomenal reals, but only in the validity of predictions. In this respect, Dewey's concept of experience is congenial to idealism, and I find myself beginning to dissent at precisely the point in which idealism is in general most swift to agree.)

IV. Experience and Reality

"Reality" like "experience" is a weasel word; but, also like "experience," it is better to call it double-barrelled.

In one sense it is coextensive with experience. Everything which enters experience, whether physical object, feeling, illusion, dream, system of metaphysics, is real as experienced, *i.e.*, in its psychological englobement. And on this level of reality, cognition, as Dewey has rightly insisted, has no privileged place.

In the other sense, "reality" is an *object of search,* and, by that sign, not on the surface; and certainly not identical with whatever is had and enjoyed. In this sense the "real" is in contrast to whatever puts up a false show of self-sufficiency, and (to be dogmatic for brevity) may be defined as *independent being, on which other being depends.* It is an inescapable concept simply because this relation of dependence is itself a matter of experience; we keep finding out that things which look, and may feel to themselves, independent (as we ourselves feel in our more robust moments) are not so, but depend on something else.

In so far as things depend on the real, it *explains* them; and conversely, whoever seeks explanation seeks the real, whether under that name or under some other name he may like better. Since independence is a matter of degree, and C may depend on B, while B in turn depends on A, there are *degrees of reality.* And since there are degrees of reality, there may be degrees of approach to reality; enquiry might conceivably approach reality forever without reaching it.

In so far as enquiry moves toward understanding (as distinct from mere description) it moves by definition toward the real; its organ for so moving is "hypothesis" or "theory."[3] Hence follows the dictum: *the more theory the nearer reality.* This is in direct contrast with the rule: the more thought the more artificial the construction and the more subjective the result. It is in direct contrast with the whole Kantian assumption that whatever is categorized by the mind is by that fact altered or veiled away from the condition of the thing-in-itself. Philosophies evidently split at this point.

The philosophies of Dewey, Bradley and Bergson, diverse as they are, agree in this one respect, that they all distrust conceptual judgment as arriving at reality. For Dewey, as I read him, the man who in a moment of insight leaps to an hypothesis which

---

3. By definition this is cognitive enquiry. Cf. Schilpp, 525.

afterwards proves to be valid is not at that *happy moment of successful induction* in any particularly close contact with reality; the truth of his achievement only arrives as its value appears, in the full process whereby it is (1) verified and (2) shows its power to bring about adaptations, controls, integrations. The other alternative, to which I adhere, is that the moment of insight is without further process a moment of grasping reality. The more theory, if it is true theory, the more reality. Let me develop this point.

Accepting the maxim that the ingredients of experience are first *had* and then *thought about,* this subsequent thinking deals in general with the enquiries "What is this object?" "On what does it depend?" In the course of these enquiries, which are always pertinent, the relative immediacy of the experience of "having" is lost; the immediate becomes charged with "mediation." This is a definite change within experience, a psychological change; the boy's experience of the locomotive as somehow understood is far removed from his first admiring impression of dark concentrated might. But this psychological change must be compatible with the identity of the object as meant throughout the enquiry, otherwise the enquiry is not *about something.* Hence the maxim: The psychological non-identity of the immediate and the mediated must be compatible with their objective identity.

(Psychological history, so far as it is cognitive, is, on this showing, always grappling with a relatively non-historical object. Now is this relatively unchanging object merely meant, or believed in, or *is it observed?* Dewey is ready to say, if the object is a chair, and my psychological history as I walk around it and have many perspectives is still taken as a changing experience of the same physical thing, that I observe *this thing.* He is ready to take this into the total of gross experience, and regards the analysis which severs the perspectives from that of which they are perspectives as a vicious and unreal kind of empiricism from which he wishes to depart. But, if the object is a molecule in the wood of the chair, or an atom in the molecule, or an electron in the atom, Dewey will not say that I observe that, but only that I think it. I agree. But is the atom, then, less real than the chair which I observe? The difference seems to be simply this: that the single chair, which

I at no time see, is assigned an invariant position in *space;* and I am inseparably aware of space with my awareness of the several perspectives. I have no such direct intuition of the atom as explanatory of the many actual aspects of the chair. Nevertheless, the atom has, not a place, nor a region, but a spatial reference, and is at least as real as the chair, and on the same ground; there is a variety of phenomena which depend on it, and which it "explains" or unifies; with reference to them it is the independent being and the independent variable; it endures through their changes.)

I am prepared to carry this principle to its consequences. For example, in spite of the impossibilities of imagination into which we are led by recent advances in physics, I must maintain (as against such operationalists as Bridgman) that the reality with which we are concerned lies not in the operations or eventualities but in the entities whose behavior responds to our differential equations. It is quite evident that we have not yet finished defining those entities, or formulating our equations; but this is very different from saying that there are no such entities. There is no way of building up a philosophy which believes in the overt phenomena of gross experience and disbelieves in the X's indicated by the intermediate theoretical structure. Operationalism is a counsel of despair where despair is not allowable; and, however congenial such philosophies may be to the subjective temper, we must decline their comfort.

That Dewey is unwilling to follow the subjectivist way of escape he has amply indicated. He states his belief, for example, that there is a physical world which antedates the arrival of consciousness, and to some extent conditions that arrival; this is to give credence to thought as providing an outlook on reality beyond the reach of observation and indeed of possible verification.

But the consequences of accepting the two principles I have here put forward—(1) the more thought the more reality; (2) the objective identity of mediate and immediate—are far-reaching. One of these consequences is that, if theory severs the original amalgam of experience and nature into two aspects, the mental and the physical, that *severance must be accepted* as a better version of truth. It divides the original unity, but it is a step toward the real, not away from it.

V. The Mental and the Physical

Now my belief is that theory does require this separation, and that Descartes was on a true scent when he made it as sharp as he did. Dewey and Whitehead agree in making Descartes responsible for much of the modern metaphysical confusion. He split asunder what experience had joined together. And since mind was in his view not body, and body was not mind, he had to attempt a mending of his world out of materials which would not take his solder. Not alone could mind not affect body, nor body mind; the possibility of knowledge became dubious, and a whole host of artificial problems sprang up which a true empiricism would never encounter. Dewey's philosophy has as one of its main motives the rejection of these sophistic puzzles.

I wish that I could accept this liberation from the metaphysical burden. Chinese philosophy has been celebrated by some of its exponents because it has never sundered mind and body, matter and spirit. My own feeling is that it is to that extent an undeveloped philosophy; it has not suffered the pain of dualism, and it will be unable, until it has done so, to work its way toward a remedy. We cannot solve our metaphysical problems by preventing them from arising. We cannot reject the analysis of water into hydrogen and oxygen solely on the ground that it is much better for drinking purposes in its undivided state.

The principle which required the Cartesian distinction was not due to Descartes; it was embedded in the new science. It was nothing less than the modern conception of causality. The resolve to clear final causes out of our theories of nature carried all the other consequences with it. What replaced final cause was a causality which required (and could use) *no goal* because the next stage of events was always completely determined. This new and severely self-sufficient mode of scientific description was supposed (at first) to be a sort of *identity in change;* cause and effect were equal in amount, and to be equal in amount they had to be alike in kind. But where there is complete likeness of kind (an ideal which reached its completion in the description of all physical change as flux of energy) *quality cancels out of the equations,* and we are dealing perforce with pure mathematics; in the real world of modern physics the differential equations (including constants and coefficients) describe all that happens.

It is just this neat result which has been the charter of liberty to scientific speculation, at the same time that it has been fraught with profound metaphysical embarrassment. One of its first implications in this field was the "bifurcation of nature"; for, if the qualities of nature are no part of the business of scientific description, these qualities find themselves relegated to the subjective, and the integral Nature of experience is split in two, primary properties in the real, secondary in the mental appearance. Against this bifurcation, Berkeley made the first ringing protest; then Hegel; then Fechner; then Dewey; then Whitehead. Dewey's expressions on this point seem to me the most vigorous and eloquent as well as the most extreme; for he would put back into Nature not alone colors, sounds, tastes and smells, but qualities commonly ascribed to feeling: beauty, ugliness, loveliness, terribleness, and the like.

He can do this, in part, because he detaches these properties from subjectivity—at least from the subjectivity of the private mind—and allows to Nature the impersonal possession—I will not say enjoyment—of traits which earlier centuries could conceive only in terms of the individual subject.

Now all these protests against mutilating Nature are well justified; they recall us to sanity of judgment both about what unsophisticated experience is, and about what we mean by Nature. But the various remedies of the scandal of bifurcation miss fire, I believe, because of a misconception of the difficulty.

This difficulty appears most patent when we try to explain *perception* in terms of the physical order as an effect of qualityless causes. We can explain everything except the qualities which appear in perception; that is, we can explain everything except the only thing that matters; that is, we do not and cannot explain perception at all in these terms.

But then it may occur to us with some relief that the modern conception of causal order *was not intended* to do this work. Its whole function has been to formulate quantitative aspects of sequence. In this it has been a complete success. And this is all we should have expected from it. Those mathematical relationships are valid: and in so far as this is the case, the theoretical construction which gives the terms of our equations is a move toward "reality."

It would indeed be an error to dignify this construction with the name of "*the real*," which would be to assert that this mathematical order could exist by itself. This claim science does not make, for it does not raise the question. This error *was made;* and all the metaphysical difficulties we have mentioned followed from it.

The remedy lies in recognizing (1) that the qualityless and desiccated Nature is an abstraction from full and concrete reality; but also (2) that this abstraction has an invaluable significance for the life of the mind. The remedy does not lie in the Berkeleian direction, of refusing to space and its substance-contents any relative autonomy. Nor does it lie (if I am right) in the direction taken by Dewey and Whitehead, of ascribing to Nature a plenum of qualities commonly regarded as mental. It lies rather in recognizing that this very autonomy of Nature, its impersonality and exactitude, its absence of quality and sense, are requisites for the free life of the mind; and are themselves to be understood as dependent aspects of a total mental life.

For observe—an old observation—: unless there is a realm of regular nature, no habits can be built, no cumulative mental mastery of Nature be accomplished. And then an observation not so old: unless there is a realm of being, empty of life and quality, impersonal and desiccated, we could not plow a field nor fell a tree without the sense of destroying life and value. The moral freedom to exploit nature is the requisite background for the moral unfreedom to exploit one another. There is thus a positive meaning in the existence of a realm of the meaningless; and, in this sense, a perception of the meaninglessness of physical nature is a radical step toward an idealist interpretation of reality.

Thus the scandal of bifurcation is only genuinely repaired by a type of objective idealism (still to be worked out in detail); and the extraordinary generosity with which contemporary naturalism enriches the concept of Nature with the attributes of the soul (which I might irreverently describe as a sort of give-away!) is striking evidence of the need for such a philosophy.

VI. Experience as Dialectical

Let me now in conclusion recur briefly to the concept of experience, and to the place of thought in experience.

Thought is indeed an enquiry devoted to the resolving of problematic situations; it is also true that thought often creates the dilemmas which further thinking has to resolve. The abstraction of nature from experience was one of those thought-begotten dilemmas. The historical conception of thinking will recognize some of these dilemmas as natural, perhaps inevitable, stages of growing insight; and such recognition is the source of the "dialectic" in its modern form, according to which experience *is* dialectical. Experience, in being remade by thought, is remade in a certain order of cumulative meaning.

I should like to recommend a view of the "dialectic" as an empirical method in philosophy, a sort of *consecutive induction*. In its simplest form it is a succession of hypotheses about the nature of the world, each one tested in experience, each one in turn found inadequate and replaced by a better one, when mankind has been fortunate enough to find a thinker. It assumes racial persistence in continuing its metaphysical enquiry; its nerve is that there is a reality to be apprehended by thought, and that thinking may under favorable conditions continue to approach it.

(In its more detailed form, the reporters of the dialectical progress of mankind have been prone to point out that new hypotheses tend to arrive, not in a sporadic or linear fashion, but commonly in pairs of contrasting views, as if thought in exploring a distinction in experience, as between universal and particular, mind and matter, fact and value, lost its balance and became partisan on two sides at once. Thus, as Dewey has well pointed out, the same situation (Descartes' dualism) produced the subjectivist and the materialist movement in philosophy; and again the same situation which permitted the spread of Hegelianism begot the revolt of the Left Wing and the Marxian version of history.)

But let these formal peculiarities of experience as a thinking process be what they will; what I wish now to consider is the temporal *arrival* of that thinking. Is it possible that the dialectic should reach a goal? And that experience should thereby contain an element which is not transitional? My belief is that two things can be said of the dialectic of experience: it never arrives and it is always arriving.

It never arrives in the sense that its task is finished, the last hypothesis verified, and interest in the temporal aspect of thought thereby lost. Since every idea by its nature is a member of the total system of ideas, to experiment with any idea is to experiment with the system; in this sense all ideas are undergoing experiment all the time. On the other hand, *truth is reached;* and all truth is in one sense eternal truth. We have only to consider how revolting a world it would be if all insight and valid judgment were reserved for those who come in at the end of an infinite time-series, that is, who never come at all, to perceive that this is not the world we live in. There is a sense, and I can quote Dewey for it, in which we *know;* that is, knowing is an experience which is *had.* But if it is knowing which is had, and not merely supposing we know, then in some sense there is *certainty and absolute knowledge,* for in this phrase the adjective "absolute" merely emphasizes without changing the fact.

There is a difference which every man knows by experience between believing it probable that something is so and seeing that it *must be so.* We do have the occasional experience of perceiving necessity; and when we have it, the time-process has produced something free of time. This is, in fact, the normal result of experimentation. The Egyptians did a lot of good experimentation with astronomy and surveying; then the Pythagoreans saw the law of the hypotenuse, and further experimentation became at once superfluous. Once we see that the diagonals of a square must be equal, to continue measuring them to see if they are equal is a sign not of intelligence but of stupidity.

We experiment with many a more complicated object in which certitude is difficult. We are experimenting, for example, with democracy. We have not made a complete success of democracy. Some have given it up as a bad job, and are experimenting with something radically different. Now if our attitude toward the matter were purely empirical, we could have no manner of objection to having anyone experiment with anything, for instance, with killing off the surplus population, as one humanitarian old Pharaoh is said to have done by throwing 80,000 beggars into a quarry, both for their sake and for that of the survivors. Why not? A simon-pure empiricism should admit the possibility that any effect might come from any cause; the singing of a tea-kettle may cause the grain to sprout in the fields. But *we do not believe it;* nor do we believe that rulers who cannot rule without frequent purgings of party and army and populace are on the right scent. That is, *we are not pure empiricists.* If our version of democracy is not working too well, we shall not try the full totalitarian program; we shall try another version of democracy. There is a *lurking conviction which guides the choice of the next hypothesis.* Something about democracy, we fancy, is necessary. That something is not expressed in the supposed axiom that "all men are created equal." But there may be a better formula; some kind of equality is assumed in conversation, in small groups of friends, in coöperation of all sorts; and if we could capture *that* we might have the key to the larger equality. We can abandon any formula for our absolute; we cannot abandon the thing itself without being swung back to it. The principle which has been appealed to in discourse that there are some propositions which we cannot deny without in some way implying their affirmation, and that such propositions must be true—this principle has its experimental expression, illustrated in this compulsory return to some incorporation of equality. Such compulsory return is the experimental sign of an absolute, hidden but doing its work, and some day we shall see it; and it will then appear to us as an *a priori* truth.

Our philosophical era has, I believe, accepted too easily a defeatist attitude in regard to its certainties. Having to surrender a formula, it has surrendered its meaning. And this is serious, for it is essential that truth be cumulative; and it cannot accumulate unless something of what is achieved can *last.* Our concept of experience then will be incomplete unless it contains this element of stability, this backbone. Vitality indeed requires that even the backbone have its metabolism; and our certitudes are perhaps best held, less in the shape of inflexible axioms, than in the shape of that persistent and mystical sense of direction in the succession of our hypotheses which is the secret of induction, and— shall we say?—the spinal cord of experience.

Appendix 3
Dr. Dewey's Stand Disputed
Binghamton Ban on Rugg Social Science Textbooks Is Approved

To the Editor of the *New York Times:*

Dr. John Dewey of Columbia University has a letter in the *Times* in which he admits that "any elected body of representatives has the right to look into the methods and practices in force in schools supported by public taxation."

But he senses a vagueness that he does not like about the pending State investigation into the New York public school system, and that of the Dies committee into the political and social affiliations of the nation's textbook writers. And he speaks of the recent removal of the Rugg Social Science textbooks from the public schools of Binghamton, N.Y. "at the instigation of the president of the New York State Economic Council, Inc.," as itself "subversive of the best public interest."

If the Rugg Social Science textbooks, which are intended for children of the impressionable ages of 12 to 15, were limited to presenting the theories of Karl Marx, Lenin and Trotsky, there might be some who would approve such a course; although most persons would not agree that such young persons were competent to appreciate the respective merits of various social systems, or, even if they were competent, that junior high schools are a proper place to teach them.

Collectivism Seen as Aim

But a survey of the author's background, and of much of the contents of the books themselves, has indicated to me and to many others that these Rugg books not only teach the pupil

[First published in *New York Times,* 9 May 1940, p. 22. For Dewey's letter to which this is a reply, see this volume, pp. 370–72, and for Dewey's rejoinder, see p. 373.]

about collectivism generally, but actually aim to indoctrinate the pupil with collectivistic ideas.

Professor Rugg and his associates clearly believe that school teachers should be indoctrinators of new social doctrines. He frankly states his philosophy in his book *The Great Technology.* On page 24 he says: "Our task, therefore, is to launch a nation-wide campaign of adult education, to create swiftly a compact body of minority opinion for the scientific reconstruction of our social order." And Professor George Counts, also of Teachers College, Columbia, said in his book, *Dare the School Build a New Social Order?* (page 28) "That the teachers should deliber-ately reach for power and then make the most of their conquest is my firm conviction."

Elsewhere in his book Professor Rugg pictures his belief in an intellectual Blitzkrieg. And his statement on page 231 that "This program will include . . . the doubling, even the quadrupling, of the national educational budget," raises the question whether the enormous rise in school budgets in recent years is not a phenome-non for which the theories of Professor Rugg, and other advocates of so-called progressive education, are not partly responsible.

On page 258 Professor Rugg says: "As we believe, so we teach. What we believe, the loyalties to which we hold, subtly determine the content and method of our teaching."

No words could better interpret what Professor Rugg is trying to get over to the youth who are today required to read his text-books in over 4,000 school systems in the United States. For it is a fair statement that many passages in these books play down most of the great accomplishments of American private enter-prise and speak at length and approvingly of the social planning of Soviet Russia. The seamy side of American life is emphasized in picture and text. Advertising is held to be a waste. Govern-ment planning, close government control, these are the inevitable substitutes for free private enterprise.

Example Cited

Just a single illustration. With each of the six Rugg text-books there is a teacher's guide and a pupil's work book. The teacher's guide is designed to tell the teacher what answer to re-quire of the pupil.

In one of the pupil's work books the question is asked, "Is the United States a land of opportunity for all our people? Why?"

The following is quoted from the corresponding teacher's work book:

"Studies show that the opinions of most pupils are founded on a lack of facts—on little more than prejudice—as the following responses of a group of 315 high school pupils illustrate:

"2. Of the 315 pupils, 88 per cent said that the following statement was true: 'The United States is unquestionably the best country in the world.' There is little doubt that if these two statements were laid before thousands of pupils in our high schools today, most of them would say that they were true. Now the attitude expressed by most of these pupils is one that we decidedly do not want to develop in our classes."

I believe it is a fair statement that these Rugg books, while containing some excellent parts, tend clearly to undermine the faith of the pupils in private enterprise—in the American system out of which American public education, the costliest in the world, is maintained.

That, I think, is why Binghamton removed these books from its schools. And that is why we are receiving daily from parents all over the United States requests for information and advice as to how they can protect their children from these books.

Dr. Dewey says these textbooks are "conducive to unfettered thinking." This, in my opinion, is untrue. They are, I think, rather part of that program Professor Rugg advocates—namely, "to create swiftly a compact body of minority opinion for the scientific reconstruction of our social order." As such, they have no place in American schools.

MERWIN K. HART,
President, New York State Economic Council
New York, May 7, 1940

Notes

The following notes, keyed to the page and line numbers of the present edition, explain references to matters not found in standard sources.

141.22   Carus Lectures] In conjunction with the annual meeting of the American Philosophical Association, Evander Bradley McGilvary delivered the fifth series of Carus Lectures, entitled "Toward a Perspective Realism," at Columbia University on 27, 28, and 29 December 1939.

262.11   Robert Morss Lovett] Lovett was elected president of the LID in 1921, at the time the Intercollegiate Socialist Society adopted the new name League for Industrial Democracy, and served until 1939. See Lovett, *All Our Years* (New York: Viking Press, 1948), pp. 207–22.

320.24; 330.5   anthropology] Margaret Mead spoke on "Lessons from the War—in Anthropology" on 23 November 1941.

328.26   Sorokin] Pitirim A. Sorokin, sociologist at Harvard University.

358.14   Mayor] Fiorello LaGuardia.

374.1   Statement on Academic Freedom] At an assembly of faculty on 3 October 1940 Nicholas Murray Butler, president of Columbia University, urged "members of his academic staff to resign if their convictions brought them into open conflict with the university's pursuit of its ideals in 'the war between beasts and human beings.'" For a report on the reception of his statements see "Dr. Butler's Edict Scored in Senate," *New York Times*, 5 October 1940, pp. 1, 7. Other critics included Senators Bennett Champ Clark of Missouri and Rush Holt of West Virginia; H. G. Wells; James Marshall, president of the Board of Education; John Haynes Holmes, pastor of the Community Church and board chairman of the American Civil Liberties Union; Charles J. Hendley, president of the Teachers Union, Local 5; and the executive council of the New York College Teachers Union. See also "Dr. Butler's Address to the Columbia Faculties," *New York Times*, 4 October 1940, p. 14.

Checklist of Dewey's References

This section gives full publication information for each work cited by Dewey. Books in Dewey's personal library (John Dewey Papers, Special Collections, Morris Library, Southern Illinois University at Carbondale) have been listed whenever possible. When Dewey gave page numbers for a reference, the edition has been identified by locating the citation; for other references, the edition listed here is his most likely source by reason of place or date of publication, general accessibility during the period, or evidence from correspondence and other materials.

Allport, Gordon W. "Dewey's Individual and Social Psychology." In *The Philosophy of John Dewey*. Library of Living Philosophers, edited by Paul Arthur Schilpp, 1:263–90. Evanston and Chicago: Northwestern University, 1939.

Banfi, Antonio. "The Thought of George Santayana in the Crisis of Contemporary Philosophy." In *The Philosophy of George Santayana*. Library of Living Philosophers, edited by Paul Arthur Schilpp, 2:475–94. Evanston and Chicago: Northwestern University, 1940.

Beard, Charles A., and Mary R. Beard. *America in Midpassage*. Vol. 3. New York: Macmillan Co., 1939.

———. *The Rise of American Civilization*. 3 vols. New York: Macmillan Co., 1927.

Benedict, Ruth. "Animism." *Encyclopaedia of the Social Sciences*, 2:65–67.

———. "Bertrand Russell and Marriage." *New York Herald Tribune Books*, 20 October 1929, p. 5.

Bentley, Arthur F. *Behavior, Knowledge, Fact*. Bloomington, Ind.: Principia Press, 1935.

Boas, George. "Santayana and the Arts." In *The Philosophy of George Santayana*. Library of Living Philosophers, edited by Paul Arthur Schilpp, 2:241–61. Evanston and Chicago: Northwestern University, 1940.

Broad, Charlie Dunbar. *Scientific Thought*. International Library of Psychology, Philosophy and Scientific Method, edited by C. K. Ogden. New York: Harcourt, Brace and Co., 1923.

Brownell, Baker. "Santayana, The Man and the Philosopher." In *The Philosophy of George Santayana*. Library of Living Philosophers, edited by Paul Arthur Schilpp, 2:31–61. Evanston and Chicago: Northwestern University, 1940.

Clapp, Elsie Ripley. *Community Schools in Action*. New York: Viking Press, 1939.

Cohen, Morris R. "Some Difficulties in Dewey's Anthropocentric Naturalism." *Philosophical Review* 49 (March 1940): 196–228. [*The Later Works of John Dewey, 1925–1953*, edited by Jo Ann Boydston, 14:379–410. Carbondale and Edwardsville: Southern Illinois University Press, 1987.]

Collingwood, Robin George. *An Autobiography*. London: Oxford University Press, 1939.

Cory, Daniel M. "Some Observations on the Philosophy of George Santayana." In *The Philosophy of George Santayana*. Library of Living Philosophers, edited by Paul Arthur Schilpp, 2:93–112. Evanston and Chicago: Northwestern University, 1940.

Cowdry, Edmund Vincent, ed. *Problems of Ageing: Biological and Medical Aspects*. Baltimore: Williams and Wilkins Co., 1939.

Dennes, William Ray. "Santayana's Materialism." In *The Philosophy of George Santayana*. Library of Living Philosophers, edited by Paul Arthur Schilpp, 2:417–43. Evanston and Chicago: Northwestern University, 1940.

Dewey, John. *Art as Experience*. New York: Minton, Balch and Co., 1934. [*Later Works* 10.]

———. *Democracy and Education*. New York: Macmillan Co., 1916. [*The Middle Works of John Dewey, 1899–1924*, edited by Jo Ann Boydston, vol. 9. Carbondale and Edwardsville: Southern Illinois University Press, 1980.]

———. *Experience and Nature*. Chicago: Open Court Publishing Co., 1925. [*Later Works* 1.]

———. *The Influence of Darwin on Philosophy*. New York: Henry Holt and Co., 1910.

———. *Logic: The Theory of Inquiry*. New York: Henry Holt and Co., 1938. [*Later Works* 12.]

———. *The Quest for Certainty: A Study of the Relation of Knowledge and Action*. New York: Minton, Balch and Co., 1929. [*Later Works* 4.]

———. *The Significance of the Problem of Knowledge*. University of Chicago Contributions to Philosophy, vol. 1, no. 3. Chicago: University of Chicago Press, 1897. [*The Early Works of John Dewey, 1882–1898*, edited by Jo Ann Boydston, 5:3–24. Carbondale and Edwardsville: Southern Illinois University Press, 1972.]

————. *Studies in Logical Theory*. Chicago: University of Chicago Press, 1903.

————. *Theory of Valuation. International Encyclopedia of Unified Science*, vol. 2, no. 4. Chicago: University of Chicago Press, 1939. [*Later Works* 13:189–251.]

————. "Introduction." In *Essays in Experimental Logic*, pp. 1–74. Chicago: University of Chicago Press, 1916. [*Middle Works* 10:320–65.]

————. "The Need for a Recovery of Philosophy." In *Creative Intelligence: Essays in the Pragmatic Attitude*, by John Dewey et al., pp. 3–69. New York: Henry Holt and Co., 1917. [*Middle Works* 10:3–48.]

————. "Pragmatic America." *New Republic* 30 (12 April 1922): 185–87. [*Middle Works* 13:306–10.]

————. "Religion and Our Schools." *Hibbert Journal* 6 (1908): 796–809. [*Middle Works* 4:165–77.]

————. "What I Believe: Living Philosophies—VII." *Forum* 83 (March 1930): 176–82. [*Later Works* 5:267–78.]

Dewey, John, and James Haydon Tufts. *Ethics*. Rev. ed. New York: Henry Holt and Co., 1932. [*Later Works* 7.]

Dewey, John, and Horace M. Kallen, eds. *The Bertrand Russell Case*. New York: Viking Press, 1941.

Edman, Irwin. "Humanism and Post-Humanism in the Philosophy of Santayana." In *The Philosophy of George Santayana*. Library of Living Philosophers, edited by Paul Arthur Schilpp, 2:293–312. Evanston and Chicago: Northwestern University, 1940.

Ford, Paul Leicester, ed. *The Writings of Thomas Jefferson*. 10 vols. New York: G. P. Putnam's Sons, 1892–99. [Vol. 2, 1893; vol. 7, 1896; vol. 10, 1899.]

Friess, Horace L., and Henry M. Rosenthal. "Reason in Religion and the Emancipated Spirit." In *The Philosophy of George Santayana*. Library of Living Philosophers, edited by Paul Arthur Schilpp, 2:351–76. Evanston and Chicago: Northwestern University, 1940.

Geiger, George Raymond. "Dewey's Social and Political Philosophy." In *The Philosophy of John Dewey*. Library of Living Philosophers, edited by Paul Arthur Schilpp, 1:335–68. Evanston and Chicago: Northwestern University, 1940.

Hart, Merwin Kimball. "Dr. Dewey's Stand Disputed." *New York Times*, 9 May 1940, p. 22. [*Later Works* 14:427–29.]

Hartshorne, Charles. "Santayana's Doctrine of Essence." In *The Philosophy of George Santayana*. Library of Living Philosophers, edited by Paul Arthur Schilpp, 2:135–82. Evanston and Chicago: Northwestern University, 1940.

Hocking, William Ernest. "Dewey's Concepts of Experience and Nature." *Philosophical Review* 49 (March 1940): 228–44. [*Later Works* 14:411–26.]

James, William. *Essays in Radical Empiricism.* New York: Longmans, Green and Co., 1912.

———. *The Principles of Psychology.* 2 vols. New York: Henry Holt and Co., 1893.

———. *Talks to Teachers on Psychology: and to Students on Some of Life's Ideals.* New York: Henry Holt and Co., 1899.

———. "Does 'Consciousness' Exist?" *Journal of Philosophy, Psychology and Scientific Methods* 1 (1904): 447–91.

Jefferson, Thomas. *The Writings of Thomas Jefferson,* edited by Paul Leicester Ford. 10 vols. New York: G. P. Putnam's Sons, 1892–99. [Vol. 2, 1893; vol. 7, 1896; vol. 10, 1899.]

———. *The Writings of Thomas Jefferson: Being His Autobiography, Correspondence, Reports, Messages, Addresses, and Other Writings, Official and Private,* edited by H. A. Washington. 9 vols. New York: Taylor and Maury, 1853–54.

Kallen, Horace M. "Behind the Bertrand Russell Case." In *The Bertrand Russell Case,* edited by John Dewey and Horace M. Kallen, pp. 13–53. New York: Viking Press, 1941.

Kallen, Horace M., and John Dewey, eds. *The Bertrand Russell Case.* New York: Viking Press, 1941.

Lamprecht, Sterling P. "Animal Faith and the Art of Intuition." In *The Philosophy of George Santayana.* Library of Living Philosophers, edited by Paul Arthur Schilpp, 2:113–34. Evanston and Chicago: Northwestern University, 1940.

Laplace, Pierre Simon. *A Philosophical Essay on Probabilities.* Translated from the 6th French ed. by Frederick W. Truscott and Frederick L. Emory. New York: John Wiley and Sons, 1902.

"Liberty and Common Sense." *New Republic* 99 (31 May 1939): 89–90.

McGeehan, John E. "Appendix I. Decision of Justice McGeehan." In *The Bertrand Russell Case,* edited by John Dewey and Horace M. Kallen, pp. 213–25. New York: Viking Press, 1941.

Macintosh, Douglas Clyde. *Social Religion.* New York: Charles Scribner's Sons, 1939.

Mannheim, Karl. *Man and Society in an Age of Reconstruction.* New York: Harcourt, Brace and Co., 1940.

Munitz, Milton K. "Ideals and Essences in Santayana's Philosophy." In *The Philosophy of George Santayana.* Library of Living Philosophers, edited by Paul Arthur Schilpp, 2:183–215. Evanston and Chicago: Northwestern University, 1940.

Murphy, Arthur E. "Dewey's Epistemology and Metaphysics." In *The*

Philosophy of John Dewey. Library of Living Philosophers, edited by Paul Arthur Schilpp, 1 : 193–225. Evanston and Chicago: Northwestern University, 1939.

Otto, Max C. *The Human Enterprise: An Attempt to Relate Philosophy to Daily Life.* New York: F. S. Crofts and Co., 1940.

Parodi, Dominique. "Knowledge and Action in Dewey's Philosophy." In *The Philosophy of John Dewey.* Library of Living Philosophers, edited by Paul Arthur Schilpp, 1 : 227–42. Evanston and Chicago: Northwestern University, 1939.

Pepper, Stephen C. "Santayana's Theory of Value." In *The Philosophy of George Santayana.* Library of Living Philosophers, edited by Paul Arthur Schilpp, 2 : 217–39. Evanston and Chicago: Northwestern University, 1940.

———. "Some Questions on Dewey's Esthetics." In *The Philosophy of John Dewey.* Library of Living Philosophers, edited by Paul Arthur Schilpp, 1 : 369–89. Evanston and Chicago: Northwestern University, 1939.

Piatt, Donald A. "Dewey's Logical Theory." In *The Philosophy of John Dewey.* Library of Living Philosophers, edited by Paul Arthur Schilpp, 1 : 103–34. Evanston and Chicago: Northwestern University, 1939.

Randall, John Herman, Jr. "Dewey's Interpretation of the History of Philosophy." In *The Philosophy of John Dewey.* Library of Living Philosophers, edited by Paul Arthur Schilpp, 1 : 75–102. Evanston and Chicago: Northwestern University, 1939.

Rees, J. R. "Sexual Difficulties in Childhood." In *A Survey of Child Psychiatry,* edited by R. G. Gordon, pp. 246–56. Oxford Medical Publications. London: Oxford University Press, 1939.

Reichenbach, Hans. *Experience and Prediction: An Analysis of the Foundations and the Structure of Knowledge.* Chicago: University of Chicago Press, 1938.

———. "Dewey's Theory of Science." In *The Philosophy of John Dewey.* Library of Living Philosophers, edited by Paul Arthur Schilpp, 1 : 157–92. Evanston and Chicago: Northwestern University, 1939.

Rice, Philip Blair. "The Philosopher as Poet and Critic." In *The Philosophy of George Santayana.* Library of Living Philosophers, edited by Paul Arthur Schilpp, 2 : 263–91. Evanston and Chicago: Northwestern University, 1940.

Rosenthal, Henry M., and Horace L. Friess. "Reason in Religion and the Emancipated Spirit." In *The Philosophy of George Santayana.* Library of Living Philosophers, edited by Paul Arthur Schilpp, 2 : 351–76. Evanston and Chicago: Northwestern University, 1940.

Russell, Bertrand. *Education and the Modern World.* New York: W. W. Norton and Co., 1932.

————. *An Inquiry into Meaning and Truth.* New York: W. W. Norton and Co., 1940.

————. *Marriage and Morals.* New York: Liveright Publishing Corp., 1929.

————. *Principles of Social Reconstruction.* London: George Allen and Unwin, 1916.

————. "Dewey's New *Logic.*" In *The Philosophy of John Dewey.* Library of Living Philosophers, edited by Paul Arthur Schilpp, 1: 135–56. Evanston and Chicago: Northwestern University, 1939.

————. "The Philosophy of Santayana." In *The Philosophy of George Santayana.* Library of Living Philosophers, edited by Paul Arthur Schilpp, 2:451–74. Evanston and Chicago: Northwestern University, 1940.

————. "As a European Radical Sees It." *Freeman* 4 (8 March 1922): 608–10.

"The Russell Decision." *New York Herald Tribune,* 1 April 1940, p. 14.

Santayana, George. *The Life of Reason; or, The Phases of Human Progress.* 5 vols. New York: Charles Scribner's Sons, 1905–6.

————. *Scepticism and Animal Faith: Introduction to a System of Philosophy.* New York: Charles Scribner's Sons, 1923.

————. *Three Philosophical Poets; Lucretius, Dante, and Goethe.* Cambridge: Harvard University Press, 1910.

————. "Apologia Pro Mente Sua." In *The Philosophy of George Santayana.* Library of Living Philosophers, edited by Paul Arthur Schilpp, 2:495–605. Evanston and Chicago: Northwestern University, 1940.

————. "A Brief History of My Opinion." In *Contemporary American Philosophy,* edited by George P. Adams and William Montague, pp. 239–57. New York: Macmillan Co., 1930.

————. "Dewey's Naturalistic Metaphysics." In *The Philosophy of John Dewey.* Library of Living Philosophers, edited by Paul Arthur Schilpp, 1:243–61. Evanston and Chicago: Northwestern University, 1939.

————. "A General Confession." In *The Philosophy of George Santayana.* Library of Living Philosophers, edited by Paul Arthur Schilpp, 2:1–30. Evanston and Chicago: Northwestern University, 1940.

————. "Tragic Philosophy." *Scrutiny* 4 (March 1936): 365–76.

Savery, William. "The Significance of Dewey's Philosophy." In *The Philosophy of John Dewey.* Library of Living Philosophers, edited by Paul Arthur Schilpp, 1:479–513. Evanston and Chicago: Northwestern University, 1939.

Schaub, Edward L. "Dewey's Interpretation of Religion." In *The Philosophy of John Dewey.* Library of Living Philosophers, edited by Paul Arthur Schilpp, 1:391–416. Evanston and Chicago: Northwestern University, 1939.

————. "Santayana's Contentions Respecting German Philosophy." In *The Philosophy of George Santayana*. Library of Living Philosophers, edited by Paul Arthur Schilpp, 2:399–415. Evanston and Chicago: Northwestern University, 1940.

Schilpp, Paul Arthur. "Santayana on *The Realm of Spirit*." In *The Philosophy of George Santayana*. Library of Living Philosophers, edited by Paul Arthur Schilpp, 2:377–98. Evanston and Chicago: Northwestern University, 1940.

Schilpp, Paul Arthur, ed. *The Philosophy of George Santayana*. Library of Living Philosophers, vol. 2. Evanston and Chicago: Northwestern University, 1940.

————. *The Philosophy of John Dewey*. Library of Living Philosophers, vol. 1. Evanston and Chicago: Northwestern University, 1939.

Soskin, William. "Books on Our Table." *New York Evening Post,* 15 October 1929, p. 15.

Souriau, Paul. "La conscience de soi." *Revue Philosophique* 22 (1886): 449–72.

Strong, C. A. "Santayana's Philosophy." In *The Philosophy of George Santayana*. Library of Living Philosophers, edited by Paul Arthur Schilpp, 2:445–49. Evanston and Chicago: Northwestern University, 1940.

Stuart, Henry W. "Dewey's Ethical Theory." In *The Philosophy of John Dewey*. Library of Living Philosophers, edited by Paul Arthur Schilpp, 1:291–333. Evanston and Chicago: Northwestern University, 1939.

Sullivan, Celestine J., Jr. "Santayana's Philosophical Inheritance." In *The Philosophy of George Santayana*. Library of Living Philosophers, edited by Paul Arthur Schilpp, 2:63–91. Evanston and Chicago: Northwestern University, 1940.

Vivas, Eliseo. "From *The Life of Reason* to *The Last Puritan*." In *The Philosophy of George Santayana*. Library of Living Philosophers, edited by Paul Arthur Schilpp, 2:313–50. Evanston and Chicago: Northwestern University, 1940.

Washington, H. A., ed. *The Writings of Thomas Jefferson: Being His Autobiography, Correspondence, Reports, Messages, Addresses, and Other Writings, Official and Private.* 9 vols. New York: Taylor and Maury, 1853–54.

Watkin, E. Ingram. "Bertrand Russell—Religious Atheist." *Catholic World* 11 (6 March 1923): 731–42.

Whitehead, Alfred North. *Adventures of Ideas*. New York: Macmillan Co., 1933.

————. *Process and Reality: An Essay in Cosmology*. New York: Macmillan Co., 1929.

————. *Science and the Modern World*. New York: Macmillan Co., 1925.

Index

natural, 86; scientific, 20–25, 28, 61–62, 80–83, 103–5, 151–52, 196–97; and subject, 132–35

Objective: vs. subjective, 25–26, 26n, 28, 189, 192–93, 196–97, 198–200

Observation: and calculation, 198; importance of, to science, 151; operational character of, 181; role of, in inquiry, 172–74

Occasions of experience: Whitehead on, 127–28, 132, 133, 134

Old Testament, 288

"Ontological Relativity" (Quine), xv and n

Ontological Relativity and Other Essays (Quine), xvn

Ontology: Cohen on, 386–87, 388–90; modern problem of, 197

Operationalism: defined, 151–52; in Dewey's propositions, xvi; Hocking on, 420

Optimism: Dewey's, 407

Organicism, 34–35, 35n, 37n

Organisms: individuality in, 102–3; influenced by environment, 15–16, 40, 64 and n; relation of, and environment, 158, 161, 167, 185–86

Otto, Max C.: relates philosophy to mankind, 289–92

Oxford University, 334

Parmenides, 398, 399

Parodi, Dominique: Dewey replies to, 80–83; on Dewey's theory of truth, 5, 56n

Past: immanence of, in present, 131, 135; influences philosophy, 312–15

Pasteur, Louis, 342

Patriotism: in U.S., 250

Pearl, Raymond, 391

Peirce, Charles Sanders, x, xiii, xiv, xviii, 5, 390; compared with Dewey, 387 and n; definition of truth of, 56–57, 57n; on experience, 21n; fallibilism of, 171

Peking, China, xx, xxi

People, the: as foundation of government for Jefferson, 209–10, 214–15, 216–18

Pepper, Stephen C., 5, 306; criticizes Dewey, 15; Dewey replies to, 34–38

Perception: James on, 160, 161; and observational propositions, 54, 170–71; role of behavior in, 20–21, 24–25

Person: defined, 27–28

Personal identity: James on, 156–57, 157n, 165–66

Personality: theory of, 40

Perspectives: philosophical, 141–42, 154

"Philosopher as Poet and Critic, The" (Rice), 300–301

Philosophes, 205, 209

Philosophical Review, xxiii

Philosophy: analytical, xvii; characteristics of Greek, 192–94, 195, 199, 316; Chinese, 421; circularity in, xiii–xiv; classical, 313; Cohen on, 394–95, 398–400, 402–6, 407, 408, 410; definition of, 381; Dewey's, ix–x, xxiii, xxiv; experience related to, 124–26, 138; fact vs. value in, 323; genetic-functional method in, 147n; in Germany, 313, 322–23; history of, 3, 4, 98–101, 142, 313; human nature related to, 324–25, 333–34; of individ-

A Note on the Text

The following correction has been made in this reprinting:

166.18   case]   vase